TO REPAIR A BROKEN WORLD

TO REPAIR
A BROKEN WORLD

The Life of

Henrietta Szold

FOUNDER OF HADASSAH

DVORA HACOHEN

Fountaindale Public Library District
300 W. Briarcliff Rd.
Bolingbrook, IL 60440

▌▌▌
Harvard University Press

Cambridge, Massachusetts & London, England   2021

First printing

Library of Congress Cataloging-in-Publication Data
Names: Hakohen, Devorah, author. | Gertel, Shmuel Sermoneta, translator. |
Ginsburg, Ruth Bader, writer of foreword.
Title: To repair a broken world : the life of Henrietta Szold, founder of Hadassah / Dvora
Hacohen; translated by Shmuel Sermoneta-Gertel ; foreword by Ruth Bader Ginsburg.
Description: Cambridge, Massachusetts : Harvard University Press, 2021. |
First edition published in Hebrew as Manhigah le-lo gevulot : Henriyeṭah Sold :
biyografyah = To repair a broken world : the life of Henrietta Szold. Tel Aviv :
Am Oved Books, 2019. | Includes bibliographical references and index.
Identifiers: LCCN 2020045447 | ISBN 9780674988095 (cloth)
Subjects: LCSH: Szold, Henrietta, 1860-1945. | Jewish Agency for Israel.
Youth Aliyah Department. | Jewish women—Biography. | Zionists—Biography. |
Zionists—United States—Biography.
Classification: LCC DS151.S9 H3413 2021 | DDC 320.54095694092 [B]—dc23
LC record available at https://lccn.loc.gov/2020045447

To my beloved children
Meron, Aviad, Hagit

And my grandchildren

CONTENTS

FOREWORD

*I*N MY GROWING-UP YEARS, my mother held in highest esteem three Jewish women: Emma Lazarus, Lillian Wald, and Henrietta Szold. She praised their devotion to the public good, their brave efforts to repair a broken world. My mother hoped I would be inspired by Lazarus, Wald, and Szold in caring about the well-being of members of my family, students and teachers at schools I attended, and people in the communities and world in which I live. As a child, I was indeed inspired by those way-paving women, and I remain touched by their example to this very day.

Emma Lazarus was cousin to the great jurist Benjamin Nathan Cardozo. Twenty-one years Cardozo's senior, Lazarus wrote constantly, from her first volume of poetry published in 1866 at age seventeen until her tragic death from cancer at age thirty-eight. Her poem "The New Colossus," inscribed on the base of the Statue of Liberty, welcomed legions of people newly arrived in the United States, among them my father and grandparents. A Zionist before that word came into vogue, Emma Lazarus conveyed in her poetry and prose her love for her people and appreciation for their endurance.

Lillian Wald, nurse, humanitarian, civil rights activist, and writer, born in 1867, lived until 1940. Initiator of public health nursing, she is best known for founding the Henry Street Settlement on New York's Lower East Side. The settlement provided neighborhood and home health care, accessible without regard to race, gender, or age, and it promoted paid employment for women, enabling them to support their families. For my mother and her siblings, the settlement, including the Neighborhood Playhouse associated with it, served as a center for young people's social life. Affiliated with the American Civil Liberties Union (ACLU), Wald was also a founding member of the National Association for the Advancement of Colored People (NAACP); that organization's first major public conference was held at the Henry Street Settlement.

Henrietta Szold, born in 1860, was a contemporary of Lillian Wald. In the United States, Szold is known principally as founder of the women's Zionist organization Hadassah, in which I am enrolled as a life member.

From Dvora Hacohen's comprehensive biography, I learned how much more Szold had accomplished in her eighty-four years on earth. In 1889, for example, Szold launched night schools for immigrants, mainly from Russia and Eastern Europe, but also from Germany and Italy. Open to people of all faiths, the schools taught English, familiarized attendees with life in the United States, and provided training in a variety of vocations. Beginning with Baltimore, the schools spread to other cities, including New York. My father, whose childhood home was a shtetl near Odessa, arrived in New York in 1909 at age thirteen. He learned English at a night school modeled on Szold's initiative. Apart from religious instruction, it was the only formal education he and countless other new Americans ever received.

In talks about inspiring women, I have several times quoted from Szold's letter explaining why, when her mother died, she declined the offer of a male friend to recite the mourner's kaddish in her stead. Hacohen sets out an excerpt from Szold's letter on page 161. Never have I come upon a more gracious plea for understanding, for celebrating one's shared heritage while tolerating—even appreciating—the differences in religious observance among us.

Hacohen's meticulously detailed account of Szold's life devotes many pages to her work and days in Palestine, where she resided most of the time from age sixty until her death some twenty-four years later. Szold's unparalleled efforts to improve health care, social services, and education in Palestine, when the land was still a British mandate, were as prodigious as they were fraught with challenges. When storm clouds gathered over Germany, then all of Europe, Szold founded and directed Youth Aliyah, a venture that saved many thousands of children from the Holocaust by bringing them to Palestine and placing them in suitable communities.

Hacohen portrays Szold's rich but often stressful public and private life with notable sensitivity and keen insight. The book is a reading and learning treasure trove of the kind Szold's story well deserves.

Ruth Bader Ginsburg
January 9, 2020

TO REPAIR A BROKEN WORLD

INTRODUCTION

ENRIETTA SZOLD, the most important American Jewish woman of her era, was born in Baltimore in December 21, 1860.[1] She lived a life bounded by two wars, coming into the world as the Civil War was about to erupt, and passing away shortly before the end of World War II. Her long life, from the mid-nineteenth to the mid-twentieth century, spanned some of the most turbulent years in modern history, when great waves of immigration transformed the United States into a powerful nation, and social revolutions and two global conflicts played out on the world stage. Szold was witness to these momentous political events, which shook and shaped the lives of millions of people. These events are woven into the fabric of her life story.

Szold followed many different paths before ascending to the highest echelons of American Jewish leadership. I first encountered her exceptional personality during the course of research on Youth Aliyah, which she established in Palestine in her final years, when she was already in her seventies and eighties. Youth Aliyah cared for and educated some 30,000 children rescued from the clutches of the Nazis and the horrors of the Holocaust. Szold established hundreds of educational institutions for these orphaned children, and they operated under her constant supervision.[2] My curiosity was piqued by the efforts she exerted and the battles she waged against powerful institutions for the sake of the humanist and pedagogical values she believed in, and by her dynamism and accomplishments at a time when women did not ordinarily play such prominent public roles. I found myself drawn to the story of her life, eager to gain a deeper understanding of this complex and multifaceted personality. When I could not find a satisfactory scholarly biography of Henrietta Szold, I began to peruse the documents I came across in the archives. What I discovered was a life divided into two distinct parts, so different from each other as to appear to belong to two different people. Henrietta spent the first part of her life, her formative years, in her parents' home in Baltimore. She was the eldest of eight daughters born to Sophie Schaar and Rabbi Benjamin Szold. Her father was her first teacher. He taught her to read and write German, the spoken language in their home, as well as Hebrew, and introduced her to Jewish literature and the ways of the intellectual world— unintentionally shaping the course of her life. As a child, Henrietta developed a love of learning and excelled at her studies, which she would have loved to continue were it not for the barriers women faced when pursuing higher education. Despite having finished high school with honors and being fluent in four languages, she was unable to attend Johns Hopkins University in Baltimore, which did not admit women at the time. Although there were universities and colleges in other cities open to women, such as Vassar (specifically founded as a college for women), where Henrietta would gladly have applied, her parents could not afford the high cost of an out-of-town education. Henrietta was frustrated but did not give up. She studied on her own, acquiring a broad education. At the age of seventeen, she began to write columns for the *Jewish Messenger*—a popular weekly published in New York—under the pen name Sulamith. She published articles in other local and Jewish papers as well, generally under a pseudonym.

Rabbi Szold, who was the spiritual leader of Congregation Oheb Shalom in Baltimore, earned a modest salary and struggled to support his growing family. Henrietta went to work as a teacher to supplement the family's income. Even as a teacher, she employed innovative pedagogical methods and stood out among her colleagues. Circumstances in the Szold household were thus somewhat unusual. Henrietta helped support the family and helped her father translate his correspondence from German to English—a language in which he was not fluent. She also stood by his side when he feared losing his livelihood due to an ongoing conflict with his congregants over the introduction of Reform practices into the synagogue. Her mother, Sophie, was busy taking care of the children and running the home. Henrietta encouraged her sisters to pursue higher education, which she paid for from her own salary. She supported them in every possible way, offering them advice and a helping hand whenever they needed it. Henrietta thus came to acquire a special position of authority within the family—one she would retain over the years.

Throughout this time, Henrietta, deeply influenced by her father's engagement in public affairs, took an interest in events in her hometown of Baltimore and elsewhere. Driven by a sense of mission and a commitment to repairing the world, she strove for great things. In the 1880s, when she was in her twenties, large numbers of Jewish immigrants from Russia and Eastern Europe began to arrive in the United States.[3] She encountered many immigrants on the streets of Baltimore in search of work to support their families. Most people simply ignored them, but Henrietta set her mind to finding a way to help. She came to the conclusion that the best way to do so was to teach them English, as she saw language as the key to social, economic, and cultural integration. A young woman without means or financial support thus decided to establish an English school for immigrants, volunteering her own time to teach them. Her biggest challenge was to raise money for classrooms, desks, chairs, and other essential expenses. She appealed to the Jewish community but met with indifference, which she attributed to a lack of respect for work done by women, confessing to her sister that it brought back her childhood longing to be a man. Her aspiration to become a writer was also an expression of her desire to be independent and free to make her own decisions.[4]

With great effort, Szold managed to establish a night school for immigrants, which she determined would be open to everyone, regardless of religion, gender, or age. The school grew quickly. Within the space of a few years, thousands of immigrants—men and women, young and old—had passed through its doors. The humanistic and egalitarian values at the heart of Szold's first project would come to distinguish all her endeavors over the years. The many projects Henrietta took upon herself filled her days. She was used to getting up early and working well into the night—a habit that stuck with her throughout her life.

The life story of Henrietta Szold is filled with contrasts and tensions that had a profound influence on her public activities. Szold encountered situations in which women were excluded time after time in the workplace. But during the first half of her adult life, Szold passively accepted this discrimination without objection or protest. At the Jewish Publication Society (JPS), she edited and translated numerous works by some of the world's greatest Jewish scholars. Her work was widely appreciated and admired, yet she was very rarely credited in the published volumes. Her formal title was "secretary" when in fact her job was that of editor in chief. Similarly, despite editing the *American Jewish Year Book* and contributing dozens of articles to it, her name was hardly mentioned, nor did she receive any additional payment for her work on the annual publication. She loved her work at the *Year Book* and considered it extremely important at a time when the only way to reach large numbers of people was through the printed word. The *Year Book* allowed her to convey her messages to a sizable readership, especially her concerns regarding the alarming ferocity of antisemitism in Europe, which had also spread to American shores. Szold believed that antisemitism, which demonized Jews with the goal of legitimizing their annihilation, posed a grave threat to the Jewish people. She could not have been more prescient. Szold fought for the eradication of antisemitism, and praised writers and thinkers of all faiths who raised their voices against it. She called attention to this phenomenon in every issue of the *Year Book,* even dedicating an entire volume to the subject. She highlighted the achievements of Jews and their many contributions to society, giving prominence to the important roles played by Jews in the US military, both houses of Congress, and American political life. She also drew attention to the accomplishments of Jewish women in the fields of literature and science in the United States and in Europe.

While determined and resolute in her literary work, even standing up to the directors of the publishing house when necessary, Szold was surprisingly passive when it came to standing up for her own rights in matters such as fair pay and due credit. This pattern of exclusion and discrimination repeated itself in her early efforts on behalf of the Zionist movement, for which she received no recognition, despite her important contributions. Oddly, she never refused an assignment. Was it her way of coping with the need to operate as the only woman in a male-dominated environment?[5] Even when she moved to New York, after her father's death, and sought admission to the Jewish Theological Seminary, she agreed to declare that she had no intention of serving as a rabbi.

While at the seminary she continued her work at JPS and began to translate and edit Louis Ginzberg's *Legends of the Jews.* During the course of their work together Henrietta fell in love with Ginsberg. When her love was not requited, she sank into a deep depression; to aid her recovery, she embarked on a trip to Europe and Palestine. Palestine was still under Ottoman rule in 1909. Szold, though an ardent Zionist from an early age, found the "land of dreams" she had hoped to see a far cry from the reality she encountered there. She was shocked to discover that most of the Jewish inhabitants of the land lived in abject poverty, plagued by endemic disease and a high rate of mortality. She understood that the Yishuv—the Jewish community of Palestine—could not develop and thrive under such conditions. Friends had warned her, before her trip, that visiting Palestine would cure her of her Zionism. On her return voyage she wrote, "The prophecy has not been verified. I am the same Zionist I was. In fact, I am more than ever convinced that our only salvation lies that way. The only thing I admit is that I now think Zionism an ideal more difficult of realization than ever I did before, both on account of the Jews themselves and on account of Oriental and world conditions."[6] The trip galvanized Szold's desire to change the situation in Palestine even as it failed to alleviate the pain of her failed romance. Her depression worsened upon her return to New York, and she suffered a deep crisis that left her unable to function for months; it ended only when she concluded that her approach to life had been mistaken. She experienced an internal upheaval and made a dramatic decision to change her priorities.

Szold wrote to a friend that henceforth she was determined to excise parts of her past life and open a new chapter. She began socializing again and enthusiastically joined public efforts to achieve women's rights. This was a turning point for Henrietta. No longer would she allow others to infringe on her rights or take credit for her work. In 1912, she established Hadassah, an organization of American Zionist Jewish women, and was immediately elected president of the organization. It was the first time in her life that she received the recognition she deserved. Hadassah would become a crucial part of her struggle for women's empowerment and equality.

When Henrietta was growing up, there were prominent single women who dedicated their lives to public life. Szold, however, would not have chosen to remain single. She had a number of romantic involvements, all of which ended in disappointment. By the time she was fifty and her last unrequited love affair ended, she seems to have given up the idea of marrying and starting a family, though her desire to do so remained a constant source of pain and frustration throughout her life. Even her many achievements in the public sphere could not compensate for her perceived loss. Szold continued to live with her mother in New York. Although current feminist research has highlighted various aspects of mother-daughter relationships, some of which are difficult and painful, such as conflict, distance, and the desire for independence, I did not find one word of complaint about her mother in any of Henrietta's letters or diaries.[7] In any case, it would be anachronistic to apply such characterizations to the relationship between Henrietta and her mother a century and a half ago, when family relationships, norms, and values were quite different.[8]

In 1920, at the age of sixty, Henrietta traveled to Palestine once again, in order to establish the kind of modern healthcare system she had envisioned at the time of her first visit to that country. Szold shuttled between Palestine and the United States, working in both places but never settling in one. She was always on the move, from the United States to Europe to Palestine and back again. "For me apparently there will be no salvation but to live on the ocean," she wrote. Her many voyages stemmed from the need to raise funds for the projects to which she devoted her energies. Her activities in Palestine were supported by US philanthropists. She met frequently with American Jewish leaders with whom she had forged close personal ties—ties that served her well in all her public endeavors. There was more to her constant travel between the United States and Palestine, however—she never felt quite at home in either country. When she was in one, she would yearn for the other. This is but one example of Szold's dual nature: despite being a decisive leader in all her public roles, she found it hard to make decisions when it came to her personal life or field of focus in her career.

She went to Palestine to lay the foundations for a modern healthcare system, but over the years she also became involved in education, social work, and more in that country. She once remarked that she did not seek out the tasks she undertook: "I did not choose the tasks; they came to me." Although the tasks were indeed precipitated by events she witnessed, she found herself drawn in, incapable of focusing on any single endeavor, as if compelled by some force beyond her control. In fact, she herself once remarked, "It seems to me I have lived not one life but several, each one bearing its own character and insignia."

A source of considerable concern to Szold over the years was the Jewish-Arab conflict in Palestine. She witnessed the riots in Jaffa in 1921, in which Arabs killed a number of Jews and injured many others. Her visits to the clinics and hospitals scattered around the country also brought her face-to-face with the aftermath of Arab attacks against Jews. A proposal had been raised to establish a single binational state in Palestine, one in which the Jews would live as a minority, dominated by the Arab majority.[9] Szold disagreed with this approach, believing that such an arrangement would spell the end of Zionism, as Zionist Jews would not come to Palestine to live under Arab rule.

Szold sought an equitable solution for all. Her familiarity with the situation in Palestine and her study of bitter conflicts and subsequent resolutions between factions in other parts of the world led her to conclude that the chances of reaching a binational arrangement with the Arabs were practically nil. She characterized the Jewish-Arab conflict as a war of life and death between two peoples clinging to the same piece of land. Nevertheless, she always believed that an equitable solution must be sought. The observations she made about the conflict nearly a century ago are still relevant today.

THE STORY I TELL HERE is based on thousands of documents found in archives in the United States, Europe, and Israel.[10] These include Szold's professional correspondence; her personal correspondence with friends and with her sisters, in which she shared her plans, difficulties, and frustrations; and her diaries, in which she recorded her intimate feelings. Most of the archival documents have never been published. Among the sources I consulted when writing about Szold's early years were the letters she wrote as a child, in German, to her grandmother in Hungary. In Baltimore I was privileged to meet with the granddaughters of Henrietta's sister Bertha, who generously shared many details of Henrietta's childhood that have been passed down in the family but never published. I have also drawn upon a wide range of relevant historical literature, much of which is in Hebrew, especially memoirs of people who lived in Palestine and were witness to the historical events there. This biography is also the first to provide a comprehensive account of Szold's remarkable and still underappreciated work in Palestine in the last decades of her life. The many and various sources on which it is based reveal, for the first time, the figure of Henrietta Szold in all its richness and depth, as well as the winding path she followed to the pinnacle of twentieth-century Jewish leadership.

HENRIETTA SZOLD was the daughter of nineteenth-century Central European immigrants to the United States. Her history speaks to the many changes that have occurred in the lives, status, and achievements of women since that time. How did Szold, who lived through some of these changes, experiencing exclusion and discrimination firsthand and fighting for the rights of women and those in need, stand out from other women leaders?

Szold became one of America's most memorable leaders, admired in the United States, Palestine, and many other countries.[11] Her personal life, however, was not a source of comfort: although surrounded by many friends, she suffered constant loneliness. The dramas and tragedies she experienced during the course of her life left scars, and she was plagued by a sense of personal failure. On her deathbed, she remarked, "I lived a rich life, but not a happy life."[12]

1

BEGINNINGS

ENRIETTA SZOLD was the best-known American Jewish woman leader of the twentieth century, but her path to the pinnacle of Jewish leadership ascended through many tortuous years. Henrietta was born on December 21, 1860, about a year after her parents, Sophie and Rabbi Benjamin Szold, arrived in Baltimore from Hungary. Henrietta was the Szolds' first child, born in a period that was to become one of the stormiest in modern history and in the history of the Jewish people.

From earliest childhood, Henrietta Szold lived in the shadow of her father, a melancholy man whose influence on her was immeasurable. Benjamin Szold was born in 1829 in the small Hungarian village of Nemeskürt, east of Pressburg (today Bratislava, Slovakia), the former capital of the Habsburg kings of Hungary. The Jews of the region spoke German. Benjamin excelled at religious studies from a very young age, and his parents saw a bright future for him as a Torah scholar. But by the age of eight, he had lost both his parents. He and his brother Solomon were sent to their uncle in Freistadt, where they lived and studied at the Talmud Torah religious school, returning to their uncle's house for the Sabbath. Benjamin later recounted that as he and his brother approached their uncle's house, the non-Jewish children would tease and bully them, making him aware of anti-semitism from an early age. On reaching the age of bar mitzvah, he was sent to the yeshiva in Pressburg to continue his studies.[1] Though he enjoyed his studies, it was a life filled with poverty and privation.

After five years of study in Pressburg, Benjamin was ordained as a rabbi and moved to Vienna to further his education at university. He was soon caught up in the revolutionary spirit of 1848 sweeping through Europe. Benjamin joined his friends in Vienna who went to the aid of the revolutionaries by setting up barricades in the city streets, but they were astounded to discover the wrath of their erstwhile revolutionary partners turned on them.[2] The blows he suffered left an emotional scar on the young Szold.

European rulers struck back hard against the revolutionaries, their measures particularly destructive for the Jews. Pogroms, looting, and calls to expel the Jews contributed to feelings of helplessness and despair, leading in turn to the start of a mass migration of Jews from Central Europe to America, where they hoped to find freedom and true equality. Benjamin hastened to leave Vienna before he was arrested, returning to Pressburg, where he made a living as a private tutor in the city itself and in the surrounding towns. In 1849, he came to work for the Schaar family, in the nearby village of Cziffer (today Cifer, Slovakia), as instructor to six boys and two girls, Minna and Sophie.[3] When two of the Schaar boys went to Breslau, Germany, to continue their education, Benjamin gladly accompanied them, for he had long wanted to study at the city's rabbinical seminary.

The seminary was headed by Zacharias Frankel, who advocated combining traditional Torah study with a critical scientific approach to the development of Jewish law over the course of history, in contrast to prevailing Orthodox views.[4] Benjamin was witness there to a revolutionary attempt to find a golden mean between Orthodoxy and Reform, one that would be open to external influences without sacrificing fundamental values of Jewish law and tradition.

Benjamin had no means of support, but the seminary offered free tuition and accommodation. As in Pressburg, students ate lunch at the homes of the local Jewish community. The young scholar, who had not lived with his family since childhood, was again compelled to eat his daily meal—usually a meager one at that—in the homes of strangers, suffering hunger pangs the rest of the day. Privation plagued him once again, leaving him with a sense of insecurity and dependence on others that remained with him for the rest of his life.

On completing his doctoral studies in 1859, Benjamin began to look for a permanent position. The Stockholm Jewish community invited him to give several sermons, but the position ultimately went to a Reform rabbi. At about the same time, the Oheb Shalom congregation in Baltimore in the United States was advertising for a rabbi. With a warm recommendation from Rabbi Frankel, Benjamin was offered the position there. While Benjamin was pleased with the opportunity, his heart was heavy. He did not know the congregation or its leaders, had no relatives or friends in America—a distant and foreign land—and had no idea what awaited him. Before he left, he married Sophie Schaar, of whom he had fond recollections from his days in Cziffer as tutor to the family. Now twenty, Sophie was an intelligent, fair-haired, and pretty young woman.

Benjamin and Sophie landed in Baltimore on September 21, 1859, making their way to a two-story house at 207 South Eutaw Street, where the second-floor apartment had been rented for them. The day after his arrival, Rabbi Szold met with Simon Cohen, the Oheb Shalom vice president, and quickly realized he had come to a congregation fraught with problems. He had unwittingly found himself in the middle of a serious dispute between Orthodox and Reform members.

The first Jewish congregation in Baltimore, founded by Jews of Spanish and Portuguese heritage, was established in 1830, although Jews had first arrived in the city, albeit in small numbers, several decades earlier. Other congregations followed, as the 1850s saw a significant increase in the city's Jewish population, especially a wave of Jewish immigrants mainly from Central Europe. Oheb Shalom, founded in 1853, had already seen considerable turnover in its rabbis. The more Benjamin heard about the congregation, the more he worried, as he realized the synagogue had begun to shift toward Reform Judaism even in its early days.[5] Fully aware of the reality of Jewish life in America, he was not averse to change, but he was leery of the Reform movement, which had relinquished the national aspect of Judaism, as well as fundamental precepts such as observance of the Sabbath and the dietary laws.

Benjamin feared a clash with a congregation leaning toward Reform Judaism and prepared his first sermon carefully. Though it was well received and was even printed for distribution, it immediately drew criticism from Rabbi David Einhorn of Baltimore's Har Sinai Reform congregation, who mounted a fierce attack against Szold.[6] As many traditional synagogues were moving toward Reform Judaism, Benjamin saw little chance of finding a position at another synagogue. Though he did everything in his power to avoid a rift with his congregation, he remained deeply concerned about his future. He feared returning to a life of poverty, the bitter taste of which he had experienced as a child. He also feared for Sophie, whose pregnancy was well advanced. The reality in which he found himself exacerbated the anxiety that gave him no peace and hovered over him like a dark cloud.

The nation in which Benjamin and Sophie welcomed their first child that December 1860 was about to experience its own dark days. In

Oheb Shalom temple, Baltimore, Maryland, c. 1903

April 1861, the Civil War broke out between the Union North and the Confederate South over the issue of slavery. Even in the North, there was considerable opposition to the war in general and to the abolition of slavery, primarily for economic reasons. In Maryland, as in other border states along the North-South divide, many opposed the war, while others supported the Confederacy. The Oheb Shalom congregation was split between the two camps, with some supporting the continuation of slavery for economic reasons and others advocating abolition based on Jewish and liberal values.[7]

Rabbi Szold, who became aware of the slavery issue after his arrival in Baltimore, supported abolition, identifying with the oppressed and the disenfranchised, as he himself had suffered discrimination in Europe. He was aware that his position would anger the anti-abolitionists in his congregation, and he studiously avoided the issue in his sermons. Although he kept to himself his membership in a group that aided freed slaves, word got out and his critics derisively dubbed him "the rabbi of Timbuctoo," after the name of the group in question.[8] Sophie identified with her husband's positions on this matter, although she generally avoided expressing her opinions on contentious matters in public. Both Szolds greatly admired President Abraham Lincoln and his opposition to slavery.[9]

The war claimed many thousands of casualties, and deserters were sentenced to death. Rabbi Szold received a request from Washington to meet with a young Jew who had deserted from the Union Army, had been sentenced to death by firing squad, and wished to see a rabbi before his sentence was carried out. Szold went to visit the prisoner in jail and read from the book of Psalms with him. The young man asked the rabbi to stay with him until the end, and Szold remained by his side until his execution.[10] The sight of the frightened young man just before his death did not leave Szold for a long time. He was disgusted by the war, the tragic destructiveness of which led him to embrace the cause of pacifism. Henrietta would later follow in her father's footsteps, opposing all wars.

Little Henrietta did not understand what was happening around her, but as the war progressed she could sense her parents' anxiety. Sophie worried not only about the war but also about its financial implications. The price of basic commodities soared even as her husband's salary was cut dramatically, from $125 a month to only $75. He was told that the cut in his salary stemmed from the difficult economic circumstances in which the congregation found itself as a result of the war. Sophie wondered whether the real reason might not have been the rabbi's positions on the war, which were not to the liking of the congregation's leaders. In letters to her mother, she wrote about the rising cost of living and the need to reduce her household expenses as much as possible.[11]

Lincoln's election to a second term as president, in 1864, was music to the Szolds' ears. The April 9, 1865, surrender of Confederate general Robert E. Lee took place on the eve of Passover, and Rabbi Szold saw a symbolic connection between the Jewish festival of freedom, marking the Israelites' liberation from slavery in Egypt, and the victory of the pro-abolition forces. Only a few days later, however, Abraham Lincoln was shot as he sat with his wife in Ford's Theatre and died of his wounds the following day. News of the assassination spread like wildfire, stunning the entire country.[12]

Henrietta heard her parents talking and realized something momentous had taken place. For many years she remembered Lincoln's cortege passing through Baltimore on its way to Springfield, Illinois. It passed along their street, and family friends came to their house to watch it go by. Sophie stood by the window, lifting five-year-old Henrietta up so that she could see the procession, an event that became etched in her memory. Sometime later, Rabbi Szold hung a large portrait of Lincoln in his study, and he told Henrietta the president had been killed as a result of his fight for the abolition of slavery. On another occasion, when Henrietta and her mother were walking down their street, they passed an old house in which black families lived, and Sophie told her daughter that they were freed slaves. Henrietta was too young to fully understand the concept of slavery but became conscious of it years later. She read Harriet Beecher Stowe's *Uncle Tom's Cabin* and identified with Tom and his harsh fate, and her admiration for Lincoln grew. She would later copy the words of Walt Whitman's poem "This Dust Was Once the Man" into her notebook:

This dust was once the man,
Gentle, plain, just and resolute—under whose cautious hand,
Against the foulest crime in history known in any land or age,
Was saved the Union of These States.[13]

The sympathy Henrietta developed from childhood toward African Americans would accompany her throughout her life. She believed in freedom and equality, and she opposed discrimination in all its forms. When she visited Palestine years later, she decided that the doors of the clinics and hospitals she helped to establish there would always be open to Arabs and people of all faiths, races, and genders. All would receive the same medical treatment as Jews—a principle later adopted by the Israeli healthcare system and upheld to this day.

CHANGES

Optimism was in the air. With the war over, life began to return to normal. Food prices that had soared during the conflict gradually came down, and it was widely believed that rapid development and economic stability would follow. Baltimore's population grew, as did the number of Jews in the city. When Rabbi Szold arrived in Baltimore in 1859, there were 6,000 Jews in Baltimore. By the end of the war, the number had doubled and membership at Oheb Shalom had increased significantly.[14]

Changes had also come to the Szold family. After Henrietta, Sophie gave birth to two girls, Rebecca and Estella, who died in infancy. When Henrietta was five, her sister Rachel was born—a fair-haired child who resembled her mother. Until Rachel's arrival, Henrietta was an only child and, as such, was the sole object of her parents' attention. She was an alert and inquisitive child who took in all of the conversations she heard in the house and was particularly attached to her father. She loved to sit beside him in his study, at a small table on which she put her drawing papers. He was her first teacher, who taught her to read and write in German, the language they spoke at home. Every now and then he would read to her works by his favorite poets, Goethe and Schiller. He also taught her Hebrew, read the Bible with her, and told her tales from the Talmud and its commentaries. In the years that followed, he opened up the world of Jewish literature to her, preparing her for the life of an intellectual—a kind of training that was, at the time, reserved exclusively for boys.

Attending the Misses Adams' School for Girls marked the beginning of a new chapter in Henrietta's life. The Misses Adams were two sisters who came to Baltimore from the South, after having lost everything in the war, and founded a private school for the daughters of their friends. The school, at 222 West Madison Street, soon gained a reputation for academic excellence. The school opened up a new world for Henrietta. She learned English and was a diligent student. She also learned to play the piano and, when she was older, enjoyed going to concerts and listening to the works of the classical composers. She began taking out books from the municipal library near the family's home and became a bookworm. Every time she brought a book home, she would sit in a corner and not put it down until she had finished it. During her years at school she would exchange library books every day, reading anything she could lay her hands on.

The Szold family continued to grow. Three years after Rachel's arrival, Sadie was born. Sophie's mother, Miriam Schaar, repeatedly asked the Szolds when they were coming home, since the Schaar family in Hungary still expected Sophie and Rabbi Szold to return to Europe. When they had left for America, Rabbi Szold and Sophie at first had no intention of settling there, planning to return to Europe after a few years. Now Sophie told her mother that they had decided to remain in America permanently, for a number of reasons. Sophie noted, "In America a father of three daughters can look into the future with less worry than he can in Europe, since here the only thing necessary for a girl to be able to marry is a good education. No one even mentions dowries."[15] Sophie honestly believed this to be the case in America. She had yet to learn that many of the traditions Central European Jews had brought with them from the old country were still maintained. In Sophie and Rabbi Szold's view, "a good education" meant encouraging their daughters to study and broaden their horizons in the fields of literature, history, the arts, music, and so forth, while ensuring that they were also well mannered, as befit girls from a good family. Henrietta internalized her parents' values, which, alongside her own desire to excel at everything she did, would inform her entire life. The idea of being "a girl from a good family" may offer some explanation of her behavior later in life—not only her modesty but also her reluctance to stand up for her own rights and oppose being discriminated against as a woman, despite the indignation she felt in her heart.

The next few years saw two more additions to the Szold family, Johanna and Bertha. The apartment was now too small for the family, and they decided to move to a bigger house, at 207 West Lombard Street, not far from where they lived, and the Szolds knew other Jewish families in the neighborhood. On the ground floor was a large entrance hall, with Rabbi Szold's book-lined study off to one side, and the dining room and kitchen to the other. The bedrooms were on the upper floor. The move to Lombard Street marked the beginning of a new period in the Szolds' lives. Their house became a meeting place for young people and scholars in Baltimore and for visitors to the city. On the Sabbath, numerous guests would join the family around the large dining room table. Henrietta would listen attentively to their conversations about current events and matters concerning the Jewish community, sometimes even taking part in the discussions. It was here that she first became acquainted with Jewish affairs.[16]

A short time after they moved to Lombard Street, the family was struck by tragedy. Four-year-old Johanna contracted scarlet fever. Her whole body was covered with a red rash and her temperature soared. Dr. Aaron Friedenwald, a family friend, visited her every day and gave her the best of care, but the child succumbed to the disease. Her death cast the entire family into deep mourning. Johanna was a happy chatterbox of a child who laughed a lot and loved to sing. Her absence was felt in every corner of the house. The family found some consolation a year later, when Adele was born. The Szold family now had five surviving daughters.[17] Henrietta spent time with her sisters whenever she could, playing with them and reading them stories. On weekends, she took them for walks in the forest at the edge of the city and taught them the names of the plants and trees growing there. Henrietta developed a very close relationship with her sisters, which she maintained throughout her life.

Henrietta was on friendly terms with the girls at school, but especially enjoyed the company of Harry, Aaron Friedenwald's eldest son. The Friedenwalds lived near the Szolds, and Harry would often come over after school. He was two years her junior but looked older than his age. He was bright, inquisitive, and interested in a wide range of topics—a boy after Henrietta's own heart. They both loved reading, they shared the hobby of stamp collecting, and Harry liked the atmosphere in the Szold home. They remained friends even as adults.[18]

In her letters to her mother in Hungary, Sophie painted an idyllic picture of their life in Baltimore. She failed to mention the constant tension in their lives and the effect that Congregation Oheb Shalom's Reform tendencies had on her husband. Rabbi Szold, who was reluctant to adopt Reform practices, did everything he could to win over the congregation, initiating a wide range of activities. His sermons and affable personality attracted many new members and Oheb Shalom grew rapidly, becoming one of the largest synagogues in the United States. In the 1880s a large wave of Jewish immigration from Russia and Eastern Europe brought a further 40,000 Jews to Baltimore, changing the face of the Jewish community there.[19]

Henrietta grew up in the shadow of her father's anxieties. Her close relationship with him influenced not only her values, but also the path her life would take.

2

NEW HORIZONS

PARENTS, FACULTY, and numerous guests gathered at Ford's Grand Opera House in Baltimore for the Western High School graduation ceremony. Seated on the stage were the forty-eight graduates, dressed in white, with flowers braided in their hair. The commencement address, delivered by seventeen-year-old Henrietta Szold, was received with loud applause and was published in the local English- and German-language press. It was her first appearance before a large audience.

Western High School was a prestigious school whose curriculum included literature, history, botany, mathematics, Latin, and French. Szold, the school's only Jewish student, excelled in both natural sciences and the humanities, and wanted nothing more than to continue her studies at an institution of higher learning. Johns Hopkins University had recently been established in Baltimore, in 1876, and already enjoyed a fine reputation, but it did not admit women. There were many colleges and universities in other cities that did admit women at the time, but Henrietta's parents could not afford the tuition outside of Baltimore.

Baltimore's new university attracted students from other cities as well, including acquaintances of the Szold family, such as Rabbi Dr. Marcus Jastrow's son Joseph (Joe), the Flexner and Halperin brothers, and Cyrus Adler from Philadelphia, who would all become regular guests at the Szolds' Sabbath table. Henrietta envied them their college education, but she had to make do with public lectures at Johns Hopkins, which were little consolation. The frustration she felt at missing out on a higher education stayed with her for many years.

Szold was well aware of her parents' precarious financial situation and wanted to help provide for the family. Soon after graduation, she returned to the high school when asked to substitute for a teacher who was ill. Before long, she was offered a full-time teaching position at the Misses Adams' School for Girls, where she also had once been a student. Sophie and Rabbi Szold had no objections to her working as a teacher, although, as a rule, girls from middle-class Central European families did not work outside the home. To do so was considered undignified and an indication of financial difficulty, which hurt the girl's marriage prospects.[1] The money Henrietta brought in, however, was vital for the family. She also took on extra work giving private German lessons. Her workday began early in the morning and went on until late in the evening. As her sisters grew up, she encouraged them to study at women's colleges, paying their tuition from her own wages.

Henrietta helped her father translate his correspondence from German into English, learning from him that letters must not be written in a careless fashion but should be made interesting and original, employing rich, articulate language. Later in life, she wrote a great many letters, putting care and thought into each and every one. Her father talked to her about political and social events around the country, and shared with her news he received from his former classmates in Europe. Her fields of interest were constantly expanding in this formative period in her life.

At the age of seventeen, as she embarked on her teaching career, Szold also began writing articles for local papers and sending essays to the *Jewish Messenger,* a widely distributed weekly published in New York. At first her columns for the *Messenger* appeared every few weeks, under the heading "Our Baltimore Letter." She used the pen name "Sulamith," and wrote about Jewish and general affairs in the city, not merely reporting but expressing her opinions as well. In one of her columns, she criticized the attitude of many congregants toward their respective synagogues: "While the services are woefully neglected on Friday eve when there is usually a ball at one of our principal club houses . . . Saturday mornings, however, our ministers deliver their sermons to large numbers." She explained the phenomenon as follows: "Apparently there are but two central ideas to which all is subservient: business and pleasure, the fluctuation of prices or a round of dissipation. . . . The very mention of Jewish literature and history is sufficient to blanch their faces and strike their hearts with terror."[2] Similarly, she noted, when a lecturer concluded his talk at the local Young Men's Association, "there was a general uproarious movement as if the audience had been liberated from prison."[3]

Henrietta Szold as a
young woman

There is more than a hint of immaturity in Szold's early articles, but her writing quickly improved. A year later, she wrote another long column on the poor attendance at synagogue services, attributing it not to the summer heat but to a lack of understanding of the value of prayer. This column was far more sophisticated, featuring quotes from rabbinical sources and a legend about Hillel the Elder, which conveyed her message without undue moralizing.[4]

The more she wrote, the more polished her articles became. Their rich language, lucid style, and varied content attracted considerable attention. The editors of the *Jewish Messenger* asked her to write a regular column, and she became the weekly's Baltimore correspondent. Some of her articles were also published in the general press.

"I think I might have become a writer," she later said, and that was indeed her greatest ambition at the time—to gain entry into the intellectual and creative world without having to sacrifice her independence. She devoured literature; she was familiar with the works of Shakespeare and could quote from his plays. In addition to English and German, she was also fluent in French, and showed a keen interest in European literature, as well as intellectual essays and articles on current affairs. She wrote reviews of literary and philosophical works for newspapers and journals, and occasionally published articles of her own, many of which have been lost. She did not sign these articles with her own name but used pseudonyms.[5]

At the Misses Adams' School, Szold taught literature, history, English, and German, and was later asked to teach algebra, botany, physiology, and other subjects. She would remain at the school for nearly fifteen years, teaching eight hours a day, and was elected president of the school's alumni society. Not one to follow the beaten path, she constantly sought to improve her teaching methods, and her pedagogical insights were out of the ordinary. In a lecture she delivered to the state teachers' association, she remarked: "Do we constantly bear in mind that conveying information is only a subordinate part of the teacher's work? Do we always labor with the sole end in view of *training* the minds entrusted to our care? . . . In every study he [the true utilitarian] must be shown growth, which is life. . . . Take a flower one day, an insect the next, dwell upon such familiar things as rain and dew, make it a rule never to overstep the horizon of the child's actual or possible experience . . . There is one study that should be found in the curriculum of every boy and girl—the study of how to read the newspaper."[6]

Szold's lecture was reported in various newspapers. The innovative pedagogical principles she advocated at the time and the way in which she applied them in the classroom proved successful. Many years later, one of her students, Harriet Jones, recalled how Szold would arouse her students' curiosity, offering new perspectives on the material at hand. She enjoyed what she taught and sought to share that enjoyment with her students, for whom she was a source of inspiration. Harriet also recalled Szold's warm relationship with her pupils.[7]

Szold gained a reputation as a gifted teacher and was offered a position at the prestigious Oldfields School, a boarding and day school located in Sparks Glencoe, some thirty miles from Baltimore. Several times a week, after completing her teaching day at the Misses Adams' School, she would take the train to Oldfields, where she would teach German, classical literature, and philosophy.[8] In addition to teaching at two schools and giving private German lessons, Henrietta also found time for other activities. She would maintain this kind of busy schedule throughout her life.

At one point an opportunity arose for Rabbi Szold to finally leave the congregation that had given him so much heartache. He was offered the vacant position of rabbi at the German-immigrant Congregation Rodeph Shalom in Philadelphia, but ultimately he decided to decline the offer, choosing to remain at his congregation in Baltimore. He felt that eventually the traditional synagogues in Philadelphia would also turn to the Reform movement, and he would be no better off than before. The Rodeph Shalom position was then offered to Rabbi Marcus Jastrow, who had served as a rabbi in Warsaw and possessed a broad Jewish and general education. Rabbi Szold traveled to Philadelphia to greet Rabbi Jastrow and his Berlin-born wife, Bertha, and they became fast friends; several years later the two families would later become related by marriage.

The Jastrows' sons, Morris and Joe, often visited the Szold family home in Baltimore, and Henrietta and Morris became friends, writing to each other when they were unable to meet in person. While studying at the University of Pennsylvania, Morris was also an East Coast correspondent for a San Francisco newspaper. He asked Henrietta for information on Baltimore, and she sent him news of various events, along with her analysis of them. She worded her reports so cogently that Morris told her he was forwarding them directly to his paper without changing a word. Both of them were well informed about events in Europe, and they exchanged views on the subject.[9]

Reporting was merely a sideline for Morris Jastrow. He was about to graduate from university and spent most of his time preparing for his final exams. In a letter to Henrietta, he complained about his workload and grumbled that he was unable to complete all of his assignments. Based on her own experience, she suggested that he get up at 5:00 a.m. Aghast, Morris replied that the very idea made him shudder: "I cannot imagine getting up while everyone else is asleep, when it is still dark and the house is not yet heated. Sitting and studying in the cold seems ridiculous to me." He viewed getting up before seven as both physical and mental torture, explaining that he barely managed to get up at eight and, if possible, preferred to rise at nine. "If you do not want my blood to freeze, my hair to stand on end, and my skin to turn to goose bumps, do not ever mention getting up at five in the morning," he wrote. At Christmas break, Rabbi Szold invited Morris to come stay with them in Baltimore. Morris had a good sense of humor and was liked by the whole Szold family. After graduation, he decided to go to Breslau in Germany to continue his studies there.[10] Henrietta, who liked him, must have been disappointed, but she did not talk or write about it.

The twenty-fifth anniversary of Oheb Shalom was celebrated in 1879. The congregation elected a new president and a new generation of leaders, who decided to renovate the sanctuary in the Reform style. The leaders of the congregation also wished to cultivate closer ties with the non-Jewish population of the city, with the aim of integrating into general society. To

Rabbi Benjamin Szold,
father of Henrietta

this end, non-Jewish clergy and dignitaries were invited to festive events at the synagogue. Henrietta saw nothing wrong with efforts to remove barriers between Jews and non-Jews, as long as religious observance was not affected. To her mind, there was no reason to prevent contact between Jews and non-Jews in secular contexts such as lectures and encounters of various kinds, as the necessary separation of church and state in no way implied that members of different faiths must be separate from one another. In the religious sphere, however, she believed that there must be a clear separation between the public and private domains. Religious law must be shaped not by public comparisons between the religions but rather by the respective religious authorities.[11]

Rabbi Szold had not internalized the fact that a new generation had taken charge, and he was deeply frustrated by the changes at Oheb Shalom. Sophie believed that a break from the congregation would do Benjamin some good. She suggested he travel to Europe with twenty-year-old Henrietta, to visit her mother and other relatives. While they were still considering the idea of going to Europe, Sophie received the news that her mother was gravely ill. Her brother Heinrich, a doctor, was summoned to the bed-side, and her sister Pepi also came to care for their mother, but two days later Miriam Schaar passed away and was buried beside her husband in Cziffer. Sophie's brother wrote to her that they were thinking about post-poning the headstone unveiling, in the hope that either she or Rabbi Szold might attend. Sophie had visited her mother two years earlier, so she sug-gested that Benjamin go. He agreed, and Henrietta was glad of the op-portunity to travel to Europe.

A EUROPEAN TOUR

In June 1881, Henrietta and her father set sail for Europe. It was the first time she had ever set foot outside the United States. The stormy crossing excited her, and the passengers promenading on the deck aroused her cu-riosity, but she spent most of her time reading the books she had brought with her to learn about the cities they planned to visit.

After two weeks at sea, the ship docked at Bremen, Germany, from where Henrietta and her father traveled to Hamburg and Berlin. Rabbi Szold did not want to linger in Berlin, and after only two days in the city they went on to Dresden. Henrietta sensed that her father was troubled by his renewed encounter with German cities. He was pensive and his mind seemed flooded by memories, but perhaps that was to be expected on his first trip back to Europe since his arrival in America more than twenty years earlier. From Dresden they sailed southward on the Elbe River. The changing scenery, the townships and villages they passed, seemed to her like illustrations from a fairy-tale book. On their arrival in Prague, then part of the Habsburg Empire, Rabbi Szold decided to stay awhile and tour the city.

As they walked through the narrow alleys of the Jewish ghetto, Henri-etta felt as if she had been there before, as if the stories and legends she had heard from her father during her childhood had come to life. At the Synagogue of the Maharal (Rabbi Judah Loew ben Bezalel, the purported creator of the Golem of Prague), she looked up at the small door leading to the attic and imagined she could hear the footsteps of the Golem. At the old cemetery, she saw ancient headstones on the verge of collapse. On each stone was etched not only the names and dates of birth and death of the deceased but also the circumstances of their passing: an infant who had died of the plague, which had claimed so many lives; a young man murdered by rioters who had attacked the inhabitants of the Jewish quarter; a woman who had died giving birth to her son. The headstones were like pages of history that had stood as silent witnesses for centuries. "The main impression of my first journey to Europe," Henrietta later wrote, "was my profound sense of belonging with my father's and mother's people." On this trip with her father, she was able to experience Jewish communities and places about which she had read so much—their brooding darkness as well as their glorious splendor.[12]

In Pressburg (today Bratislava, Slovakia), her father confidently led her through the city where he had studied for several years. He pointed out the gateway leading to the ghetto. The gate was no longer there, "but he recollected the time when it used to close upon the last belated Jew . . . with the spiteful click that all prison doors know how to produce." The city's rulers later allowed the ghetto gates to be left open, and from time to time Jews would slip out, establishing themselves beyond its confines. It felt as though the walls of the ghetto had been pushed back a little farther, allowing in a sense of more fresh air and sunlight.

The visit left a profound impression on Henrietta. She wrote in her diary that when she had read about Jewish suffering in the past, "pity and sympathy filled out my whole heart," leaving "no room for anger," but now when she "stood in the place where gloom had brooded, where misery had flourished, where men and women had existed hermetically sealed up . . . such reflections could not but arouse the resentful feelings of a Shylock."[13]

In Pressburg, Henrietta discovered what her father had kept locked deep in his heart for many years. She knew that his mother had died when he was five years old, and that his father had passed away when he was eight, but not much more of his personal history. As they walked through the city streets, he told her quite candidly about his childhood as an orphan, his studies at the yeshiva in the city, the midday meals provided for the yeshiva students by members of the community. He recalled how, in one such family, relations between the husband and wife were so strained that they often quarreled in his presence, and he, in his embarrassment, would make himself small in a corner and wait for the storm to abate. On more than one occasion, in the heat of the argument, the woman forgot to serve his meal, and after waiting in embarrassment, he went back to the yeshiva hungry. His experiences at other homes also filled him with a feeling of helplessness. Henrietta now understood the source of her father's anxieties as an adult.

As they continued their journey, Henrietta looked forward to visiting Cziffer, the village where her mother had grown up and where her parents had met. The village was nestled among wooded mountains. Pretty little houses, surrounded by vegetable gardens and fruit trees, were reflected in the crystal-clear waters of a stream that flowed through the village. Beyond the houses lay vineyards and wheat fields. At the village center was a small old church, and everything seemed so peaceful and pastoral.

The encounter with the Schaar family was an emotional one. Her mother had always spoken fondly of them, and now Henrietta was meeting them face-to-face. Aunts and uncles and cousins from other towns and cities in the area came to embrace her. The warmth and affection she felt all around her were unlike anything she had ever experienced in Baltimore. She went to the cemetery with her aunts and uncles, and as she stood at her grandmother's graveside she was choked by tears. She had begun writing to her grandmother at the age of five, as soon as she had learned to read and write, and had always longed to meet her. Now she was attending the headstone unveiling at the grave of the grandmother she had never seen.

Henrietta asked to meet other relatives in Vienna. There the American Szolds were welcomed by Sophie's sister Minna Kien and two of their brothers, Heinrich and Naftali, whom their mother had sent to Breslau with Benjamin Szold to study at the university there. Henrietta also enjoyed meeting Minna's son Ignatz, a chemical engineering student at the Vienna Institute of Technology, who took her on a tour of the city. He hired a carriage and they drove along the Ringstrasse, the circular boulevard around the city center. Henrietta gazed in amazement at the parks and monuments on both sides of the boulevard. They also saw many magnificent homes and famous public buildings. Ignatz told her about the buildings they passed: the magnificent opera house; the Hofburg, the imperial place of Vienna; and the Gothic St. Stephen's Cathedral, all in the first district. The streets of the quarter were lined with bookshops and cafés, and Henrietta did not know where to look first.

In the second district, they reached Praterstrasse, with its broad paving stones and spacious mansions. Some of these houses belonged to affluent Jewish families, home to men such as Theodor Herzl, Sigmund Freud, and Arthur Schnitzler, who were still young and unknown at the time. Henrietta was impressed by the elegant structures, with their tall windows and carved stone jambs, and by the trees that towered over the rooftops along the banks of the Danube River. In the passing carriages, they saw fashionable ladies in all their finery heading toward the Prater promenade. Ignatz stopped the carriage and invited Henrietta into one of the cafés, and as they entered she was aware of the looks directed at her. With her dark complexion and black hair, she stood out beside the fair-haired women sitting there. Although they did not say a word, she could sense their hostility. She asked Ignatz if they could leave, for she had never experienced anything like this in America.

Henrietta had mixed feelings about her brief visit to the city, which had left a deep impression on her. The trip had opened up a new world to her, exciting her curiosity: the vibrant, cosmopolitan atmosphere, the palaces, theaters, and concert halls—all so different from everything she knew in Baltimore. She liked Ignatz's Viennese manners and enjoyed his company. He suggested that she stay with them in Vienna, where she would be able to study at an institution of higher learning, and he promised that he would accompany her on a trip to Italy in the winter. Henrietta was excited by the prospect. This was like an offer of marriage. In fact, Ignatz's parents thought Henrietta would be a perfect match for their son and urged Rabbi Szold to leave her with them for a year, or even a shorter period. But Benjamin wanted Henrietta to return to Baltimore with him. "The little ones will miss you," he told her. Henrietta felt a twinge of sadness. She was attracted to Ignatz and wanted very much to remain with her aunt, but she obeyed her father without argument: she packed her suitcase, and they left Vienna.[14] Henrietta kept this memory for a long time as a great loss of an opportunity to marry. She mentioned it in her diary many years later when she met Ignatz and his wife in France on her travels to Europe in 1909.[15]

On their way home to America, Rabbi Szold and Henrietta stopped off in Munich, where he met some of his friends from his student days in Breslau. They reached Paris in August, and Henrietta was dazzled by the large shop windows lit up with electric bulbs. The main streets were crowded even late at night, and the city was so alive and exuberant that Vienna seemed almost sleepy by comparison. When they visited the Great Synagogue, they found a wedding taking place, and the beadle suggested they stay and see "a four-thousand-franc wedding." The bride was the daughter of a member of the Consistoire, the representative council of French Jewry. The wives of the community's grandees, all decked in finery and jewels, reminded Henrietta of the nouveau riche women back in Baltimore, although the splendor she witnessed in Paris was beyond anything she could have imagined. Henrietta thus experienced yet another aspect of the multifaceted nature of European Jewry. After a brief visit to London, the Szolds sailed back to Baltimore. Henrietta's European tour left a lasting impression on her, and she hoped to return to the continent someday.[16]

After her summer-long absence, Henrietta was glad to get home and see her friends and acquaintances. She was also happy to see Harry Friedenwald, who told her he had decided to follow in his father's footsteps and study medicine. She went back to work and to her various other activities; her articles continued to appear in the *Jewish Messenger* and elsewhere. Although overworked, she was in good spirits and looked toward the future. She always remembered what Harry's mother, Bertha, had once said jokingly: We have five boys in our family and the Szolds have five girls. Perhaps we should match them up. Deep in her heart, Henrietta hoped that this wish would come true, at least as far she was concerned.

When Harry started medical school, he told her all about the fascinating world he had discovered. Szold expressed her frustration at being prevented from studying at university in an editorial she published in a bimonthly periodical called *Education: An International Magazine.* She wrote: "If, at the same time, a superior college for young women could be endowed in Baltimore, whose advanced students could be admitted to the great opportunities of the University for special study, all plans might be happily harmonized and the monumental city add to its other attractions the fame of a great university town."[17] Her remarks elicited considerable attention and were reported in newspapers and journals around the country, as far west as San Francisco, but her desire was no closer to being realized.

In addition to her work, Szold continued to dedicate time to pursuits close to her heart. She joined the Baltimore Botanical Club (part of the Maryland Academy of Sciences) and convinced Harry to join as well. Henrietta was an active member of the club, organizing meetings and proposing topics for discussion. She also delivered the occasional lecture, including presenting the paper "Growth, Mechanics of, Tensions and Mutations of Plants" in October 1890.[18]

Henrietta's love of botany remained with her throughout her life. Even after she settled in Palestine, she noted in her diary that she longed to stand in the shade of the forests on the outskirts of Baltimore, and she mentioned the trees by name, as if they were close friends: "oaks, elms, maples, beeches, chestnuts, planes, and liriodendrons."[19] She also recalled how the memory of the forests in all their radiant beauty in the fall, the leaves painted in a palette of colors, filled her with longing: "I sometimes feel the need to fly and see them," she wrote years later. On her travels in Palestine, when she visited the Hadassah clinics and Youth Aliyah institutions, she would ask her driver to stop the car so she could get out and identify plants she saw on the roadside or climb the slope of a path to hunt for herbs.

THE TREFA BANQUET OF 1883

On July 11, 1883, more than a hundred leaders and rabbis gathered at the magnificent Bene Yeshurun synagogue in Cincinnati, at the invitation of Rabbi Isaac Mayer Wise, in order to form a representative body of all the Jewish religious movements in the United States. Wise believed that American Jewry stood at an important juncture in terms of its religious organization, in which he hoped to play a leading role. It did indeed turn out to be a historic moment, but not quite in the way Wise had expected. The leaders and rabbis invited to the event—including Rabbi Szold, who was accompanied by Henrietta in her role as correspondent for the *Jewish Messenger*—represented seventy-six congregations from all over the United States. It was a splendid affair. Benjamin Szold was one of the rabbis invited to address the audience. Musical pieces were performed between the speeches by a small choir of five women and three men, accompanied on the organ.[20]

The event marked the ordination of four graduates of the first class of the Reform movement's Hebrew Union College in Cincinnati, as well as the tenth anniversary of the Union of American Hebrew Congregations, founded by Wise. Wise's aim in convening the gathering was to advance his plan to bring all the Jewish congregations in America under the umbrella of the Reform movement's rabbinical organization. Wise observed the audience of rabbis listening to his speech and believed his vision was about to be realized. He could not have imagined that his dream would instead soon be shattered.

In the evening, a festive dinner was held at the exclusive Highland House restaurant, overlooking the Ohio River. In addition to the meeting participants, many other guests were invited, including Christian clergymen and professors from the University of Cincinnati. On each beautifully laid table was an ornate nine-course menu that included littleneck clams, soft-shell crabs, shrimp, frogs' legs, chicken, pigeons, cheeses, assorted cakes, and ice cream, all accompanied by five different wines.

On reading the menu, the Orthodox rabbis were dumbstruck. All of the dishes were *trefa*, forbidden by Jewish dietary law. The menu broke almost every rule, serving seafood, non-kosher meat, and meat and dairy at the same meal. Henrietta was absolutely stunned. What she saw was diametrically opposed to everything she knew. Some of the traditionalist rabbis got up and angrily left the restaurant, while others simply sat frozen in their seats, not eating and not joining in the applause for the speakers.

What soon came to be known as the Trefa Banquet was reported in the Jewish press throughout America, creating a storm. The large papers published articles criticizing Wise. Rabbi Marcus Jastrow, of the Rodeph Shalom congregation in Philadelphia, accused Wise of disgraceful and contemptible behavior, claiming that he was not a rabbi at all, as he held no academic degrees and had never been ordained. In the *Jewish Messenger*, Henrietta expressed her disgust that traditionalist rabbis had been invited to the event and served non-kosher food, which in her view crossed every imaginable line. She was disappointed by the fact that only a few people had left the restaurant.[21]

The organizers were surprised by the heated reactions to the event and insisted that it had not been meant as a provocation. The catering, they explained, had been entrusted to a Jewish caterer by the name of Gustav Lindemann, who did not observe Jewish dietary laws but had been instructed to prepare kosher food for the event and had failed to do so. Still, the storm did not abate, and the attacks against Wise and the Reform movement continued for weeks. Tensions mounted when Wise failed to apologize and instead replied with his own attacks, accusing some of his rabbinical detractors of hypocrisy, as they themselves did not observe the dietary laws. His supporters rallied to his defense.

Wise did not foresee the impact the Trefa Banquet would have on American Jewry or the developments to which it would give rise, further shattering his hope of creating an umbrella organization under his leadership. Following the Trefa Banquet, a number of congregations left the Union of American Hebrew Congregations, and voices were heard in the Jewish press—New York's *American Hebrew* and Philadelphia's *Jewish Record*—calling for the establishment of a modern, traditionalist rabbinical seminary that would compete with the Reform movement's Hebrew Union College.[22] The Trefa Banquet was not the cause of the rift between the different movements in American Jewry, but it served as a catalyst and helped demarcate the boundaries.[23] The controversy in the Jewish press did not abate, and the dispute between the two camps escalated. Some radical Reform rabbis decided to further define their position and, in 1885, convened a conference in Pittsburgh. After three days of discussions, some twenty rabbis, including Isaac Wise, published the Pittsburgh Platform, which constituted a radical departure from traditional Judaism.[24]

Congregations that opposed the platform decided to hasten the establishment of a rabbinical seminary committed to the preservation of Jewish law. A short time after the Trefa Banquet and the Pittsburgh Conference, the Jewish Theological Seminary (JTS) was founded, counting Rabbi Jastrow among its supporters. Sabato Morais, the rabbi and cantor of Congregation Mikveh Israel in Philadelphia and one of the driving forces behind the establishment of the seminary, was elected president. The seminary's founders stressed that while the new institution was traditional, it was prepared to accept changes mandated by modernity, as long as they did not contravene Jewish law.[25] The establishment of JTS also laid the foundations of the Conservative Judaism movement in the United States, which grew rapidly.

Henrietta had become increasingly exposed to public affairs, and her presence at the Trefa Banquet and involvement in the ensuing controversy afforded her particular insight into the diverging approaches among American Jews. She followed the processes unfolding around her, taking a keen interest in the individual leaders and movements active within the American Jewish community and in their respective roles in the shaping of American Jewry.[26]

She also took note of a new force that had already begun to change the face of American Jewry. A large wave of Jewish immigration from Eastern Europe to America began in the final decades of the nineteenth century, gaining momentum in the 1890s. Between 1881 and 1914, more than 2 million Jews immigrated to America from Russia, Eastern Europe, and the Austro-Hungarian Empire. The large number of traditionalists among these immigrants served to reinforce the traditionalist camp in the United States. The movement for Conservative Judaism thus grew apace with its Reform counterpart.[27] Rabbi Szold, a supporter of the Conservative movement, was prepared to adapt to the modern world on condition it did not entail deviating from the basic principles of Jewish law. Henrietta followed in her father's footsteps and joined the public struggle for the preservation of traditional Jewish heritage, never imagining that she would one day become an object of that struggle as the first woman to study at JTS.

HARRY FRIEDENWALD IN BERLIN

On Sunday evenings, the Szold house on Lombard Street was abuzz with young people gathered there. Around the table sat students from Johns Hopkins and local friends. Lively conversations on current affairs sometimes turned into heated arguments. Henrietta took part and freely voiced her opinions, standing out with her knowledge, analytical skills, and articulate expression, earning the respect of all present. Harry Friedenwald, a regular participant in these evenings, graduated from medical school in Baltimore and decided to specialize in ophthalmology in Berlin.[28] Henrietta was sorry to see him go, but they kept in touch through regular correspondence. Harry wrote to her from Berlin about his internship, his experiences, and his impressions of his new city.

Henrietta knew that had it not been for the exclusion of women at Johns Hopkins University, she too would have been able to fulfill her ambitions, scholarly and otherwise. Harry, Morris Jastrow, Cyrus Adler, and others in her circle had all followed this path, first studying at an American university and then going on to specialized education in other cities or countries, thereby ensuring professional success, financial rewards, and social status. This path was closed to her, although her talents may have been greater than theirs. Men who took part in public life were given impressive titles, invited to join committees, and entrusted with key positions in the institutions. Women stood no chance of realizing their ambitions or gaining equal status.

Szold remained in Baltimore and continued with her work, but her social life was limited to the Sunday evening gatherings at her family's home. Among the regular visitors was Joe Jastrow, who was studying psychology at Johns Hopkins University. Like many visitors to the Szolds' home, he greatly admired Henrietta's intelligence and talents, but he was romantically drawn to her sister Rachel, a beautiful, elegant, and exuberant young woman. He proposed marriage, and she accepted. Sophie and Rabbi Szold liked Joe and were happy to link their family to that of their friend Rabbi Jastrow through their children's marriage. According to Jewish custom, parents generally sought to marry off the eldest daughter first, followed by the other daughters in order of age. Sophie and Rabbi Szold did not try to dissuade Rachel or ask her to postpone her marriage in the hope that Henrietta might, in the interim, find a suitable partner. If Sophie and Rabbi Szold felt uncomfortable with Henrietta being skipped over, so to speak, they did not show it. Preparations for the wedding got under way, and the house became a hive of activity as excitement mounted over the family's first wedding.

While everyone was busy preparing for Rachel's wedding, Henrietta found her thoughts going to Harry Friedenwald, whose letters she eagerly awaited. The correspondence between Harry and Henrietta contains many indications that they truly missed each other. From Berlin he wrote to her about his studies and work, his teachers and fellow interns. He described the latent antisemitism at the clinic, and the thin veneer of politeness that barely concealed his colleagues' contempt for him. Antisemitism was endemic among the German and Austrian intelligentsia, so Harry passed his free time in the company of other young Jews. He became friends with Leon Bodenheimer, a Jewish student he had met at the kosher restaurant where they dined, and was happy to spend weekends with him when he was not on duty at the clinic.

The marriage of Joe and Rachel was celebrated in Baltimore in 1888, attended by a large number of guests. Joe had completed his psychology studies and was offered a post in Madison, Wisconsin, where the couple settled after the wedding. When the joyous occasion was over and silence had settled on the Szold household once more, Henrietta wrote to Harry about the wedding, and Sophie added a few sentences to the letter, telling him that they were sorry he had not been able to be there.

The correspondence between Harry and Henrietta continued. Harry took pains to describe Berlin, the magnificent concert halls and the performances he attended on Sundays, when he was not at the clinic. He also described his weekend walks in Berlin with his friend Leon, and reported to her on current affairs—political events and the mood in Berlin, the Jewish community and its relations with non-Jews, and the constant presence of antisemitism.[29] The subject of antisemitism appears frequently in their correspondence: "Why are we so hated?" she wondered in a letter to Harry.[30]

When Harry had been in Berlin for two years, Henrietta wrote him a long letter, which she ended with the sentence "I must confess that some evenings are altogether incomplete without you." She also mentioned that his name occasionally came up in conversations at home. Harry hastened to reply that he was glad his name was mentioned at the Szolds': "I have never ceased to think of the pleasant evenings I spent in your home. . . . It is one of the nicest reminiscences of many of the most important years of my past life. I have reason to look to coming years for much pleasure from the same source."[31] Henrietta kept all his letters.

One day, Henrietta called on Bertha Friedenwald and told her about the letters she had received from Harry. Bertha understood that they had been corresponding intensively and feared they were developing a romantic relationship. Trying to dissuade Harry, she wrote to him saying that he should remember Henrietta was older than he was, and intimated that he should stop writing to her. Although Harry had a warm relationship with his parents and was attentive to their wishes, his correspondence with Henrietta did not stop. When Bertha heard from Cyrus Adler that two of his relatives, pretty young women from affluent families, were going on a tour of Europe and would be visiting Berlin, she sent a letter to Harry suggesting he meet them and spend time with them while they were in the city. Harry acceded to his mother's request and toured the city with the two young ladies, but Bertha did not stop there. She wrote to Harry that many people were going to visit Paris to see the Eiffel Tower, erected in March 1889. "I have no doubt that you will meet lots of people from Baltimore this season. . . . Among them is Miss Birdie Stein, a daughter of Sam Stein, the banker," she commented, adding, "This Miss Stein is an awfully sweet girl," and otherwise singing her praises.[32]

In 1889, the Friedenwald family was invited to Rabbi Szold's sixtieth-birthday party, at the Szold home. Aaron Friedenwald, who was still mourning the death of his brother and had not left the house for a long time, accepted the invitation, since he liked and admired Rabbi Szold. The table was laden with dishes and delicacies all made by Sophie. The main event at the party was a performance of Dickens's *The Old Curiosity Shop* by the Szold girls, Sadie, Bertha, Adele, and Henrietta—the last of whom played the lead role and also directed the play. Henrietta was outstanding, with wonderful acting and diction. The play was amusing and the guests burst into laughter every now and then. Bertha Friedenwald wrote to Harry about the lovely party at the Szold home, praised the performance and the actresses, and again urged him to avoid a close relationship with Henrietta. Prior to his return to Baltimore, however, Harry wrote to his mother about how much he missed his family and the city, adding that were he to return to Baltimore that very day, he would spend his first evening with the family and the second with the Szolds. Bertha was alarmed and once more reminded him that Henrietta was both older and not a suitable partner.[33] Despite his mother's urgings, Harry and Henrietta continued to correspond, and as time went by, her anticipation for his return to Baltimore grew.

At the conclusion of his ophthalmology internship in Berlin, Harry left for the United States, stopping in several places in Europe along the way, including Vienna and Capri. He sent Henrietta a letter from the Italian island, in which he enclosed some flowers he had picked. He then spent two weeks in London, with Henrietta counting the days to his return to Baltimore. He reached the city on March 16, 1890, and received a warm welcome from his parents and the entire family. He did not linger long with his family before going to the Szold home. His meeting with Henrietta was emotional; they were happy to see each other again. Harry resumed his Sunday evening visits to the Szolds' but felt that the house and its atmosphere had changed in his absence. The group of Jewish students that had previously visited the house, animating it with their passionate discussions of public affairs, was no longer there. Some had left Baltimore after graduating from Johns Hopkins, moving away to other cities or to Europe to continue their studies. Those who had been offered positions had embarked on their professional lives. Even Henrietta seemed less vibrant than she had before his departure for Europe. He wondered whether her work was beginning to take a toll or whether his own pleasant memories of her had simply been magnified during his absence.

Bertha persisted in her efforts to persuade Harry to break off his relationship with Henrietta. Although Henrietta came from a respected family and possessed some admirable qualities, Bertha wanted her son to marry an attractive young woman who would devote herself to home and family. An educated and talented woman involved in public affairs would, in all likelihood, spend a good deal of time outside the home, which could not but affect her family. Bertha thus sought to introduce Harry to eligible young women in Baltimore. At one such meeting he met Birdie Stein, one of the women his mother had tried to interest him in earlier. Stein was a beautiful, elegant young woman who dressed in the latest fashion, and Harry asked her out. On November 29, 1891, a celebration was held at the Chizuk Amuno synagogue in honor of the ninetieth birthday of Jonas Friedenwald, patriarch of the Friedenwald clan. Among the many people who came to congratulate Friedenwald and deliver speeches in his honor was Rabbi Szold. A few months later there was another festive event at the synagogue, when Samuel Stein invited his many friends to celebrate the marriage of his daughter Birdie to Harry Friedenwald.[34]

Henrietta did not show her profound disappointment and frustration. She neither talked nor wrote about her feelings, and her grief remained locked in her heart. Her sisters took pity on her for being so troubled and neglecting her appearance. Unlike so many young women, Henrietta paid little attention to what she wore, and she had no patience for girlish behavior. She was not a natural beauty and did nothing to enhance her appearance. Her long hair was drawn back and tied with a ribbon, and she appeared graceless. Her sisters urged her to reduce her workload, to make time to buy some fine clothes, but she refused. She worked ever longer hours and threw herself into new challenges. She seemed to be trying to drown her sorrows in hard work—a pattern that would repeat itself at similar junctures throughout her life.

"NO JEWS ALLOWED"

An advertisement for a New Jersey hotel published in the *New York Tribune* included the caveat "No Jews Allowed." Austin Corbin, who owned a hotel chain, declared in 1879, "We do not like Jews as a class," and he barred Jews from his Brooklyn hotels.[35] Some hotels in the Catskills—a resort area favored by the Jewish middle class—and elsewhere barred Jews, posting signs with the warning "No Dogs or Jews Allowed." And in 1877, Joseph Seligman, a prominent Jewish banker and businessman, had been denied entrance to the Grand Union Hotel in Saratoga Springs, a well-known summer resort, and when the incident was publicized in the press, it provoked fierce reactions.[36]

Even in her early twenties, Henrietta was troubled by antisemitism, and her European tour had further heightened her sensitivity to it. The ghettos she saw there, coupled with her father's stories about his own experiences, reinforced her views regarding antisemitism in Europe. She was more optimistic about American society, hoping that the ideals of freedom and tolerance so close to its heart would prevent it from allowing harm to come to the Jews. Many American Jews shared her feeling that occasional attacks against Jews in the United States were merely a passing phase, alien to a society committed to the principles of freedom and equality. Not everybody agreed. The winds blowing in Europe at the time certainly did not bode well. The granting of equal rights to the Jews with the unification of Germany in 1871 and the establishment of the Reich by Otto von Bismarck had not put an end to the flagrant discrimination against Jews in that country, and the situation had only grown worse in the years that followed.

Henrietta's attention was drawn to the growing antisemitism in Europe and Russia, and she foresaw the danger it posed to the Jewish people. She knew the problem needed to be addressed as soon as possible, and felt she was up to the task. She was not one to shrink from global problems, and often acted as if she bore the weight of the world on her shoulders. Szold perceived antisemitism not as a specifically Jewish problem but as a phenomenon that undermined the very foundations of American society, running counter to its core value of freedom and equal rights for all, without discrimination. She viewed the struggle to eradicate antisemitism as a patriotic duty incumbent upon every American citizen. She dissociated herself from the angry public reaction to the Seligman affair, since she believed that it stemmed from the fact that Seligman was one of the wealthiest men in America. She felt that discrimination should be fought wherever it occurred and that action must be taken to uproot it. She was convinced that antisemitism in America had more to do with Shylock than Judas—that is, it was more economic than religious. The entrepreneurs developing the country were highly regarded in America, as they promoted productivity, physical labor, and industrial efficiency, and many Jews had met with success in the fields of industry and commerce.[37] In times of crisis, however, hostility toward them increased, as it had during the Civil War, when Jews were accused of war profiteering and black marketeering.

It was now clear to Henrietta that hatred of the Jews was far more complex than she had previously imagined. She came to understand that the claim that the financial success of Jews was the primary cause of antisemitism was simplistic and specious. From European newspapers and journals, she learned about the wave of antisemitism sweeping through Germany, with its false claims about Jews who slaughtered Christian children to use their blood in religious rituals—accusations similar to the medieval blood libels.

The tide of antisemitism moving through Germany, Austria, and France—countries that had reached great heights in science and culture—worried Henrietta. She held fast to her belief that the humanistic values of

American society would not allow this kind of sentiment to flourish in the United States. She feared, however, that the reaction of the Jewish community to the antisemitism they did encounter in America would lead to self-segregation, and she believed that avoiding conflict was defeatist. Only facing the danger head-on would ultimately be successful. For that reason she proposed meetings between Jews and non-Jews, as a way of challenging anti-Jewish prejudice.

During Passover in 1881, pogroms erupted in southwestern Russia after the Jews were accused of the murder of Tsar Alexander II. Angry mobs broke into Jewish homes in dozens of cities, towns, and villages, murdering men, women, and children, looting and raping, burning and destroying. This brutal outburst of violence left entire communities in ruins and tens of thousands of Jews reeling from the horrors they had seen and heard. Szold was stunned as she read the reports in the widely circulated British weekly *Jewish Chronicle,* which were accompanied by illustrations of the dead and wounded and of the still-smoking ruins of Jewish homes, vividly conveying the magnitude of the disaster.

The pogroms struck Russian Jewish communities like the eruption of a volcano. There had been pogroms in the past, but the Jews were accustomed to believing that they were simply attacks by unruly mobs and that the authorities would protect them. While previous pogroms had consisted mainly of looting and vandalism, the pogroms of the 1880s also included acts of murder, rape, and abuse of infants and the elderly. With the prolonged and expanding wave of pogroms it became increasingly clear that the authorities not only were not protecting the Jews, but were actually encouraging the perpetrators. The terror and fear engendered by the pogroms became an integral part of the Jews' lives, lives that could be taken with impunity, and it was then that they began to acknowledge that there was no place for them in Russia.[38]

Szold received a German copy of Judah Leib Pinsker's pamphlet *Auto-Emancipation,* written in the wake of the pogroms and published in Berlin in 1882.[39] The pamphlet was subtitled *An Admonition to His Brethren by a Russian Jew.* The author's name did not appear, but it was widely known Pinsker had written it. According to Pinsker, "Judeophobia is a form of demonopathy, with the distinction that the Jewish ghost has become known to the whole race of mankind, not merely to certain races, and that it is not incorporeal, like other ghosts, but is a being of flesh and blood, and suffers the most excruciating pain from the wounds inflicted upon it by the timorous multitude who imagine themselves threatened by it." Theodor Herzl later confessed that he had not read Pinsker's pamphlet when it was published, and that had he read it, he would not have published his *Der Judenstaat.*[40]

Szold was impressed by Pinsker's pamphlet, but she did not share his pessimism. It was difficult for Szold to espouse Pinsker's "diagnosis" that antisemitism was an incurable disease. His explanation of Jewish detachment from general society ran counter to her thinking. She herself did not feel detached from American society and, like many Americans of goodwill, believed that all injustice could be eradicated. She continued to believe it was possible to fight antisemitism.

Henrietta saw in Emma Lazarus a shining example of activism in both Jewish and general causes, a woman whose voice rang clear and true and reached the hearts of many. Lazarus was a gifted poet from a wealthy Sephardic family that had come to America in colonial times. Her father moved in non-Jewish intellectual circles, and Emma was unfamiliar with Jewish life. This changed when she learned of antisemitism and the pogroms in Russia. She was shocked by the sight of the Russian Jewish refugees who arrived in New York. She proudly embraced her Jewish identity and dedicated herself to fighting antisemitism. Lazarus raised her voice against the anti-immigration faction in the United States, led by the Immigration Restriction League, which sought to bar Russian refugees—most of whom were Jews—from entering the United States.[41] Lazarus called upon her country to open its gates to refugees, and in this spirit she composed the sonnet "The New Colossus," later inscribed on a plaque at the base of the Statue of Liberty in New York Harbor.[42]

Szold was impressed by Lazarus's courage and ability to stir the public conscience, and respected her for breaking down the barriers that kept women out of public life. She saw Lazarus as a model for other women, although her circumstances were far from those of most women. Moses Lazarus had encouraged his daughter's literary talents since she was a child, and his contacts in non-Jewish social circles facilitated the introduction of Emma's works into general society. The family's favorable economic circumstances also allowed her to devote all her energy to writing and public affairs, and she never married. After her Jewish awakening, Lazarus threw herself wholeheartedly into the study of Jewish culture and history, as well as the Hebrew language. Beyond defending immigrants seeking refuge in the United States, Emma also believed in the rebirth of the Jewish people and its return to its ancient homeland.

Szold followed Lazarus's activities closely, taken by the fact that the other woman subscribed to the notion of a Jewish "return to Zion." She shared Emma's views and poems in the non-Jewish circles she frequented, and she believed that Lazarus's influence on public opinion would only grow in the years to come. Szold was stunned by Lazarus's death from cancer in November 1887, at the age of thirty-eight, and mourned her loss. The *American Hebrew* decided to publish a commemorative issue in memory of Lazarus, inviting various writers and intellectuals, including Henrietta, to contribute.[43] Henrietta believed that the struggle championed by Lazarus must not be abandoned. Szold herself was neither an author nor a poet, but she believed that antisemitism had to be challenged in public, by every possible means.

3

THE IMMIGRANTS ARE COMING

ALTIMORE SAW THE ARRIVAL of many Jewish immigrants from Russia, Eastern European countries, and other places. Some of the Jewish immigrants came from the lower classes, but they were not entirely destitute, because some resources were required to make the long journey across the ocean, and they needed money for the first weeks in America until they found work. However, the established German Jews were ambivalent about their newly arrived co-religionists. They sympathized with them, but also felt a certain aversion toward them. The Jews from Central Europe who had already managed to set down roots and adopt the customs and manners of their non-Jewish neighbors were afraid that the newcomers from Eastern Europe would tarnish their own image. To the Jews from Germany, the Yiddish spoken by the immigrants sounded like a bastardized version of the elegant German of which they were so proud. They were prepared to assist those in need, from community charity funds.[1] But the established Jews were concerned that the continued influx might impose an excessive economic burden on them. Henrietta saw this attitude as a slap in the face to immigrants who had fled adversity abroad.

The Russian immigrants also differed in their religious practices. While some American Jews adhered to traditional observances, among others there was a large variety of identities. From time to time, Rabbi Benjamin Szold, who felt sympathy for the immigrants, would go out to the pier,

The Jewish Quarter of Jerusalem in Ottoman-ruled Palestine, c. 1900

where he himself had landed some twenty years earlier, to greet the new-comers as they disembarked. Henrietta often accompanied him.

Some 2.4 million Jews emigrated from Russia and Eastern Europe be-tween 1881 and 1914. Nearly 2 million of them went to the United States. Others headed for England, France, Argentina, Canada, and South Africa. There were also a few groups of idealistic Zionists who preferred to join agricultural settlements in the land of their fathers: some 65,000 Jews settled in Ottoman Palestine between 1880 and 1914.[2]

The mass migrations of the late nineteenth century were facilitated by improved modes of transportation. Railways across the continent and ship-ping lines based in ports such as Hamburg, Liverpool, and Rotterdam shortened the duration of the journey from Eastern Europe to America to

A ship full of immigrants to the United States passes the Statue of Liberty, 1887

around two weeks. There were no restrictions on the admission of immigrants to the United States, except for those with chronic illnesses. Most of the Jewish immigrants from Eastern Europe were referred to by US immigration officials as "Russians," including the many who were actually from Poland and the smaller numbers from Lithuania and other provinces of the Russian Empire. Ships full of immigrants anchored in the major harbors on the East Coast, mainly New York, but also Philadelphia, Boston, and Baltimore; many of the immigrants went no farther than their port of debarkation and settled there.

The Jewish population of Baltimore from the 1880s doubled four times, with thousands more arriving in the city over the course of the following decades. Many of them found homes near the harbor in the eastern part of the city.[3] Peddlers circulated, crying out their wares. Some people relied on odd jobs and lived hand to mouth, while others wandered the city searching for work.

When Henrietta encountered unemployed immigrants, as so many others did, she racked her brain for a way to help them find jobs and a place in society. Of the many immigrants in Baltimore, one group of young people in particular drew her attention. Their conversation revealed that some of them were well educated, fluent in Hebrew, and familiar with modern Hebrew literature. She proposed that they organize a literary society. They

named it for Isaac Baer Levinsohn, one of the pioneers of modern Hebrew literature in Russia. Others soon joined the new organization and its
activities expanded. They also agreed to Henrietta's suggestion that they
establish a Zionist association, one of the first in the United States, and
her friend Harry Friedenwald joined too.[4] This was well before Theodor
Herzl founded the Zionist Organization in Europe in 1897.

At the meetings of the Hevrat Zion, or Zion Association, Henrietta met
Saul Bernstein, an ascetic young man with a beard and blazing black eyes.
He told her he had studied art in Lithuania and was eager to continue his
studies and paint but was quite penniless. Impressed by the paintings he
showed her, Henrietta tried to help by selling them for him. When Bernstein decided to continue his studies in Paris, he kept contact with Henrietta, writing her desperate letters complaining of his poverty and loneliness there. She suggested he send her sketches of his paintings and prints
and asked her acquaintances to support him. Some responded and bought
his works, providing money that Henrietta sent Bernstein to help him fulfill his dream to enroll in the Académie Julian.

Bernstein continued to send her letters bemoaning his acute shortage
of funds, including the fact that he could eat only once a day and was constantly forced to move from one dismal apartment to another. He again
urged Henrietta to sell more of his prints. Despite all of her other activities, Henrietta became his patron, making strenuous efforts to sell his
works to her acquaintances and send him money. She kept writing him
letters and encouraged him not to give up hope and to keep painting, for
his situation was sure to improve. Their lively correspondence continued
for a number of years.[5] Henrietta organized exhibitions in Baltimore, where
some of his works were sold, and he began to make a name for himself.
Sadly, Bernstein died in 1905, at the age of thirty-three, before he could
realize his dreams. She made similar efforts to assist other immigrants to
overcome the obstacles that stood in their way. Her friendship with Bernstein and other young immigrants made Henrietta even more aware of
the hardships suffered by the refugees from Russia.

Every day on her way to work, Henrietta passed immigrants wandering
the city to find a job. Many relied on charity from the Jewish community
to survive. Henrietta saw charity as a stopgap form of assistance that was
of little benefit and did not really help the immigrants better their situation. What was more, living on charity increased their dependence and
sense of inferiority and humiliation. She did not merely observe the immigrants from the sidelines, but felt obligated to take concrete steps to help
them. She came up with the idea of creating a kind of gateway to the labor
market and American society. She was certain that the young, educated

immigrants of the I.B.L. Hebrew Literary Society could help her implement the plan she had devised. When she shared it with them, they quickly endorsed it and enthusiastically took up the great challenge.

A NIGHT SCHOOL FOR IMMIGRANTS

Szold immediately got to work on her new project: evening classes where immigrants could learn English. She believed that acquiring command of the language would provide them with the means to enter American society. She asked the members of the literary society to circulate information about the English classes among the immigrants. They produced flyers in Yiddish and distributed them on the streets where the immigrants lived. Henrietta also published announcements in Italian and other languages, for non-Jewish immigrants. Before long, thirty people had signed up. Expecting more immigrants to register, she began working out the details in order to anticipate any potential problems.

The preparations took almost a year. Major efforts were required to raise sufficient funds to rent premises and to buy tables, chairs, books, slates, pencils, and fuel for heating. The first class began in November 1889, in a rented room on North Gay Street, with Henrietta herself teaching. Every day, after she finished work at Misses Adams' School, she rushed off to teach the immigrants English. She also provided them with information about Baltimore and its institutions, about the Jewish congregations there, and about the types of jobs that were available.

News of the language class spread among the immigrants, and the number of potential students rapidly increased. By the end of the first semester, in April 1890, 150 new students, ages thirteen to forty-five, had already registered for the next semester. She had to find a larger location with room for additional classrooms. Because money was tight, she rented an apartment with several rooms, on the second floor of a rundown building. The stairwell was filthy, the long corridor that led to the apartment was dark, the paint on the walls was peeling, and the floors were badly stained. The young Russians rolled up their sleeves, whitewashed the walls, painted the window frames and doors, sanded down the floors, and found old benches and tables. The students were divided into three classes. Two young women volunteered to help Henrietta—Grace Bendann and Russian-born Deborah Cohn. Classes met for two hours every evening, Monday through Thursday. There were no classes on Friday or Saturday evenings, out of respect for the Sabbath, or on Sunday, the official day of rest in America.

Expenses ballooned and Henrietta sought donations from the wealthier members of the established Jewish community, but they were indifferent to the venture. She was disappointed, because she believed that it was up to the wealthiest among the Jews of Baltimore to support the English school.[6]

Szold was well aware of the efforts by American nativists, who opposed immigration and sought to put a stop to it. One of their proposals was a law that would make fluency in English a prerequisite for naturalization. This threat drove many immigrants to study English. The number of those signing up for the language classes increased, and Henrietta continued to expand the project. Because the volunteer teachers could not cope with the pressure and sometimes failed to show up, Henrietta decided to pay her staff a salary of $15 a month. Once again she turned to her friends, asking them to contribute and to solicit funds from their friends. A donation of $1,000 by an anonymous benefactor made it possible for her to hire certified teachers instead of relying on volunteers, and to keep the school running until the end of the year.

Her plan was to open additional English classes and to add courses in bookkeeping as a way to help the immigrants find employment. As the night school continued to expand, the expenses grew accordingly. Henrietta wrote to her sister Rachel, who lived in Madison, Wisconsin:

> I am sure I shall wear you out with the only subject I am able to write about. . . . I eat, drink, and sleep Russians. *Ergo*, there is nothing to do but to write Russians also. . . . As was predicted, a tremendous rush of pupils came in on Monday after the holidays: 340 have been enrolled. As we can with difficulty shelter 300, a great many were turned away. But the rush has been so great that we have determined to rent two rooms elsewhere and open two new classes. This is of course a serious matter, for the simple reason that we have no money or none worth talking about. We shall want two new teachers, seven dozen schoolbook slates, chalk and pencils, besides the rent. In the face of all this, our community remains cold and indifferent. If we decide to open two new classes, we have more than sufficient material in the way of pupils. We shall have seven English classes, a bookkeeping, an arithmetic, a Hebrew, and a dressmaking class running. That is tremendous, is it not?[7]

Henrietta agreed to open the two extra classes because the young Russians wanted to expand the school, although she was not sure it was a good idea. "But whenever I go to a board meeting, I carefully refrain from influencing my Russian friends on any subject under discussion. This is their school and they must run it."[8] In addition to the financial issue, she was worried about her ability to supervise the classes that would be held in a different building, two blocks away. Her solution was to assign her best and most experienced teachers, whom she did not have to keep such a close eye on, to the annex. Despite a natural tendency toward direct control and involvement in every detail of the project, Henrietta sought, as a matter of principle, to cooperate with anyone who could contribute to the school's success. She did not impose her opinions on them and gave them freedom to act, but she supervised their work in order to ensure the best possible outcome.

The school's expansion and constant shortage of funds weighed on Henrietta, but she would not be deterred. She added a dressmaking course for women (made possible by a contribution from Bertha Rayner Frank) so that they would have the necessary training to find work and achieve economic independence without having to rely on someone else for their livelihood. Henrietta was enthusiastic about the rapid growth of her night school for immigrants and saw her dream coming true.

The large numbers of immigrants enrolling in the school proved its importance but also exacerbated its financial difficulties. Fundraising was Henrietta's greatest challenge, and everything depended on it. She set up a committee of friends of the school to lend an air of public-spiritedness, in the hope that it would have a positive effect on fundraising, but the results were disappointing. The committee was slow to act, and Szold could wait no longer.

With no alternative, Henrietta decided to seek assistance from the Baron de Hirsch Fund in the United States. Baron Maurice de Hirsch, who lived all his life in Europe, came from a family of bankers. He married Clara Bischoffsheim, daughter of the director of the Bischoffsheim and Goldschmidt Bank in Brussels, embarked on various business ventures, and amassed a fortune. He demonstrated deep solidarity with his fellow Jews and focused on the "productivization" of the Jews who emigrated from Russia, investing heavily in the establishment of agricultural settlements in Argentina, where Jewish immigrants could receive occupational training and acquire productive vocations.[9] He also established several agricultural colonies in the United States, in the hope that immigrants there would go into farming. Hirsch was adamant about investing his money in agricultural colonies rather than supporting immigrants who settled in cities. He saw no future for Jews who made their fortunes in commerce or intellectual pursuits if they continued to live in the antisemitic swamp that rejected them. After the death of his only son at the age of thirty, he devoted most of his vast fortune to philanthropy. Following the baron's own death, his wife administered the foundations he had established. She was more open to assisting projects in categories that her husband had avoided.

In 1891, Szold invited representatives of the Baron de Hirsch Fund to visit her school. They came and were impressed by the packed classrooms and the sight of immigrants diligently working through their books. They sent Szold a letter full of praise for her dedicated efforts and achievements—but no money.[10]

Every night she returned home close to midnight, exhausted, and got up early the next morning. Some days she barely had time to eat. She described one such day in a letter to her sister Rachel:

> I rose at 5:30 on Monday morning. At 6:30 I was at my desk, writing to my teachers to meet me earlier than usually, and writing a lengthy letter to two new teachers whom I wish to engage, an answer to the Y.M.H.A. refusing to lecture before them, and other letters. This before breakfast. Then to [the Misses Adams'] school where I am nowadays busy, recess and all, until three o'clock. Thence I rushed to Cushing's to order the extra books, slates, pencils, etc., for the two new classes, and uptown again for the meeting of the Botany Club, which lasts until six. Rushed home for supper, and at seven I was at the Russian school. That evening I had 300 people to manipulate with, but I am thankful to say that by a quarter of nine everybody was at work. I reached home at 11:30.[11]

In another letter to Rachel she wrote: "Perhaps you can do some missionary work among your friends." In order to illustrate the immigrants' plight, Henrietta sent her *Darkest Russia*, a collection of articles and reports about the pogroms in Russia that had first appeared in the London *Jewish Chronicle*.[12]

The shortage of funds continued to be a problem. The teachers had to work an entire summer without pay and without vacation. Henrietta confessed to her sister: "The Russian business so absorbs my thoughts that I have gone back to my early girlish longing to be a man. I am sure that if I were one I could mature plans of great benefit to them. . . . Our community remains cold and indifferent."[13] The problem, she believed, was that volunteer work by women tended to go unnoticed, so the community failed to appreciate the achievements of the night school for immigrants.

Szold again contacted the Baron de Hirsch Fund's educational committee. This time it agreed to underwrite the school's rent. She was thus able to sign a contract for a building on Front Street and move the school there. The entire building was at her disposal, and the classrooms filled up quickly. It was a moving sight—so many young people poring over their textbooks after an exhausting day at work, side by side with gray-haired immigrants who wanted to become acclimated to their new country. Sometimes there would be a husband and wife or father and young son sitting next to each other on a bench, studying together. The doors of the school were open to non-Jewish immigrants as well, including Germans, Italians, Russians, Poles, and others.

In addition to the money from donations, the school also managed to raise a modest sum from student tuition. Henrietta did not believe in "free lunches." The tuition was low, only 30¢ a month, and those who could not pay were not required to. Tuition revenue for the entire year came to $217. The school also took in small amounts from various appeals by the members of the I.B.L. Hebrew Literary Society at social events. Henrietta was delighted with their cooperation and encouraged them to continue, although the sums they provided were small.

A young lawyer by the name of Benjamin Hartogensis came to Henrietta's assistance. He was inspired by her vision and impressed with her organizational abilities. He volunteered to help her keep the institution's books or provide any other administrative assistance she might need. When necessary, he paid urgent bills out of his own pocket. When he did not have time to speak with Henrietta at the school, they corresponded after hours. Working closely with Henrietta, Hartogensis grew fond of her. When he suggested that they go for a walk in the woods on the weekend, Henrietta declined. Several weeks later, when Hartogensis repeated the invitation, she replied, "Today indeed, I have little heart left to contemplate any pleasure of my own. I have two or three cases on my mind, that trouble me greatly and I can do nothing to relieve."[14]

THE NIGHT SCHOOL CONTINUED to grow. Enrollment increased, additional classes were opened, and more teachers were hired. Henrietta, forced to dedicate even more time to fundraising, gave up teaching in the evenings, but she continued to manage the school, supervise the classes, and make sure that the premises were maintained. Her notebook was full of entries about items that required attention—repairs by a plumber, a carpenter, and a painter; the purchase of kerosene for the lamps and coal for the stoves in the classrooms during the frigid winter; and more books, notebooks, and pencils.

In its fifth year, the night school had an enrollment of 700 immigrants. An increased grant from the Baron de Hirsch Fund made it possible to open additional classes in the building of the Talmud Torah Association on Front Street and in rented rooms in an adjacent building. Every evening, the classrooms and corridors were filled with hundreds of students—men and women, Jews and non-Jews, teenagers through senior citizens. Then, thanks to the assistance provided by the Baron de Hirsch Fund, the school was able to move into larger premises, at 1208 East Baltimore Street. The English classes continued, taught by salaried teachers. The bookkeeping and dressmaking classes also attracted many students. Henrietta supervised all of the school's activities, on a strictly voluntary basis.

She kept meticulous records of every penny received and every penny spent. Her watchword was frugality: she carefully considered every expenditure, so as to remain within the school's budget. In 1893, the school's fifth year, expenses amounted to $1,800 a month, of which $1,000 was covered by the Baron de Hirsch Fund, with much of the remainder coming from the donations raised by the Russian Jewish Night School Committee established by the literary society. There was also the students' tuition, as well as donations by various other groups, which totaled $458. The last category reflected increasing public appreciation of the night school. Henrietta was gratified to see that the school finally had a balanced budget.

In the midst of all of this frenzied activity, Henrietta experienced a great personal tragedy. Her younger sister Sadie, who was twenty-five years old, had become engaged to Max Loebel, an immigrant to New York from Prague. Sophie and Benjamin Szold were very fond of the young man and had heard about his distinguished family in Prague, and they gave their blessing to the marriage. The Szold household was busy with preparations for the wedding when Sadie came down with rheumatic fever. Everyone was sure she would recover, and so they continued to get ready for the special day. The wedding gown was finished and everyone was looking forward to the celebration, but the bride-to-be did not get better. Henrietta did everything she could to encourage Sadie, including sitting by her bedside and reading her favorite books to her. When Sadie's condition improved slightly, everyone was convinced that the danger had passed. Within a few days, however, she took a turn for the worse and succumbed to her illness. The family was in shock, scarcely able to deal with its loss. Instead of leading Sadie to the bridal canopy, they carried her to her grave.

The family was brokenhearted and the house was filled with gloom. Sophie and Benjamin fell into a depression, and Henrietta found it difficult to return to her normal routine. She decided to quit the night school, which had become a full-time occupation, in order to spend more time with her parents. Henrietta knew that the school was on stable footing and felt that it could now survive and grow without her.

Over five years, thousands of immigrants had passed through the night school's classrooms and had been encouraged to continue their studies even after they had acquired a basic command of English. The curriculum for advanced students was expanded. In addition to English, there were courses in American history, using English-language textbooks. For the most advanced students, there was also a course in English literature. The night school exerted an even greater acculturating influence after the young Russians of the literary society, with Henrietta's encouragement, established a library in the building. Its collection included books and newspapers that the students could sit and read. On long winter Sunday nights, Henrietta had organized lectures, turning the school into a vibrant community center for the immigrants.

Later, summing up the school's first five years, Henrietta noted that her main goal had been to teach the immigrants to read, write, and speak English, but that the vocational training had been an important addition. She stressed that with the exception of the bookkeeping teacher, all the teaching and administration at the school had been done by women. Henrietta titled her summary "The Night School of the Hebrew Literary Society" and attributed its success to the fact that "it was established for those who need it by those who need it, and it remains virtually theirs."[15] In subsequent years, the method that Henrietta employed to establish, organize, and run the night school would come to characterize her activities in her other fields of endeavor: defining a goal and then pursuing it with determination, investing maximum effort, and coping with the difficulties that emerge along the way. Henrietta had assumed full responsibility for the project and supervised every detail. Her ability to galvanize people and get them to take part in her projects, as well as her scrupulous management of finances, would also become hallmarks of her work. Henrietta did everything on a volunteer basis, never accepting any financial remuneration—a principle she would adhere to in all of her later public positions.

In 1898, the night school was taken over by the city of Baltimore, but it continued to operate in the same format devised by Henrietta.[16] The city subsequently established additional night schools for immigrants in other neighborhoods, and cities and states elsewhere soon followed suit, establishing similar institutions in ever-growing numbers, as the wave of immigration to the United States continued. The idea was adopted in other countries as well. It is doubtful whether any of the other organizers in other locations knew who had originated the concept.

4

THE INTELLECTUAL WORLD

AS THE NINETEENTH CENTURY DREW TO A CLOSE, a spirit of optimism pervaded the United States. New technologies and fast-developing industries inspired hope in the future. The 1893 Chicago World's Fair—the biggest exhibition of the century—was on everyone's lips. The fair commemorated the 400th anniversary of the discovery of America by Columbus and was officially known as the World's Columbian Exposition. It covered a large expanse of land and looked like a city in its own right. The dozens of pavilions housed the latest technological innovations, including a dishwasher, picture postcards, the world's first Ferris wheel, and neon lighting. There were also demonstrations of the telephone, electric lights, an electric motor, and more. America's industrial advances were a source of great pride, and millions flocked to the fair from all over the country and the globe. The fair's organizers, who sought to imbue it with cultural and scientific significance as well, organized a number of special events, including a Congress of Mathematicians, the World's Parliament of Religions—attended by representatives of religions from the West, Asia, and the Far East—and the World's Congress of Representative Women, held in the Woman's Building.[1]

Hannah Greenebaum Solomon sought to organize a Jewish women's congress at the fair. Solomon, the daughter of an affluent Chicago family affiliated with the Reform Sinai Temple, was active in both Jewish and general public life in the city. Five years earlier, she had come up with the

Ferris wheel at the Chicago World's Fair, 1893

idea of establishing a national council of Jewish women, and asked Henrietta Szold to serve as its president, in the hope that such a move would both afford the council prestige and attract women to join its ranks. At the time, Szold was extremely busy organizing the night school for immigrants and was forced to decline Solomon's invitation.[2]

Solomon planned to establish her national council at the fair's congress. Rabbis and community leaders attempted to prevent the appearance of Jewish women on the fair's stage, suggesting that they participate in the capacity of hostesses—a suggestion that Solomon rejected outright. She recognized the magnitude of the challenge and was determined to bring her plan to fruition. She chose to hold the opening of the Jewish Women's Congress within the framework of the Parliament of Religions rather than the Congress of Representative Women, arguing that it was incumbent upon the Parliament of Religions to afford a place to Jewish women as well. Solomon's choice of venue may also have stemmed from the fact that Elizabeth Cady Stanton was slated to appear at the Congress of Representative Women. Stanton, a social activist and suffragist, was notorious for her attacks against the Jewish religion for its treatment of women, and Solomon wanted to avoid a confrontation with her.[3] Solomon invited Szold to be the guest of honor at the Jewish women's congress and to address the Parliament of Religions.

Szold was of two minds about accepting Solomon's invitation, since she was still recovering from her grief over the sudden death of her sister Sadie. When her sister Rachel heard about the invitation, she urged Henrietta to accept it, adding that it would also give her an opportunity to visit the fair. Rachel's heart went out to her sister, trapped in the gloomy atmosphere at home, and she thought it would do Henrietta good to go to the fair. Henrietta decided to take Rachel's advice.

Hannah Solomon was pleased with Henrietta's choice of subject for her address, entitled "What Judaism Has Done for Women." Szold went to Chicago early and visited the various exhibits at the fair, which astonished her. In a letter to Rachel she enthusiastically described the exhibits as fruit of the irrepressible human imagination and ability to harness the forces of nature.

In her lecture before the Parliament of Religions, Szold spoke of Judaism's attitude toward women and the admiration they enjoyed in the family and the community. Szold asserted that Judaism's admiration for women and appreciation of their spiritual potential had served to encourage them in all their endeavors, including those particular to nineteenth-century women. She chose to focus on attitudes toward women in the Bible: "Our question calls for the spiritual data about the typical women whom Judaism has prepared for nineteenth-century work. To discover them we must go back to the women of the time of Abraham. Abraham stands out in the historic picture of mankind as the typical father. He it was of whom it was known that he would command his children and his household after him that they should keep the way of the Lord to do righteousness and justice." The Bible describes the exceptional status of Sarah and Rebekah in their households and their significant influence on the education of their children. Szold was familiar with the commentaries and homiletic interpretations critical of the matriarchs—of Sarah, for example, for the expulsion of Hagar, and of Rebekah for counseling Jacob to deceive his father—but in her lecture chose to present only the positive side of women in the Bible. On Sarah's role in the realm of educational endeavor, she quoted the verse from Genesis in which Abraham is told: "In all that Sarah hath said unto thee, hearken unto her voice."⁴ In the generation after Abraham as well, Isaac and Rebekah hold different views on the subject of education, but Rebekah is the more energetic of the two, combining sentiment and perception with a practical approach and far-reaching vision; she was convinced that humankind would benefit far more from Jacob's gentleness than from Esau's barbarism. Szold explained that Judaism valued women's moral competence and responsibility and did not prevent them from engaging in intellectual activity. It permitted women to advance in the new world of the late nineteenth century, assume additional duties, accept responsibility, and enjoy the broad spectrum of possibilities, all while preserving their honor. She concluded her lecture with the following: "My Sabbath lamp shall ever be a-light; in its rays you will never fail to find yourself, your dignity, your peace of heart and mind."⁵ The audience burst into thunderous applause. The organizers later asked her permission to publish the lecture in a large tome, along with the other addresses and papers presented before the Parliament of Religions.

The Chicago World's Fair had a profound impact on the millions who visited it, instilling in them a sense of pride in the technological advances exhibited there. The general atmosphere in the United States at the time also heralded the direction that American Jewry would take in the coming decades. The establishment in Philadelphia of the Gratz College for teacher training, which opened its doors to women and encouraged them to pursue a career in teaching and education, was revolutionary in the way it contributed to changing women's perception of their place in Jewish public life. Women's groups mounted the public stage and began voicing their views. This awakening of Jewish women, influenced by the prevailing mood in American society as a whole, also gave rise to the creation of women's organizations within a variety of different frameworks.⁶

From the fair, Henrietta hurried back to Baltimore to hear Rabbi Szold's last sermon at the Oheb Shalom synagogue on Hanover Street. Her eyes followed her father as he stepped down from the pulpit and slowly made his way, bent and seemingly defeated, to the main door of the synagogue he had served for thirty-four years. At home Rabbi Szold was depressed, as was the atmosphere around him. The previous year had been filled with grief and bitterness, affecting the entire family. In this difficult period, much to Henrietta's surprise, she received an offer to take up a challenging and promising position that would change her life.

THE JEWISH PUBLICATION SOCIETY

In 1893, the directors of the Jewish Publication Society asked Henrietta Szold to come work for them. She found the offer extremely attractive. It was a great challenge, and she believed in the society's aims. What was more, the offer came at a time when she was ready for a change in her life. Yet she hesitated.

JPS was a prestigious and ambitious enterprise founded by the American Jewish leadership.[7] The idea of establishing a Jewish publishing house in America was first raised by a committee headed by Rabbi Marcus Jastrow. The committee members hoped to transfer the centers of Jewish culture that had developed in Europe to America, using the publishing house to produce English translations of Jewish historiography and the literary output of the Wissenschaft des Judentums movement. Despite these discussions and good intentions, however, the plan went no further. The publishing house lacked money and resolute leadership.[8] Members of New York City's Reform Temple Emanu-El were among the first to show interest in the publishing house. They believed that the acculturation of the Jews in America was a matter of the greatest importance. The rabbi of Temple Emanu-El, James K. Gutheim, translated the fourth volume of historian Heinrich Graetz's eleven-volume *History of the Jews,* titled *From the Downfall of the Jewish State to the Conclusion of the Talmud.* It was published in New York and, in the wake of its publication, the nascent American Jewish Publication Society expected its subscriptions to increase. The book had been put together hastily, however, without professional editing, and lacked an index. A thousand copies of Gutheim's translation were printed, but only a handful were sold over the course of the following two and a half years.[9]

Szold was aware of this history. The situation had changed, however, when the project was joined by a number of well-educated and influential leaders and wealthy backers, capable of putting the idea into practice. They had every reason to be confident that their efforts would be successful, but Szold still hesitated, as she had reservations about some of the people involved in the project.

The group was headed by Jacob Henry Schiff, who was born in Frankfurt am Main to a respected family of merchants and rabbis. He immigrated to the United States in 1866 and soon joined the private banking house of Kuhn, Loeb & Company as a senior partner. Kuhn Loeb was one of the largest banks in America, specializing in railroad finance and international investment. Schiff also married into the moneyed American Jewish aristocracy. At the heart of the publishing house initiative stood a

Temple Emanu-El, at the corner
of Fifth Avenue and 43rd Street,
New York City, 1868

group of wealthy families of German origin, who formed a sort of clan. Not only were they partners in business, but they were related to one another by marriage as well: Schiff was married to Solomon Loeb's daughter Therese, while Loeb was married to Abraham Kuhn's daughter. Paul Warburg, the son of a wealthy banking family in Hamburg and a partner at Kuhn Loeb, was married to Loeb's sister, and thus related to Schiff as well, while Warburg's younger brother Felix was married to Schiff's daughter Frieda. The banking families thus formed a close-knit group that worked together, moved in the same social circles, and worshiped at Temple Emanu-El, the prestigious Reform synagogue on Manhattan's Fifth Avenue.[10] They also led similar lifestyles. Most of them resided in Manhattan, their children attended the same schools, and the younger members of the families became friends and married one another. The wealthy Jewish elite in

America resembled similar groups in Germany and England, like the Rothschilds, who sought to keep their vast wealth in the family.

Schiff's family connections further bolstered his status among the wealthy elite. He stood out due to his forceful personality, acumen, and strong opinions, which he did not hesitate to express even at the highest levels—as, for example, when he demanded that President Theodore Roosevelt rescind the American alliance with Russia in light of the persecution of the Jews there. Schiff, who had become one of the wealthiest Jews in America, was deeply involved in public affairs, and was seen as a sort of father figure for two generations of Jewish immigrants. Famed for his immense wealth, he donated generously to Jewish charities and educational and cultural enterprises, hospitals, and universities, and was among the driving forces behind the establishment of institutions for the promotion and development of Jewish culture in America, such as the Jewish Publication Society. The most powerful and influential figure in the American Jewish community was thus the chief backer of JPS and the decisive voice in its management. Schiff himself was too busy to deal with the day-to-day management of the institutions with which he was connected, so he delegated this responsibility to those close and loyal to him—men such as attorney Mayer Sulzberger, whom he asked to chair the JPS publication committee in Philadelphia.[11]

Although born in Germany, Sulzberger was raised in Philadelphia, where he was greatly influenced by Isaac Leeser, a man of broad intellectual interests who sought to preserve Orthodox tradition. Leeser was not entirely inflexible on religious matters, recognizing that certain minor changes were warranted to accommodate life in America, but he fought against the Reform movement throughout his life. He was a prolific author and translator who wrote and edited numerous books, and he published a monthly magazine, the *Occident and American Jewish Advocate*, in which he propounded his views. Leeser left a lasting impression on the young Sulzberger, who later in life acted in Leeser's spirit and strove to continue his work.[12]

Sulzberger apprenticed in the law office of Moses A. Dropsie, one of Philadelphia's preeminent lawyers, who, like Leeser, was an advocate of traditional Judaism. Sulzberger quickly made a name for himself, leading to financial as well as professional success. He was elected a judge in Philadelphia's Court of Common Pleas, in which capacity he served for twenty years, becoming the court's presiding judge. He played a part in revising the Pennsylvania state constitution, was active in the Republican Party, and was a personal friend of President William Howard Taft. Sulzberger's friendship with Schiff was a stepping-stone to leadership roles within the American Jewish community and its institutions, including Schiff-sponsored initiatives such as JPS.

Sulzberger's home housed an impressive library, estimated to be the largest private collection of Jewish books and journals in America at the time. He later donated most of his collection to the Jewish Theological Seminary. Sulzberger devoted his spare time to expanding his own and others' knowledge at Jewish institutions he was instrumental in establishing. He was the first president of the American Jewish Committee (AJC), and chairman of the JPS publication committee. He was once described as "a mean old cuss with a tongue as sharp as a dagger, and a degree of conceit that would break all records," but he was also known as a brilliant and generous man.[13]

Following Sulzberger's appointment as chairman of the JPS publication committee, it was widely hoped that the project would finally get off the ground. Szold was already familiar with the society, as her father was a member of its English Bible translation committee. Rabbi Szold was also on friendly terms with Solomon Schechter, Rabbi Joseph Herman Hertz, and other scholars, whom Henrietta came to know through him, and she knew the people working there. She had also been asked to write books for the publishing house. Schechter, for example, suggested that she write about Jewish women in recent centuries, particularly the *tkhines* (private devotions written primarily for women), since she had written an article on this subject for a journal. On Schechter's recommendation, Sulzberger also suggested to Szold that she write a book on Jewish values for children and adults.[14]

Henrietta was occasionally invited to meetings of the JPS publication committee and was asked to review manuscripts submitted for publication. Her reviews were clear and well reasoned, and her opinion was respected. The views she expressed were independent, unaffected by passing trends. Even when an author's books were popular, she did not shy away from swimming against the tide. This was the case with Israel Zangwill's *Children of the Ghetto*, which was very popular in England. She was not impressed by it, deeming the plot shallow and predictable and the characters stereotypical.[15] Every now and then she was asked to edit books and to translate French and German books selected by the publication committee into English, winning high approbation. Szold, who had previously done all this on an occasional basis, was now offered a full-time position at JPS. She was very much taken by the idea of working with the prominent scholars and researchers on the organizing committee, many of whom she knew.

Szold was a great believer in the acculturation of the masses of Jewish immigrants. This had, in fact, been the idea behind the night school for immigrants she had founded, which strove to open a gateway for them into American society and culture. She also firmly believed in promoting scholarship in Jewish studies in America, to make it accessible to the younger generation of English-speaking Jews. The invitation to work at JPS was, to Henrietta's mind, both challenging and inspirational, and she was flattered. The work was interesting and suited to her talents and was a breath of fresh air after the long hard years she had spent teaching and running the night school.

The Jewish Publication Society sought to publish research in Jewish studies by the world's leading Jewish scholars. Most of these books were hundreds of pages long, and in her new position Szold would be required to read them, as well as manuscripts submitted to the publication committee, and give her opinion on their quality and suitability. She would also be required to translate manuscripts and books from German and French into English, and edit each one. In addition, she would have to write progress reports on JPS activity for the publication committee and the trustees. All of these assignments, which required several people working full-time, were offered to Szold as a single job. Her title was to be "secretary to the publication committee," although the job description was actually that of a manager and editor in chief. Her salary would be $1,000 per annum, which was commensurate with a secretary's pay scale but very low for someone of her abilities and, above all, for the complex position she was expected to fill. Cyrus Adler, a member of the JPS executive, later said that had Szold bargained they would have been prepared to go up to $1,200, "but a dignified woman in her position would never do that."[16]

Jacob Schiff pulled the strings at JPS, although never holding any official position there. Schiff always seemed to be looking over the shoulders of the society's president and trustees, keeping an eye on everything they did. At publication committee meetings, the members gravely considered every one of Schiff's comments or requests, inevitably doing their best to satisfy him. Without his large contributions, the publishing house would probably cease to exist. Schiff demanded that the money he provided be used in accordance with his instructions, and so it was. The JPS staff felt they owed him a debt of gratitude not only because of his financial support but also because of the investment advice he gave them, telling them what to buy and when to sell on behalf of JPS. Nonetheless, the main objective of JPS was to publish books, and that task was for the most part in the hands of the chairman, Mayer Sulzberger.

Szold was to work directly under Sulzberger, which was the main reason she hesitated to take the job. She had met him during her earlier work at the publishing house and was repulsed by his arrogance, impatience, and aggressiveness. Cyrus Adler believed that Szold possessed the necessary qualities for the job, so he tried to allay her fears and persuade her to accept the position. He was an old friend of the Szold family and had been among the visitors to their home when he was a student at Johns Hopkins.[17]

Adler was neither wealthy nor a member of high society. He also lacked Sulzberger's influence and force of personality. He owed his place on the JPS board to his family ties with Sulzberger, through whom he had also met Jacob Schiff and become friendly with him. Szold, who knew Adler well, did not consider him an original thinker, but she appreciated his qualities as a pleasant, sociable man who had a way with people and played an active role in Jewish public affairs. He would later serve as chairman or president of many Jewish associations and institutions.[18]

There were also personal reasons behind Szold's reluctance to accept the position at JPS. The publishing house was in Philadelphia, which meant that she would have to leave Baltimore. Henrietta wanted to stay at home to help her parents at a very difficult time for them. Her father had been dejected ever since he lost his position at Oheb Shalom, and he occasionally sank into depression. Sadie's death further compounded her parents' distress. The decision to move to Philadelphia was thus a difficult one.

Szold wrote to her sister Rachel about her deliberations, and Rachel quickly replied, urging her to accept the position. Rachel believed that Henrietta should not sacrifice her life for their parents, and thought that moving away from their parents' home would raise her spirits and do her good. She was certain Henrietta would find a new circle of friends in Philadelphia and, deep down, also hoped that Henrietta would meet a potential mate. Rachel was more than a sister to Henrietta. She was a close friend on whose sage counsel Henrietta had come to rely whenever faced with a difficult decision. Rachel's advice made an impression on Henrietta, and she decided to take the job. She later said that had her father asked her to stay in Baltimore, she would have done so. Such was her sense of duty toward her parents.

AT THE PUBLISHING HOUSE

In the summer of 1893, Henrietta resigned her teaching positions, ceased her remaining activities at the night school for immigrants, said goodbye to her private students, and prepared herself for a new life in Philadelphia. It was unthinkable, at the time, for an unmarried woman from a respectable family to live on her own in the big city. Henrietta was thus invited to live with the Jastrow family—old family friends and in-laws of the

Szolds, through their son Joe's marriage to Rachel. The gossip in Baltimore was that Henrietta was to marry Morris, the Jastrows' eldest son, but Morris was in Breslau studying at the rabbinical seminary and the university there. He and Henrietta had been friends years earlier and corresponded. There were also three Jastrow daughters, but Henrietta did not see much of her hosts, since she left the house early in the morning and returned late at night.

A great deal of work awaited her at JPS, and her first experiences in her new job were less than encouraging. She was given a small, miserable office with bare walls, sparsely furnished, with only a desk, a chair, and an old bookcase. Henrietta felt ill at ease in such a room, so she painted the bookcase, sewed a curtain for the window, hung pictures on the walls, and immediately got to work. She was responsible not only for the content and language of the books she edited, but also for the references and sources and any missing details. Her work was meticulous and involved corresponding with the authors—a source of considerable aggravation to her. When she suggested revisions or rewording, some authors accepted her suggestions, while others vigorously rejected them, refusing to change a single letter. Since Szold was responsible for the finished product, she found such refusals to cooperate extremely distressing. She knew that she would be blamed for any errors, inaccuracies, or stylistic shortcomings.

Her task was to translate and edit the manuscripts, but she was a perfectionist and also became responsible for preparing the manuscript for printing, reading the proofs, and compiling the index. Furthermore, she had to contend with all of the problems and mishaps that regularly plagued the printing process. On one occasion, Szold complained: "I had to go to the printing office to give the foreman a blowing up. . . . Some wrongly stupid commas have gotten mixed up with the others, and was four hours today picking them out of some 40–60 pages of proof. My eyes feel queer after that hunt."[19]

Such snags were an annoyance and a waste of time, but they were also a source of anxiety to Henrietta, as she knew that she would be held responsible by the chairman of the publication board for every delay. She described her frustration in daily letters to her parents. In one such letter, for example, she wrote: "The book is not out yet and I am afraid it may be delayed another ten days. I am receiving blame left and right for it. . . . I was on the point of giving up the whole job on Sunday, but I feel better about it now on mature reflection."[20]

The publication committee met once a month, except during the summer. Sulzberger conducted these meetings in a high-handed manner. He went over the new manuscripts that had arrived, and then asked for the members' opinions on each one they had been asked to read and review. The committee decided which manuscripts would be published—usually four or five every year. Szold, the "secretary," did most of the administrative work as well. At the monthly meetings, she gave a progress report on each of the books—where things stood in terms of translation, editing, and the printing process. In addition to Szold, there were only two other staff members involved in administration: Charles Bernheimer, who was in charge of subscriptions, which he was constantly trying to boost in order to balance the society's budget, and Maurice Dannenbaum, the treasurer, who took care of accounts and payments.

Sulzberger oversaw everything and, as Szold had expected, working under him was not easy—so much so that she dubbed him the "Grand Mogul" and was apprehensive before every meeting. The work inevitably failed to go as smoothly as the irascible chairman expected, and Szold would emerge from the committee meetings dejected and hurt. Sulzberger always seemed sour and grumpy. Nevertheless, Szold enjoyed her work immensely, taking great pleasure in the research involved in editing and translating.[21]

She was also gratified to receive letters of thanks from authors for her painstaking work or praise for her translations and indexes. Through her work, she came in contact with public figures, academics, and eminent authors and thinkers in America and Europe. She was in touch with the scholar Moritz Lazarus, for example, when she translated the two volumes of his *Die Ethik des Judenthums,* which enjoyed considerable success in the United States.[22] Szold edited and indexed Gutheim's translation of part of Heinrich Graetz's *History of the Jews,* which became an immediate bestseller. She also translated and edited the works of Solomon Schechter and other scholars, and greatly enjoyed her interaction with the authors. She earned the respect and admiration of all the authors whose works she translated and edited, both for her erudition and for the richness and clarity of her writing.

She eventually fell into a routine, with days of immense satisfaction and others best forgotten. There were days on which she would rather have done anything but work. On one such day, she described her discomfort to her parents: "It is hot, and Philadelphia is dirty."[23] Her social life in Philadelphia was dismal: she had no time to meet people and make new friends, and she was cut off from all her friends and family in Baltimore. She spent all day either hunched over a manuscript in her office or running to the printer. She sometimes took work home, working until well after midnight.[24] She was a perfectionist in everything she did.

Henrietta was lonely in Philadelphia, although she went home every weekend. She did not stay in Philadelphia for long, however. Rabbi Szold soon fell ill with intestinal cancer. He was in a great deal of pain and in low spirits, and Henrietta decided to return to Baltimore. She hesitated to go directly to Sulzberger, preferring to write a letter to Cyrus Adler explaining her father's condition and her desire to return to Baltimore and continue her editorial work there. Her request was approved, and she moved back to Baltimore in 1895.[25] She continued to travel to Philadelphia to oversee printing and attend publication committee meetings. There were also meetings of the board of trustees, which took place two or three times a year at Sulzberger's grand office in Philadelphia. One by one, the trustees would enter, wearing expensive suits and fashionable ties, and sit down. Some took out their pipes and others smoked cigars as they talked about current affairs in a pleasant atmosphere, not unlike a gentlemen's club. Szold sat at the end of the table and, as secretary, took the minutes.

At her parents' home in Baltimore, she continued her work for JPS. The assignments that piled up on her desk demanded her attention from early morning until late at night. Occasionally she was given an extra assignment, such as writing press releases for books published by the society, in order to promote sales. Some days, when she was completely exhausted, the thought of resigning would cross her mind. Sometimes she would even write a letter of resignation but would wait to mail it. After a day or two, she would change her mind, consoling herself that even before she started working for JPS, her work life had hardly been relaxed.

In 1898, on the tenth anniversary of JPS, a surprise awaited Henrietta. The board decided to hold a special meeting in honor of the occasion. The meeting took place, as usual, in Sulzberger's office, and began with a review of the society's achievements, the books it had published, public response, and the ever-increasing number of subscribers. JPS president Maurice Neuberger spoke in praise of Szold, calling her "a secretary whom the Lord himself seems to have provided for the Society." He was followed by Sulzberger, who in the five years she had worked at JPS had never uttered a single word of praise. But on that day Sulzberger said the following:

> The word secretary is severely strained to describe her duties. Do you read a work in idiomatic English that originally appeared in French or German? It is the secretary who has rendered it into English. Do you find that errors in expression, in punctuation, in references, are almost non-existent in the books? It is the secretary who has read the proofs and has spent weary hours and days and nights in verifying citations and correcting them. Do you find expressions that seem rough and uncouth? It is again the secretary who has had the trouble to suggest the corrections and the grief to have them rejected

by the author. Do you look at the great index volume of Graetz, with its chronology and maps? It is the secretary who has been the chronologer and the index-maker, and has not been without influence on the maps.[26]

The "secretary" was overjoyed. It was the first time she had ever heard words of approbation from the board. She was particularly surprised by Sulzberger's fulsome praise of her work. She wrote excitedly to her parents: "To me it was the reward of my work, reward sufficient for two times as much work. . . . I am a very fortunate person."[27]

DESPITE THE ACCOLADES SZOLD RECEIVED for her work at JPS, her title and salary remained the same; she did not dare demand the status and remuneration she deserved. This can probably be attributed to her upbringing in a cultural milieu in which even the most talented women tended to internalize society's disparagement of their abilities. The young men who had studied at university and earned degrees and appointments also acquired self-confidence and were ultimately rewarded with important positions. The women were excluded from all of these positions and the honors that went with them. What is more, Henrietta's name did not even appear in many of the books she translated and edited for JPS, thereby denying her the public recognition she deserved, for her hard work and remarkable achievements.

Henrietta's parents had raised her in the Central European Jewish tradition, which demanded impeccable manners from girls. Haggling, raising one's voice, and making demands were unbecoming of a girl from a good family, and Henrietta had no wish to be seen as a rebel. She took particular care not to harm her father's standing as a rabbi with behavior that might dishonor him in the eyes of his congregation. She was familiar with the feminist ideology in the United States and Europe and its leaders, but she passively accepted being discriminated against and denigrated; she neither objected nor protested.

THE *AMERICAN JEWISH YEAR BOOK*

While still as busy as ever translating and editing at JPS, Szold was asked to work on another project as well: the *American Jewish Year Book*. The *Year Book,* like the publishing house itself, was meant to play a role in the solidarity of all of the Jews of America, including the many immigrants from Russia. This program was, for the most part, the brainchild of long-established Reform leaders with a Central European background, who had initially been ambivalent toward the immigrants arriving from Russia in the 1880s and 1890s. While they pitied the poor and the unemployed, they also saw the immigrants as their cultural inferiors and did not want to be identified with them. They preferred to associate with one another, and aspired to integrate into the broader American elite, but that was not to be. Wealthy Jews such as Jacob Schiff had business dealings with their non-Jewish peers but quickly discovered that these relationships never went beyond the office. The American Protestant elite would not allow the wealthy Jews into the elegant clubs around which their social lives revolved.

The established Jewish elite recognized the importance of welcoming the immigrants into the Jewish community and reinforcing Jewish unity, and thus embarked on a campaign to help them integrate into American society. This included taking a public stand against attempts by American Protestants to restrict Jewish immigration—attempts that gained momentum in the 1890s. Szold had long been of the opinion that the immigrants from Russia and Eastern Europe should be integrated into the established Jewish community. She had learned to respect the immigrants she had met in Baltimore at her night school, and also hoped to attract those who had moved away from Judaism.

American Jewish leaders sought to revitalize Jewish culture, which was languishing beneath layers of neglect and ignorance. They sought to awaken the interest of members of the established Jewish community and immigrants alike by providing them with easily accessible and up-to-date information about Jewish life in the United States, its achievements, and its institutions. In this way, they hoped to bring Jews closer to the Jewish community. This was no simple task in the late nineteenth century, which lacked the kind of communication technology that we take for granted in the early twenty-first century and which constantly inundates us with the very latest information. The printed word was virtually the only means they had at their disposal to reach large numbers of people scattered throughout the United States.

The *American Jewish Year Book* was meant to offer readers up-to-date information on topics of interest to the American Jewish community, from noteworthy social and cultural events in the United States and elsewhere to information about Jewish organizations, institutions, and associations, including their functions and the services they provided. Cyrus Adler was appointed editor of the *Year Book,* and it was to be published by JPS. Adler, who was familiar with Szold's talents and admired her broad knowledge and insights, requested that she assist him. Asking her to work on the *Year Book* in addition to her already heavy workload at JPS was, in itself, a huge burden, and no additional pay was forthcoming, yet she accepted; she seems to have been incapable of turning down any position offered to her. She quickly threw herself into work on the *Year Book,* exerting considerable influence on its content from the outset.

Szold was enthusiastic about the *Year Book* and considered it a valuable tool, well suited to the goals it was intended to achieve. She believed, however, that it should not only address the Jewish community, but also be used as a vehicle for influencing American public opinion in general. The rise of antisemitism in Europe at the end of the nineteenth century continued to trouble her. She closely followed events in the Jewish world and feared that the wave of anti-Jewish hatred mounting in Europe would also reach American shores. There were indeed signs that this was already happening—most notably in the increasing number of initiatives to restrict immigration, which targeted Jewish immigration in particular. Szold feared that antisemitism would determine the fate of the Jewish people for generations to come, with catastrophic consequences. She was also ahead of her time in understanding the importance of shaping public opinion to achieve social and political objectives. She believed this would be an effective way of shattering the stereotypes propounded by antisemites and refuting the delegitimization of Jews. Furthermore, she understood the importance of public opinion as a means to influencing the American administration and its policies—including immigration policy.

BOTH ADLER AND SZOLD were deeply committed to Jewish tradition, which they aspired to preserve and disseminate. This commitment is clearly evident in the nature and content of the *Year Book,* which was published each year before Rosh Hashanah. On the first pages of each volume was a Jewish calendar in Hebrew and English, with the dates of the festivals and High Holy Days in bold print; its inclusion there was meant to emphasize the importance of the calendar as the backbone of ancient Jewish tradition. Similar yearbooks published in England and other countries did the same thing.

Szold's influence can be seen in the choice of subjects and the *Year Book*'s incisive prose. At the beginning of the first volume, published in 1899, are two brief overviews, one on the Jews of the United States by Rabbi Abram S. Isaacs, and the other on the Jews of Europe by Joseph Jacobs. These essays provided the necessary background for the volume's numerous articles describing the activities and fields of endeavor of a wide range of American Jewish organizations, for the benefit of its Jewish readership. The articles written by Szold included a detailed overview of the American Jewish press, as well as articles aimed at non-Jewish readers.

As an ardent believer in Jewish solidarity, she also included a number of essays on events in Europe, Russia, and other countries. These elements reflected two objectives Szold believed the *Year Book* was capable of achieving: buttressing Jewish solidarity among the various circles of American Jewry and strengthening the links between them and Jews in Europe and other countries.

Most of the *Year Book*'s articles and overviews were thoroughly researched and painstakingly written by Szold herself. One of the *Year Book*'s most interesting features was Szold's review of the most significant events for Jews in the United States and around the world during the course of the previous year, titled "A List of Leading Events." The review was based on a variety of sources: Jewish newspapers and magazines published in English, German, French, and Hebrew in the United States and Europe, as well as institutional and organizational publications. Szold gathered all of the information she provided in her article by carefully combing through the many publications on which her review was based. The events she published in her list were those she deemed most significant, and pertained mainly to topics close to her heart, such as the emergence of the Zionist movement and Jewish social and cultural life.

Antisemitism occupied a central place in the first *Year Book*. Szold had been stunned by the accounts she had read of the Dreyfus trial in France, which had sparked a virulent outburst of antisemitism. Alfred Dreyfus, a French Jewish artillery officer, was accused of treason. He denied the charge but was convicted by a secret court-martial and sentenced to life imprisonment on Devil's Island in French Guiana. The Dreyfus trial lasted from October to December 1894. Theodor Herzl, who attended the trial as a correspondent for the Viennese *Neue Freie Presse,* was astounded by the force of hatred for the Jews that emerged during the trial, although he had not yet drawn any practical conclusions from it.[28] The Dreyfus Affair returned to the fore of public opinion in France after Bernard Lazare, a sharp-tongued Jewish publicist, demanded that Dreyfus be given a retrial, since his conviction had been based on forged documents. In a trenchant article, Lazare argued that Dreyfus's conviction had been motivated by antisemitism. He concluded his article with the phrase "J'accuse," which would later become the headline of the famous open letter published in the widely read French daily *L'Aurore* by one of France's greatest authors, Émile Zola. In his letter, Zola criticized the army and the judicial system and, like Lazare, demanded a retrial. Zola paid a heavy price for *"J'accuse . . . !"* He was sued for libel and, in order to avoid arrest, had to leave for England, suffering a severe blow to his reputation and his finances as a result. The Dreyfus Affair was the subject of intense debate in France between those who opposed a retrial, fearing that it would tarnish the army's reputation, and those who demanded justice. Léon Blum, who would later become France's first Jewish prime minister, said about the Dreyfus Affair, "It was as if life had been suspended . . . those two years of commotion, of passion, of veritable civil war."[29]

More than any other event of its day, the Dreyfus Affair symbolized the potency of antisemitism and its deleterious effects. Western European Jewry and Jews around the world were particularly shocked by the fact that it had taken place in France, a nation that was founded on the principles of *liberté, égalité, fraternité* and had been the first country to grant Jews full emancipation. That the Dreyfus trial had unfolded in France was thus perceived as clear evidence that neither equal rights nor assimilation could resolve the problem of antisemitism.

Szold viewed the Dreyfus Affair as a reaffirmation of the great power of public opinion, which had been galvanized by the involvement of famous authors and intellectuals in the fight against antisemitism. In the "List of Leading Events" for that year, which filled dozens of pages, Szold reviewed the antisemitic events that had occurred throughout Europe: the expulsion of 5,000 Jews from Kiev; an attack against the Jews of Kosov in eastern Galicia, during the course of which ten Jews were murdered; the torching of a Jewish neighborhood in Iasi, Romania; pogroms in Náchod (in Bohemia) and in Kherson (in Russia); and antisemitic rioting and demonstrations in various other countries. In her article on Zionism, she reported on the Third Zionist Congress, held in Basel on August 15, 1899; on Herzl's appearance before an audience of thousands in London; and on Max Nordau's address before 2,000 people in Vienna.

Another subject close to Szold's heart was the unique contribution of Jewish women to science, literature, public affairs, and so forth. She regularly included this subject in the year's leading events in the United States and other countries. In the first *Year Book,* for example, she mentions Amelia Rosselli, who received a prize of 2,000 lire in Turin for her play *Anima,* and Elsa Neumann, who was awarded a doctorate from the University of Berlin, "the first woman so distinguished." There were also reports on the activities of women's organizations, such as the participation of representatives of the National Council of Jewish Women in the conference of the National Council of Women of the United States, held in Washington, D.C.

In the list of events for 5660, she also mentions the publication of Zangwill's latest book, *They That Walk in Darkness,* by JPS, as well as other forthcoming books. The cultural events listed for 5659 (1899–1900) include important publications in the field of Jewish studies, such as Solomon

Schechter's study on the Cairo Genizah; *The Nineteen Letters of Ben-Uziel* by Samson Raphael Hirsch, translated into English by Bernard Drachman; and Professor Moritz Lazarus's *Die Ethik des Judenthums* (The ethics of Judaism), in two volumes, which Szold herself translated from German—and she did not mention that she was the translator. The "List of Leading Events" also included a necrology of Jewish writers, intellectuals, and public figures who had passed away that year. Among the deaths listed for 5659 are those of Baron Ferdinand de Rothschild in England and Baroness Clara de Hirsch in France.

When the first volume of the *Year Book* came out in August 1899, the name of the editor, Cyrus Adler, appears on the title page, but Szold's name is nowhere to be found, although she wrote numerous articles for it, contributed to shaping its content, painstakingly edited and proofread it, and oversaw the entire publication process. Szold's "List of Leading Events" also included reviews of literature, Jewish art, and education, all of which were of special interest to her. Among the cultural events listed for 5661 (1900–1901) is a theatrical production of Israel Zangwill's *Children of the Ghetto,* which aroused considerable public interest, with some praising it and others condemning it. Despite her own criticism of the book, Szold considered the staging of the play an important event, as it presented the difficult problems that Jews faced to the general public.

All of the work that Szold did on the *Year Book* was, as previously noted, in addition to her other duties at JPS, and her workdays became even longer than before. She worked until late at night and was forced to give up her summer vacation, since the book's proofreading and printing had to be completed before Rosh Hashanah. When her sister Adele saw the finished book and realized the amount of work that Henrietta had put into it, she scolded her for driving herself into the ground and for not being paid for her efforts. She also rebuked her for waiving credit for her work.

Relationships within the Szold family were complex. Sophie was aware of Henrietta's difficulties and always treated her gently, never commenting or criticizing. Rachel, who knew how sensitive Henrietta was, was careful not to offend her, and Bertha treated her with a kind of reverence. Adele, on the other hand, the youngest of the Szold sisters, held nothing back and spoke her mind. She was the only member of the family who did not shy away from criticizing Henrietta.

The second volume of the *Year Book* came out just before Rosh Hashanah in 1900. In the introduction, Cyrus Adler offered thanks "above all to the Secretary to the Publication Committee, Miss Henrietta Szold, to whose painstaking and indefatigable labors much of the accuracy and many of the improvements in this volume are due." The second volume was twice as large as the first and opened with a long article by Szold for which she was credited: "The Year 5660, by Henrietta Szold."[30] It seems that she took Adele's reproaches to heart, albeit not entirely, since her name does not appear on the many other articles and reviews she wrote for this volume. Adele herself was occasionally asked to translate or edit articles for the *Year Book,* with pay and credit, naturally.

In Szold's lengthy article on the year's events that appeared in the second volume, she provides a broad overview of the manifestations and character of antisemitism in German, Austrian, Hungarian, and especially Russian cities. The article includes a report on the latest developments in the Dreyfus Affair and notes the decision regarding a retrial. The second trial took place on August 7, 1899, and Dreyfus was once again found guilty, but his sentence was commuted to ten years. He continued to protest his innocence and sought to have his conviction overturned. In September 1899, he was pardoned by the president of France, but Dreyfus and his supporters were still not satisfied and continued to demand his complete exoneration—a demand that would be satisfied only years later. Szold highlights and lauds the Jewish response to antisemitic events. When antisemitism reared its ugly head in France, both Jews and non-Jews decided to take concerted action not only in defense of Jewish life and property, but also to safeguard Jews' honor and dignity.[31]

The question of defending one's honor, as it appears in Herzl's journals and in works such as *The New Ghetto,* often involves challenging the offender to a duel—a common theme in European literature of the time.[32] Szold took a very different view of Jewish honor, stressing the importance of the national organization of Jews in every country for exerting political and other pressure.[33] Szold greatly valued Jewish solidarity, as manifested in the increasing awareness of Jewish leaders of the fate of Jews everywhere. She expressed the hope that demonstrations of Jewish solidarity would set an example for similar initiatives and that non-Jews would also take action against "the incubus of the 'ritual murder' charge and of anti-Semitism."[34]

Relations between Jews and Christians preoccupied Szold, and she mentioned a number of eminent professors and respected clergymen who had raised their voices against antisemitism. Although she lavished praise on non-Jews who strove to eradicate antisemitism, she did not delude herself that articles and protests by non-Jewish intellectuals and writers alone could eradicate antisemitism. She did, however, believe that the increasing number of voices raised in protest would be heard, influence public opinion, and dull the edge of antisemitism's evil effects.

Szold's article on the year's events concluded with a report on the Fourth Zionist Congress, held in London. The great importance she ascribed to what was happening in the Zionist movement was also manifested in her interest in the development of the Jewish community in Palestine. One important event she deemed noteworthy was the transfer of the *moshavot* (agricultural colonies) from the aegis of Baron Edmond de Rothschild to the Jewish Colonization Association (JCA) in January 1900: "These occurrences have one meaning: Palestine colonization has passed from the stage of a private charity to that of world-wide philanthropy; from the stage of an experiment to that of an enterprise whose publicity precludes long-standing maladministration, or even the long-standing imputation of maladministration: from the stage at which every traveler's tale about the fertility or barrenness of the soil, the salubrity or noxiousness of the climate, is accepted as endorsement or condemnation, to the stage at which, for better or for worse, Palestine colonization is a fact. This transition is the achievement of Zionism. . . . Political Zionism has forced Philanthropic Zionism into self-conscious assertion and dignity."[35]

At the turn of the century, Szold looked back at the past year and saw more shadow than light: "In the annals of Jewish history, the closing year of the nineteenth century will occupy a prominent though not an honorable place. Marked in Austria by anti-Semitic excesses and 'ritual murder' charges, in Galicia by continued distress, in Bessarabia by famine, in Romania by an accumulation of indignities and hardships, it may almost be said to epitomize the Jew's martyrdom in the Christian centuries. The generation whose years are full goes to the grave with the disappointing knowledge that the visions of '48 were, many of them, will-o'-the-wisps."[36]

Looking forward, it was hard for her to forecast what the new century held in store. She was not optimistic, but she chose to conclude on a hopeful note, with the wish that the Jews might step into the new century conscious of their mission: "However much he may share in the prevailing degeneration, the Jew . . . [is] still occupied with the questions, political, social, ideal, that are at once summed up and solved in the word Zion—Zion, that is, the mountain of the house of the Lord, to which the nations shall flow to be taught the ways of the God of Jacob, and to walk in His paths."[37]

The *Year Book* was widely distributed in hundreds of communities throughout the United States. In its second year, the number of subscribers exceeded 5,000, and subscriptions continued growing in the following years. The annual volume became a prime source of information on the Jews of America in every sphere of activity: society, culture, research, and literature. It contained reprints of up-to-date articles from Jewish newspapers and magazines and the titles of new publications in the field of

Jewish studies and belles lettres. The *Year Book* also included information on religious activities; its second volume, for example, noted the establishment of more than forty new synagogues in America in the preceding year.[38]

The *Year Book*'s statistics section presented data on the number of Jews
around the world at the start of the new century. The Jewish community
in the United States numbered more than 1 million and was twice as large
as that of Germany. In Russia, there were close to 6 million Jews—the
largest concentration of Jews anywhere in the world, followed by Austria-
Hungary with some 2 million and Romania with 1.3 million. At the turn
of the twentieth century, there were some 12 million Jews in the world.

Szold continued to write, edit, and deal with the subsequent volumes of
the *Year Book*. Her articles in the third volume (published in 1901) were
aimed at highlighting the achievements of Jews and their contribution to
humankind in all fields of cultural endeavor: science, philosophy, and art.
The subsequent volumes included biographical sketches of successful Jews
in the professions, the sciences, and philosophy, as well as in the world of
business and industry. There was a list of Jews who had attained high
public office in the American courts and in Congress, as well as those who
held high political office in Europe, and a list of high-ranking Jewish officers in the American military. All these lists sought to underscore the loyalty and contributions of American Jews to their country. Szold hoped
that these messages would provide a response to the antisemitic propaganda that portrayed Jews as demonic creatures and would refute the
delegitimization of Jews, which prepared the ground for harming them.
This was intended not only for the general public, but also for Jews themselves, so that they would appreciate and be proud of the achievements of
their fellow Jews, boosting their confidence and self-respect.

This third volume also included an extensive report on the activities of
JPS—the new books it had published and those planned for the coming
year.[39] Similar reports were published in the subsequent volumes as well.
Although they were written by Szold, she is not given credit as their author. Szold meticulously notes Bernheimer's name, on the other hand, as
the compiler of the list of subscribers.

In his preface to the fourth volume (published in 1902), Adler once again
expresses his gratitude to "Miss Henrietta Szold, Secretary to the Publication Committee, whose valued aid renders the annual publication of this
volume possible"; so too in the fifth volume (published in 1903). Nevertheless, Adler's name continues to appear as editor, without ever crediting
Szold as the co-editor. Szold's decisive contribution to all of these volumes
remained shrouded in anonymity. Adler enjoyed the honor that went with

being the editor of the *Year Book*, and he was loath to share it. He knew that Szold would not demand recognition as his co-editor, just as she had not demanded the credit she deserved on previous occasions.

In the *Year Book*'s sixth volume (published in 1904), Szold did all the work and Adler added her name below his as a co-editor, as was also the case in the seventh volume (which appeared in 1905). The year 1907 saw the founding of Dropsie College for Hebrew and Cognate Learning, named after Moses Aaron Dropsie, who donated substantial funds for its establishment, and Adler was appointed its first president. Consequently, in the eighth and ninth volumes of the Year Book (which appeared in 1906 and 1907, respectively), Henrietta Szold was credited as the sole editor.

The eighth volume, the first Szold edited entirely on her own, she subtitled *From Kishineff to Bialystok,* which was embossed on the front cover. This is also the title of a long article she wrote for the book, which is unsigned.[40] It is strange that Szold's name did not appear on the articles she wrote and all the lists she compiled for these volumes of the *American Jewish Year Book.* She was in charge of every stage of publication, from editing to printing, so she could easily have signed them, as well as noted her own name as translator of some of the works she listed among the books published by JPS. Such recognition would have been no more than that she accorded to Isaacs and Jacobs, who wrote the two overviews that appeared in the first volume, or to other writers and translators whose work appeared or was listed in subsequent volumes she edited.

Why, then, did Szold not sign the lists she compiled and the articles she wrote, or note her own name as the translator and editor of works published by JPS? Was it because the frequent appearance of her name seemed like conceit to her, or was there another reason? She was conscious of her weaknesses but felt unable to overcome them—something she grappled with and agonized over in her diary. Szold was well aware of her abilities and talents and erudition. Ever since she was a young girl, she had been an outstanding student, and she possessed a wealth of knowledge in the fields of literature, philosophy, and history. She was an independent thinker, not afraid to voice her opinion when asked to assess manuscripts and books for publication by JPS, or in the lectures she delivered and proposals she made to the various organizations in which she would later be active. Even when her views did not coincide with those widely held around her, she never avoided expressing them and defending them, ultimately winning the admiration of many public figures and scholars.

There was a huge gap between Szold's talents, education, abilities, and extraordinary professional achievements, but we have to remember that her standing was a consequence of a social, cultural, and professional world that was entirely dominated by men. And despite being a woman with no formal education, she ultimately succeeded in playing a significant role at the forefront of American Jewish life. Szold, who had an exceptional personality and many remarkable achievements, was a trailblazer who needed every ounce of courage and resourcefulness she could muster in order to succeed. Perhaps her decision not to sign everything she did stemmed from her desire not to stand out too much. Or perhaps Cyrus Adler prevented her from taking the credit.

IN LIGHT of the success enjoyed by JPS and the *Year Book*, it was suggested that a Jewish encyclopedia be published in English. Leading scholars were asked to contribute entries, as was Henrietta Szold, who was widely respected in the academic community even though she held no degrees. The first volume of the encyclopedia was published in 1902 and was a repository of ideas and subjects in the spheres of interest of Jewish scholars at the turn of the century. Szold contributed a total of fifteen entries to the encyclopedia, which appeared alongside entries by the most eminent scholars in America and around the world.

The *Year Book* and its publication passed into the hands of the American Jewish Committee in 1908, when Szold abruptly ceased editing the annual volume due to her personal situation.

5

TRANSITIONS

HE HOUSE on Lombard Street was shrouded in gloom. Rabbi Szold
was depressed, and it affected everyone. Sophie understood that
his depression was due not only to his illness, but also to the dispirited-
ness that had come over him ever since his congregation had forced him
into retirement. She believed he would feel better if they moved to an apartment far from the synagogue that had been taken from him. The move
would also ease their financial situation: Rabbi Szold's pension was modest
and the family had to reduce their expenses. Instead of the big house on
Lombard Street, they rented an apartment on Callow Avenue, a quiet side
street some distance from the city center, and moved in.[1] Apart from Rabbi
Szold and Sophie, Henrietta and Bertha lived there too, while Adele was
away at college most of the time.

Henrietta was constantly anxious about her father's health, and in her
letters to Rabbi Joseph Herman Hertz told him about the ups and downs in
Benjamin's condition. Rabbi Hertz had become friendly with Rabbi Szold
when both were members of the publication committee for the English Bible
translation, with each of the scholars on the committee translating the book
closest to his heart. Rabbi Szold chose the Book of Job and Rabbi Hertz
chose Joshua. Hertz visited the Szold home in Baltimore, where Henrietta
met him and was profoundly impressed by his personality.

Hertz and his family had immigrated to the United States from Hungary in 1885. He studied at Columbia University and, at the same time,

was a member of the first class at JTS. Following his ordination, he was appointed rabbi of the Adath Yeshurun congregation in Syracuse, New York.[2] When Rabbi Hertz was invited to South Africa to serve as rabbi of the Witwatersrand Old Hebrew Congregation in Johannesburg in 1898, he continued to correspond with Rabbi Szold. When writing became too difficult for Rabbi Szold, Henrietta replied to Hertz's letters, writing about public affairs and news. All of Henrietta's letters to Hertz were clouded by the state of her father's health. The contact between Rabbi Hertz and Henrietta Szold continued after his return to New York, and after his appointment as chief rabbi of the United Kingdom.[3] She never imagined that she would one day find herself in a fierce confrontation with Rabbi Hertz.

Rabbi Szold's health further deteriorated in the summer months, and the atmosphere in the Szold home was heavy and sad. One ray of light was Bertha's announcement that she had decided to accept the marriage proposal of Louis Levin, an educator and editor of the Baltimore *Jewish Comment*. Rabbi Szold was able to take part in the wedding festivities, and the young couple rented an apartment in Baltimore, not far from the family. Rabbi Szold's condition continued to deteriorate, and Sophie and Henrietta cared for him devotedly, but after a few months he passed away (July 13, 1902). Henrietta grieved over the death of the father she had been so close to since she was a small child.

The funeral was attended by hundreds of members of the Oheb Shalom congregation, rabbis, and Baltimore dignitaries, as well as friends of the family from other cities. Rabbi Marcus Jastrow came from Philadelphia and eulogized Szold with tear-filled eyes: "A great man, who was a holy ark for the entire Jewish community."[4] Szold was laid to rest in the cemetery in Baltimore next to the graves of his four daughters. Throughout the seven days of mourning, the apartment was filled with friends and acquaintances who came to console the grieving family, and each day saw the arrival of dozens of telegrams and letters of condolence.

When the Shiva was over, Rachel returned to Wisconsin, Sophie and Adele remained in the apartment, and Henrietta, who concealed her pain, went back to her work at JPS. In the *Year Book*, edited by Henrietta, Rabbi Szold's name appears in the "Necrology" section, together with the names of other leading figures who passed away that year. She added nothing beyond what she usually wrote about others, noting only briefly: "Rabbi Benjamin Szold, of Baltimore, aged 72."[5] Rabbi Szold's personality and spirit had filled every corner of the house, and after his death everything changed; an era had come to an end. Every year afterward, family and friends would gather in Baltimore on the anniversary of Rabbi Szold's death. After Henrietta settled in Palestine she tried to get to Baltimore for

The Szold family. Seated (*left to right*): Henrietta, her mother, Sophie, and sister Rachel; standing: Adele and Bertha.

the occasion as often as she could. On the twentieth anniversary of Rabbi Szold's death, she was unable to do so, and wrote to her sisters from Jerusalem: "I cannot say that I thought of him more today . . . for I think of him every day."[6]

After the death of the head of the family, the Szold household felt empty, and Henrietta was dejected and restless. After a few weeks, Sophie suggested that she move to New York, where she would be able to enroll at JTS and thus realize her ambition of studying at an institution of higher learning. Henrietta was thrilled at the prospect and waited impatiently to move to New York, the largest Jewish community in America, the center of Jewish public and cultural life, and she looked forward to studying at JTS. There was one problem, however: JTS was a rabbinical seminary and at the time did not admit women.

Szold approached Professor Schechter, president of JTS, and asked to be allowed to study at the seminary. She had met him the previous year when he came to JPS at Sulzberger's invitation. Schechter was friendly with Rabbi Szold, and when he first met Henrietta in Philadelphia and told her he had been invited to deliver a lecture at Johns Hopkins, she immediately invited him to be the family's guest when he came to Baltimore. He was familiar with her work at JPS, admired her broad knowledge and her range of talents, and so he had accepted her invitation. Now Schechter gave her his approval to study at JTS—a revolutionary decision for a non-Reform institution. The idea of women in the rabbinate was inconceivable at a traditional institution such as JTS. While the JTS executive did not challenge Schechter's decision, they asked Szold to declare that she had no intention of serving as a rabbi, and she did so willingly. She was not interested in the rabbinate but sought only to broaden her knowledge at an academic institution, after having been denied the possibility of studying at a university. She was thus free to study at the seminary with some of the greatest scholars in the field of Jewish studies, finally realizing one of her fondest dreams.

ANTISEMITISM AND ZIONISM

The move to an unfamiliar city after so many years in Baltimore was not easy. In the summer of 1893, Henrietta went to New York to look for an apartment for them, preferring a location close to the seminary where she was going to study, then came back to Baltimore to make arrangements for the move. For Henrietta the winter months in Baltimore were filled with work at JPS and on the *Year Book,* but she remained as aware as ever of events around her. She continued her efforts to influence the non-Jewish public to renounce their antisemitic attitudes toward the Jews.

Szold lectured at the Woman's Literary Club of Baltimore, which drew its members from the city's intellectual elite. Among them were writers, poets, and the wives of financiers—a circle in which antisemitism was all too common. She did not preach, but gave them her impressions of her visit to the Woodbine agricultural settlement in Cape May County, New Jersey, which had been established for Jewish immigrants from Eastern Europe. The immigrants were settled on farms created by the Baron de Hirsch Fund with the aim of encouraging productivization among the Jewish immigrants. Hirsch's intention was to return them to tilling the soil, the occupation of their forefathers in the Land of Israel. In the census taken in 1900, Woodbine had 2,700 inhabitants, and Szold described the young people she met there as "strong, brawny, energetic, idealistic, [and] intelligent."[7]

The ladies of the literary club were surprised by what Szold had to say, which disproved the prevailing stereotype of Jews as hustlers and shopkeepers, people who were far removed from productive work and more inclined toward commerce and moneylending than physical labor. They heaped praise on her and lauded her lecture, which was even reported in the *Baltimore Sun.* In another lecture she delivered to an elite circle in Baltimore, at the home of her former classmate Bessie Smyth, she reviewed the religious motives and political circumstances that formed the backdrop of the emergence of the Zionist movement, and expressed the hope that the Jews in Palestine would compete as a nation with other nations.[8]

Szold continued to speak to non-Jewish groups in an effort to eradicate antisemitism, while at the same time working to expand and strengthen the Zionist movement. She was troubled by the precarious state of the movement in America, which had few members and was in disarray. From Baltimore, far from the center of events in New York, she closely followed its vicissitudes.[9] The movement's dwindling numbers stemmed from organizational instability and the constant splits that characterized it in American Jewish communities.[10] With the appearance of Herzl and the convening of the First Zionist Congress came an awakening in the Zionist movement. The congress raised expectations among the Jews, and more people joined Zionist societies, which now numbered several dozen. In Baltimore too, membership in the Zionist Association increased with Herzl's appearance and the preparations for the First Zionist Congress, but the movement remained small and unstable. When one of the delegates to the congress was asked if he knew any American Zionists, he replied, "There are only two: Rabbi Stephen Wise, New York's eminent Reform leader, and Henrietta Szold of Baltimore—and they are both mad."[11]

Szold, who was imbued with a keen Zionist consciousness and was among the founders of Baltimore's first Zionist society, was dispirited by the dwindling of the American Zionist movement. In a long article she wrote for the *Year Book,* she examined its various strands of the American Zionist movement and presented ideas that might improve the situation, but she had no control over its competing factions.[12]

The American Zionist organization was founded in February 1898 and was soon joined by other Zionist associations. The American organization was headed by Richard James Horatio Gottheil, a Semitic scholar and the son of Rabbi Gustav Gottheil from Temple Emanu-El in New York; both were Zionists. It was then suggested, however, that Zionist activity be put on hold, since the United States was fighting the Spanish-American War at the time, and people felt that membership in a Zionist organization could be construed as showing a lack of American patriotism. They felt that a Jew should not consider America as simply a refuge or a place of temporary exile. Even among the Reform Jews, there were those who, like Rabbis Bernhard Felsenthal from Chicago, Stephen S. Wise, Judah Magnes, and Gustav Gottheil of New York's Temple Emanu-El, saw no contradiction between American patriotism and the Zionist idea. Louis Marshall, an eminent attorney, one of American Jewry's great leaders, and a founder of the American Jewish Committee, believed that Zionism did not run counter to American patriotism.[13] Marshall and some of his colleagues did not support the political Zionism led by Herzl, but they backed the revival of Jewish culture in the Land of Israel in the spirit of the Zionist thinker Ahad Ha'am (born Asher Ginsberg).[14] In Baltimore at that time, there was significant Zionist activity, inspired by Szold. There were meetings and lectures, mainly delivered by her, and she formed study groups devoted to disseminating the Zionist idea. Dr. Aaron Friedenwald was a known Zionist and his son Harry followed in his footsteps, and while Rabbi Szold had also supported Zionism, Henrietta was far more actively involved than he ever was.

In 1898, a general meeting of representatives of the Zionist associations was convened in New York to found the National Federation of American Zionists; the name was shortened a year later to the Federation of American Zionists (FAZ).[15] The FAZ was meant to incorporate the dozens of Zionist societies and clubs, but it did not succeed. Incessant disputes between the Russian and German factions led to constant splits between associations and activists, which sabotaged any efforts to establish a nationwide Zionist federation. The energizing effect of Herzl's leadership and the First Zionist Congress gradually waned, and the number of FAZ members dwindled. The situation continued in this vein for another year, with the blame falling on Gottheil for not being a "real" Zionist and for the organizational disorder in the FAZ executive. Beyond New York, the situation was no better. The Zionist movement was in disarray and losing members.[16] Szold was concerned about the sad state of the movement, which was due to the lack of organizational skills among FAZ's leaders, who failed to communicate with the various groups and unite them in a common cause.

AT THE SZOLD FAMILY HOME, the winter months of early 1903 passed quickly, and Passover was fast approaching. The holiday preparations were tinged with sadness, as it would be the first Passover they would celebrate without Rabbi Szold. Each page of the Haggadah they read evoked memories of his interpretations of and commentary on the story of the Exodus; he had always accompanied the readings, especially the phrase "Next year in Jerusalem," with a topical allusion.

Before the holiday was over, news arrived of the pogroms in Kishinev (Bessarabia), which erupted on the last day of Passover in 1903 and shook the Jewish world. Southern Russia had a rapidly growing Jewish population. The Jews, many of whom were poverty-stricken, lived not just in small towns and villages but also in cities, where they eked out a living from shopkeeping and various crafts. The rapid growth of the Jewish population heightened the hatred felt by the non-Jewish population. Expulsions and pogroms became an almost everyday occurrence for Jewish communities in southern Russia, but what took place in Kishinev exceeded anything they had experienced up to that point. There was widespread alarm at the murderous brutality of the perpetrators, who did not stop at robbery and vandalism but killed 49 Jews, including children and infants, wounded some 500, and raped 600 women and girls. Some 1,500 shops and work-shops were looted, and hundreds of houses were left in ruins. Shattered furniture was left everywhere, and the yards were strewn with feathers from torn bedding. The cries of women and children echoed through the rubble. [17]

The Hebrew poet Hayim Nahman Bialik, who heard about the atrocities, committed his own anguished cry to paper, in his poem "On the Slaughter," which includes the famous lines "Even Satan created no quittance/For a small child's blood."[18] Bialik condemned the perpetrators and their brutality, as well as the wretchedness and helplessness of those Jews who were unable to defend themselves. The poem was written in a spontaneous outburst several days after the pogrom. Bialik published it in the Hebrew monthly *Ha-Shiloah,* and it quickly spread throughout the Jewish world.

Bialik's poem left a strong impression on Jews everywhere—in Russia, Europe, America, and Palestine—including Szold. Two weeks after the pogrom, writers in Odessa, including Ahad Ha'am and Bialik, published a clandestine manifesto in which they called for the establishment of a Jewish self-defense organization in Russia, arguing that "it is a disgrace for five million human souls to unload themselves on others, to stretch their necks to slaughter and cry for help, without as much as attempting to defend their own property, honor and lives."[19] There was a mixture of anger and shame in their words. Kishinev was not just another pogrom but a national trauma, which exceeded previous pogroms by its murderous brutality, and in its wake both the Zionist movement and the socialist Bund were strengthened. Young people started to organize for self-defense. Kishinev was a symbol not only of helplessness but also of attempts at defense against the rioters.

Later, Bialik wrote "In the City of Slaughter," a lament for both the victims and the survivors. Writer and Zionist activist Ze'ev Jabotinsky translated the poem into Russian, which brought it to a large readership that did not know Hebrew, and it had a powerful effect on many young Jews who took to heart the message regarding the need for Jewish self-defense. After Jabotinsky emigrated to Palestine he continued his activities for self-defense there.[20] In the coming years it was this idea that germinated into the initiative to establish a Jewish defense force in Palestine.

Bialik's cry continued to resonate for many years in the Jewish people's collective memory. The powerful expression "Even Satan created no quittance/For a small child's blood" would resurface during and after the Holocaust. In many communities all over the world Jews condemned and protested against the pogroms in Russia.

Szold was among the first in the United States to call for a protest. She organized a meeting in Baltimore on May 17, 1903, to protest the terrible brutality in Kishinev. Harry Friedenwald answered her call and cooperated with her in preparing the meeting. His participation was important, since he was president of the Baltimore branch of the Alliance Israélite Universelle, a position previously held by his father. He was also in touch with non-Jewish leaders and sought their cooperation in order to raise public awareness of and outcry against the atrocities being committed against Jews. The governor of Maryland, members of Congress, and clergymen such as Reverends Hodges and Scobell also answered the call and sent Harry letters condemning the slaughter in Kishinev and calling upon the Russian authorities to prevent further events of this kind. The meeting was held in an auditorium at the Baltimore Academy of Music, which was filled to capacity, one of the first of seventy-seven such meetings held in twenty-seven states, in cities including Cincinnati, San Francisco, St. Louis, and New York.[21] Protests came from the entire Jewish spectrum in the United States and were reported in articles and editorials in the leading American newspapers, which attacked the Russian regime for its encouragement of the pogroms.[22]

Fundraising appeals were launched for the victims, and steps were taken to get the American administration to respond to the pogroms. A B'nai Brith delegation met with President Theodore Roosevelt and the secretary of state to demand American intervention, to ensure that Russia protected the Jews. The president hesitated at first but, after additional pressure was exerted, ordered his representatives to submit a protest to the tsar. The Russian Foreign Ministry rejected the protest as interference in its country's internal affairs. Furthermore, the Russian minister of the interior took punitive measures, ordering the cessation of the Zionist movement's activities in Russia and prohibiting Zionist meetings and fundraising. In the *Year Book,* Szold continued to urge influential Jews not to cease their efforts to persuade the governments of the United States and other countries to take action on behalf of the Jews of Russia. The harsh reaction of American Jews to the Kishinev pogrom attested to their power and their solidarity with their brethren throughout the world. In a commemorative volume, Cyrus Adler documented all the meetings, decisions, and newspaper editorials, as well as the aid extended to the victims of the pogroms.[23]

The continuing pogroms there upset Szold, and each year she reported on dozens of them in the *Year Book*. She also noted the pogroms in other European countries, North Africa, and Persia. She would later return to the subject of Kishinev and subsequent pogroms in a special volume of the *Year Book*.[24]

The reverberations of the Kishinev pogrom and those that came after it, as well as the protest and condemnation meetings held in Jewish communities in Europe and the United States, constituted a turning point in Jewish consciousness, especially in Russia. The fact that the authorities had collaborated with the perpetrators compelled the Jews to acknowledge that they had no future in Russia. The pogroms galvanized tens of thousands to take their fate into their own hands and leave the "vale of tears," and their number increased in the following decades, most of them flocking to the United States. In the early twentieth century, Jews who had emigrated from Eastern Europe came to constitute over 80 percent of American Jewry, and Jews from Central Europe became the minority.[25]

THE UGANDA CONTROVERSY

The pogroms and expulsions drove Herzl to take urgent action to find a refuge for the masses of Jews fleeing Russia. After failing to receive permission to settle Jews in Palestine and the Sinai Peninsula, he considered the British proposal of settlement in East Africa, where it was thought the victims of the pogroms could easily be absorbed.[26] He hoped that Jewish philanthropists around the world would support efforts to establish the new settlement. Herzl had yet to obtain the approval of the Zionist Congress for the new settlement program in East Africa but had faith in his own powers of persuasion.

The Sixth Zionist Congress convened in Basel on August 23, 1903. Harry Friedenwald was a member of the American delegation, as vice president of the FAZ. He wrote to his mother about the reactions at the congress when Herzl brought up the proposal of an autonomous Jewish settlement in East Africa under British auspices. In view of the opposition to the proposal, Herzl explained that the settlement would be "a night shelter" for the Russian Jews who needed it urgently, and not a substitute for settling the Land of Israel. Harry wrote that it was the big surprise of the day and that it was followed by a stormy dispute.[27] It was decided to recommend sending a survey team to East Africa that would submit its report to the executive, and the findings would be presented at the next congress.

The decision to send a survey team to investigate the feasibility of the Uganda Plan also sparked a fierce debate. A majority voted in favor of sending the team.[28] The result was welcomed with applause, but the Russian delegates fiercely opposed it. As the tumultuous applause continued, the opponents of the proposal left the hall with their supporters and walked to another hall, where hysteria ensued: women wept and men sat on the floor lamenting as if it were the Ninth of Av, the date of the destruction of the Temple.[29] When Herzl heard of this, he hurried to them and spoke earnestly with them, assuring them that, indeed, Uganda was not a substitute for the Land of Israel, merely a temporary solution mandated by reality. Harry Friedenwald deliberated over the Uganda question but did not voice his opinion. Szold firmly supported the Russian delegates and vehemently opposed the Uganda Plan, which she viewed as a dangerous deviation from the Zionist idea, and she did not accept Herzl's explanation that Uganda was to be only "a night shelter" for the Jews forced to flee the pogroms.[30] In her opinion the supporters had engaged with the Uganda question as if it had been a trivial matter, rather than something that lay at the very foundations of the Zionist movement. She believed that they should strive toward the settlement of the Land of Israel in every possible way and not be lured by empty solutions.

Ahad Ha'am leveled scathing criticism at Herzl and won over many of the Central and Western European delegates who had long supported his position in contrast to Herzl's, who had long supported his position that the Land of Israel should be solely a spiritual and cultural center, with the majority of the Jewish people continuing to live in the diaspora.[31] Szold was conversant with the writings of Ahad Ha'am and had translated several of his articles into English, and while she espoused his approach on some subjects, she did not agree that the Land of Israel should be solely a spiritual and cultural center, with the majority of the Jewish people continuing to live in the diaspora. She believed that the return of the Jewish people to its land and the building of the country were vital and would, in turn, provide the momentum for its spiritual rebuilding.

Szold briefly mentioned the Uganda Plan in her "List of Leading Events" that year, without further elaboration.[32] She followed the Uganda controversy with great concern, as it threatened to split the Zionist movement. Szold would have liked to attend the Zionist Congress and be at the center of Zionist activity, but in the summer of 1903 she was overloaded with work on the *Year Book,* needed to meet its annual Rosh Hashanah deadline.

In the fall, she was also busy with preparations for the move to New York, about which she had mixed feelings. She was looking forward to a change in her life, but it was hard for her to say goodbye to Baltimore, the city where she had spent nearly all of her forty years. She had rented an apartment at 528 West 123rd Street, not far from JTS. The move to New

York forced Sophie and Henrietta to make some difficult choices as they packed up their Baltimore home. Since there was not enough room in the New York apartment, they had to part from objects and furnishings that were very precious to them. It was at this time that they received the happy news that Bertha had given birth to a son, named Benjamin after his grandfather. He was the first grandchild born to the Szold family and was the cause of great excitement and joy, especially for Sophie, who had been waiting for a grandchild for many years. In the coming years Bertha would have four more children, two boys and two girls. In late 1903, Rabbi Marcus Jastrow, the Szolds' loyal family friend and in-law, passed away, and Henrietta again felt personal bereavement. She admired his scholarship and integrity and wrote a moving eulogy. Bertha named her son Marcus after him.

THE NEW WORLD OF THE JEWISH THEOLOGICAL SEMINARY

In November 1903, Sophie, Henrietta, and Adele left Baltimore and moved into their new apartment in New York. Adele continued to work as a translator and editor for the *Jewish Encyclopedia*. She was young, critical, and outspoken, and she did not hesitate to express her views on matters of public concern to the city and the Jewish community.

For Henrietta, a new world opened up in New York, and she quickly threw herself into social and community activity. Her dream of studying at an institution of higher education was about to come true. In addition to her studies, she found a vibrant social life and a number of impressive friends, whose influence on her life cannot be overstated. The first of these was Solomon Schechter, whom she had met before she came to the seminary, but her close personal relationship with him and his wife, Mathilde Roth Schechter, only developed after she moved to New York. She was a regular visitor at the Schechters' home, and the experience she had there was unlike anything she had previously known.

Schechter, who was described as the "most wonderful combination of learning, wit, and spiritual magnetism," was the dominant figure at JTS, which was known to many as "Schechter's Seminary."[33] Schechter boasted a Hasidic background, a broad rabbinic education acquired during his studies in Germany (where he was ordained), as well as a first-class secular education and doctorate from the University of Berlin. While he adhered to Jewish tradition, his worldview was modern. In 1882, he went to England at the invitation of Claude J. Montefiore, who awarded him a grant that enabled him to work on his research. At first he taught at Jews' College in London, where he met the woman who would become his wife.

Professor Solomon Schechter

Mathilde Roth was born in 1857 and grew up in Breslau, Germany. Her father died when she was still a child, and she was sent to a Jewish orphanage. Due to her natural talents, intellectual ability, and ambition, she continued her studies at the Breslau Teachers' Seminary, where she acquired a broad education and a teaching certificate. She also studied French and English, which she taught at school, but she wished to develop further. In 1885, she went to England to study at Queen's College, in London. It was in the Jews' College library that she met Schechter, who helped her find books, while she helped him with translations from French and English, and their friendship eventually led to marriage.[34] Mathilde would become a full partner in Schechter's public activities and leadership, and in developing his ties with the academic and cultural elite in England and the United States.[35]

Mathilde later recounted that when Schechter first arrived in England, he did not speak English, but learned it with characteristic speed. According to Mathilde, he was a "compulsive reader" who especially loved the works of Schiller and Heine, which he had studied in Germany and frequently quoted. Once he gained a good command of English, Schechter read articles on philosophy, theology, and history, and took a great interest in everything pertaining to the French Revolution and the American Civil War, becoming a great admirer of Abraham Lincoln.

In 1890, Schechter moved to Cambridge University, where he was appointed to the faculty and served as lecturer in Talmudic studies and reader in rabbinics, and it was there that he reached the peak of his achievements. He was captivated by the treasures he found at Cambridge, and the university library and the British Museum were the inspiration for his studies on the Cairo Genizah—fragments of thousand-year-old papyrus scrolls that revealed excerpts from the foundational works of Jewish literature, including the Old Testament, the prayer book, and more. The variant readings found on these scrolls provided scholars with important insights into ancient biblical and other textual traditions. Schechter's research gained him renown and earned him a place among the world's leading scholars in the field of Jewish studies.

Mathilde identified completely with her husband's work. She was entirely fluent in English, and assisted him with translation of his books from German. Schechter's reputation preceded him, also thanks to Mathilde's social activities, as she carried on the tradition of their hospitality. Schechter must have cut a very odd figure indeed as he strolled through the streets of Cambridge: "With his bushy, red-tinted beard, unruly hair, and tendency to gesticulate broadly as he spoke, Schechter had been known to set off in the broiling heat of midsummer wrapped up in a winter coat and several yards of scarf." He also had, his wife would write years later, "'a genius for friendship; he loved people and they loved him.' . . . Schechter gained the deep respect and affection of the town's leading intellectuals."[36]

In 1901, Schechter was invited to New York to head JTS. The seminary had been founded in 1886, but by the end of the century it found itself on the verge of bankruptcy. A number of leading figures, such as Jacob Schiff and Louis Marshall, decided to back the seminary. They hoped to bring most of New York's diverse Jewish community to identify with the seminary and, ultimately, to turn American Jewry into an important academic and intellectual center in the Jewish world. The support of men such as Schiff and Marshall for JTS ensured its financial security, and they saw in Schechter a leader who would not only turn the seminary into an important academic institution but also make it a central force in American Jewish life.[37]

The seminary reopened in the spring of 1902, after the reorganization that accompanied Schechter's arrival, and was renamed the Jewish Theological Seminary of America. Szold welcomed Schechter's appointment enthusiastically.[38] A delegation of JTS dignitaries came to welcome Schechter and his wife when they arrived, and he wasted no time in telling them about what he viewed as his mission.[39] He decided that the seminary's crest would be a burning bush with the legend "And the bush was not consumed."[40] It quickly became clear that the hopes placed in Schechter were well founded. His importance for the advancement of Jewish studies in New York cannot be overstated. At JTS, he continued with the extensive research that had won him international renown, and he also proved to be a natural leader.

Schechter and Mathilde continued their tradition of welcoming guests, as they had at Cambridge, and their home became a meeting place for scholars, seminary faculty, and visitors from abroad, all of whom widened Schechter's circle of friends and admirers. It was at their home that his great charm was revealed in bringing colleagues and intellectuals closer to one another. Their guests were impressed by both spouses: as Mathilde later described it, "[Solomon] brought them and I kept them."[41]

Szold had been struck by Schechter's erudition and captivating personality when she met him for the first time on his visit to the United States. He admired her as well. Schechter was consistent in his position on the integration of women into Jewish studies, and it was in this spirit that he decided to allow Szold to study at JTS.

When Szold met Mathilde in New York, she was as charmed by her as she was by Solomon, and soon she became a regular guest at their home. Schechter held her in high esteem, and she and Mathilde became close friends. Of her hosts and the atmosphere in their home, Szold wrote, "So many, many of us basked and were transformed."[42] Szold viewed them as the ideal couple, and her close relationship with them would provide her with support in difficult times, particularly the great trauma she would later experience—support for which she would be grateful to them for the rest of her life.[43] In addition to his research and work at the seminary, Schechter was also active in the wider Jewish community, spending a great deal of time lecturing and expressing his opinions on various matters. He believed that the Jews had to accommodate the new reality in America—a guiding principle behind many of the innovations he introduced at JTS, particularly with regard to women. For example, he demonstrated considerable openness and courage in allowing Szold to study at JTS.

Even before Schechter came to America, he showed a keen interest in the role of women in the Jewish community. This stemmed from his liberal thinking and possibly from a desire to broaden the scope of Jewish history to include women, largely excluded from Jewish public life for generations. This position was reflected in some of the articles he wrote, such as "Women in Temple and Synagogue" and "The Memoirs of a Jewess of the Seventeenth Century," which he composed after the publication of the memoirs of Glückel of Hameln.[44] It may be assumed that these views were influenced by the enormous presence of his wife in his life.

Szold was extremely enthusiastic about her studies at JTS. She was also involved in cultural activities and met many new people, including members of the JTS faculty, whose personalities and scholarship inspired her and filled her world. Schechter traveled to Europe to invite a number of brilliant young researchers in Jewish studies with a general higher education to JTS—notably Alexander Marx, Israel Friedlaender, and Louis Ginzberg. Their research achievements proved the wisdom of Schechter's approach. These scholars enhanced the seminary's reputation, and the institution flourished. All of them became Szold's close friends.

Alexander Marx was the son of an old German Jewish family. He studied at the Rabbinerseminar zu Berlin and the University of Berlin, and was a dedicated student with a great love of Jewish books and manuscripts.[45] Schechter decided to build a large library at the seminary for the use of scholars and faculty, and he appointed Marx to establish and manage it. Marx donated some of his own books and manuscripts, and the library grew and expanded with the help of Judge Mayer Sulzberger of Philadelphia, the greatest collector of Jewish books in America, who donated his own library and rare manuscripts to the JTS library. The JTS collection went on to become the largest and most impressive in America. It was at the Schechters' home that Szold met Marx and was impressed by his graciousness and generosity; their acquaintance developed into a friendship that lasted for decades.

Schechter invited Israel Friedlaender to lecture at JTS in 1903. Friedlaender was born in Ukraine, where he received an Orthodox education, and subsequently studied in Germany at the Hildesheimer Rabbinical Seminary, where he was ordained, while studying Semitic languages at the University of Berlin.[46] He was a brilliant and charismatic young man of whom great things were expected. Schechter invited him to serve as Sabato Morais Professor of Biblical Literature and Exegesis, and to lecture in philosophy and Jewish history. Szold met him at the Schechter home, and his impressive appearance captured her attention. He quickly became one of the leading intellectual Orthodox figures in American Jewry and was in great demand as a speaker. Szold discovered that he was a passionate Zionist, and this brought her closer to him. Like Szold, Friedlaender was also a member of the FAZ executive.[47]

Marx and Friedlaender were in their twenties, while Szold was already over forty, but that did not stop them from becoming fast friends. Szold met them at the Schechter home and in the synagogue on Saturdays. Both men were bachelors and their families did not live in America, so they were occasionally invited to the home of Sophie and Henrietta for the Sabbath meal. They asked Szold to help them with their English, and she was only too happy to oblige. Every Saturday evening they came to the Szold apartment to learn English, further cementing their friendship.

A prominent figure among the JTS faculty was Louis (Levy) Ginzberg.[48] He was born in Kaunas (Kovno) in Lithuania, then part of the Russian Empire, and was educated at the famed Lithuanian yeshivot. From a young age he had a reputation as a Torah prodigy, with a brilliant future ahead of him in the yeshiva world. His father was greatly disappointed when he left the yeshiva and went to university in Germany, where he studied ancient history and Semitic languages. After being awarded his doctorate in 1899, he decided to go to the United States. Mayer Sulzberger suggested that he write a book on the Jewish legends relating to the Bible, to be published by JPS. Sulzberger offered him an advance of $1,000, which Ginzberg accepted. Szold wrote to him on behalf of JPS, informing him that the society had decided to accept his book proposal. They asked that it be research-oriented but also accessible to educated readers who were not scholars. They envisaged a popular collection of ancient legends, along the lines of the work done by the Brothers Grimm. Ginzberg sent JPS a few sample pages. His English was poor, and so he wrote in German, but that was not a problem, since Szold had agreed to translate the book into English. Ginzberg signed a contract with JPS, and after he was offered a professorship in Talmudic studies at JTS, he decided to remain in the United States.[49]

Ginzberg, a brilliant Jewish studies scholar, was the leading light on the JTS faculty. Szold recalled meeting Ginzberg for the first time in 1903, not long after her arrival in New York, at the Clara de Hirsch Home for Working Girls. Before that meeting, she had heard about Ginzberg from Rabbi Marcus Jastrow, who admired his erudition and described him as a great researcher and an original thinker. As part of her work at JPS, Szold corresponded regularly with Ginzberg. A short time after signing the contract with JPS for the publication of *Legends of the Jews,* Ginzberg informed them that the book would be more comprehensive than he had initially thought. Rather than write "like the Brothers Grimm," he intended to produce a comprehensive research volume. He collected the commentaries and ancient legends from multiple sources, including rare manuscripts, medieval Jewish works, and the writings of Church fathers.[50] He asked that the contract with JPS be amended to include an extension of the deadline for submission of the manuscript and an increased fee.[51] Mayer Sulzberger's letter in reply was succinct and unequivocal: JPS was not prepared to amend the contract under any circumstances. The cost of translation, editing, and other attendant expenses would be greater, precluding an increase in Ginzberg's fee. JPS also demanded that Ginzberg submit his final manuscript within the timeframe stipulated in the original contract.[52] In the end, Ginzberg did not uphold the contract with JPS, and over the coming years, the book, which was supposed to be about 300 pages long, turned into six volumes, taking some twenty years to write.[53]

DESPITE HER HEAVY WORKLOAD, Szold continued to make time for public affairs, in particular the Zionist movement. The effects of the Uganda Plan controversy continued to plague the movement, threatening to destroy it from within. Herzl found himself under unexpected attack, but he managed to maintain his status at the congress and continued his efforts in the European political arena.[54] The strain and disappointment were beginning to take their toll, however, on his already poor health. His heart disease worsened, and on July 3, 1904, he succumbed to pneumonia. He was forty-four, and only nine years had passed since he first came to prominence with the publication of *The Jewish State*.

News of Herzl's death spread like wildfire and sent the Zionist world into turmoil. A sense of irreparable loss pervaded all his admirers. Eighteen-year-old David Ben-Gurion wrote: "There will not again rise such a marvelous man."[55] "What is to become of us?" lamented David Wolffsohn, Herzl's close friend and confidant, who would become the second president of the Zionist Organization.[56] Numerous eulogies appeared in the newspapers over the course of weeks. Even Herzl's adversaries acknowledged the magnitude of the loss. Ahad Ha'am, Herzl's fiercest opponent, wrote of him: "But one thing Herzl gave us involuntarily, which is perhaps greater than all he did on purpose. He gave us *himself,* to be the theme of our Hymn of Revival, a theme which imagination can take and adorn with all the attributes needed to make of him a Hebrew national hero, embodying all our national aspirations in their true form."[57]

Like many in the Zionist movement, Szold was stunned by Herzl's death at the height of his efforts on behalf of the Zionist cause. The man who had captured the imagination of the masses and convinced them to follow him had left the stage, and no one knew what would become of the Zionist movement. The Uganda Plan controversy, which had split the congress delegates, now undermined the movement's very foundations. The survey team that had gone to East Africa to examine the plan from a practical standpoint announced that its findings were negative, leading to the plan's final rejection. Szold increased her activities in disseminating information on Palestine and its great potential as the only national home for the Jewish people. In her articles, lectures to the Daughters of Zion in New York, and other forums, she did not cease extolling settlement in Palestine as a central component of bringing the Zionist idea to fruition.

As Szold continued her involvement in Jewish community affairs and in the Zionist movement, she was also captivated by the atmosphere at JTS, which had begun to occupy a central place in her life. Her studies and the people she met there, many of whom became her close friends, gave her immense satisfaction. Her work with Louis Ginzberg translating and editing *Legends of the Jews* grew into a close friendship that would take her to dizzying heights—and nearly destroy her.

6

LOVE AND MISERY

NEW YEAR HAD BEGUN, and Szold's expectations soared. When she began her studies at the Jewish Theological Seminary in 1904, she signed up for Louis Ginzberg's course in ancient Jewish history. Aware of his reputation for brilliance, she looked forward to his lectures, but was disappointed when Ginzberg frequently showed up late and often not at all, because he was ill. To fill the gap, Dr. Alexander Marx taught Aramaic. Szold enjoyed his class and respected the breadth of his knowledge, his character, and his decency. On Seder night, Szold and her mother were guests of the Schechter family, along with Marx, Israel Friedlaender, Ginzberg, and other members of the JTS faculty. When the assembled company left at the end of the evening, a violent storm was raging. Marx and Friedlaender gallantly offered to see Szold and her mother home. Ginzberg apologized that he could not join them because he was still weak from his illness.

Marx and Friedlaender came to Szold's house every Saturday night to improve their English under her tutelage. The two men were congenial and pleasant, and Szold enjoyed their company. Her sister Adele knew Ginzberg, having translated articles for him from German to English, and was repelled by his arrogance.

In the summer of 1904, Marx wrote to Szold that he was engaged to Anna, the daughter of Rabbi David Zvi Hoffmann, one of the leading lights of the rabbinical seminary in Berlin and a leader of Orthodox Jewry in

Germany. Szold quickly congratulated him and his fiancée.[1] Israel Friedlaender married Lilian Bentwich, the daughter of an old and respected London family and the sister of Norman Bentwich. The Friedlaenders' home was always full of guests, including Szold. Her circle of friends and acquaintances continued to expand.

Szold and Ginzberg became better acquainted through their encounters in the corridors of the seminary, at the Schechter home, or in synagogue on the Sabbath. Ginzberg asked her to translate into English a eulogy he had written in German to mark the first anniversary of the death of Marcus Jastrow.[2] Jastrow and his memory were very close to Szold's heart—he had been a friend and was related to the Szold family by marriage—so she readily agreed and did not ask for payment. After that, Ginzberg would sometimes ask her to translate letters and articles for him. He never offered to pay her and she never asked him to.

At the start of 1905, Ginzberg invited Szold to attend his course on the Talmudic tractate *Kiddushin,* which deals with the laws of betrothal and marriage. When she hesitated, he added that there would not be anything in the course material that might embarrass her. One day he asked whether she would transcribe his course lectures, because he was planning to publish them as a book, and once again she agreed. She was flattered by Ginzberg's frequent requests for her assistance. As she continued her labors on the translation of his work *Legends of the Jews,* she consulted with Ginzberg from time to time about various issues related to the project. Their conversations also dealt with his manuscripts and the translations and transcription that Henrietta had done for him. When Ginzberg went to visit his parents in Europe, in the summer of 1905, Szold was surprised to receive personal letters from him.

Ginzberg described the voyage to Europe and complained that throughout the crossing he had been surrounded exclusively by women, whose husbands were always at the card table. "[Given that] 'bad company spoils good manners,'" he wrote, "I acquired some weaknesses of the fair sex, among others the custom of changing the mind. When we came near Cherbourg it suddenly occurred to me that it would not be a bad idea to visit Paris. . . . The weather and the sea were splendid all the time of my voyage. I spent all my time in sleeping, walking and dreaming. . . . As to my dreams in the state of waking, they were not of a very pleasant mind. The grandeur and monotony of the sea has always a melancholy-producing effect on me." He concluded the letter with "kind regards to you, Mrs. Szold, and Miss Adele."[3]

In his next letter, Ginzberg again referred to the ocean crossing, his visit to Paris, and the melancholy that came over him when faced with the grandeur and vastness of nature: "Such a sight is the best demonstration of how little and insignificant this little creature is which in its stupidity calls itself 'homo sapiens.' Of course I do not deny that moral indignation at the men gambling below and resentment of being left in the company of chattering geese drove me to Paris. This is again an illustration for the philosophical theory according to which there is neither evil nor good in itself. The bad company had the good result for me to enjoy the art treasures of Paris."[4]

Szold was glad to receive his letters, even though they made her wonder about their author's character and values. She answered him and included the news from America, such as the death of attorney Moses Dropsie, who had bequeathed his entire fortune for the establishment of a college for Jewish studies.[5] Ginzberg replied: "If I were rude I would have said what a pity that Dropsie did not die a few years earlier, but as I am too gentle to make such remarks, I will deplore only the fact that his will was not known four years ago. We would have had a Jewish Academy instead of a Theological Seminary. But 'das Geschehene lasst sich nicht mehr un- geschehen machen' [what has been done cannot be undone]."[6] It seems that Ginzberg would have preferred to teach at a university or college rather than at a "theological seminary."

In another letter, he wrote: "I believe that a woman can't master more than one strong feeling at once. When in love, nothing but the object of her love exists for her, while the man is strong enough to love a woman and have other passions at the same time." Szold felt uncomfortable with the many cynical comments he made about people he encountered, especially his ridicule of women and contempt for them, and could not decide how to react. She avoided sharp replies, however, limiting herself to weak reservations in one letter about his language. Szold, who knew the other scholars at the seminary—Schechter, Marx, Friedlaender, and others—as refined and gentle souls, found it hard to reconcile the scholar she had imagined to be just like them and some of the things he wrote to her in his letters. She could not simply break away from him, as she had a commitment to the publisher to translate his book on Jewish legends, and had to continue working with him.

Szold invested great efforts in translating and editing *Legends of the Jews*. Every Tuesday, after he finished teaching his courses at JTS, Ginzberg would come to the Szold house, which was not far from the seminary, and they would go over her translation. He also read the notes she had taken at his lectures and proposed corrections and additions to the text. He dictated to her in German, English, or Hebrew, as appropriate, which she later translated and edited. Sophie often invited him to stay for dinner, and this soon became his regular custom. He enjoyed Sophie's cooking, which was a pleasant change from his bachelor's fare. He and Henrietta would sometimes go for a walk in the nearby park, discussing his *Legends of the Jews* and other matters. Gradually, Ginzberg got into the habit of coming to the Szold house on other days as well, sharing their meals as if he were a member of the household.

Ginzberg returned to Europe from time to time, and upon coming back to the States would often bring Henrietta a gift: a book, an inkwell, a pen, and so forth. His letters also gave Henrietta the impression that his feelings for her were warmer than she had imagined. Despite her misgivings about his arrogance and disdain for people, she began to be attracted to him.

In her regular visits to the Schechter home, Szold noted the central role Mathilde Schechter played there. She saw that household as a model of the kind of married life she longed for, and was saddened by the fact that she had missed out on such a wonderful experience. As her feelings for Ginzberg grew stronger, she began to entertain hopes that it might not be too late after all. She worshiped Ginzberg for his vast erudition, phenomenal memory, and immense talents, and was swept away by the thought that all her happiness in life depended on that man. In her imagination, she saw herself running a home similar to the Schechters', where leading Jewish studies scholars would gather around Ginzberg's brilliance, and she would be his devoted helpmate, as Mathilde was to Solomon.

In one of his letters from Europe, Ginzberg added regards to Henrietta from his mother, "*unbekannterweise* [though she has never met you] and my father also said that if it were not against the Talmudic law . . . he would like to send his regards to you." His family knew that he was a frequent visitor to the Szold house and that he often dined there, and they were grateful for Henrietta's hospitality. By chance, Szold met his brother's wife, who lived in New York, not far from her own house. Ginzberg's sister-in-law praised her for the help she gave him with translations into English and for inviting him to eat with them. Szold felt as if she had been accepted into his family. In all her dealings with Ginzberg, she perceived special attention on his part that went beyond their professional relationship. She became increasingly enthralled by everything Ginzberg said and wrote.

Still, Ginzberg's letters persisted in the same vein as before. Whenever she mentioned some event or person, he responded with critical sarcasm: "I do not understand such indignation at Krauskopf's [an American Reform rabbi] remark that the thread uniting the Jews is purely social . . . If I were in America I might have written on the subject: What is social? The Zionistic movement is mainly due to social reasons and if Krauskopf were not a fool or a charlatan he might have become a Zionist."[7] Szold, an avowed Zionist, never expressed her irritation with Ginzberg's contempt for the movement.

IN 1904, Szold's old friend Dr. Harry Friedenwald was elected president of the Federation of American Zionists. It was hoped that Friedenwald, whose forebears were from Germany, would attract the older, more established segment of the American Jewish community to Zionism.[8] In the summer of 1905, the Seventh Zionist Congress, the first after Herzl's death, would take place in Basel. Judah Magnes and Israel Friedlaender attended, and they became friendly with Friedenwald; after the congress adjourned, they went on holiday together in the Swiss Alps, further cementing their friendship. Friedenwald garnered additional support during the congress and buttressed his standing in the FAZ. Szold had longed to participate in the Seventh Congress but could not leave New York. Chained to her desk at the Jewish Publication Society and constrained by the need to edit the *Year Book,* she felt frustrated. While others were relaxing in Europe, she was trapped in the stifling heat of a New York summer, translating, completing articles, proofreading them, and sending them off to the printer. The pressure was especially great in the summer, just before the *Year Book,* with its inflexible deadline, had to be sent to press.

After Herzl's death there was a sharp decline in the membership of the Federation of American Zionists, and attempts to rebuild the organization had been unsuccessful. Upset by this development, Szold suggested to Friedenwald that the federation put out pamphlets explaining the Zionist idea, in order to reach out to the American Jewish population.[9] He agreed but did nothing to implement the idea. The federation continued to tread water or worse. Abandoned by most of its members, it found itself in a financial and organizational crisis. Friedenwald, who did not know how to revive the organization, submitted his resignation as president in 1906. Because no consensus candidate to replace him emerged, however, he agreed to stay on.

No one proposed Szold for president of the federation. Although she was well known as a devoted Zionist, was highly intelligent, and was blessed with extraordinary organizational talents, it never crossed anyone's mind that a woman could fill such a high position, and all the more so because she had no academic credentials. Friedenwald continued to serve as president and then honorary president until 1918, and the federation continued to wither. In order to bring some order to the office and revitalize the federation, it was decided to hire an executive secretary. Friedenwald recommended Joseph Jasin. The members of the board demurred, not knowing what his skills and experience were, but Friedenwald pressed, and Jasin was given the job. He proved unable to deal with the chaos in the office and was an utter failure. The federation reached rock bottom. Its organizational and financial situation could not have been worse, and further attempts to mend the organizational problems came to nothing.[10] At this point the board turned to Szold, believing that she was the only person who could save the organization from ruin; even so, they did not offer her the title of president of the FAZ. Appreciating the magnitude of the crisis, Szold concluded that she would have to dedicate all of her time and energy to the job. Given her many previous commitments, she felt compelled to turn down the offer.

THAT YEAR ALSO SAW a major change at the *Year Book*. Cyrus Adler had resigned as co-editor because of his other engagements, leaving Szold as sole editor of the eighth volume.[11] She devoted many pages to topics that interested her and were of central importance to the Jewish world. In Kiev, the capital of Ukraine, uniformed Cossacks joined the attacks on the Jews, shooting any they encountered on the streets, killing and wounding dozens. Staying indoors was not safe either. The Ukrainians broke into their homes, arresting, plundering, vandalizing property, and sowing panic and destruction everywhere. Those who could run away did. Among the refugees was the author Sholem Aleichem, who left with his family for Lvov, then London, and finally New York.

The Jews who remained in Russia were targeted by pogroms. Szold stayed abreast of the situation and knew no rest. She was impressed by the charismatic personality of Vladimir Ze'ev Jabotinsky, one of the Jewish leaders during the pogroms in Odessa. Disgusted by the helplessness of the Jews who were being assaulted, he again organized self-defense groups of young Jews to fend off the pogromists. Szold predicted that he would have a brilliant future as a Jewish leader.

Szold watched events in Russia with great concern. In her introduction to a table published in the eighth volume of the *Year Book* that she edited, detailing the pogroms from 1903 to 1906, Szold warned that the upheaval in Russia presaged a bitter future for the Jews. The pogroms, she said, were a symptom of what was wrong with Russia.[12] The long arm of European antisemitism, which reached as far as the United States, troubled her, and cracks began to develop in her faith in the freedom and equality promised by the US Constitution. She was also apprehensive about the fact that antisemitism in the United States led Jews to deny their heritage. Szold believed that there was only one solution: Zionism. Antisemitism would disappear when the Jews had their own country. When millions of Jews emigrated from Eastern Europe in the late nineteenth century, however, most went to the New World rather than to their ancestral homeland. Even had large numbers of Jews wanted to settle in Palestine, the country was too poor to absorb them. The problem of antisemitism remained, and Szold believed that it had to be faced head-on. She never stopped sounding the alarm and spurring American Jews to action.

In the *Year Book,* Szold cast a spotlight on the important contribution that the Jews of the United States were making to their country, as she did in previous volumes. She included a section on "The Government of the United States and Affairs of Interest to the Jews, 1905–1906," as well as a list of the five Jewish members of the Fifty-Ninth Congress.[13] She also printed information about Jews who had served in the American armed forces, some of them as senior officers, along with the names of intellectuals, authors, poets, and others who had contributed to American culture.

THERE WAS A JOYOUS EVENT in the Szold family that year, when Adele, the youngest sister, married Thomas Seltzer. The Russian-born Seltzer, brought to America as a child, was affiliated with a circle of socialist and anarchist intellectuals and also tried his hand at journalism and translation. Seltzer later established a publishing company that specialized in contemporary authors, both Jewish and non-Jewish. Unlike most publishers, he was interested not in famous writers, but in bringing young talents to public attention.

The only daughter left at home now was Henrietta. She had not yet given up her hopes of marriage, and set her eyes on Ginzberg, with whom she had, by now, fallen in love. Her work on *Legends of the Jews* and Ginzberg's other works had brought them closer, leading Szold down a dizzying path.

THE CRISIS

In the summer of 1906, Ginzberg vacationed in Tannersville in the Catskill Mountains. He sent Szold regards from Schechter, who was also there. Others from the seminary were attending the FAZ convention, taking place at a resort there. Ginzberg wrote about them: "Dr. Benderly is sitting to my right while Dr. Marx spreads his wings to my left and in such surroundings you cannot expect from me a well [w]ritten letter." About himself, Ginzberg added toward the end of the letter: "I am still trying to live the life of the Hindu but I am sure it would be easier for me to adopt the mode of life of the Dervish than of the Hindu."[14]

Ginzberg's ability to laugh at himself only slightly mitigated his contempt for the people he met, while his chauvinist comments made Szold cringe. "When I happen to look at the well fed and well-dressed Jewesses sitting in the park I can not help asking with the prophet Ezekiel '*Ha-tyhyenoh ha'azamos ha-eyleh!*' [Can these bones live?]. Is there any hope for Israel if its representative elements are so degenerated? And now how are you? Do you take your daily walks at the Riverside Drive? Many a time I thought of our walks which I would prefer to those in the mountains."[15] If she began having doubts about his character and how he might treat his future wife, she did not share them with her diary. Every brief personal comment directed at her, like his reference to their walks, electrified her and stuck with her.

Year after year, summer was the season of Szold's greatest frustration. She yearned for a break as she read the letters from her friends, especially Ginzberg. At the end of the summer, the vacationers returned to New York from Europe and elsewhere in the United States, and Szold returned to working with Ginzberg on his books and articles. Their meetings became even more frequent. Every Saturday, at the end of services, he would look up at the women's gallery in the synagogue and try to catch Szold's eye. When their glances met, he would nod at her, as if inviting her to meet him outside so they could go for a walk in the park. Seeing them together so frequently, their acquaintances treated them as a couple headed for the marriage canopy. From time to time they received joint invitations for Sabbath dinner at the Marxes' or the Friedlaenders'. Szold entertained the hope that Ginzberg's marriage proposal was only a matter of time.

In late April 1907, Ginzberg was suddenly called away to his father's sickbed. He sailed to Amsterdam and remained there with his parents for five months. It was the most intensive period of his correspondence with Szold. She inquired how his father was doing and updated him about developments at the seminary. She wrote about the Schechter family wedding, about the bride and groom and guests, and added a maternal scolding: "At Ruth Schechter's wedding I was told that you were not well—that you were sick, in fact. Your anxiety, to be sure, is sufficient to account for a breakdown. But do you not see that you must be particularly careful of yourself? Won't you be good to yourself, and not add to the apprehensiveness your friends already feel in your behalf?"

As for herself, Szold was tired and in very low spirits, writing, "Did I enjoy *myself*? I had had to interrupt my Year Book work for half a day to go, and in the crowd I remembered keenly that I was all alone in New York, for the Seltzers have left, too. To-day I worked harder than ever to make up for the time lost. All feelings vanished—I am again a machine. It is better so."[16]

From Amsterdam, Ginzberg reported to Szold on the tension with his father, who was still disappointed that his son had left the yeshiva, where great things had been expected of him, to attend university instead, and also by the fact that he was still a bachelor. Ginzberg wrote that he was not at all sorry that he had become an academic.[17]

Their letters became more personal. Ginzberg wrote to Henrietta's mother, who had gone to Baltimore to help Bertha, and suggested that as much as she enjoyed her grandchildren, she should really rest and take a vacation. Henrietta answered Ginzberg and sent regards to his mother, adding, "I don't know if your father would be pleased if I sent regards to him." Ginzberg asked Szold to urge his sister-in-law in New York not to put off the operation she needed. Szold came away with the impression of a very close bond between her and his relatives, and between Ginzberg and hers, as if they were family. At the end of July, Ginzberg informed Szold of his father's death, and she replied at once with a condolence letter. During the Shiva, she wrote to him every day. He answered at the end of the week of mourning, in a letter full of suffering. He mentioned their walks in Riverside Park, and said that they could resume them in three weeks' time, when he would be coming home. When the month of mourning was over, however, Ginzberg was in no hurry to go back to New York. First he went to Berlin and then Königsberg, and from there to Memel, to visit and comfort his father's mother. Then he went back to his mother in Amsterdam, and stayed with her until after the fall holidays.

The day Ginzberg landed in New York, he went to Szold's house and invited her out for a walk in the park. On Tuesday, he resumed his old routine, coming to lunch and then staying to work with her for four hours, after which they went for a walk. They returned to her house for supper and he remained the entire evening. Throughout the winter they continued to work intensively on what would become Ginzberg's *Geniza Studies*, which she transcribed and edited. As always, he dictated to her in three languages, German, English, and Hebrew, after which Szold translated as necessary and edited the result. In May, he began to write the preface to *Geniza Studies*, which he said would be only ten pages long. It turned out to be much longer than that, and Henrietta worked night and day to translate and edit it. Because the book was going to be published by the seminary and not the Jewish Publication Society, Szold received no payment for her many hours of work on it, which consumed so much of her precious time.

In 1908, the hot and humid summer months again sent many New Yorkers flocking to the mountains. Szold's friends sailed for Europe on vacation or to visit relatives. Ginzberg left for Germany in early August. Szold remained in New York, completing the translation of a volume from French, editing books for JPS, and fully immersed in the work of getting the *Year Book* ready for the printer. She was burdened by the monotony of summer, with the oppressive heat and enervating humidity, and did not feel comfortable in the half-empty seminary synagogue. She was also worried about her mother, whose illness weighed on her.[18] Ginzberg's absence, too, left her feeling out of spirits. Before his departure, her daily hope had been that he would propose to her, but his departure for Germany had frustrated her expectations. During this trip, his letters were infrequent. When he landed in Europe he sent her a short letter, followed only by a spate of postcards, although she wrote him long and frequent letters. Szold began to doubt his love for her, but then she received a warm letter that dispelled her concerns. His first letter to her was dated the Ninth of Av, a day of collective mourning, commemorating the destruction of the ancient Temple in Jerusalem. He wrote that her letters gave him so much pleasure that the fast day had passed easily. She replied in a long letter in which she expressed her joy in his friendship, her happiness in being part of his work, and her pride in his rising career. She added that her walks in the park were dull without him. Ginzberg replied to only some of her letters. From Berlin he sent her a book about Jewish literature, with the dedication "To my dear friend, Miss Szold, regards from Berlin, 28.8.1908." Szold was excited by the dedication, especially the word "dear," which could be viewed as the conventional opening to a letter but could also be taken as an expression of affection. Szold opted for the second interpretation and was overjoyed that he had written in a more intimate style than ever before.[19]

After that, she received a number of letters that worried her. In one of them Ginzberg wrote that he was going through a crisis. He was sorry for the pain he had caused her but felt the need to pour out his heart to someone, and she was his "victim."[20] Henrietta wondered what he meant by "victim" and was afraid that he had fallen into a serious depression. In his next letter, Ginzberg teased her about her fears and said she should not pay attention to what he had written about a crisis. In fact, he was "the same old egotist." Szold thought that the crisis stemmed from his grief over his father's death, now a year in the past. Ginzberg wrote that she should stop worrying, that his crisis had passed, and that he would be returning to New York on the SS *Minneapolis*. This did not assuage her misgivings. She sensed in her heart that something was amiss.

A letter by Henrietta Szold to "Dearest friend"

Before he returned to New York, Ginzberg wrote her another letter to reassure her that he had returned to himself, and sent her his best wishes for the New Year.[21] Her optimism returned and her heart was full of song. The letter was sent two weeks before his return, but as the date of his arrival in New York approached, she sank into dark thoughts, overcome by uncertainty. She sensed that the tone of his letters had changed. Just then Szold received a letter from Judah Magnes, informing her of his engagement to Beatrice Lowenstein. Her heart shrank, for though her friends shared news of their happiness with her, she could not reciprocate.

Szold's tension peaked on Tuesday, the day Ginzberg was scheduled to arrive. He had told her what time he would be disembarking. For a moment she thought about going to the window to see whether he was on his way, but gave up that idea. Then she heard a knock at the door, and there he stood. Szold was busy working with her secretary. He asked her to accompany her to the next room. "I have something to tell you," he said. Her heart was pounding, and she could feel her pulse throbbing in her temples: The great moment had come at last! When they were alone, he told her, without delay: "You will be surprised, I am engaged."[22]

Her blood froze. The room turned dark and she was sure she was about to faint. Seeing her pallor, he told her, "You know that I always do the unexpected." Then he went on to tell her the story. He had been staying with a friend and went with him to the synagogue, where he noticed a young woman who attracted his attention. His friend told him who she was. That very afternoon she came to visit, and within a few weeks they had decided to marry. He showed Szold a photograph of his fiancée. She mustered all her strength so as not to collapse in front of him, though it was as if she had been struck by lightning. He saw this and said, almost without thinking, "You'll get over it," and went off.

After he left, Henrietta crumpled into a chair. The tension and expectations that had welled up in her for so many months had disintegrated in a flash. For weeks she was unable to express, even in her diary, the profound pain she felt, until she finally wrote, "I was cold as ice outward, inside I was consumed by heat and rebellion." She blamed herself: "I had been blind—I had been mistaken, he had never loved me. . . . [I] sat down and made a pretense at eating—practically nothing passed my lips for ten days."[23]

Her mother, seeing her grief, said nothing, and tiptoed about the house. For weeks, Szold was overwhelmed by her pain and tormented herself incessantly. A torrent of questions coursed through her, all running together: How could he have done this to her? Why had she deluded herself? Was she blind? Had he ever loved her or was it all in her imagination? And if he had never had any thoughts of marriage, but only of a professional relationship, why had he piled so many translation and editing jobs on her and enslaved for years, day and night, and never offered to pay her? Most unsettling was the question of whether he had deceived her intentionally. Szold simply could not make a sharp transition in her feelings for a man she had worshiped and loved so deeply. She found no way to escape her despair and find the exit from the labyrinth of questions in which she was trapped. Her anguish intensified and left her no rest. Weeks passed until she found the strength to set her thoughts down on paper and organize the chaos in her mind. At last she opened her heart to her diary.

Szold wrote: "Today it is four weeks since my only real happiness in life was killed by a single word. . . . Today for the first time I have been calm. Since then I have hardly been conscious of living. There has been only suffering, nights and days, and days and nights of suffering . . . Today for the first time I have been calm, at least outwards. For the first time I have been aware of what I was doing at a given moment. Almost I slept all night. All these weeks composed of minutes of misery I have done nothing but remember—and it has been a thorny crown of sorrows, this remembering bittersweet days. . . . If I put all my memories down perhaps it will help me to adjust myself to the new cold loveless life I must henceforth live."[24]

But she did not adjust. She kept torturing and tormenting herself, blaming herself for her vain delusions and for allowing them to sweep her away till she lost all sense of proportion. She could not shake off the painful questions: Was it possible that he had never loved her? And if he had never had any serious intentions about her, why hadn't he made her aware of her mistake years earlier? Certainly he had seen she was in love with him. What was more, he had even encouraged her feelings. Szold repeated the same questions obsessively, writing in her diary almost every day—sometimes only a single page, sometimes several, recording her feelings and thoughts and terrible pain.

Szold saw Ginzberg as a genius, blessed with tremendous abilities and a vast store of knowledge—a truly extraordinary individual of the highest moral character. That perspective affected her judgment: she could not believe that Ginzberg had deliberately deceived her because he wanted to enjoy the fruits of her labors without paying for them. She could not make the switch from the idol she worshiped to a despicable human being. Although the entire business left her frustrated and humiliated, she felt obligated to keep a promise she had made to Ginzberg and write a letter of congratulations to his fiancée, when he told her that he was engaged. In fact, the very request filled her with disgust, but she did sit down and write to her: "Dr. Ginzberg told me so many things I wanted to know about his future wife and companion. He showed me your picture. You are the last person I need to tell what a fortunate woman you are to have won the love of such an extraordinary man. I have been in almost daily contact with him for five years and I know every fibre of his being for true and upright. A gift of God indeed is his clear, penetrating, and richly stocked mind. For you, life at his side will be a sacred and beautiful feat. And when you come to follow him to America in a short time then you must promise to become my friend even as your fiancé has been up to now."[25]

Despite the kind words she put on paper, Szold was furious with herself for having agreed to write to the young woman. Her pain was redoubled by her inability to renege on this foolish promise and lack of control over her actions. In her mind she relived the countless conversations with Ginzberg over the years. The more she thought about them, the clearer it became that he was not at all the man she had imagined. She was torn.

Her rational mind understood, but her heart insisted otherwise. The unrelenting pain and disappointment were mixed with self-condemnation.

She continued to love Ginzberg despite everything and spoke up in his defense when others excoriated him. She could not make her peace with the gulf between her love for him and her anger at his offensive traits. She wanted to protect him but could not forgive the cruel humiliation and the cold indifference to her feelings. She revisited the terrible moments after he had told her about his fiancée, and she remembered his dismissive response—"You'll get over it"—when he saw her deep pain. "Does he understand what a broken heart is?" she asked in her diary.

Szold's mortification and pain were worse because she saw herself as a fool. How could she not have understood that he was playing with her? How could she, a mature and intelligent woman with the ability to understand a man's personality and character, have allowed herself to be deceived for so long? Had she been out of touch with reality all that time? Had she been blind? She was quite broken and found it impossible to resume her routine or go back to work. Szold resolved to leave the *Year Book,* which she had been editing without any additional remuneration from the Jewish Publication Society beyond her regular salary. Mayer Sulzberger, the chairman of the JPS publication committee and one of the founders of the American Jewish Committee, arranged for the *Year Book* to be transferred to the AJC. The ninth volume (published in 1908) was edited by Herbert Friedenwald, Cyrus Adler's brother-in-law.[26] But Szold could not simply pass on her duties at JPS to someone else. Her ingrained sense of responsibility forced her to stay. Her heart ached when she received a letter from Ginzberg several weeks later: "I have finished my preface to the *Geniza,* and I would like to ask you whether you have any objection to my reference to your kind assistance, without which the book would never have been published in English. I do not think I have any right not to mention it; on the other hand, I have no right to mention your name in connection with the book without asking your permission."[27]

Szold could not find the strength to answer him. Ginzberg sent her the rough draft of the preface he had written, asking her to edit it. When she saw that her name did not appear there, it was like salt in her wounds. She sent him back the edited copy with comments and corrections. Ginzberg wrote with other questions, and she was helpless to ignore them. Ginzberg's *Yerushalmi Fragments from the Geniza* was published by JTS in 1909. Szold's name does not appear on the title page or in Ginzberg's preface, nor is there any mention of her translations, careful editing, and meticulous proofreading. Outside their immediate circle, no one knew about her crucial contribution to Ginzberg's book, and it was soon forgotten.

Having finally had too much, Szold found the strength to inform Ginzberg that she would not work on volume 3 of *Legends of the Jews*. But this was not the end of their professional relationship, because Szold felt she had to honor her commitment to complete her labors on Ginzberg's other books, which she had already edited, and prepare them for printing, including reading the proofs. The galleys, with Szold's corrections, were sent for Ginzberg to approve, so their correspondence dragged on, despite the torture it involved.

Unable to wall herself up in her misery, Szold shared her unhappiness with close friends. She poured out her heart to her devoted friend Mathilde Schechter. When Schechter's husband learned about Szold's mental state, he and Sulzberger came up with the idea of asking her to edit a book about women, thinking that perhaps this topic might attract her and ease the pain. Szold felt that she could not take on another commitment, however. She was already overworked beyond her capacity and committed to seeing Ginzberg's works through to publication.

The Szold-Ginzberg drama was the talk of the day at the seminary and within her circle. Everyone knew how close the two had been and had been certain they would marry. When people learned of Ginzberg's engagement, they were indignant about his treatment of Szold and felt sorry for her. They knew how deep her pain was. Szold asked Schechter whether she should stop coming to the seminary synagogue, which Ginzberg attended, and perhaps even leave New York. He advised her not to break with all her friends and to try to channel her relations with Ginzberg into a friendship.[28] When Szold told Marx of Schechter's suggestion about remaining friends, he rejected it forcefully. Marx thought that Szold's mistake had been to idealize a human being, to see Ginzberg as a paragon of virtue.[29]

Marx told Szold that she did not have to treat Ginzberg as a friend when what she really felt was love. He suggested that she analyze the sequence of events rationally. She might conclude that had she married Ginzberg her life would have not have been the bed of roses she had imagined. She might find she had been saved from a bitter fate that was worse than being jilted.[30]

Szold found it hard to accept these rationalizations, and she continued to fill her diary and correspond with her closest friends. Many people who knew Ginzberg condemned him for having misled her and for the callous manner in which he told her of his engagement. For years, this was the dominant opinion at the seminary and among her friends and acquaintances. Their horror at Ginzberg's conduct increased when they learned that he had wanted to continue working with her after his marriage, as if there had never been anything between them. They blamed Ginzberg for his lack of sensitivity toward her and for his refusal to acknowledge the wrong he had done her.

Ginzberg was not oblivious to the climate among his colleagues at the seminary. When he and Adele Katzenstein were married in London in May 1909, he did not inform any of his colleagues of the wedding date. He introduced her to them only after the couple arrived in New York. Szold suffered every time she encountered the Ginzbergs. It was like a knife being twisted in her heart. Their mutual friends tried to avoid inviting them to the same events. Adele Ginzberg recalled that once, when they found themselves by chance in the same house as Szold, the hosts hustled her off to a side room until Szold had left. The entire episode, which made waves at the seminary and elsewhere, cast a heavy shadow on the Ginzberg family for many years.

In his biography of his father, Eli Ginzberg noted that two episodes in his father's life had been taboo topics in the family: Ginzberg's aborted appointment to the faculty of Hebrew Union College and his relationship with Henrietta Szold. "An Exceptional Friendship" was the title Eli Ginzberg gave the chapter about that relationship. He endeavored to refute the charge that his father had deceived Szold, insisting that their long collaboration, and especially her exceptional dedication to Louis's writings, were an expression of friendship. This, he said, was how his father had seen matters.[31] Eli Ginzberg interpreted the story this way:

> Miss Szold early fell in love with my father but, realizing the discrepancy in their ages, she was careful to keep tight rein on her emotions and aspirations. As the years of friendship lengthened and the ties of intimacy deepened, she found it increasingly difficult to control her emotions, but she succeeded nevertheless. From 1903 to 1907, the relationship remained in reasonable balance. It was a close working friendship as far as my father was concerned, and Miss Szold did not permit herself to admit more than that.
>
> But in the spring of 1907 my father had to be at his father's side during his terminal illness. These were very hard weeks that stretched into months. In his anguish, he needed solace and broke through his own reserve. The letters between him and Miss Szold take on a deeper hue. No longer are they limited solely to manuscripts and galleys, current events, and pleasantries. They become introspective, personal, emotional.[32]

Louis Ginzberg opened his heart to Szold and wrote about his distress at the thought that he had disappointed his father by choosing the university over the yeshiva. His father was also hurt by his break with religious tradition. "He bare[d] all this and more in his letters to Miss Szold and she did her best to steady and reassure him. And slowly, he regain[ed] his composure and his equilibrium. But at what a price for her!" The biography reveals that during that summer of 1907, the Ginzberg family discussed not only whether he should marry, but also the implications of his marrying a much older woman: he was thirty-four, Szold forty-seven.[33]

Eli Ginzberg recounted that many years later his father had uncharacteristically opened up about the subject and told his daughter-in-law (Eli's wife) "that he could never have contemplated marrying Miss Szold, for the simple reason that his pride would never have permitted him to marry a woman so much his senior, and that one reason for his ever marrying was his desire for children, a desire that could not have been fulfilled by Miss Szold."[34] For Louis Ginzberg, everything was ordered, planned, rational. To judge by his son's account, Ginzberg was aware of Szold's strong feelings but never made his intentions clear to her and allowed her to wallow in her illusions for too many years.

In the Szold family, too, the whole incident was avoided like the plague. For many years, they trod lightly around the whole subject of her relationship with Ginzberg. In Lowenthal's biography of Szold, which was published in her lifetime and relied heavily on her family as a source, the episode was barely alluded to. Even after her death, the family was reticent on the subject. Alexandra Lee Levin, who was married to Henrietta's nephew Marcus Levin, wrote a composite biography of the family, *The Szolds of Lombard Street*. Henrietta takes center stage, but the Ginzberg episode is mentioned only briefly.[35]

Ironically, Eli Ginzberg met a young woman whose family name was Szold. Her relatives warned her "to be on guard" about a Ginzberg. But the couple married anyway and named their only son Jeremy Szold Ginzberg. According to Eli Ginzberg, it eventually became a family joke that Louis Ginzberg was the father of Hadassah: "Szold's disappointment in love propelled her to find new meaning and direction in her life"—as the mother of the Hadassah Women's Zionist Organization.[36]

Szold's agony proved intractable. Her friends tried to help ease her pain. Schechter spoke with Sulzberger and they agreed to grant her a leave of absence from JPS. Edwin Wolf, the president of JPS, persuaded the board to offer her six months' vacation at full pay, until February 1910, so she could travel to Europe. They added another check for $500 so that she could continue on to Palestine. The vacation was intended to get her far away from New York and from the milieu in which she had been linked to Ginzberg, so that she could recover her strength and equilibrium. She accepted and expressed her gratitude in public.[37] However, her diary told a different story. Nothing could calm her seething heart, as her anguish continued to ferment inside her. Even the preparations for the trip gave her no respite. Yet another blow fell when it was the seminary press that sent her a copy of *Geniza Fragments,* not Ginzberg himself. Her wretchedness swelled and grew worse.[38]

Szold continued to prepare for her trip to Europe and Palestine, but her thoughts were elsewhere: "Tomorrow will be a year since he called me up on the telephone and told me he wanted to speak to me once more before he sailed [to Europe]. As he stood with his grip in his hand. Tomorrow will be a year since he saw the tears streaming down my cheeks as I bade him farewell at the post office. I did not look upon it as humiliation then that I should weep. But in the light of all the humiliation he has put upon me since then publicly and privately, it too was humiliation—I cannot yet free myself of that feeling of degradation." She resolved to stop tormenting herself. She had thought that she could put the entire sorry chapter in her life behind her if she got it all out of her system before leaving for Europe, but she was wrong. "Inside of myself nothing has changed, outwardly I have been completing all arrangements for the European flight, inwardly I have been weeping. I miss him, I long for him, I dare not think that he is with another woman—her husband." A few days before she sailed she wrote: "The last few days I've reached the insight that he never intended to marry me."[39] Not only did the candor fail to assuage her pain, but it added fuel to the fire in her heart.

On July 30, 1909, Henrietta and her mother, Sophie, sailed for Europe. She had intended to keep a travel diary, but her heart was elsewhere and her impressions of the journey were mingled with confessions and expressions of the feelings that continued to seethe within her. The vacation did not help her get over her grief. Instead, her misery peaked without warning in 1911, after her return to America, and caused a sharp change of direction in her life. This part of Henrietta Szold's story has never before been told.

7

THE LAND OF DREAMS

ENRIETTA AND SOPHIE SET SAIL from New York on the Scotland-bound SS *California*. The atmosphere on the ship was thoroughly Scottish: "Scotch speaking, Scotch names, Scotch songs, Scotch dances, and Scotch patriotism. I am being put into the proper frame of mind for Glasgow, the lochs and Edinburgh," Henrietta wrote.[1] Most of the travelers were Scots who had immigrated to the United States and were now going to visit the old country. The travelers seemed cheerful, conversing and passing the time with music, dancing, and card games. Henrietta sat by herself, immersed in reading and writing for hours on end. On the eve of their departure, Henrietta and Sophie had received thirty letters and fourteen telegrams from friends, as well as baskets of fruit and packages with various items for their journey. As was her wont, Henrietta did not leave a single letter unanswered or gift unacknowledged. People on the ship saw her constantly reading and writing and wondered who she was. When Sophie told her that some of the passengers had speculated that she was a follower of the feminist activist Emma Goldman, Henrietta was amused.[2]

Henrietta and Sophie were assigned a very spacious cabin on the ship, thanks to someone they knew. "It is important for a person to have friends with good connections," Henrietta wrote. Her friends went out of their way to make her journey comfortable so she could rest from the trauma she had suffered. On second thought, however, the possibility that they would be charged for these extras on the ship and would have to pay out of pocket troubled her. She worried that their money would not last their six-month journey. She praised the kosher food on the ship, which she described as including "fish, vegetables, and fruit in abundance." To satisfy her literary appetite, Henrietta had taken an ample supply of poetry and prose with her, including books about the places they would be visiting.

The book she read about Mary Queen of Scots fascinated her and filled Henrietta with pity for the hardships that befell the beautiful young queen and for her bitter fate.[3] She wondered why she had never before given much thought to the fate of the people she encountered through literature. She supposed it was due to the fact that she had been overburdened with work for so many years, and she began to agonize, asking, "Is there something wrong with me?" She then tried to comfort herself, reasoning that had she really been such a complete failure in her life, would she have received such a large bundle of letters and telegrams and so many gifts from people who had written to her with affection and wished her well for the journey? Similar thoughts returned to trouble her from time to time, and she never stopped criticizing herself. Her self-confidence was severely shaken.

Henrietta had brought along the proofs of Bentwich's book, *Philo-Judæus of Alexandria,* and, more absurdly, the proofs of the second volume of Ginzberg's *Legends of the Jews,* to look over while she was away. Her trip to Europe was meant to calm her nerves after the trauma she had experienced with Ginzberg, and here she was taking with her the very seeds of the crisis that had nearly driven her mad. She had hoped to read the books she had brought with her during the voyage but found herself distracted by thoughts she would have preferred to avoid. She wrote in her diary that the vast ocean around them had failed to deliver the calm everyone had said it would.

In Glasgow, Henrietta inquired into local Jewish history, as she often did when visiting a new place. She was shocked to learn that Jews had, in the past, been imprisoned under harsh conditions in the tower of the old cathedral until their deaths.[4] She was impressed by Edinburgh, which she found to be "both solemn and gay": the modern architecture on the wide boulevards, the old quarter and the history on display in the old castles, the gardens and vast parks. They also visited the Scottish lochs, and she marveled at the sights.

From Scotland, Sophie and Henrietta continued by train to England, making a few stops along the way. In the city of York, they heard a man speaking Yiddish in the market. They asked him about the Jewish community, and he pointed to a woman, saying, "She knows and can tell you." She was the wife of a well-to-do merchant, and she explained to them that the community consisted of thirteen families, most of whom lived in poverty. The synagogue, located at the end of a narrow alley, looked poor and neglected, and there was no sign of the old cemetery. From York, they continued on their journey to Lincoln. While they found evidence that Jews had lived in the city in the past, when Henrietta and Sophie visited not a single Jew remained.[5]

When they arrived in London, they found rooms in a guest house, and Henrietta went out to survey their surroundings. It felt like she was walking in the footsteps of Dickens and Thackeray. Henrietta hoped that she would have an opportunity to meet members of the Jewish community in London and to talk with them, but she was disappointed. She had an impression that everyone had gone on holiday. Fortunately, though, not everyone had left. Henrietta and Sophie enjoyed the hospitality of their friends in London, especially the Bentwiches, who gave them a very warm welcome. Henrietta was friendly with Norman Bentwich and had edited his book for JPS.[6] Israel Friedlaender and his wife, who was Norman Bentwich's sister, graciously invited Henrietta and her mother to spend the weekend with them at Carmel Court, the Bentwich family estate, located in a seaside village in Kent. Henrietta effusively wrote of the heartfelt hospitality they received there, and she described the house and the surrounding gardens. Before they left the estate, their hosts informed Elkan Adler of their arrival in London, and when the Szolds got to the city they spent a pleasant evening at his home.[7]

Elkan Nathan Adler, the son of British chief rabbi Nathan Marcus Adler, was a lawyer and collector of Jewish books and ancient manuscripts. Adler was among the first scholars to study the material found in the Cairo Genizah, having visited Egypt and brought back a large number of text fragments.[8] Henrietta had planned to go to Cambridge, not merely as a tourist, but also in the hope of visiting the university's vast library and collection of ancient manuscripts cited in the books she had edited. Adler referred her to the Cambridge manuscript librarian. The visit afforded her a unique experience. She was impressed by the beauty of the city of Cambridge, the river Cam crossing it, the ancient cathedrals, and the well-kept lawns and gardens that lent it a pastoral air. In a letter to Mathilde Schechter, Henrietta wondered how she and Solomon could ever have left such a place.[9]

Henrietta seems to have enjoyed their trip to England, but her pleasure was marred by the thoughts that troubled her. In her letter to Mathilde, she shared her impressions of the things she had seen, but she also unburdened her soul. The pain still gnawed at her heart and gave her no peace. From Cambridge they traveled to Oxford, where once again Henrietta marveled at the ancient buildings and their beautiful gardens. On the way, they met a group of students dressed in gowns striding purposefully to the ceremony marking the end of the academic year. She visited the Bodleian Library and its collection of ancient manuscripts, which attracted scholars from around the world.

On their return to London, Dr. Hochman, whom they had met at the home of the Bentwich family, joined them on their tour of the city. They visited castles and parks, St. James's Church, and Westminster Abbey, but they were unable to visit the Houses of Parliament, from which women were barred at the time, due to fears of disturbances by the suffragettes— women who demanded the right to vote and often resorted to violence that led to clashes with the police. Dr. Hochman accompanied them to the British Museum and arranged the necessary special permission for them to see its library. She marveled at the spectacular collections that had been brought from far-off lands, and was particularly impressed by the large sarcophagi from Egypt. Even in her excitement, however, she did not neglect to mention that so many of these treasures had been stolen from other nations.[10]

From England, Henrietta and Sophie sailed across the English Channel to France, disembarking at Saint-Aubin-sur-Mer, a small town on the Normandy coast.[11] They were greeted by Sophie's nephew Ignatz, who was vacationing at his family's country house in the town and hosted them there. Henrietta had met Ignatz on her first trip to Europe with her father, at the age of twenty, when they had stayed with his family in Vienna. Ignatz's pretty wife graciously welcomed them. He went with Henrietta to see the sights in the nearby towns and city, visiting the old churches they saw on the way.

Her attention was caught by the paintings depicting the Madonna and Child. She thought that it would have been fitting to continue her European tour in Italy, "where there are many more and richer Madonnas, with the babies and the angels, in paintings and in sculpture," and added: "If a note of dissatisfaction creeps in, it is that this opportunity did not come earlier in my life, many things might have been different."[12] This was a reference to her earlier meeting with her cousin Ignatz, then a university student, who had showed her Vienna and tried to convince her to stay at their house, promising that he would take her on a trip to Italy. Henrietta regretted turning down his offer, which had been a kind of invitation to become his wife. She imagined that had she responded positively to him, her fate would have been different, and she would not have remained alone and unhappy for the rest of her life.

During Sophie and Henrietta's visit to Hungary and Moravia they met many relatives. Their visit to Vienna was especially exciting. Henrietta was fondly reminded of her earlier visit with her father, recalling the places and museums that they had visited, and was overjoyed to see the works of Botticelli, Rembrandt, Velasquez, and Rubens again. In addition to her descriptions of the beauty of the city, she added to Marx, "My mother is a tireless traveler, curious and interested; no tower is too high for her to climb up its many stairs, no distance is too great, no tour too tiring." Henrietta marveled at her mother, and also felt sorry for the seventy-year-old woman dragging herself through foreign lands in order to ease her daughter's pain.

As their journey continued, Henrietta began to miss her friends in New York. "The holidays provided me with an opportunity to see and feel so much of the Jewish life that enlivened my experience," she wrote to Mathilde Schechter, but added, "I miss the prayers at the Seminary synagogue, and I hope that my absence will be felt there as much as I pine here for my friends in New York."[13] This thought troubled Henrietta, who feared losing her friends after such a long separation. She turned her attention to the proofs she had brought with her, noting, "This is the first time since the winter that I have found more free time than ten or fifteen minutes to work on a book."[14] Still, she found it hard to work.

From Europe, they turned their thoughts to Palestine. Henrietta wanted to go there in the autumn, and not during the searing summer days. She planned to enter the country from the north, first visiting Jewish communities in the Upper Galilee and the pioneering settlements about which she had heard so much. Henrietta wanted to save Jerusalem for the end of the trip, as it would be the crowning moment of the journey, and she wished to spend more time there. The route that Henrietta chose extended their journey. Instead of departing by ship to Alexandria and from there continuing on to Jaffa, they went to Istanbul.

Henrietta was impressed by the great city, which seemed so different from Europe in its architecture, in the spacious and richly ornamented mosques, in the streets crowded with people, in the women's colorful clothes, and in the arcades of the Grand Bazaar—one for carpets, one for spices, others for produce and meat, and more. They were surprised at the sweets market and the great variety of candies there, in all the colors of the rainbow. From Istanbul they went to Beirut and Damascus, beautiful cities that Henrietta enjoyed as well.[15] From Syria, they made their way to Palestine, the pinnacle of Henrietta's dreams, which she had yearned to visit for so long. She had read so much about the country and about people who had visited the Holy Land, and she had heard accounts by friends who had been there—Harry Friedenwald, Cyrus Adler, Judah Magnes, Richard Gottheil, and others. All this increased her curiosity, but she did not foresee that this visit would one day change her life.

THE PROMISED LAND

The mountains of the Galilee were a sharp contrast to European landscapes rich with lakes and forests. As far as the eye could see were bare mountains and hills without rivers or groves. The small Arab villages with their low houses seemed rooted in the earth, and the Bedouin, with their tents and flocks, seemed as if they had been frozen in time. Before Henrietta set out on her journey, she had read about Palestine and heard from her friends what a poor, backward, and malaria-ridden land it was, but seeing it for herself was quite another thing. At the time, some 80,000 Jews lived in Palestine, mostly in the cities of Tiberias, Safed, Jerusalem, Hebron, Jaffa, and Haifa. About half of them were members of the Old Yishuv (the pre-Zionist Jewish community of Palestine) and were supported by the *halukah*—charity funds donated by Jewish communities in the diaspora for religious scholars in Palestine.[16]

The Szolds' first stop in Palestine was the hilltop city of Safed. From a distance, it seemed shrouded in ancient glory, but when they finally entered the city, they saw the devastating poverty of its inhabitants, packed together in courtyard after courtyard. Wherever they turned, they saw women in long dresses carrying heavy baskets up and down the steep stairs between the houses.

From Safed, Sophie and Henrietta went to Tiberias, in the Lower Galilee. There were no paved roads in the Galilee, and no comfortable mode of transport. Travel was by donkey or mule, and sometimes in a horse-drawn carriage. The journey was exhausting, and Henrietta gazed at her long-suffering mother, who uttered not a word of complaint as the carriage jolted and lurched along the derelict roads. Henrietta hoped that when they reached Tiberias, Sophie could stay in the hotel for a day or two to rest while she went sightseeing in the city and the surrounding area, but things did not go according to plan.

When they approached Tiberias, they saw the black basalt rocks on the stony hills—remnants of the lava that had flowed throughout the Lower Galilee from a nearby volcano thousands of years before. The old walls of Tiberias were built of the same rock, as were the city's houses, giving it a unique appearance. Tiberias was a small city. At the beginning of the twentieth century, it had a population of some 2,000 residents, half of whom were Jews. Henrietta and Sophie were shocked to see the poverty and neglect in Tiberias, where most of the streets were unpaved. When they arrived at the hotel, they found an old and dilapidated building, and the room they were offered was not clean. Sophie could not stay there even a single day, and Henrietta had to change her plan.

While Henrietta was weighing in her mind how they could continue their journey, a thin man of average height, with a long, distinguished-looking beard, arrived with a letter. At the time, she did not know who Yehoshua Hankin was; she was later told he was known as "the redeemer of the land," because he purchased land in Palestine on behalf of the Jewish National Fund, particularly in the Jezreel Valley. Manya Shohat, a revolutionist in Russia and a Zionist leader in the socialist movement in the Yishuv and in Israel, had asked Hankin to deliver a letter of apology to Szold for being away from home, and to help plan their tour of the Jewish settlements.[17] Szold asked to visit Sejera, near Tiberias, to see the collective community where Manya herself lived. Hankin proposed they travel by carriage from Tiberias and arranged for a driver with a horse-drawn carriage to take them on their journey.

Szold had met Manya two years earlier in New York, when she had arrived armed with letters of introduction addressed to Szold and Magnes, asking for their aid in raising funds for the pioneering settlements of the Galilee. During their meeting in New York, Manya told her excitedly about Sejera, where she had settled with her husband and a group of workers who lived cooperatively—an innovative enterprise intended to make life easier for the pioneers. Henrietta was impressed by the young, passionate woman who wanted to promote the pioneering settlement of Palestine.[18]

When Henrietta and Sophie got to Sejera, Manya's husband, Israel Shohat, greeted them. He gave them a tour of the small community, describing the collective life of its members. Most were young and unmarried, and the collective was intended to facilitate the division of labor and organize their lives as if they were a single family. Shohat accompanied Henrietta and her mother on their tour of the agricultural colonies. The charismatic Shohat greatly impressed Szold. From him she learned of the sorry state of the colonies, and of the farmers' complete dependence on the Baron de Rothschild's agents. Henrietta and Sophie continued traveling to Zichron Ya'akov, to visit its vineyards and winery. Szold observed the Arab laborers who worked for the farmers, living in small shacks on the edges of their courtyards. She was reminded of Ahad Ha'am's article "Truth from the Land of Israel," in which he warned that the Zionists were coming to a land that was not unpopulated—Arabs lived there, and they should not be dispossessed of their country.

On the way, she met farmers who told her of their difficulties, especially the malaria that had struck down so many. Her visit to the nearby cemetery and the farmers' houses in Zichron Ya'akov demonstrated to Szold the extent of the devastation wrought by the disease. Beside the gravestones of the young men and women who had fallen victim to the disease, she found a plot with the small gravestones of children and infants who had died. Henrietta had been aware of the scope of the disease in the country, but the sight of the many victims in the cemetery shocked her.

They continued on their trip, reaching the small colony of Meir Shfeyah, nestled in the verdant hills near Zichron. From there they went on to Hadera, where again they heard gloomy stories of malaria victims. The entire population of a neighboring Circassian village had died of the fever. Elsewhere, no family was left unscathed. Most of the victims were children, including infants who had not yet been named and those whose names were unknown because their parents had died before them. According to Zvi Saliternik, one of the pioneers of the battle against the disease in the 1890s, this was still the case in Hadera at the beginning of the twentieth century. The summer was terrible and bitter, and Hadera's best and brightest succumbed to the disease.[19]

Szold had two Palestine guidebooks that provided her with interesting and sometimes amusing material. One she had received from Cyrus Adler, who had visited Palestine during his tour of Egypt and the Mediterranean. Adler told her of the changes under way in the country during the previous decades, when Palestine was transformed from a forgotten and pitiful place to a land that attracted many travelers. He gave Szold the Palestine guidebook published by John Murray in conjunction with Thomas Cook, who had founded a travel agency and organized tours to the Holy Land and Syria.[20] The English-language guidebook was mainly intended for the many Christian pilgrims and tourists who began to visit the country toward the mid-nineteenth century, following a change in Ottoman policy.

Szold also brought a guidebook written by the journalist and scholar of Palestine Avraham Moshe Luncz, who had emigrated from Russia with his parents and settled in Jerusalem. Following in John Murray's footsteps, Luncz published the Hebrew-language *Moreh derekh be-Eretz Yisra'el ve-Suriyah* (Guide to Palestine and Syria) for Jewish tourists. The booklet was small enough to be carried in one's pocket, and contained useful information and instructions: a list of the Jewish hotels in Jaffa and Jerusalem, information on the currency in Ottoman Palestine and its value in relation to European and American currencies, local systems of measurement, and the postal and telegraph rates to various countries. These details pointed to the diverse character of visitors to the Holy Land. Luncz warned travelers against common local diseases, including malaria, and even suggested remedies: "The method that is best tested and most widely accepted among doctors for treating malaria is quinine powder." He recommended that every traveler procure a supply of quinine before arriving. According to Luncz, eye infections were also common.

Therefore, travelers were advised to wear dark glasses and cover their heads with cork hats, or at least put white covers over their hats, as the local inhabitants did. In his book, Luncz also noted that the most comfortable seasons for visiting the country were from the beginning of the Hebrew month of Adar (February-March) to the end of Iyar (April-May), and from the beginning of Tishre (September-October) to the end of Heshvan (October-November).[21] He mentioned the two routes for reaching the country: traveling from Beirut and Damascus, visitors could enter the country from the north, or they could go by sea to Jaffa and then travel inland. From Jaffa, one could travel to Jerusalem by coach at any time of the year: in the morning during the winter, and in the evening in summer.[22]

Szold was not looking for shortcuts. She had not wanted to arrive in Jaffa and go from there to Jerusalem, preferring to first tour the Galilee. Luncz explained why the Jaffa route he proposed was the better choice: "On the country's other roads, the traveler will be forced to ride, going by horse, mule, and donkey. However, the local horses, as well as the mules and donkeys, are used to traversing over rocks and obstacles, climbing mountains and descending valleys, and the traveler can sit easily on his or her horse, mule, or donkey, with no fear or fright."[23] Luncz's reference to "fear or fright" was apt, as mules and donkeys tended to walk on the sides of the roads, and some of the mountain roads in the Galilee ran alongside sheer drops into deep chasms, which terrified riders. Luncz's reassurances notwithstanding, Sophie and Henrietta traveled by carriage.

Mother and daughter went to Jaffa on their tour but did not linger there, as they planned on visiting the city as their final stop before leaving the country, and departed for Jerusalem straightaway. In order to get from Jaffa to Jerusalem, they did not need a horse and carriage, as Luncz recommended. He had published his guidebook in 1891, a year before the Jerusalem railway line was completed. The train trip to Jerusalem lasted nearly five hours. Henrietta was used to train travel in the United States and in Europe, but the train to Jerusalem was not a pleasant experience. The cars were dirty and uncomfortable, the windowpanes were dusty, and the travelers packed into the carriages were noisy. She thought that they were fighting, "but I soon understood that this was the accepted manner of conversation," she wrote in her diary. Overflowing baskets of all kinds of food were piled in the train's passageways, and the local travelers did not stop eating throughout the entire journey. Notices forbidding spitting were hung on the walls of the carriages, but the majority of passengers paid them no heed. The train slowly climbed. A glance outside at the landscape revealed rocky hills, the grass that grew on them yellowed and withered in the burning sun. The train pulled

Jaffa, seen from the sea

into the Jerusalem railway station, and on November 16, 1909, they entered the city. Professor Richard Gottheil greeted them and accompanied them to their hotel.

The morning after arriving in Jerusalem, Henrietta and Sophie went sightseeing in the Old City, accompanied by Gottheil. They entered through the Jaffa Gate. On the plaza inside the gate, they found a mass of people, and donkeys and camels with their owners. On the ground at the edge of the square sat peddlers hawking their wares in loud voices. Beggars, their hands outstretched, were all around. The Arabs' colorful clothes, the noise, and the packed crowd mixed with the sound of the donkeys' braying and the donkey-drivers' calls to clear the way.

The alley opposite Jaffa Gate led to the Church of the Holy Sepulcher. They did not stay there long, and continued to walk in the direction of the Western Wall—down a flight of steps and through a narrow alley flanked by open, stinking sewers on both sides. They found themselves among porters carrying goatskins filled with water, while boys leading donkeys heaped with goods walked up and down the steps. The small shops on either side of the steps were filled with merchandise of all kinds. In one, there were sacks of spices that filled the air with their different scents, in

Jaffa Gate in the Old City, Jerusalem

another an array of brightly colored vegetables, followed by a haberdashery and a kind of alcove festooned with long dresses decorated with multicolored embroidery. On a side alley was a row of butcher shops with sides of mutton hanging at their entrances, attracting swarms of flies. They continued to descend the steps until they reached a narrow alley that led toward the Western Wall. Beggars dressed in rags, blind men, and cripples stood on the sides of the stairs, all of them with hands outstretched, expecting alms.[24] Henrietta found a similar scene next to the Wall. She felt a sense of excitement mixed with disappointment. The Western Wall that she had seen in photographs had seemed tall, wide, and magnificent, and looked nothing like the one she saw before her. In front of the Wall was a kind of elongated, narrow courtyard, and behind it were closely packed houses in which Muslims lived. Jewish men and women who gathered in front of the Western Wall to pray did not leave room for others to pass by. And beggars asking for handouts were everywhere, pouncing on the passing tourists.[25]

Henrietta was shocked. Was this "the land of dreams"? Travelers who had preceded Szold had reacted in a similar way. Mark Twain had visited the Holy Land on a journey of Christian pilgrims. His description of

Jews praying at the Western Wall in the Old City, Jerusalem

walking in the narrow alleys of the Old City reflects his harsh impression of Jerusalem: "Rags, wretchedness, poverty and dirt, those signs and symbols that indicate the presence of Moslem rule more surely than the crescent-flag itself, abound. Lepers, cripples, the blind, and the idiotic, assail you on every hand."[26]

Even Herzl, who came to Jerusalem to meet Kaiser Wilhelm II on his visit there in 1898, had recoiled when he saw such desolation and poverty on the route to the Western Wall. His tone after visiting the Tiferet Israel synagogue was more optimistic: "From the gallery of an ancient synagogue [Tiferet Israel] we enjoyed a view of the Temple area, the Mount of Olives, and the whole legendary landscape in the morning sunshine. I am quite firmly convinced that a magnificent New Jerusalem could be built outside the old city walls."[27] The conspicuous foreignness of European and other Western travelers set them apart from the local population. Szold was surprised that so many tourists visited, despite the poverty of the city. At the beginning of the nineteenth century, Jerusalem had been a small city, part of the Damascus province of the Ottoman Empire, and did not have any economic significance on account of its location, far from international trade routes. The city began to recover with new reforms and improvements instituted by the Ottoman government in 1856, and public order and personal security improved. European powers, who saw in Jerusalem the potential to increase their influence in the Middle East, compelled the sultan to open the city to Christian activity, including tourism and commerce.[28] This transformed the city into an international religious center. In the space of a few decades, Jerusalem became an important city with an international standing, and its population quickly increased.

With the increase in pilgrimages and tourism to Jerusalem, missionaries, archaeologists, painters, writers—including Herman Melville and Mark Twain—and prominent individuals such as the British politician Benjamin Disraeli visited the city. Ulysses S. Grant, the eighteenth president of the United States, as well as the extended Roosevelt family from New York, including fifteen-year-old Theodore, the future president, also came to Palestine. Kaiser Wilhelm's visit to Jerusalem garnered widespread publicity. Many Jewish travelers from Europe and the United States also continued coming to the Holy Land in the late nineteenth century. Public transportation was improved, and the establishment of the railway connection to Jerusalem initiated an important change in the city's economic progress.

During their stay in Jerusalem, Szold and her mother became acquainted with the physicians Chana and Naphtali Weitz, and were invited to stay in their home. There they met other Jerusalemites who told them of the city's difficult economic situation and its complicated medical problems. In addition to malaria, trachoma was widespread among the population. Harry Friedenwald, who had visited the country the previous year, had been appalled at the prevalence of the disease. As an expert in eye ailments, he had decided to extend his stay in the country for a week in order to treat patients, especially children, most of whom suffered from trachoma. Anyone who did not receive appropriate medical treatment was likely to go blind.[29] Sophie and Henrietta visited the Tiferet Israel synagogue and toured the alleys of the Jewish Quarter of the Old City and the first neighborhoods established outside its walls some decades earlier. Szold's impression was that much work was necessary in order to promote development of the Jewish presence in the city.

Their return trip to Jaffa from Jerusalem afforded them a special experience. Szold wanted to visit the girls' school in Jaffa. As they were approaching, they spied a group of children. Clouds of flies swarmed around the children's faces and eyes. It was a terrifying sight. But when they entered the school, they were surprised to see that none of the schoolchildren's eyes were infected. They asked the principal, Dr. Nissan Touroff, how it could be that the children in the school were healthy while those outside were in a terrible state. He said: "The answer is obvious. We have a doctor who visits twice a week and a nurse who comes every day, and they care for the children's eyes."

Henrietta wrote in her journal: "When we left, my mother said, 'This is your task, yours and that of the women's group, "Benot Zion." You must provide practical help to Palestine.'"[30] Henrietta wrote to her sisters not only of the poverty, desolation, and neglect that she saw in the Holy Land, but also of the pioneers and the fledgling Jewish Yishuv, in which she saw such great promise: "How much I shall have to tell you when I return, of the misery, of the beauty, the interest, the problems of the Holy City. If I were twenty years younger I would feel that my field is here. As it is, there are heroic men and women here doing valiant work. The colonies and the cities of Palestine, they have taught me so much that for the first time I feel the impulse to speak out in public."[31]

Szold wrote to her friends about the depressing aspects of life in Palestine, particularly in the cities. She was pleased that she had not taken the recommended tourist route: "Traveling on a wagon gave me the opportunity of smelling the very soil and rubbing shoulders with the people. The result is I am still a Zionist, but I think Zionism a more difficult aim to realize than I ever did before, and finally that I am more than ever convinced that if not Zionism, then nothing—then extinction for the Jew."[32] She reached the conclusion of her visit to Palestine: "They warned me that a visit to Palestine would put an end to my Zionism. But I am now convinced more than ever that there our redemption lies."[33]

IN JAFFA, Sophie and Henrietta boarded a ship to Alexandria, and from there sailed to Italy, where they planned to embark on their return journey to the United States. They decided to spend a few days in Italy. Henrietta enjoyed visiting the museums and the art galleries, the cathedrals and ancient churches, but remained all the while transfixed by her experiences in

Palestine. From Italy, Henrietta wrote to her sisters of her impressions: "In Jerusalem there was pulsating life, and life coupled with misery, poverty, filth, disease, and there was intellectual life, coupled with idealism, enthusiasm, hope. Here in Italy I have no responsibility, I may enjoy, I need not weigh and criticize and doubt and wonder—or if I do, I wonder only at the rich beauty poured out upon this favored land."[34]

Even as Henrietta regaled her sisters with her Italian adventures, her thoughts wandered elsewhere. Her deep melancholy had not faded, and she wrote in her diary: "I still pass many nights without sleep, and inside I know now that I will never be again as I was before."[35] The closer that Henrietta came to her return home, the more often anxiety that her friendships in New York might have frayed after her long absence began to rear its head in her letters to Mathilde Schechter. In that same spirit she wrote to her friend: "It has been five months since I've heard from anyone who is connected to the Seminary, and for that reason I hesitated before writing to you. I hope nonetheless that everything is as it should be between us, and that our connection has remained as it was before I left."[36] She had no idea what awaited her in New York.

8

THE DEPTHS OF MISERY

SURPRISE AWAITED SZOLD and her mother when they returned to America: an invitation to a festive banquet in their honor at the Premier Hotel in New York, to be held on February 10, 1910. The invitation bore a circle with a Star of David at the center and the Hebrew date in large letters: 1 Adar 5670.[1] The nominal excuse for the party was Mrs. Sophie Szold's seventieth birthday. But the real goal of the organizers (who included Mathilde Schechter, Judah Magnes, and Alexander Marx) was to cheer up Henrietta. The warm embrace and party took her quite by surprise.

Over the next few weeks, Szold settled back into her work at the Jewish Publication Society and the Federation of American Zionists and had frequent get-togethers with her friends. She resumed teaching the Zionist idea to the Daughters of Zion group in New York. Various organizations invited her to talk about her trip to Palestine. In these lectures and conversations with her friends, she tried to enlist them to support Jewish settlement there. She noted in her diary that Friedlaender had good ideas, that her friend Ida Guggenheimer was sympathetic to the concept, and that the Altmayers seemed to be interested and might even become Zionists. She continued to promote various ideas and projects, as she had before her trip, and there was a constant stream of friends and acquaintances dropping by her home to socialize or ask for advice.

Outwardly, Szold seemed to have regained her emotional equilibrium, but her apparent composure was deceptive and short-lived. She noted in her diary that an ecstatic Emily Belmont had shown up in New York to celebrate her first wedding anniversary. The sight of a woman beaming with marital bliss was like salt poured on her still-open wound. "I am broken up in the effort and disappointed in myself."[2]

Her family believed that the best way to relieve her recurrent bouts of depression was to keep her surrounded by friends. During the first two weeks of March, when she was busy morning to night with meetings and other obligations, Szold recorded her activities in her diary. A short letter from Ginzberg, however, was enough to put an end to her equanimity: "I broke my glasses over a letter of his, the second or third this week. But not having seen him on Saturday, I am able to withstand the letters though they bring back many details I have not been thinking of lately. The letters are necessitated by the change of plan, lengthening his work to five volumes. He now seems to notice that a change requires a number of changes. Of course not! He has been accustomed to my relieving him of all such drudgery. But I sent him his draft and told him what had to be done."[3]

Szold's solution was to invest all of her time and energy in her work. Fortuitously, a new project turned up just at that time. A few weeks after her return to New York, she was introduced to Aaron Aaronsohn, who was visiting America in search of funds to help him establish a botanical research station in Palestine. He told her about his agronomy studies in France; about his parents, who were among the founders of the colony of Zichron Ya'akov; and about his lovely sister Sarah, fluent in five languages and an expert equestrian who galloped over the hills with a sword hanging from her waist, like a Hebrew of old. A few years later, during the First World War, Sarah Aaronsohn gained renown as a member of the Nili underground (established by her brother Aaron), which engaged in espionage for the British against the Turks.

Some years earlier, Aaron Aaronsohn had discovered emmer, an ancient species of wild wheat that proved to be the ancestor of the modern cultivated variety. His discovery made him famous throughout the world of science. The United States Department of Agriculture sought his advice on how emmer might be used to improve cultivated strains of wheat. Aaronsohn told Szold about his field trips to study flora throughout the Levant and Ottoman Empire, including Transjordan, Syria, the Galilee, and the Hauran. He recounted his meetings with famous botanists such as George Post, an American who taught at the forerunner of the American University of Beirut; the German Georg Schweinfurth, known for his research on the flora of Egypt; and William Ashbrook Kellerman, director of the botanical station in Ohio. Aaronsohn described his huge collection of 10,000 plant species, augmented by as many more purchased in Europe and America, which he stored at his home in Zichron Ya'akov. He was hoping that Szold could help him raise enough money to establish a botanical research institute, which would be the first in the Middle East. Szold had loved botany from childhood and was very taken with Aaronsohn, whom she described as a man of unusual intellectual stature, fluent in several languages, charismatic, and with a winning personality, and agreed to meet him again.

Szold acceded to Aaronsohn's request that she serve as the botanical institute's representative in the United States and organize meetings for him with Jewish leaders and wealthy potential donors. She introduced him to Louis Brandeis (on whom he made a strong impression), Felix Frankfurter, Louis Marshall, and Judge Julian Mack, as well as Judah Magnes and Cyrus Adler. Aaronsohn also met the wealthy philanthropists Julius Rosenwald, Nathan Straus, Jacob Schiff, and Morris and Albert Loeb, whom he asked for help in setting up his planned research station.

Some did not trust Aaronsohn and tried to dissuade Szold from assisting him. Katzman did not think he was honest, and had angered Morris Loeb and his brother-in-law Jacob Schiff. Despite the constant attacks on him, Szold held firm in her support for Aaronsohn. She noted in her diary that Louis Lipsky had compared him to a clever politician who tells everyone what he thinks they want to hear: to the American patriot Schiff, he talked about improving the quality of American wheat; to Louis Marshall, about Jewish Palestine; to Herbert Loeb, about scientific progress; and to Lipsky himself about advancing Zionism.[4]

Szold made every effort to counter the accusations against Aaronsohn, and met with some of his supporters to consider how best to help him. Schiff was opposed to the project because he had been told that the botanical institute would be built on land belonging to the Jewish National Fund, an organization he did not support. Marshall understood the true source of Schiff's opposition: "Mr. Schiff is very insistent about not accepting the National Fund, not to be a tail to the Zionist kite."[5]

Herbert Friedenwald suggested that Aaronsohn go back to Europe and leave the Loeb/Schiff faction to him and to his other supporters in America. Aaronsohn decided to stay on in New York, however, to confront his opponents and further develop ties with his supporters. Julian Mack tried to move Morris Loeb, and Magnes promised to work on Jacob Schiff. The campaign to win support for Aaronsohn continued for several weeks, with special efforts made to win over Schiff.

Aaronsohn wrote in a letter to Mack that he thought of Szold "not only as a very sweet soul, but as the greatest Jewess it was my lot to know."[6] Aaronsohn became a regular at the Szold house and told her about all of his meetings.[7] She was impressed by a memorandum he had written in French, noting that it showed that he was a man who had something to say and knew how to say it. She became increasingly fond of him. She also delighted in his quick mind. After she arranged for him to meet with Schechter, in the hope that the latter could be persuaded to exert pressure on Schiff, Aaronsohn reported back to her on his interesting encounter with the "dean of American Jewry." Schechter had declined to intercede with Schiff on his behalf, and Aaronsohn understood that he did not want to risk the philanthropist's support for the seminary. Szold, who always followed the dictates of her conscience, wondered at this: "Queer world, what a queer world in which I have to go around."[8]

Outwardly, it seemed that the drama that had upended her life was over: Szold continued to work at JPS, lecture, and help Aaronsohn and others. But the pain would not vanish, and the slightest spark was enough to reignite the flames within her: "Only yesterday afternoon at the meeting of the Publication Committee all my depths were stirred up again. There was a letter from him [Ginzberg] addressed to Judge Sulzberger. His material for 'Moses' so abundant that he asks for a fifth volume. He has been careless about the book—no planning. The sentence of the letter was brief—the old arrogance was in it—indeed the whole letter is himself, and I am beginning to see him as they want me to see him. He says 'I have no personal means to have the second volume divided in two. I will be ready long before the translator will have translated the 150 pages awaiting him.' When did he give the 150 pages to the translator? It is the old spirit of boastfulness that he used toward me too. And I did not remonstrate, although it was not justified. But he got his way, there will be five volumes."[9]

Szold was revolted by the implicit accusation that she was lagging behind in her translation and felt that Ginzberg was persecuting her relentlessly: "I cry out against fate! I feel so deep a capacity in me for happiness and making happy, and I must seal myself up. The books and wise people tell you to help others and you will forget yourself. Am I not putting most of my time into other people's work?"[10]

Visiting the seminary synagogue became a torment to her: "Going to the synagogue this morning was painful as ever. He was there without her; that stimulates the old feeling. I almost expected his eyes to invite me for a walk. Instead he slipped off without either Dr. Friedlaender or Dr. Davidson, who both live a block from him and I walked alone in the sunshine along

Riverside."[11] Of another visit to the synagogue she wrote: "What a dreadful day yesterday was! I had to leave the synagogue after the prayer for the New Moon, the prayer that always excites me beyond measure, and he came in gaily with his wife just before the prayer was to be said."[12] And sometimes she felt that she simply could not handle seeing Ginzberg and his wife at all: "Saturday morning, though it was Rosh Hodesh [a minor holiday, marking the new moon] and Parshas shikolim [a special Torah portion read in the synagogue at or prior to the beginning of the month of Adar], I stayed away from the synagogue, and took a walk through Morningside Park . . . and walked back, staring at the greengrocer's, fruiters' and florists' shop windows. It was like a walk in a foreign city, and all the time I had a sense of relief of not having had to face him and her in their happiness."[13]

Whenever she saw Ginzberg, the emotional spasms that had tormented Szold before her trip returned, along with the questions that drummed insistently in her mind: Why had he misled her if he had not thought of marriage? Why had he given her presents and dedications? Why had he made her his slave, demanding work without compensation? And why had he come to her home so often and eaten at her table? Was that part of a normal working relationship? Her conviction that he had deliberately deceived and abused her grew stronger: "I confessed my weakness of the morning to Mrs. Schechter, and then the memories came crowding back, stimulated by the freely displayed joy of those we visited—first Mollie Jackson who is to be married in a week, and who spoke with unrestrained freedom of her forward-looking delight."[14] Furthermore, she wrote: "Not only has he ruined my life, he has ruined me. Did I ever envy before?—This morning I am like a burnt out crater, headache, shame, and lassitude."[15]

Yet when Szold heard some of her friends condemn Ginzberg, she found it hard to bear. Could it really be that the man she had worshiped, not only as a great scholar but also as a paragon of virtue, was a rank scoundrel? She revived the accusation she had hurled at herself in the past: perhaps it had all been her imagination? She was confused and felt trapped by her emotions, unable to find a satisfactory answer. At such times, she went out for walks, hoping they would serve as a diversion and ease her pain, but all the streets around her house reminded her of the days when she had walked there with Ginzberg, and the pain actually increased. Sophie and Henrietta thought about moving and finding a different synagogue, but her friends counseled against it. They believed that losing their close support would hurt Henrietta more than the change of scenery would soothe her. As long as she was surrounded by her friends, they could distract her from her grief, and so they endeavored to keep her social schedule full.

Even after a week when she had been busy around the clock, her diary entry referred to it as a full week with no visible results. Szold was invited to dine with friends. Nathan Solis took her to a reception for the dedication of the new wing of the Metropolitan Museum of Art. She was invited to many lectures and met dozens of people during the course of the week—close friends who came to consult with her about their plans, and acquaintances who came and went, some of them staying for a meal with her and her mother.

Szold went to a party at the home of her friend Ida Guggenheimer. Ida had grown up in a well-to-do family, her husband was a well-known attorney, and their large home was in a prestigious neighborhood. She was a feminist and prominent suffragette and also active in the Zionist cause. The other guests included Sam Guggenheim, Edgar Nathan, and their wives. The conversation turned to the franchise for women and became very heated. Only Szold and Ida were in favor.[16] Szold found that she and Ida were on the same wavelength, and their friendship grew closer. They often met at each other's homes and took walks in the park together. Through Ida Guggenheimer, Szold came into contact with Jewish high society and was invited to wealthy homes from time to time. Henrietta did not feel at ease with such people, especially the women, who were so different from her.

Szold also grew closer to Alice Seligsberg, the daughter of a wealthy German Jewish family. Seligsberg was a Barnard graduate, a social worker, and a woman with strong opinions. She too had been disappointed in love and never married. She met Szold in New York and was influenced by her, and they became good friends, although Seligsberg was thirteen years her junior.

Ida Guggenheimer and Mrs. Brainin came to see Szold to discuss Magnes's plan to establish the Kehillah—a united Jewish community or federation of the hundreds of Jewish organizations and associations in New York City. Magnes wanted to combine the Jewish communal tradition with an American-style democratic organization. The first step was to overcome the fierce disagreements pitting the Orthodox against the Reform and the anti-religious socialists. Magnes was blessed with sterling leadership qualities. Drawing on his ties with different Jewish circles—he was a Reform rabbi, but he frequently met with and was impressed by his Orthodox counterparts, and he was also a supporter of Zionism—he was able to put together a twenty-five-member executive committee for the new organization. Although control remained with the Central Europeans, the body represented a wide spectrum of Jewish groups, including the Orthodox from Eastern Europe, who wrestled with frustrating community issues, such as the supervision of kosher food. In order to address the complete chaos that reigned in the field of Jewish education, the new Kehillah decided to establish the Bureau of Jewish Education.[17]

Szold was an active participant in the Kehillah initiative. Magnes was named president of the Bureau of Education, Israel Friedlaender chairman, and Szold secretary. Despite her immense talents, they would not give her a more prestigious title—the same thing that had happened at JPS. "I accepted the Secretaryship. Perhaps it is good for me to have more to do than I can do," she wrote in her diary. "It will make me hard and practical and drive out sentiment and grief."[18]

Most of the responsibility for creating the Bureau of Education—filling key positions and getting the project on track—fell to Szold. She enjoyed the challenge and noted in her diary that she found the work interesting. As always, she adopted a methodical approach and drew up a detailed course of action. She concluded that the best person to run the new organization was Dr. Samson Benderly, whom she knew from Baltimore. She contacted him and reported back to Magnes that Benderly was willing to accept the position. But there was opposition to the appointment, motivated in part by the fact that the candidate lived in faraway Baltimore.

Benderly, born in Safed, Palestine, in 1876, had come to America and studied medicine at Johns Hopkins, with the encouragement of Dr. Aaron Friedenwald. He subsequently decided to switch careers and focus on Jewish education. Some of the members of the Kehillah executive did not have a high opinion of his work or his methods, but Szold thought the world of him and endeavored to persuade her colleagues of Benderly's virtues—his fine habits, his Zionism, and his many accomplishments. He had years of experience and had been involved in every aspect of education: theoretical study; work in schools with parents, teachers, and pupils as well as the general public; and the creation of a formal system for training and accrediting teachers.

Learning that Solomon Schechter was among those opposed to Benderly's appointment, Szold tried to persuade Mathilde that he was the right man for the job, in the hope that she would pass on the message to her husband. Eventually Szold was able to persuade the Kehillah executive that Benderly was the best person to run the new Bureau of Education. She suggested to Magnes that Jacob Schiff be solicited to fund the project.[19] Her experience with the night school for immigrants had made her aware that there was no point in setting goals and building an organization without securing funding. Her choice of Benderly proved successful. He went on to become one of the best-known and most admired Jewish educators in the United States, and produced many students who followed in his footsteps.[20]

Szold had frequent meetings with the Daughters of Zion. The group continued to attract new members and her influence on them increased. She also devoted more time to the Zionist movement. Her position as a member of the executive committee of the FAZ enabled her to express her opinion even when others chose to remain silent. At one of the meetings of the FAZ executive, she lost her temper with one of the members because of his shameful and contemptuous attitude and persistent exploitation of the secretary. No one in the room raised a voice to support her. It was only after he had left the room for several minutes that other members of the executive joined her attack. She wrote in her diary that she was very sorry she had attended the meeting.

Members of the family continued to visit her. Her sister Rachel's husband, Joseph Jastrow, was regularly invited to New York to lecture, while Bertha's husband, Louis Levin, often came to the city to attend conferences on education; they would come to the house for lunch or dinner, and stay to talk about education, socialism, and idealism for hours on end. Her sister Adele also visited frequently, and she and Henrietta grew closer. Henrietta was invited to join Adele and her husband when they went to the racetrack or ballet performances; she found the latter unimpressive apart from the technical stunts, such as a pond in the middle of the stage.[21] Her family believed that their presence kept Henrietta from wallowing in her misery. They were blissfully unaware of the obsessive thoughts that continued to torment her.

Szold finally decided to sever the Gordian knot with Ginzberg: "I must give up the position with the Publication Society because I cannot, cannot, cannot bear the handling of his book and more than that I cannot bear my duty to the Society."[22] She screwed up her courage and wrote to Mayer Sulzberger: "My request is that you relieve me of the work as well as the responsibility connected with seeing volumes 3 and 5 of Dr. Ginzberg's 'Legends of the Jews' through the press, and give me permission to employ some one to do it at my expense. . . . I admit that in setting a personal feeling over against my sense of responsibility and loyalty, I am putting a strain up the latter. Let that be the measure of my present embarrassment. What it should indicate further is, that, being a human woman besides a proofreader, I may not be in a condition to do my literary duty to the author properly."[23]

Sulzberger agreed to her request. She proposed that Dr. Jacobs take over her editorial labors on Ginzberg's books, but the society preferred the seminary's Professor Israel Davidson for the task.[24] Still there was no relief from her pain, which only became more acute when she surveyed the list of books she had translated, edited, and overseen over the course of the years and realized that her name was nowhere to be found in most of them. Feeling nothing but contempt for herself, she succumbed to the effects of her self-flagellation and grew increasingly bitter, even contemplating suicide. She felt stabs of pain no matter where she turned: "Later in the afternoon we visited the Joffes and Mrs. Marx visited us. Mrs. Joffe, with her pride in her new household (which she put above her music) and Mrs. Marx with her solicitude for her baby, both such natural manifestations of wifely and maternal feeling deprived me of all calm. And in the evening I went to see the Magneses—she and he and the baby, their pride in each other, their plans—that was added to the fuel of the afternoon. And this morning Dr. Davidson said he would talk the matter over with his aide, friend, and counselor, his wife. That was too much for my pitiful human endurance."[25]

At JPS, they were expecting her to resume editing the *Year Book,* but she was angry and resentful. Her depression deepened: "Saturday I did not go to the synagogue, because I wanted to be with Rachel. Foolishly, I betrayed myself into talking about the old affair. And I stored up so much indignation and self-pity that the outburst, gathering force all afternoon and evening, came today in the presence of Dr. Davidson, who came to find out what would be expected of him with the Ginzberg manuscript. He took it with him and as soon as he got home telephoned he would not undertake to do it. Naturally he would not, when he saw the display of feeling with which I concluded a business arrangement with him. He must have felt that a part of my resentment would have been transferred to him."[26]

Szold could not find any respite from the storm raging inside her. She had always enjoyed reading, but now she found she could no longer concentrate on the printed page. Her thoughts were constantly invaded by memories and doubts she wanted to be rid of. She also began to fixate on matters that had never bothered her before. After a visit to Ida Guggenheimer's mansion, she wrote in her diary: "This evening I spent an hour at Riverside with Ida Guggenheimer. She is a lady! I wish I could be one for a couple of years. I long for gracious living. I hate all that I have built up around myself. . . . So it is fate with me! And I am meant to suffer until the end."[27]

The values on which she had been brought up—a modest life, the avoidance of display—no longer appealed to her. She wanted to throw off her past and escape to a different world. She could not shake the obsessive thoughts that continued to plague her. She wanted to regain control of herself, but once again found herself sinking in a morass of pain and frustration.

IN THE SUMMER OF 1910, the FAZ asked Szold to help rebuild the movement, which was on the verge of collapse. Its activity was sporadic, membership was down, and about two-thirds of its chapters had folded. Szold, saddened by its leaders' fecklessness, was not alone in her criticism of its president, Harry Friedenwald, and his colleagues in the leadership. She complained that they treated their titles as if they were honorary and did not accept responsibility for the work that came along with the job. Friedenwald, who lived in Baltimore, was busy with his medical practice and could not often find the time for the long train ride to New York; he came up only for board meetings and special events. Other members of the board also tended to sit on their hands. The federation's coffers were empty, and utter chaos reigned in its offices. Friedlaender, who was chairman of the federation's board, was furious with the newly appointed executive secretary, Joseph Jasin, who was often absent from the office. When the board realized that Jasin was contributing nothing and decided to fire him, Friedenwald asked that he be appointed "honorary secretary" instead.

At this juncture they turned to Szold, seeing her as the only person who might be able to rehabilitate the organization and set it back on track. They never dreamed of appointing her president of the federation, of course—although that would have been the appropriate title for the job they expected her to do—offering her the title of secretary instead. Szold was aware of the discrimination but accepted anyway. She wanted to drown herself in work so she would not have any free time to pick at her wounds, but she was willing to commit herself for only one year. Szold took over at the federation in July 1910.

In keeping with her long-standing practice when holding a public position, she refused to accept a salary. The situation in the office was, however, an unmitigated disaster. She had not fathomed the extent of the disarray that Jasin had left behind. Nevertheless, she did not renege on her promise to restore some semblance of order to the federation. She dove into the stacks of paper that had accumulated over the years, discovering many letters that had been sent with donations to the federation but had never been acknowledged with a thank-you note or even a receipt. Some envelopes had never been opened at all. Sisyphean efforts were required to sort and catalogue it all. Friedlaender had expected Szold to supervise the day-to-day running of the office, but she had no time for that. She was furious with herself for having agreed to take on such a pointless task. Szold grew short-tempered and bitter. The meetings of the federation board only made matters worse.[28] She wrote to Mathilde Schechter, apologizing for the fact that five months had passed since her last letter.[29] She was also frustrated by the situation of the Zionist movement, noting that it could not be worse. When summer came, Szold was tormented not only by the heat and humidity of New York, but also by the painful isolation when her friends went on vacation. She missed her regular social interaction with Alexander Marx and his wife, who were off in Europe, and even more so Mathilde Schechter, who had gone to Johannesburg to visit her daughter Ruth. Letters had to fill the place of meetings and heart-to-heart talks with her friends.

SOLOMON SCHECHTER was planning to take a sabbatical in 1911 and needed to appoint a temporary replacement. His first thought was Ginzberg, who stood next in line in the hierarchy of the seminary's faculty. Particular importance was attached to this decision, because it would have bearing on the choice of Schechter's successor when he retired. Mathilde told her husband that Ginzberg would be a poor choice to lead an educational institution, but Schechter was afraid that Ginzberg would pack up and leave if he was passed over now. Schechter wrote Szold to ask what she thought about Ginzberg as acting president. She replied that she had always admired Ginzberg as a scholar of the first order, and still did. Schechter saw this as support for the appointment, but his wife again argued that Ginzberg was not suited for the post because of his arrogance toward both students and colleagues and the fact that he was interested only in his own research and was totally oblivious to public affairs. Henrietta herself noted in her diary: "Took a walk with Mrs. Schechter by appointment. She asked me to walk in order that she might talk to me about Dr. Ginzberg taking her husband's place during his year's absence abroad. Dr. Schechter has spoken to me before about it. It was after Mrs. S [Schechter] had gone to Europe. He had complained to me that he was much troubled about the matter, and I announced swiftly 'If you are troubled on my account, dismiss it from your mind. You have no choice, you must leave your senior professor in charge.'"[30] Schechter, however, was persuaded by his wife's arguments, and Ginzberg did not become acting president of JTS, nor did he succeed to the position after Schechter's death.

The third volume of *Legends of the Jews* was published in 1911, listing Louis Ginzberg as author and acknowledging Szold's replacements Paul Rodin as translator and Dr. Husik of Dropsie College as "reviser and proof-reader." Szold's meticulous translation and editing of much of the book was not mentioned—like with so many others she had worked on. She believed she was "damned to ineffectuality," and felt frustrated, humiliated, and the victim of discrimination.

The thought had already crossed her mind many times that Ginzberg had deliberately misled her throughout their association, but now she could no longer dismiss it, and the realization was like an arrow through her heart. She began to see that all of the condemnations of Ginzberg's treatment of her that others had readily expressed but which she had tried to deny were in fact justified. From childhood she had been taught to aspire to excellence and the expansion of knowledge. She had grown up with the naive belief that scholars are intrinsically moral and more virtuous than others, and saw her father as a paragon of such values. She was pained to see that Ginzberg's conduct belied this faith, undermining her entire perception of the world. Her family sensed her deep distress, but no one could imagine that she would fall still further.

DARKNESS

Toward the end of 1910, Henrietta sank deeper into depression and complained about various aches and pains and extreme fatigue. Her emotional agony had reached a physical breaking point. In early 1911, she noticed that her eyesight was failing. She consulted with specialists, but they could find nothing wrong with her. Nevertheless, her vision continued to deteriorate until she was almost blind. Her world literally grew dark.

She was hospitalized for weeks, groping in the dark, stripped of her independence. Her condition did not improve, and at last her family could no longer bear the cost. The Jewish Publication Society came to her aid once again: Cyrus Adler informed the family that the society would cover her medical costs.[31] Henrietta's mother and sisters decided to send her to Mount Desert, a resort in Maine, in the hope that the new surroundings would prove beneficial. But her situation did not improve there either, and several weeks later they transferred her to Miami, hiring a private nurse to look after her.

Weeks passed, and then months, and Szold was still immersed in darkness. Every day seemed an eternity. Szold, accustomed to pouring out her heart in her diary and in letters to her closest friends, was unable to do so during those months. She could not write, books were out of the question, and the many letters that piled up on her table remained unread. She fumbled in the dark, dependent on the girl who had been hired to help her. Miami was very far from New York City, and few came to visit and dispel her loneliness. She stayed in bed most of the day, sunk in a world of gloomy silence. Her depression had defeated her.

What preoccupied her thoughts all those months when she was walled up inside herself, so far from family and friends? Did she mourn her life, with so little joy and so much pain? So many of her friends were happy, married and with children, while she had had only her work and was condemned to be barren and alone to the end of her days. Now she had something else to worry about: how would she manage if she was blind?

Did she relive her life and wonder why she had not married when she was young, like other women? Did her thoughts go to her family—to her sister Rachel, for example, who had married the talented and wonderful Joe, the love of her life, and for whom everything seemed so beautiful and promising, while a cloud hovered over her own life, and she was tormented by her childlessness? Did Henrietta think about her mother, whose marriage had been so wonderful and who had been blessed with eight daughters, but whose life had also known much pain, including the loss of four daughters and her husband's recurrent bouts of depression? Did she contemplate her mother's deep and unspoken grief that her firstborn daughter, the family's pride and joy, had never married, and remained alone, bruised by her relationship with Ginzberg?

During those long months of darkness, did Szold begin to process the trauma she had been through? Did she come to understand that the idea that she could find happiness in marriage to Ginzberg had never been more than a pipe dream, because of his personality and character flaws, which became even more apparent when he jilted her? Was she conscious of the fact that even had she married Ginzberg she would have been too old to have children anyway, and that their home could never have resembled that of the Schechters? Schechter's geniality and love of people, his warm relations with the faculty and students at the Seminary, and his involvement in Jewish public affairs were all so very unlike Ginzberg. Nor would Schechter's great love and esteem for his wife have been duplicated by Ginzberg, who was always immersed in his scholarly research and other personal matters. Did Szold reach the conclusion that the perfect marriage she had sought could never have been attained with Ginzberg and that she had in fact been saved from a bitter fate? We do not know what went through her mind during those months of perpetual night, as she could not record her thoughts in her diary, and she never spoke of them in later years.

Then, miraculously, her eyesight began to improve. The progress was slow but steady, and within a few weeks she was again able to read and write. She made a Herculean effort to answer the letters that had piled up on her table. To one friend she apologized for the delay in her response and described the travails of the last eight months. Even now she was quite unable to work because her eyes were still not back to normal; the physicians could not find the cause of her disability, so they still had no way to treat her. Writing one letter a day was the best she could do. The terrible waste of time distressed her greatly, as did the fact that she could not stay in closer touch with friends.[32]

When she began to feel that she was returning to normal, she began worrying about her job at JPS, which she had neglected for so long, and she prayed that she would not find herself without a livelihood. She wrote to Marx: "I had to have my leave of absence from the Society extended by three weeks, because I could not discern enough improvement in my eyes to justify my resuming work without the explicit permission of Dr. Friedenwald [with whom she had consulted because he was a respected ophthalmologist as well as a friend], and he does not return from abroad until the eleventh of this month. Then I expect to meet him in New York at the dock, and gain from him some sort of expression of opinion that will enable me to decide on my future course. Meantime, he writes to me reassuringly that the eyes will get well. He does not commit himself as to when and thus I am forced to keep the Society dangling. . . . Otherwise my strength has returned as well as could be expected. Perhaps New York will complete what Maine began."[33]

With the improvement of her eyesight, her words took on a new tone. She wrote to Alice Seligsberg that her mood had improved and she was optimistic. The trip to Europe and Palestine, intended to soothe her, had not addressed the root of her sadness and frustration. And for the last three years she had been fooling herself: rather than letting herself recover fully, she had tried to submerge herself in work. But her body had rebelled. Now she was determined to move on and to begin a new chapter of her life as soon as her physical condition was back to normal.[34]

For the rest of her life, Szold never again referred to the episode with Ginzberg that had so tormented her; it was as if she had erased it from her memory. She was impatient to get back to New York and plunge into her next adventure.

WHEN SHE RETURNED HOME in the autumn of 1911, Henrietta and Sophie moved to a new apartment in Manhattan, far away from the seminary, the site of her great disappointment. There was also a change in her inner circle of friends. She continued to be in contact with those who had supported her when things were at their bleakest, but now she increasingly surrounded herself with women whose interests and situations were more like her own, such as Alice Seligsberg and Jessie Sampter, who became her closest friends.

Sampter was the daughter of a well-to-do family from Germany, so thoroughly assimilated that as a child she did not even know she was Jewish. Her parents said they were atheists. She had contracted polio when she was twelve and was left with limited use of her arms. She could no longer go to school, so her mother hired private tutors for her. Sampter began writing poetry and stories that were published in major periodicals and won her a reputation as a talented poet and author. In adulthood she drew closer to Judaism. Under the influence of Szold, whom she admired greatly, she became a Zionist, and she would immigrate to Palestine in 1919. Neither Seligsberg nor Sampter was married, and Szold's friendship with the two women blossomed, although they were much younger than she was. She enjoyed their company and shared her private worries and public concerns with them.[35]

Szold regained her optimism and energy. She saw things more clearly after the trauma of her hysterical blindness had passed. My assumption about the diagnosis of Szold's condition as "hysterical blindness" has been confirmed by Israeli psychiatrist Eliezer Witztum, whom I have consulted.

Szold summoned up her strength and decided to set off on a new path, which, although she could not have known it at the time, would eventually bring her international fame. She wrote, "In the life of the spirit there is no ending that is not a new beginning." Much later this maxim was engraved in large letters over the entrance to the Hadassah Hospital on Mount Scopus, where it still greets visitors today.

9

THE HEALING OF MY PEOPLE

*S*ZOLD EMBARKED on a new path, full of energy and ambition, seeking to bring about a revolution and change the way in which things had been done for generations. She planned to create a large organization of women for their empowerment and for the struggle to gain equal rights for women.

Szold had further goals: she sought to revitalize Jewish identity among American Jews—members of the older, established families, as well as more recent immigrants who had failed to find their place in Jewish society. She strove to imbue the Zionist movement with a new spirit, capable of touching the heart of every Jew, strengthening the affinity between Jews and the land of their ancestors. Szold believed that women would play a leading role in this process, promoting the Zionist idea and taking it to new heights.

As she considered the state of American Jewry, she was still affected by the vivid impressions from her visit to Palestine. She would never forget the clouds of flies around the eyes of the children she saw in Jaffa; the headstones in the cemetery in Zichron Ya'akov, marking the graves of children and young men and women who had died of malaria; or the pained expression on the faces of the women she encountered in the alleyways of Jerusalem as they held their thin and sickly babies in their arms. These images drove her to try to find a way to help extricate the Yishuv in Palestine from the difficult circumstances in which it found itself. As a passionate

Zionist, she strove to bring about social change in Palestine, to lay the foundation for a healthy society capable of building a Jewish homeland. In establishing a national women's Zionist organization in America, she sought to address urgent tasks: the empowerment of women, strengthening Jewish identity in America, and realizing the Zionist ideal in Palestine.

Szold was impressed by the *halutzim* (pioneers) she had seen on her trip to Palestine three years earlier, and by the new agricultural settlements they had established and the improvement they had brought about in the situation of the older colonies. She was convinced, however, that as long as extreme poverty and disease persisted in the Jewish settlements in Palestine, impeding their development and progress, the Zionist dream would never be realized. Despairing of the ineffectual Federation of American Zionists, Szold approached her friends in the Daughters of Zion circle in New York, in the hope that together the women might get things under way.

The Daughters of Zion circle in New York had been founded in New York in 1898 by Emma Gottheil, wife of Richard Gottheil, president of the FAZ. Similar circles were founded in other cities to study the Zionist idea. All the circles took the name Daughters of Zion, but each had an additional name to distinguish it from the others. Most adopted the names of famous Jewish women in the Bible, such as Ruth, Rachel, and Deborah. The New York chapter had adopted the name Hadassah.

When Szold had moved to New York some years earlier, she had been invited to join the Daughters of Zion. The circle's members wanted to make Szold, already a well-known Zionist activist, their president, but she refused; she said that she had no interest in honors or sitting at the head of the table, but had come to work. Nevertheless, "wherever she sat and led the discussion, there was the head of the table," as circle member Lotta Levensohn recalled.[1] The women would simply gather around her and listen. Szold taught them Zionism, from the writings of Moses Hess, Judah Leib Pinsker, Theodor Herzl, and Ahad Ha'am.[2]

The membership of the Daughters of Zion included Szold's friends Mathilde Schechter, Emma Gottheil, Eva Leon, Alice Seligsberg, and Sophia Berger. Szold hoped that the members of the circle would serve as pioneers in the founding of the large national women's Zionist organization she envisaged. She also involved members of Daughters of Zion circles in other cities. When the project was made public, more women answered the call, and on February 24, 1912, thirty-eight of them met in a room in Temple Emanu-El on Fifth Avenue in Manhattan, where they laid the foundations for the organization. Inspired by Szold's vision, they declared that it would serve a dual purpose: "to promote Jewish institutions and enterprises in

Palestine and to foster Zionist ideals in America."[3] Since the meeting took place only a short time before the holiday of Purim, they decided to name the organization Hadassah, after Queen Esther, also called Hadassah, who brought salvation to her people.[4] It was later decided that the name Hadassah would be adopted by the entire national organization of Zionist women in America, in order to emphasize its nature as a women's organization inspired by the Jewish tradition of benevolence.[5]

Szold strongly supported the idea of equal rights for women, but she did not believe the problem would be resolved by aggressive tactics or localized struggles. She viewed the issue of women's rights as multifaceted, and felt that the best strategy was to address the root causes of the inferior status of women in society. She was of the opinion that problems within complex systems cannot be resolved by means of headlong attacks, but require lengthy processes of change and a great deal of hard work. She had personally experienced the consequences of the exclusion of women, and was keenly aware of the difficulty in eradicating long-held beliefs and practices. Szold believed that if women received a good secondary education and all universities opened their doors to them, they would be able to acquire professions and to excel at them. This would, in turn, increase their self-esteem and allow them to aspire to suitable positions in all walks of life, leading to equality with men in all fields, including politics. Szold's idealistic vision would appear to have underestimated the force with which men would resist attempts by women to encroach on their exclusive domain.

The task that Szold envisioned for the women's organization she sought to create was particularly complex, demanding simultaneous action on two geographically distant fronts, in America and in Palestine, with diverse needs, each requiring immense efforts. Szold had no illusions that any of this would be easy to accomplish, and therefore she wished to establish a large and powerful organization, capable of contending with this twofold task. The establishment of Hadassah became an anchor for Szold's efforts for the empowerment of women and for the struggle for their equal rights.

Operating in Palestine was particularly difficult. The exclusion of women weighed heavily on the weaker strata of society, such as the Old Yishuv, in which religious restrictions prevented women from acquiring a general education or vocational training. Poverty and disease also had a disproportionate effect on women—they were forced day in and day out to care for children, the sick, and the entire household, in conditions of severe hardship, leaving them drained and exhausted. The idea that they might attain occupational status and equality in society was practically unimaginable.

Szold believed that American Jews could provide financial support to the Yishuv in Palestine. It was not her intention to simply collect money and send it to the poor. Rather, she presented the women of Hadassah with a clear goal toward which they might direct their energies and resources. As the organization's first challenge, Szold proposed the provision of medical assistance—the Yishuv's most pressing need, essential to its well-being and future development. She believed that the goal of establishing a healthcare system in Palestine would touch the heart of every Jewish woman in America and, as a concrete objective, would elicit the commitment and effort necessary to make it a reality. Szold wanted to control the process itself, rather than simply transferring the funds to others and leaving matters in their hands. She expected the women of Hadassah to establish and run the project themselves, including its further development and expansion.

A few weeks after the decision to create the Hadassah national women's organization, the members met to draft a constitution, including a statement of its goals. The preamble affirmed that the organization would seek "the establishment of a system of district nursing in the towns and colonies of Palestine."[6] This was intended as a first step toward the creation of a general healthcare system in Palestine. Szold acted in the spirit of American progressivism, which sought the betterment of the lower classes through the development of public medicine, social and welfare services, and a modern education system, as well as the promotion of cultural activities.[7] Szold knew that a large organization could not rest on the shoulders of a single individual or core group of members, as dedicated as they might be. She therefore sought partners to start chapters in cities throughout the United States.

Szold approached friends and acquaintances in various cities. She wrote to Julia Felsenthal, daughter of Bernhard Felsenthal, a Zionist Reform rabbi and friend of Benjamin Szold's. Henrietta asked Julia to join Hadassah and open a chapter of the organization in Chicago. Julia accepted the challenge and went on to become one of Hadassah's most enthusiastic members. Similarly, Szold wrote to friends in Philadelphia, Boston, and Cleveland, describing Hadassah's goals and asking them to establish chapters in their own cities. Thus began the first stage of Hadassah's expansion to numerous cities and states throughout the United States. Szold then visited each of the new chapters, addressing members and encouraging them to recruit others. Szold was a well-known figure even before the founding of Hadassah, and so many women came to hear her.

Szold's manner was always unassuming, and she treated the women she met like friends, speaking heart to heart. She told them about her impressions of Jerusalem, where she had seen families of nine or more living in a single room, in appalling poverty, without electricity or running water. She described how the residents of the city draw their water from wells, which provided them with enough to satisfy only their most basic needs—drinking, cooking, and washing—leaving no water for laundry or to clean their homes. She spoke of the outhouses on balconies or in courtyards, each serving a number of families, filling the air with an overpowering stench. The hygienic conditions were extremely poor, with no sanitation services to speak of, increasing the risk of disease and contributing to a high mortality rate. When darkness fell, small kerosene lamps provided scant light, making the city look gloomy and hopeless.

At these meetings, Szold managed to convey a vivid image of the circumstances in Palestine, impressing upon her listeners the vital importance of the task before them. She promised them that every cent of the money they donated or raised would go to realizing the organization's goals, as everything would be done by volunteers, avoiding the wasteful expense of administrative overhead.

Once chapters had been established in all of the larger cities, members were asked to help start chapters in nearby smaller cities and towns. Szold visited these new chapters as well, presenting Hadassah's goals and urging the women she met to bring their friends, so that the organization might continue to grow. After meeting with such groups, she always stayed in touch with the members, by mail or in person whenever possible. When she discovered that Julia Felsenthal was moving from Chicago to Minneapolis, Szold quickly wrote to her, asking her to start a Hadassah chapter there as well.[8] She took a similar approach throughout the country.

Szold ascribed particular importance to the establishment of chapters in every city, but considered the existence of more than one chapter in a given city detrimental—a waste of energy and a source of potential rivalry. She did not want Hadassah chapters to become exclusive clubs, divided by socioeconomic class; rather, she sought to bring together intellectual, well-to-do women and less-educated, working-class women. She also strove to include both Eastern European women and women of Central European backgrounds. At the time, members of the well-established Jewish families, originally from Germany, tended to look down on the more recent immigrants from Eastern Europe. Szold saw the Hadassah chapters as places where members would focus exclusively on the goals of the organization, where each individual would contribute to the best of her ability. It was decided that the organization would welcome any woman willing to further the ideas on which it was founded.

Members were required to pay dues and were asked to solicit donations from friends and acquaintances. The membership continued to grow, as did the sums of money they managed to raise. More chapters were started, and within a few short years, there were Hadassah chapters throughout the United States, counting thousands of members. Szold managed the organization, her visits to the chapters, and meetings with members alongside her work at JPS. The burden was great, but she never faltered in her efforts on behalf of Hadassah. She spent hours at a time on trains, which she used to write dozens of letters to the members of the various chapters, encouraging them to expand the scope of their activities. When addressing the chapters themselves, she instilled in her listeners the belief that each and every one of them had the power to contribute to improving the state of the Yishuv in Palestine. In a conversation with the New York artist Ruth Light, Szold explained the unique nature and importance of settlement in Palestine as follows: "The reason that the Jews come to Palestine, the reason that you Jewish youth love to be here is that here the Jewish creative ability is allowed free play. In other lands, the Jew can perhaps put a few strokes into the background of the picture, but here he is painting the whole background."[9]

Szold was receptive to ideas expressed by the members of Hadassah regarding the questions of the day, never giving orders or imposing her own views. At every gathering, she encouraged the participants to express their opinions, in order to underscore the fact that they were all equal partners. In the pleasant atmosphere that developed, the decisions that were taken engendered neither resistance nor resentment. She strove to make every chapter a cohesive group, acting in solidarity to achieve a common goal. Even decades later, this atmosphere persisted in Hadassah chapters throughout the country. It was decided that an annual conference would be held in every state, to be attended by representatives of the various chapters. At these conferences, the accomplishments of individual members who had been particularly successful at recruitment or fundraising were recognized and celebrated. In addition to the statewide conferences, it was also decided to hold an annual national convention, with representatives of all the chapters, in order to report on the activities of the previous year and set goals for the year to come.

At the national convention held in Rochester, New York, in June 1914, Szold was unanimously elected president of the organization, to the acclaim of all the members. For the first time, Szold received not only recognition of her organizational skills and tremendous accomplishments, but an official title as well. She had asked her friend Israel Friedlaender to help choose a motto for the organization, and he suggested *arukhat bat ami*— "The healing of the daughter of my people"—from the verse "Is there no balm in Gilead; is there no physician there? Why then is the health of the

The symbol of the Hadassah
organization, founded in 1912
in New York

daughter of my people not recovered?" (Jeremiah 8:22). The Rochester convention also adopted the organization's emblem: a Star of David inscribed
with the Hadassah motto, designed by Victor David Brenner—a well-
known Lithuanian-born Jewish American medalist, creator of the Lincoln cent.[10] The convention chose three vice presidents: Mathilde Schechter,
Emma Gottheil, and Augusta Kohn. Nettie Illoway was elected treasurer.
A secretary was hired—the only paid staff member—and it was decided
to open an office. Two rooms were rented on West 42nd Street in Manhattan, and Hadassah was born.

At the time, the FAZ was in deep crisis, plagued by infighting, and its
secretary at the time, Louis Lipsky, described it as being on the verge of
collapse. In Boston, in 1913, only six of the thirty-five Zionist associations
previously active in the city remained, and membership in other cities had
dwindled as well. Lipsky looked on with a mixture of admiration and
envy as Hadassah, already a large national organization, continued to
grow. It was probably then that Lipsky came up with the idea of incorpo-
rating Hadassah, with its thousands of members and financial resources,
into the federation—an idea he would try to put into practice only a few
years later.[11]

Nothing could stop Szold. Those who knew her found it hard to believe that her health had been so poor in the previous three years. She stuck
to her decision to begin a new chapter in her life, and certainly she had no
time to dwell on the past. She threw herself completely into the task of

moving Hadassah forward, marshaling all of her strength, organizational abilities, hard work, and perseverance. Founding the organization was only the first step. The time had come to realize the goal stated in the preamble of the Hadassah constitution: "the establishment of a system of district nursing in the towns and colonies of Palestine."

It was decided that a medical unit would be sent to Palestine as soon as possible, with modern medical equipment and a large supply of medicine, in order to provide urgent aid. The hardest part was finding doctors and nurses willing to make the journey to Palestine, to work and live in a distant, poor, and disease-ridden Levantine country for an extended period. The plan was to find specialists in various branches of medicine, capable of treating patients suffering from a range of illnesses. At the time, few in the medical profession identified with the Zionist ideal. They thus looked to physicians who might agree to join the unit for humanitarian reasons. Considerable sums of money were needed to cover the living expenses and professional activities of the members of the unit, and to pay for the medical equipment and large quantities of medicine they would bring with them. Neither recruitment nor fundraising on such a scale was a simple task.

It would take some time before this large undertaking could be brought to fruition, and Szold wanted to start providing aid immediately. She therefore decided to send two nurses to Palestine without delay. She consulted with Lillian Wald, who had earned a reputation for providing medical aid to the poor in New York City. Szold was impressed by Wald's achievements and sought to lay the foundations for a healthcare system in Palestine modeled on the method employed by Wald in New York.

Lillian Wald was the daughter of wealthy Jews of German origin. Inspired by the idea of social justice, she decided to become a nurse, and successfully developed and organized programs to provide medical assistance to the poor in various cities in the United States. Wald was particularly affected by the condition of the women she saw on New York's Lower East Side, where large numbers of poor Eastern European immigrants lived in damp basements, working in sweatshops for low wages from dawn to dusk. Exhaustion, malnutrition, and poor hygiene led to the spread of disease. Wald thus established a neighborhood healthcare "district visiting nursing" center in the Lower East Side, where the nurses did not wait for the patients to come to them, but visited them in their homes, providing women with guidance in childcare and inviting them to seek medical attention at the Henry Street Settlement House.[12]

Szold asked Wald to recommend two Jewish nurses who would be willing to work in Jerusalem. Wald remarked, "You don't think you will find Jewish girls who would do that sort of work?"[13] Nevertheless, an advertisement that Szold had placed in the newspaper elicited numerous responses. Within three weeks, twenty-one candidates had been interviewed, and Szold chose two certified and experienced nurses to start work immediately: Rachel Landy, twenty-nine, and Rose Kaplan, forty-six.[14] Rachel Landy, born in Lithuania, immigrated to the United States with her parents and settled in Cleveland, Ohio. She attended nursing school in her hometown, and worked in hospitals in Cleveland and in New York City.[15] Rose Kaplan was born in Russia and immigrated to the United States when she was twenty-five. She attended Mount Sinai Nursing School in New York City, and though she wasn't a Zionist, she was highly motivated to take the assignment in Palestine.[16] Both women were unmarried (at the time, nursing positions in the United States were not open to married women). Before the nurses departed for Palestine, Szold asked them to visit the Henry Street Settlement, suggesting that they establish a similar district settlement in Jerusalem. She also asked them to send her a report from Palestine detailing the urgent medical needs of the population, so that she might better organize the planned medical unit and provide it with the necessary equipment.

Although Landy and Kaplan were ready to leave, Hadassah did not yet have enough money to fund their activities, establish a nursing settlement, and pay for the nurses' own living expenses. Szold sought donors, and Judah Magnes introduced her to Nathan Straus.

Nathan Straus was a member of a wealthy Jewish family of merchants, which came to own many department stores. Straus was a well-known philanthropist and public figure.[17] He first became involved in public health in New York in 1892, when he opened a network of milk stations for the distribution of pasteurized milk to mothers unable to nurse their children.[18] He opened shelters for the homeless, and a center for the treatment of children with tuberculosis. Influenced by Magnes, he also began to take an interest in Palestine. Upon witnessing the disease and poverty there firsthand, he decided to take action to improve healthcare services for Jews and Arabs alike.[19] He established a health center in Jerusalem, primarily for the treatment of malaria and trachoma, both endemic in Palestine at the time. Magnes told Straus about Szold's work, and she was invited to come to the home of Lina and Nathan Straus. Szold told them about Hadassah and its goals, and about the two nurses selected to go to Palestine. The following day, the Strauses went to visit Szold at her home, and Nathan asked her why the project had not yet gotten off the ground. She replied that the organization had only $273 in its coffers. Lina Straus told her to "start work" and to "have faith and the rest will follow." Szold did not get the hint; starting work before ensuring that it would be able to continue was not her way. Straus then told her that he and his wife had come to see her in order to contribute to her project. He promised that they would pay for the two nurses' expenses, the medicine that they would take with them, and their activities.[20] Hadassah's first project was about to get under way.

FIRST AID

In January 1913, Landy and Kaplan traveled to Palestine together with Lina Straus. Straus rented a small apartment for the nurses in the Meah Shearim neighborhood of Jerusalem, which they also used for their clinic. The sign they hung at the building's entrance read "American Daughters of Zion, Nurses Settlement" in Hebrew and English.[21] Szold chose to begin in Jerusalem because it was home to roughly half of the Jewish population in Palestine and because economic and hygienic conditions in the city were particularly grave. She had never intended to make do with a single settlement, but sought to replicate the model in all of the cities and agricultural colonies in the country, viewing Jerusalem merely as a first step.[22]

On March 23, the settlement opened to the public. Kaplan and Landy walked around the neighborhood, inviting women to come to them for help and advice, but no one showed up. The American nurses realized they had to break through the walls of suspicion erected by the conservative and insular society of the Old Yishuv. Some feared that they were Christian missionaries who had come to offer medical assistance to the poor in order to bring them closer to Christianity. The fact that Landy and Kaplan wore nurses' uniforms, just like the Christian missionaries, only reinforced their fears. Others said that the two nurses were advocates of the Reform movement and that had come to Jerusalem to influence Orthodox women. Only after numerous conversations and considerable explaining did they manage to convince the neighborhood women that they were indeed there only to help them. Landy and Kaplan opened a mother-and-child station, conducted home visits, and encouraged the women to come to the settlement for guidance. They distributed medicine for a nominal price, in order to attract the women, and gave new mothers diapers and baby clothes.

Thus began the first neighborhood clinic in Palestine, modeled after the Henry Street Settlement in New York. The intention was for the nurses to become an integral part of the neighborhood, providing residents with a range of services, including preventive medicine, vaccines for schoolchildren, eye treatment for the prevention of trachoma, referral of tuberculosis

A donkey carries jugs of milk in a tank of ice, for baby clinics.
On the jug: "A drop of milk" in Hebrew, English, and Arabic.

patients for medical treatment, help for women in childbirth, and a mother-and-child station.[23] The project was also influenced by Hull House, a settlement house founded in 1889 in Chicago by Jane Addams, a pioneer in the field of community work, who came to be known as the mother of social work in the United States. She engaged in a broad range of public and political activities, becoming the first American woman to win a Nobel Prize (1931).[24] Szold admired Addams and told her about the nurses' settlement in Jerusalem, which Addams visited shortly after it opened.[25]

The two nurses soon became a part of the neighborhood landscape. Landy was tall, blond, and slim, while Kaplan was short, dark, and full-figured. The Jerusalemites called them "the tall one" and "the short one." The pair visited homes and schools, checking children's eyes for bacterial infection and their hair for lice. They failed, however, to win the complete trust of the neighborhood women. The sphere of childbirth proved particularly difficult, as the women tended to prefer traditional midwives, who did not consider hygiene an important factor in safeguarding the lives of the mothers and newborns. The traditional midwives also resorted to spells and charms, such as strings of garlic hung at the head of the bed during childbirth, and other folk remedies. Dr. Helena Kagan, a young Swiss-trained doctor who began practicing in Jerusalem in 1914, described some of the methods employed by the traditional midwives: "If the birth

Jewish and Muslim mothers hold their infants at a medical clinic for
babies in Jerusalem

failed to progress in a satisfactory manner, these women [the midwives]
would pour bottles of oil into the poor mother's womb, or tie a long thread
to the holy ark of a nearby synagogue, and the mother would pull on it
[the thread] every time she felt a contraction."[26]

The Old Yishuv, which in fact comprised many different ethnic groups,
was extremely conservative and deeply suspicious of all change and inno-
vation. While the American nurses ascribed particular importance to the
training of young midwives to replace the older, traditional midwives, it
was not easy to get mothers to trust the young midwives and their modern
methods. The women were deterred by the young midwives' new approach
and were reluctant to use them, while the older midwives, who feared for
their livelihood, reinforced their clients' fears. Landy and Kaplan did everything they could to convince mothers that their approach was the correct
one, and offered them guidance in matters of hygiene and nutrition.

Kaplan and Landy sent regular reports to Szold, in which they described
the difficulties and obstacles they encountered, noting that they would have
made greater progress had it not been for the severe shortage of nurses,
doctors, and medicine in the country. Emma Gottheil's sister, Eva Leon,
joined the two nurses and helped them in their work, but they got an unexpected boost about a year and a half after the nurses first came to Palestine when Dr. Kagan arrived in the city and quickly became a prominent

figure there. Kagan was born in Tashkent, Uzbekistan, where her father, an engineer, had been sent to open a glass factory. Her mother was an educated woman and a talented musician. It was hard for Jews to get into Russian universities, and many universities in Europe did not accept women, so Helena's parents sent their children to study in Switzerland.[27] Kagan studied medicine at the University of Bern, while simultaneously attending the Bern Conservatory. Upon completing her medical studies, she interned at one of the city's hospitals. When she arrived in Jerusalem, however, the Ottoman authorities refused to grant her a license, as only men were allowed to practice medicine. Kagan began to work in the Yishuv, but she continued to seek official recognition as a physician—to which end she began to study Turkish (which is related to the Uzbek language, spoken in Tashkent). She also learned Arabic in order to be able to communicate with Jerusalem's Arab inhabitants.

Kagan proved to be a tireless, dedicated, and resourceful physician who made a significant contribution to the state of medical care, and especially pediatric care, in Jerusalem. She managed to gain the trust of the Jews of the Old Yishuv and the Arabs, as well as that of the Armenians and other Christians, by treating their children with such care. In her memoirs, she wrote: "I strove to give the Arabs [of Jerusalem] the feeling that we Jews who were returning to our homeland wished to live in harmony with all of the holy city's inhabitants."[28] Kagan joined forces with the Hadassah nurses and was an important motivating force in their work. Szold heard about Helena Kagan in the reports she received from the nurses. Her work and the principles behind it coincided with Szold's own approach, and Henrietta looked forward to meeting her.

The Hadassah nurses were also helped by the ophthalmologist Dr. Albert Ticho, who instructed them in the prevention of trachoma, which was endemic in Palestine at the time among adults and children alike (some 40 percent of the population suffered from the disease; in some villages, the rate was as high as 70 percent). Ticho had come to Jerusalem from Vienna in 1912 and opened an eye clinic, Lema'an Zion, in the city. He gained a reputation as a miracle worker and soon became a legend, greatly admired in the Old Yishuv and throughout the country. At his clinic, poor patients were treated for free. As Ticho's fame spread, patients came to see him even from neighboring countries, including Syria, Turkey, Persia, and others. His waiting room, filled with patients in a variety of traditional costumes, looked like something out of a film. Even Emir Abdullah of Transjordan came to his clinic for cataract surgery. As Dr. Ephraim Sinai, who worked with Ticho, recalled, the emir "came with an entire retinue,

The Nathan and Lina Straus Health Center, bearing the inscription
"For people of all nations and religions"

bodyguards, his five sons and two wives. He carried a pistol and a sword, and his guards were armed with daggers and swords."[29] Another important institution was the health center in Jerusalem established by Nathan and Lina Straus, bearing the inscription "The Nathan and Lina Straus Health Center, For people of all nations and religions."

Landy and Kaplan accomplished a tremendous amount with babies and young children, but the needs of the city were well beyond the capacity of just two nurses, so Szold decided to send more help. Two more nurses were selected and began preparations to leave. Szold herself planned to follow, to get a firsthand impression of the situation in Jerusalem, assess the country's needs, and complete preparations for the departure of the large medical unit and its essential equipment. Suddenly, however, everything changed.

ON JUNE 28, 1914, Archduke Franz Ferdinand, heir to the Austro-Hungarian throne, was shot by Serbian student Gavrilo Princip. The ramifications of that gunshot were beyond imagination. In the wake of the assassination, Austria-Hungary declared war on Serbia, starting a chain reaction. A month later, Germany declared war on Russia, claiming that the assassin was a Slav, and two days after that it declared war on Russia's ally France and France's ally Belgium. In August, Britain declared war on Germany, and in November, the Ottoman Empire joined the war on Germany's side. Terrified people on all sides wondered how a single shot had managed to start a world war.

The assassination of the archduke was only a pretext, of course. The true causes stemmed from the decline of the empires that ruled Europe, and the rivalries between them. No one imagined that the great powers would be drawn into a war that would go on for years, sowing destruction and killing millions of people, profoundly changing Europe and the Ottoman Empire—including the Yishuv in Palestine, which faced the risk of annihilation. From the moment the Ottoman Empire entered the war, conditions in the Yishuv began to deteriorate.

Szold cancelled the new nurses' trip at the last minute, aware of the dangers they would be facing. She explained that Hadassah did not have the power, means, or influence of the Red Cross, and had no right to put the nurses in harm's way.[30] Szold also cancelled her own plans to go to Jerusalem.

As Europe and Russia were swept into the maelstrom of war, the United States remained a beacon of light, to which the members of the Yishuv looked for help. The Zionist Organization opened an office in Copenhagen to coordinate efforts on behalf of the Yishuv; they chose that neutral site in an attempt to avoid taking sides in the conflict, though in that they were unsuccessful.

The FAZ convened a meeting to discuss providing urgent aid to the Yishuv, and an eleven-member emergency committee was established.[31] Effective action, however, required power and influence. Eyes turned to the esteemed American jurist Louis Brandeis. Brandeis was born in Louisville, Kentucky. His mother believed in ethics and honesty, and it was in that spirit that she raised her children. Louis showed tremendous potential from a young age and went on to excel in his studies at Harvard Law School, eventually becoming a successful lawyer in Boston. Like his mother, he believed in honesty and fairness. He lived a modest and frugal life at home,

Louis Dembitz Brandeis, 1910

his office was furnished simply, with "no rug or easy chair," and he donated generously to charity.

Brandeis stood out in the legal world for the role he played as a defender of consumers and labor organizations. Undeterred by employers, he followed his conscience, and became known as the "people's attorney." Wrote a contemporary, "His personality was an unusual combination of the qualities that make for a successful corporate lawyer and a passion for the little man who was likely to be shoved aside and stepped upon."[32]

Brandeis came to symbolize rare human qualities and virtue, leading some to compare him to the prophet Elijah. He was admired by Jews and non Jews alike, hailed as "the greatest Jew since Jesus Christ."[33] He was sometimes likened to Lincoln for his honesty and the principles that guided his actions. Some even saw a certain physical similarity between the two, as both were tall and gaunt, with sharp features. Brandeis had little connection to the Jewish community, and encountered Jewish tradition primarily at the home of his mother's brother Lewis Dembitz. The young Brandeis greatly admired Dembitz, to the point that he adopted his uncle's surname (which was also his mother's maiden name) as his own middle name. He never embraced Jewish tradition, however, and did not belong to any synagogue. Brandeis was far removed from Jewish life and the Zionist movement.

The leaders of the FAZ hoped to convince Brandeis to lend his support to the Zionist movement by heading an emergency relief committee, convinced that his prestige would have a significant impact on American Jews and boost fundraising at such a critical time for the Yishuv in Palestine. They believed that Brandeis would also be able to secure diplomatic assistance from his contacts in the Wilson administration. They invited him to attend the federation's annual convention, in June 1914 in Rochester, New York, and sought to convince him that his place was with them. They also hoped that his support would help convince integrated American Jews that there was no contradiction between Zionism and loyalty to the United States, and that it was by no means a foreign movement of interest only to Russian immigrants.

Brandeis hesitated to accept. As a lawyer, he had met with Eastern European Jews during the garment workers' strike in New York, and been touched by their plight. As a man of principle, however, he was concerned that there might be a conflict of interest between his loyalty to his country, as an American, and lending his support to the Zionist idea, which advocated the return of the Jewish people to its ancestral homeland. Many members of the Jewish elite in the United States had similar compunctions. Brandeis, as was his habit in all matters, studied the issue in depth.[34] Influenced by leading figures of the Zionist movement, his attitude toward Zionism became increasingly favorable. He was also deeply impressed by the American Jewish philosopher Horace M. Kallen, who coined the term "cultural pluralism" to describe the coexistence of diverse ethnic and religious groups within American society.[35] In the end, Brandeis agreed to join the Zionist movement. Szold admired Brandeis, a man after her own heart. When Brandeis later met Szold and learned of her accomplishments, he came to admire her as well, and the two became friends.

Brandeis embraced the Zionist idea of the establishment of a national home in Palestine for Jews who wished to live there and realize their national aspirations. He stressed, however, that Zionism must not advocate the forced immigration of all Jews to Palestine, and every Jew must have the right to live wherever they chose. The Zionists who wished to establish their homeland in Palestine did so, he believed, in the firm conviction that the age-old longing of Jews to return to the land of their fathers carried far deeper meaning. He thus concluded: "Loyalty to America demands that each American Jew become a Zionist. For only through the ennobling effect of its striving can we develop the best that is in us and give to this country the full benefit of our great inheritance. The Jewish spirit, so long preserved, the character developed by so many centuries of sacrifice, should be preserved and develop further."[36]

Brandeis accepted the proposal put forward by the leaders of the FAZ, explaining his agreement to join the federation's emergency committee as follows: "Since the Jewish problem is single and universal, the Jews of every country should strive for its solution. But the duty resting upon us of America is especially insistent."[37] The fifty-eight-year-old Brandeis, with his shock of white hair and the aura that surrounded his personality, was a shining star: "The advent of Brandeis on the Zionist scene was a sensation, it was the unexpected arrival of a new and 'alien' personality of immense prestige and moral authority."[38] The impetus that Brandeis gave the Zionist movement was unprecedented—as reflected in the large increase in membership of the Federation of American Zionists.

Dr. Shmarya Levin, a Zionist leader who had been visiting the United States and was unable to return to Europe because of the outbreak of war, called an "extraordinary conference" at the Hotel Marseille in New York. It was at this conference that the Provisional Executive Committee for General Zionist Affairs was established, and Louis Brandeis named chairman—effectively, the head of the Zionist movement in the United States.[39] He immediately set to work. He convened a meeting of the executive committee and federation leaders, including Henrietta Szold, in order to explore the possibilities of extending relief to the Yishuv in Palestine in its hour of need. In a letter to Isadore Biskind, a Cleveland physician who had agreed to take part in the medical unit, Szold wrote that they had sat for two days straight, from morning to night, in order to study the problems and determine a course of action. In answer to Dr. Biskind's question as to why the federation had taken this task upon itself, Szold replied that the meeting had been convened in response to appeals from various American organizations, adding: "Our supreme test is our supreme opportunity, not only for us Zionists, but for the American Jew in general. It will depend upon us now whether the Jews shall remain a gypsy nomad people, or we shall become a nation in every sense of the word. With Herzl still among us there could be but one answer."[40] Szold signed all the letters she wrote from the Hadassah office with the words "With Zion's greetings."

Brandeis's prestige helped to attract other prominent figures to the federation's leadership. Nathan Straus joined the federation, while a number of younger men, such as Judah Magnes and Israel Friedlaender, who had left the FAZ over their disappointment with its leadership, decided to return. Brandeis's friend Judge Julian Mack also joined the FAZ at that time. Born in San Francisco and raised in Cincinnati, Mack, like Brandeis, was a graduate of Harvard Law School. He moved to Chicago, where he served as a circuit court judge and was eventually appointed to the federal bench. During World War I, Mack played an active role in Jewish public life, becoming one of the foremost Jewish leaders in America. He was one of the founders of the American Jewish Congress, of which he was made president in 1917 (through the influence of Shmarya Levin and Szold). An ardent Zionist, Mack also served as president of the Zionist Organization of America from 1918 to 1921.[41] Other prominent figures who joined the Zionist movement together with Brandeis included the jurist (and later Supreme Court justice) Felix Frankfurter and the New York lawyer Bernard Flexner. Brandeis also used his influence with President Wilson, urging him to lend his support to the Balfour Declaration, Britain's promise to favor the establishment of a national home for the Jewish people in Palestine. Brandeis's influence had an immediate impact on the campaign to provide economic aid to the Yishuv, helping to stave off famine during the war.

ON NOVEMBER 19, 1915, Jewish Theological Seminary president Solomon Schechter passed away. Szold was devastated, feeling as if she had lost another parent. He had been a dear friend to her for many years, had allowed her to study at the seminary, had opened his home to her, and supported her through difficult times. Faculty and students mourned the death of their beloved and revered president, an extraordinary scholar who had led the institution since 1902, turning it into an important center for Jewish studies, respected throughout the United States and beyond. His close friends admired him not only for his scholarship but also for his shining personality and the way in which he inspired everyone around him.

Around the time of Schechter's death, Szold's life underwent a revolutionary change. Ever since her recovery from blindness, in late 1911, she had continued to work at JPS, but by 1915, her heart was no longer in it. She would have liked to dedicate all of her time to Hadassah and her Palestine relief work, but could not afford to leave JPS. A solution was provided by Judge Mack, who greatly admired Szold's dedication to the Zionist movement, and especially her work in founding, running, and developing Hadassah. He also knew of her accomplishments at JPS and the demands it placed on her time and energy, preventing her from focusing entirely on Hadassah. Mack thus came up with the idea of establishing a trust for Szold, which would provide her with a stipend for life, allowing her to dedicate all of her time to her outstanding public endeavors without having to worry about making a living. He gathered a number of his wealthy friends who shared his admiration for Szold, including the philanthropist Julius Rosenwald and the activist and philanthropist Mary Fels, wife of industrialist and social reformer Joseph Fels. The trust established by Mack was kept secret, as were the names of those who contributed.[42]

They first approached Szold and asked for her consent. She was embarrassed by the offer and considered rejecting it, but eventually decided to accept. With the establishment of the trust, Szold felt like a weight had been lifted from her shoulders. Two weeks later, in December 1915, she wrote to Cyrus Adler and Mayer Sulzberger, chairman of the JPS publication committee, informing them that she would be receiving an annuity from a trust established for her benefit, and that she wished to resign in order to devote all of her time to Jewish communal work. She assured them that she would remain until a suitable replacement had been found, adding that she would, on occasion, be willing to offer her services to JPS in the future, on a volunteer basis.[43]

Szold's responsibilities at JPS were divided among a number of people. Dr. Benzion Halper was put in charge of editing and administration and, unlike Szold, was given the title of "editor"—a title subsequently borne by all of his successors. Benjamin Alexander was appointed secretary, and George Dobsevage became assistant secretary.[44] Further editors or translators were engaged for specific books, as well as proofreaders and a copy editor. After Szold's departure, JPS began to print the names of all who had contributed to a given work—editors, translators, proofreaders, and so forth—in every volume they published. Szold, who had done all of those things for dozens of books, was not even mentioned in most of them. Her considerable contribution to the publication of the finest works of Jewish scholarship and literature during the twenty-two years she worked at JPS remained largely unknown.

Jonathan Sarna, historian of the Jewish publisher's first hundred years (1888–1988), called the chapter on Szold's work at JPS "The Henrietta Szold Era." JPS flourished during those years: in the number of titles it published, in the tens of thousands of copies it sold, and in its 14,000 subscribers throughout the United States. While Szold was there, the society published works of non-fiction and fiction for adults, as well as five children's books written or edited by women.[45] Sarna termed the years after Szold's departure the "The Lean Years," while others have called the two decades after Szold "the darkest years in the Society's history."[46] Upon her resignation from JPS, Szold was invited to join the society's prestigious publication committee, headed by Mayer Sulzberger, which counted among its other members such illustrious figures as Israel Friedlaender, Judah Magnes, and Cyrus Adler. Solomon Schechter had also been a member of the JPS publication committee.

Szold continued to publish articles in the *American Jewish Year Book*. In 1915, she wrote a long article entitled "Recent Jewish Progress in Palestine"—a comprehensive overview of the history of the Yishuv in

Palestine from the beginning of modern Jewish settlement in the country, including a detailed survey of the Jewish population, most of which resided in the larger cities: Jerusalem, Tiberias, Safed, and so on.[47] Many of her descriptions were based on her own impressions during her visit to Palestine a few years earlier. JPS president Simon Miller remarked that Szold's article "was really a book in itself."[48]

Szold was now free to focus her energies on Hadassah. She received no salary for her work, as was her practice with all of the large projects she founded and directed throughout her life. She did not wish to receive public funds, and relied only on the modest stipend she received from the trust established for her by Julian Mack and his friends.

Szold planned to take the organization by storm and greatly expand its activities, but was unable to dedicate all of her time to Hadassah and the Zionist movement, as she had planned. Her mother, Sophie, had suffered bouts of illness over the previous years, and in 1915 she took a turn for the worse. Henrietta nursed her devotedly. Her condition improved after a few months, but eventually worsened again. It was hard for Henrietta to see her mother fading before her eyes. She wrote to her friend Elvira Solis: "She was conscious to the end—spoke to me less than two minutes before her last breath was drawn, and a little while before bade me recite the Shema. I was alone with her."[49]

Sophie passed away in August 1916. It had been her wish to be buried in Baltimore, next to her husband and daughters. Her funeral was attended by members of her husband's congregation, Oheb Shalom, and by her many friends. Her daughters Henrietta, Rachel, Bertha, and Adele sat shiva at Bertha's home in Baltimore, which thronged with callers, many of whom Henrietta had known since childhood. It felt like all the chapters of her life were passing before her eyes. Dozens of condolence letters and telegrams arrived, recalling Sophie's affability and the warmth with which she received everyone who came to her home. When the period of mourning was over, the sisters went back to their respective homes. Upon her return to New York, Henrietta wrote about the difficulty she experienced in coming back to "an apartment that was a home." It was then that she was struck by the full force of her loss and loneliness. The apartment seemed empty without Sophie, who had filled it with life, warmth, and love. Henrietta had lived with her mother her whole life—first at her parents' home in Baltimore and later in New York. She grieved for the loss of a devoted mother, a wise and kind woman who had stood by her throughout the years. She hoped that she would "have the courage to reshape my own life in her spirit."[50] Haym Peretz, a family friend, wrote to Henrietta, offering to recite Kaddish (the Jewish prayer for the dead) for

Sophie throughout the traditional year of mourning, as she had no sons. Szold thanked him warmly for the offer but declined:

> It is impossible for me to find words in which to tell you how deeply I was touched by your offer to act as *"Kaddish"* for my dear mother . . . You will wonder then that I cannot accept your offer. . . . I know well and appreciate what you say about the Jewish custom; and Jewish custom is very sacred to me. . . . The *Kaddish* means to me that the survivor publicly and markedly manifests his wish and intention to assume the relation to the Jewish community which his parent had, and that so the chain remains unbroken from generation to generation. . . . You can do that for the generations of your family, I must do that for the generations of my family.
>
> I believe that the elimination of women from such duties was never intended by our law and custom—women were freed from positive duties when they could not perform them, but not when they could. It was never intended that, if they could perform them, their performance of them should not be considered as valuable and valid as when one of the male sex performed them. And of the *Kaddish* I feel sure this is particularly true.
>
> My mother had eight daughters and no son; and yet never did I hear a word of regret pass the lips of either my mother or my father that one of us was not a son. When my father died, my mother would not permit others to take her daughters' place in saying the *Kaddish,* and so I am sure I am acting in her spirit when I am moved to decline your offer. . . . I repeat, I know full well that it is much more in consonance with the generally accepted Jewish tradition than is my or my family's conception.[51]

After her mother's death, Henrietta dedicated all her time and energy to helping the Yishuv in Palestine, where conditions were very grave.

THE GREAT WAR

"On the Ninth of Av 5674, the war broke out," wrote the farmer and Hebrew writer Moshe Smilansky.[52] The ninth day of the Hebrew month of Av, traditionally associated with the destruction of the two Temples in Jerusalem, also served as a powerful symbol for the dire condition of the Yishuv under Turkish rule during the First World War. Szold followed the events in the newspapers and in letters she received from her friends in Palestine, and feared for the Yishuv's survival.

Palestine had been cut off from Europe since the beginning of the war. Imported goods such as wheat, sugar, rice, and petroleum ceased to arrive, and exports such as citrus fruit and wine were unable to reach European markets. Donations from abroad, on which a significant portion of the Old Yishuv relied for its livelihood, were blocked. Merchants and craftsmen were affected by shortages of raw materials. Fear and uncertainty led to a run on the banks. Nearly a quarter of a million francs were withdrawn from the Anglo-Palestine Bank in two days, and large sums were withdrawn from other banks as well. The authorities ordered the closing of the banks, and all assets were frozen. The absence of imported goods caused prices to rise, and many people could no longer afford to buy even basic staples. The damage to commerce led the economy to slow down, inflation to rise, and the value of the Ottoman currency in circulation to plummet. Without access to raw materials, factories closed, laying off workers. Unemployment rose, shortages of food and medicine worsened, and hunger and disease spread throughout the Yishuv.[53]

American Jews were their only hope. At the outbreak of the First World War, there were nearly 4 million Jews in the United States.[54] Wealthy businessmen and well-known attorneys used their connections with policymakers in the United States to help the Yishuv, and as long as the United States stayed out of the war, they also had some influence in Turkey.

Henry Morgenthau, who served as the American ambassador to the Ottoman Empire, had close ties to President Woodrow Wilson and important contacts in Constantinople. He had visited Palestine before the war, where he was shown around the country by Arthur Ruppin, director of the Zionist Organization's Palestine Office, and was particularly impressed by the "pioneers," whom he saw as "new Jews." At the beginning of the war, Ruppin informed him of the dire situation in the Yishuv, and Morgenthau asked Jacob Schiff, Louis Marshall, and the American Jewish Committee (of which Marshall was president) to raise funds for the Jews of Palestine, who risked starvation. Szold was asked to involve Hadassah in raising the necessary funds, which she did. Morgenthau's involvement was crucial, because he had the means to transfer the money from the United States to Palestine. Morgenthau sent a telegram to Ruppin informing him that his son-in-law, Maurice Wertheim, had departed for Jaffa on an American ship with $50,000 in gold as emergency relief. In October 1914, the ship docked at Jaffa and the money reached its destination. American ships continued to arrive from time to time, bringing money and food, and evacuating foreign nationals who wished to return to their countries. American help was the Yishuv's only lifeline.

Szold allowed the nurses she had sent to Jerusalem the freedom to do as they saw fit, but neither asked to return to the United States. She hoped, like so many others, that the war would soon be over, and she worked to hasten the departure of the large medical unit for Palestine.[55]

During the war years, a number of American warships docked in Palestinian ports, facilitating the transfer of funds to the Yishuv and alleviating the hunger and privation suffered by its inhabitants. Conditions in the Yishuv worsened when Turkey entered the war, in October 1914, as one of the Central Powers, alongside Germany and Austria-Hungary. Overnight, the Russian Jews in Palestine became enemy nationals. The non-Jewish inhabitants of Palestine also suffered at the hands of the Turks, but the Jews suffered more.

Ahmed Djemal Pasha, who was the Turkish governor of Greater Syria and commander of Ottoman forces, ordered the deportation of all non-Ottoman citizens and suspected Zionists. David Ben-Gurion and Izhak Ben-Zvi were among the first ten deportees, along with Manya and Israel Shohat and Arthur Ruppin. Cruelest of all was the expulsion from Jaffa and Tel Aviv. As Dr. Helena Kagan recalled: "On Black Thursday, 17 December 1914, 29 Kislev 5675, the expulsion order was given. The holiday of Hanukkah was transformed from the Festival of Lights to days of misery and darkness. Groups of frightened men, women, and children were taken like sheep to the Customs House near the Jaffa Port, and dragged on boats. In all the chaos and panic, some of them fell out of the overcrowded boats."[56]

These deportees joined the thousands of Jewish refugees from Palestine already in Egypt. By the end of January 1915, 7,500 people had been deported from Palestine, and an additional 4,000 were forced to leave by the end of the year. Many of those who remained in Palestine faced death by starvation and disease. The danger that the Zionist dream would come to an end was very real.

Morgenthau swung into action. With the support of President Wilson, diplomatic pressure was brought to bear on Turkey, and with the help of Austria and Germany, the deportations were stopped.[57]

The Jews who had remained in Palestine and assumed Ottoman citizenship did not fare well. They had pledged to enlist in the Turkish army, and those who hid in order to avoid being drafted or deserted from the army were sentenced to death. Dr. Kagan recalled: "I remember one of the most shocking events I witnessed one day, in the early morning hours, near Damascus Gate at the Old City of Jerusalem, the bodies of three young men were hanging. They had been executed for desertion. Around them were a group of women and children, weeping bitterly, crying and scratching their faces until they bled."[58]

Palestine was also visited by a number of natural disasters during the first two years of the war. In the spring of 1915, swarms of locusts darkened the skies. As Moshe Smilansky observed, "On the twelfth day they rose up from the earth and flew toward the sea. Green was the world before the locusts, black and desolate after their departure."[59] The locusts had wiped out the entire country's food supply, and starvation was widespread. On every street corner in Jerusalem, one could see people with bellies swollen by malnutrition. Some simply collapsed in the street and died. In addition to deportation and starvation, disease claimed numerous victims in the Yishuv. In 1916, there was an outbreak of typhus in Palestine, which took an especially heavy toll on those already suffering from starvation. Dr. Kagan recounted: "I was once called to see a family that lived near Meah Shearim. I was called by the neighbors, since they had not seen any members of the family outside in days. In the dim light of the basement where they lived, I could see the parents and a number of children, all lying on the floor, wrapped in rags. All, with the exception of one child, were unconscious, their bodies covered in typhus rash."[60]

Szold followed the desperate situation with growing trepidation, but her hands were tied. The two nurses she had sent to Jerusalem were still there, and tried to help as best they could. When Rose Kaplan discovered that she had cancer, she returned to the United States, but when her condition improved, she traveled to Egypt to help the Jewish refugees from Palestine there until her death in 1917. Rachel Landy remained in Jerusalem and worked with Dr. Ticho and Dr. Kagan. In September 1916, with the medicine at the nurses' settlement gone and Turkish attitudes toward American nationals worsening, Landy decided to close the settlement and return to the United States. Landy spent the remainder of the war serving with the U.S. Army in Egypt, attaining the rank of lieutenant colonel.[61]

Szold sought to hasten the departure of the American medical unit to Palestine, but the costs were now significantly higher than they had been when the idea was first proposed. In addition to the large number of doctors and nurses required, the need for medical equipment and supplies, such as ambulances, X-ray machines, modern laboratories, and large quantities of medicine, was very great. It was a complex project, fraught with difficulties—far more than Szold had anticipated. Currency devaluation had also taken its toll, and the sum of $20,000 originally allocated to the project was now woefully inadequate. In fact, costs were now estimated at $450,000 per year. Hadassah was unable to provide such a sum on its own, so Szold approached the Joint Distribution Committee (JDC), established in the United States at the beginning of the war to provide aid to Jews in need.[62] The JDC agreed to contribute $100,000 toward the cost of the medical unit. The unit's medical advisor was Dr. Harry Friedenwald, and Alice Seligsberg served as Hadassah's representative.[63]

In early March 1917, Szold went on a speaking tour of the United States and Canada to promote the activities of Hadassah and to raise money for the medical unit. The tour lasted six weeks and included stops in Philadelphia, Rochester, Syracuse, Toronto, Detroit, Cleveland, Youngstown, Baltimore, Texas, and Washington.[64] On this arduous trip, Szold encountered Jewish communities that had little or no interest in the Zionist idea. Many viewed Zionism as an obstacle to attaining their goals and demonstrating their loyalty to the United States. Szold realized that only a profound change of consciousness would bring them closer to Zionism and attract women to Hadassah.[65]

Szold suddenly found herself at a crossroads. On February 17, 1917, the United States cut diplomatic ties with Turkey. On her visit to Washington, she felt the tension in the air: talk of war and young men getting ready to enlist. Szold noted the sharp contrast between the preparations for war and the beauty of Washington in the springtime.[66] Shaken by the prospect of her country entering the war, her pacifism reawakened. She spoke of the horrors of war and the tragedies and disasters it provokes. Women she admired, including Jane Addams and Lillian Wald, had raised their voices against the war and joined the People's Council of America for Democracy and Peace. A number of Hadassah members, including Szold's close friends Jessie Sampter and Alice Seligsberg, also joined the People's Council, as did her sister Adele and Judah Magnes, known for his pacifist views. Szold too decided to join the People's Council.

At the time, many in the United States did not look kindly on pacifists, whom they perceived as undermining patriotism and the spirit of sacrifice exhibited by American troops. American Jews, and especially Zionist leaders, were particularly sensitive to the question of loyalty, for fear of being accused of harboring dual or divided loyalties. They went out of their way to prove their patriotism, and sharply criticized those, such as the members of the People's Council, who opposed the United States entering the war. Jacob de Haas, a Zionist leader, writer, and essayist, wrote to Szold that her position ran counter to that of the Zionist movement, which favored Jewish settlement in Palestine and the victory of the Allied powers over Germany and the Ottoman Empire. Even Brandeis, who greatly admired Szold, believed that she and those of her friends who had joined the People's Council were weakening national solidarity and undermining loyalty to the United States—especially in light of President Wilson's efforts on behalf of the Jews in Palestine from the very beginning of the war. Brandeis explained that pacifism was of course an individual prerogative, but not one that members of the Zionist movement could afford to exercise. He asserted that those who insisted on remaining in the People's Council should leave the FAZ. Szold faced an agonizing decision. Leaving the Zionist movement was unthinkable, as it would require her resignation from Hadassah. She was trapped between her conscience and her commitment to the Zionist movement and Hadassah, which was her life's work. She wanted both to continue to work for the Zionist cause and to protest against the war. Szold met with members of the emergency committee—Brandeis, Julian Mack, Harry Friedenwald, and others—to whom she explained that she was a loyal patriot, but that she believed that wars brought only death and destruction, and was therefore bound by her conscience to oppose them. Her explanations were rejected, and she was forced to make a decision. She returned home and carefully weighed Brandeis's words. With a heavy heart, she wrote to the People's Council asking that her name be removed from their membership list and that it no longer be used in their public appeals against the United States entering the war.

Meanwhile, Szold learned of the Russian Revolution, which began in February 1917. "The Russian Revolution!" she wrote in a letter to Alice Seligsberg. "Perhaps we shall still rise and bless this war. But no! Russia's gain is lessened through our loss."[67] The February Revolution would fail, to be succeeded six months later by a second revolution, the October Revolution, marking the Bolsheviks' rise to power under the leadership of Lenin.

News of the epidemics spreading throughout Palestine drove Szold to focus on sending the medical unit immediately. The operation required complex wartime diplomacy. Prior to the United States entering the war, the State Department and Henry Morgenthau had brought pressure to bear on Constantinople to ensure that the medical unit would be allowed to enter the country. Britain and France had also promised that they would grant the unit passage through their territories, and it seemed that all obstacles had been removed. Everything changed, however, when the United States entered the war alongside the Allied Powers, Britain, Russia, and France, in April 1917. The departure of the medical unit was postponed indefinitely. Szold was frustrated. She knew how urgent this assistance was for the Yishuv, and how disastrous its delay would be. She waited impatiently for the war to end so that the medical unit could finally go to Palestine, and she herself intended to follow.

The Americans' entry into the war further exacerbated conditions in the Yishuv. Djemal Pasha's treatment of the Jews worsened, and American Jews were soon ordered out of Palestine, like other foreign nationals before them. After British general Edmund Allenby's failed attempt to take Gaza, the Turks ordered the expulsion of all Jews from the south of the country, and in April 1917, 10,000 Jews were brutally driven out of Jaffa and Tel Aviv. "We will never forget that terrible sight, and we will never forgive," wrote Mordechai Ben-Hillel, a Hebrew writer, Zionist leader, and one of the founders of Tel Aviv, who witnessed the expulsion.[68] Children, the elderly, the sick, and women carrying infants were forced to depart on foot. Many reached Petah Tikva, to the east, but they lacked food and shelter. The inhabitants of the surrounding agricultural colonies tried to help, but they lacked the means to provide for such large numbers of people. Some went on to Kfar Sava, to the north, but there was no shelter for them there either. They simply huddled in the brush, waiting to return to their homes. Others went even farther north, to Hadera and Zichron Ya'akov. More than a thousand refugees reached Tiberias. In the absence of adequate shelter, they built huts on the shores of the Sea of Galilee, but there was no food for them. The people of Tiberias were already starving and were unable to help the masses of refugees.

Rabbi Moses Kliers, chief rabbi of Tiberias and the Galilee, sent desperate letters to Meir Dizengoff, head of the emergency committee in Palestine. Rabbi Kliers begged Dizengoff to send money to buy food for the refugees, who languished, destitute, on the seashore.[69] Crowding, starvation, and the poor health of the refugees led to outbreaks of disease in Tiberias: meningitis, influenza, malaria, dysentery, and, worst of all, cholera, which spread rapidly, infecting the inhabitants of the city as well. Workers of the American Red Cross, active in Palestine during the final weeks of the war, did everything they could to provide medical assistance, but about half of the people infected with cholera died.[70] Helena Kagan wrote to Henrietta Szold about the epidemics sweeping through the Yishuv, compounded by poor hygiene and malnutrition.

As the war began to go badly for the Ottomans, they toughened measures against the Jews, closing the American health centers and the Straus Health Center in Jerusalem, and intended to seize Hadassah funds. That money was transferred to Helena Kagan in time to avoid falling into the Turks' hands, however, and was immediately sent to the Galilee, to help provide for refugee women and children. Kagan gave Szold a detailed account of the expenditures, adding that she would hold on to the receipts rather than send them by mail, for fear that they might be lost.[71] Szold forwarded Kagan's report to Jacob Schiff, as head of the JDC, which had donated $100,000 to Hadassah to help finance the medical unit. Furthermore, Szold sent detailed reports to all of the donors, telling them how their money had been spent, and expressed her hope that they would continue to support the medical unit after the British conquest of Palestine, in order to provide urgent care to those in need.[72] This was Szold's standard practice: to keep a precise record of all income and expenditure, down to the last cent, and to submit it to scrutiny.

The war raged on. The British had managed to drive the Turkish forces from their positions along the Suez Canal, and they were preparing to take the Sinai Peninsula and advance into Palestine. The British considered Palestine an important strategic asset, a point of transit between the Suez Canal and the land route through Transjordan, Mesopotamia, and the Persian Gulf, all the way to India, a valuable British possession. The French and British governments, respectively represented by the diplomats François Georges-Picot and Mark Sykes, had already reached a secret agreement regarding the partition of the Ottoman Empire—allocating Mesopotamia, Transjordan, and southern Palestine to the British, and Syria and Lebanon to the French.

The Nili underground was founded in 1915, to help the British take Palestine by providing information regarding Turkish troop movements. In practice, however, Nili did not begin operations until 1917. The organization was headed by Aaron Aaronsohn, and its core members were Aaron's brother Alexander and sister Sarah, the brothers Na'aman and Eitan Belkind, Avshalom Feinberg, and Joseph Lishansky. Nili activities were coordinated from Aaronsohn's agricultural experiment station at Atlit, near the coast. The information they gathered was conveyed to a British ship that secretly approached the shore from time to time.

When the Turkish authorities exposed the spy ring, Sarah Aaronsohn was arrested by the Turks, interrogated, and tortured, but she refused to give up the names of her comrades, ultimately taking her own life. Djemal Pasha accused the leaders of the Yishuv of involvement in the espionage conspiracy. A curfew was imposed on the Jewish colonies, and innocent people were arrested and severely beaten. Some were sent to prison in Damascus. There was a growing fear that the Turks would take their anger out on the entire Yishuv.

DURING THIS TIME of terrible anxiety, a sudden bolt of news brought hope. On November 2, 1917, news arrived of the Balfour Declaration—the famous letter presented by British foreign secretary Arthur James Balfour to the prominent Zionist leader Lord Lionel Walter Rothschild. The declaration opened with the words "His Majesty's government view with favour the establishment in Palestine of a national home for the Jewish people, and will use their best endeavours to facilitate the achievement of this object."[73] Many in the Yishuv believed it was the dawning of the Messianic Era. Excitement reached fever pitch. Sara Azaryahu, a Zionist activist and feminist leader, wrote: "One day in November of 1917, I was lying down, unwell, in my room. Suddenly, the door flung open, and Azaryahu [Sara's husband] burst in, followed by a group of friends. 'The dawn of redemption!' he managed to blurt out with tremendous excitement, and began to read from the *Jüdische Rundschau* about the declaration issued by Balfour, the British foreign secretary. Silent and deeply moved, we listened with bated breath to tidings of the return to Zion; 'We were like dreamers' [Psalms 126:1]."[74]

Henrietta Szold continued to raise money, so as to increase the amount of medicine and equipment the medical unit would bring with it to Palestine. She expected the unit to depart as soon as travel restrictions were lifted. She launched a national fundraising drive, but when she encountered indifference in the Jewish communities she visited, her hopes were dashed. "*Texas* is not different from *New Rochelle* or New York," she wrote. "The British declaration passed over the heads of the Jews down here as an unseen airplane from one of the Texan aviation fields. They didn't know that something epoch-making had just happened. . . . Down here I have learnt to say a dreadful thing: 'Rather assimilation than this!'"[75]

Szold believed that "Zionism, like Judaism in general, implies or presupposes a high grade of intelligence and mental discipline. Our people, used up by the struggle for existence, do not possess that." Furthermore, Szold had reached the conclusion that "missionizing" visits to the various communities had little point and "ought to stop. Or we ought to have angels to do it. . . . I know now that I am neither angel, agitator, propagandist, orator, nor missionary."[76]

The Balfour Declaration found the Yishuv still at war. The British advance into Palestine was slow, but the Yishuv, which had suffered so terribly under the Ottomans, could not wait, and celebrated each and every British victory. On December 11, 1917, General Allenby reached the gates of the city of Jerusalem. It was the eve of the festival of Hanukkah, celebrated that year with particular joy. Some saw Allenby's arrival as a sign from heaven, and the traditional holiday prayer, "For the miracles and wonders and redemption," assumed new meaning: "In the week in which the Torah portion of Mi-ketz is read, the city was taken by the English and an end (ketz) came to Turkish rule, and the city of Jerusalem rejoiced and was glad."[77] Hearts soared, and messianic fervor was in the air.

Many Jerusalemites came to see General Allenby enter the city gates. He stopped at Citadel Gate and read a proclamation written for him by his friend Mark Sykes, the British diplomat, and by François Georges-Picot, representing the French government. Dr. Kagan wrote to Henrietta Szold that a new era had dawned—one in which the government respected the holiness of the city, the beliefs of its inhabitants, and its special status. Allenby dismounted from his horse and entered the city on foot, as a pilgrim

British soldiers enter Jerusalem, 1917

rather than a conqueror. Kagan wrote that a world full of hope and light had opened before them.[78] A few weeks later, the British also took Tel Aviv, further increasing the Yishuv's joy. Many saw it as a miracle: the city was saved from destruction, and its expelled inhabitants began to return.

The medical unit obtained all of the necessary permits, and left for Palestine. All of Szold's efforts were focused on the unit, which she planned to join at a later date. She was unwell, however, and her doctor warned her not to jeopardize her health by traveling immediately. The medical unit comprised forty-four doctors and nurses, and a small number of administrators. The equipment they had purchased included ambulances, freight trucks, and a large quantity of medicine—all sent on a separate ship. Members of the unit reached England, en route to Palestine, where they received a warm welcome from leaders of the local Jewish community. In

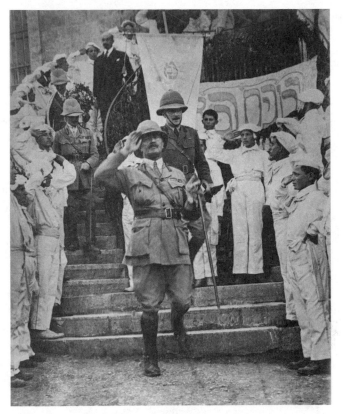

General Allenby enters the Old City of Jerusalem,
December 1917

France, representatives of the unit met with Baron de Rothschild, who gave
them permission to use the Rothschild Hospital in Jerusalem. From France
they traveled to Italy, and finally set sail for Alexandria aboard an Indian
ship. In Egypt, they met with Chaim Weizmann, and reached Palestine
some ten weeks before the end of the war.

GENERAL ALLENBY'S NORTHERN OFFENSIVE (September 14–October 12, 1918) and the
British conquest of the Galilee caused the Turks to flee in disarray, thwarting
their destructive plans. "In the Yishuv, it was widely believed that we had
witnessed one of the miracles that saved our foundering ship from the
abyss, as it was about to sink into the stormy sea," wrote Sara Azaryahu.[79]
On November 11, 1918, the armistice was signed. Word reached the United
States in the morning, and rejoicing broke out in the streets.

Szold was overcome with emotion: "The day—the day of peace! . . . From early morning until the peace news heralded by bells and whistles and joyous cries came. . . . Just then came the ringing of the bells. Our girls—we have nearly 200 in our office now—stormed in laughing, crying, dancing, jumping up and down, embracing each other; and from the street, all the way up to our office on the fifteenth floor, rose shout after shout of joy. . . . The office closed at once for the day, and we surged down Fifth Avenue. The spontaneity of the demonstration was overwhelming."[80]

Szold was swept up in the joy, but as she had feared, the consequences of the war were devastating. It soon became clear that 20 million people had been killed during the war, with tens of millions wounded and millions made refugees. The *American Jewish Year Book* reported that many Jews had enlisted in the American armed forces, and 250,000 Jews had served during the period 1917–1918. Of these, some 3,500 had fallen in battle, and 12,000 had been wounded.[81]

The First World War was the seminal event of the twentieth century. It brought about the collapse of four empires, including three that had existed for centuries. A great change came over the Jewish people as well. The Zionist leadership had been paralyzed during the war years, refraining from taking a position in a war in which Jews were fighting against Jews. The end of the war marked the beginning of a new chapter in the history of Zionism and the Land of Israel. All of Palestine had been liberated, bringing 400 years of Ottoman rule to a close. The Turks left behind a deeply troubled land and a beleaguered, starving population. There were 4,000 orphans in Jerusalem alone. The cities and towns of the Galilee were particularly hard hit. The Jewish community of Safed had numbered 7,000 before the war; a census commissioned by the Zionist Federation in 1918, however, found only 2,685 Jews left in the city—about a third of its pre-war population. Many inhabitants of Safed had perished from starvation and disease. Disease struck Tiberias as well, where cholera claimed numerous victims. There too, only about a third of the city's Jews remained.[82]

Worst of all, however, was the situation in Jerusalem. Before the war, the city had been home to some 45,000 Jews and 21,000 Arabs. During the war years, the population decreased by 25,000. British major William Ormsby-Gore, a Conservative member of Parliament who was among the authors of the Balfour Declaration and later served as colonial secretary, was appointed liaison officer between the Jewish population and the British military administration. In an official report, Ormsby-Gore wrote that some 60 percent of the population of Palestine suffered from malaria, and many were exhausted from extreme poverty and typhus. He noted that in

1917, 2,084 Jews died in Jerusalem, mostly from typhus. Of the 85,000 Jews who had lived in Palestine before the war, only 56,000 remained. Many had fallen victim to starvation or disease, while others had suffered deportation.

With the war over, everyone believed it was the beginning of a new era for humanity. The war was called at the time the Great War; no one imagined that only twenty years later another world war would break out, leaving unprecedented destruction in its path. Still, at the end of the Great War, some optimism flourished. The members of the Hadassah medical unit began operations even before the fighting had ceased. Their arrival in Tiberias, upon the city's liberation, was met with great excitement and hope.

CONFLICT

Szold's pride in Hadassah's accomplishments was tempered with concern. There was increasing conflict among the leaders of the Zionist Organization, and to Szold's great dismay, Hadassah, which she had worked so hard to build, was also in jeopardy.

The changes that followed the First World War, the Bolshevik Revolution in Russia, and the isolation of its inhabitants from the rest of the world, did not leave the Zionist Organization unscathed. The organization's center of gravity shifted from Russia westward, with the leadership concentrating in the United States and Britain. Greater weight was given in the international organization to the leaders of the Zionist Organization of America as representatives of the largest Jewish community in the free world.

Dr. Chaim Weizmann, a veteran Zionist leader, active in the movement since his youth, presided over Zionist activities in London. In Herzl's day, Weizmann had criticized the movement's founder for placing too much emphasis on diplomacy. Weizmann was among the founders of the democratic faction within the Zionist Organization, which in 1903 advocated practical Zionism—the expansion and reinforcement of Jewish settlement in Palestine. However, following his first visit to Palestine, in 1907, Weizmann came to the conclusion that action must be taken on both tracks simultaneously, the practical and the political. This approach later came to be known as synthetic Zionism.

Dr. Weizmann, who worked as a scientist at the University of Manchester, developed a new method for the production of acetone. His invention contributed to the British and Allied war effort, and thus opened doors at the highest levels. He was charismatic and witty, with a good sense of humor and remarkable powers of persuasion. He had close ties with members of the British government, and contributed to the issuance of the Balfour Declaration.[83] With the conquest of Palestine and the confirmation of the British mandate, the Zionist movement in Britain gained greater prominence, and Weizmann was recognized as its leader. He and his supporters were convinced that his place as head of the international Zionist Organization was ensured.

Brandeis's many admirers in America were equally certain that he was the most suited to lead the international movement. This was also the view of Jacob de Haas, who had been instrumental in persuading Brandeis to embrace Zionism, and Shmarya Levin, a well-known Zionist leader and friend of Weizmann's who had been visiting the United States when hostilities broke out in Europe, forcing him to remain there for the duration of the war. Both men had been extremely impressed by Brandeis's character and by the prestige he enjoyed among non-Jewish Americans. Brandeis's close ties to President Wilson and other members of the administration were also considered a strong point in his favor, as they would prove useful in the diplomatic struggle for the establishment of the Jewish national home in Palestine. Brandeis's candidacy for president of the Zionist Organization had many prominent supporters.

Brandeis visited Palestine in 1919, together with Jacob de Haas. He was inspired by the pioneer settlements but amazed at the poverty and difficult conditions in which they lived, and at the backbreaking work they did in draining the swamps.[84] He was shocked by the prevalence of malaria and the large number of victims it claimed, and he reached the conclusion that development in Palestine was haphazard, without any central plan or direction. It is at this time that Brandeis formulated the systematic approach he believed the Zionist Organization should take. He would become convinced that the organization should adopt a long-term strategic policy to create the necessary economic infrastructure for the development of Palestine and for the absorption of the tens of thousands of Jewish immigrants expected following the awarding of the Palestine Mandate to Britain. Brandeis would come to the opinion that efforts should focus on fundraising and large-scale investment of American capital for the establishment of public corporations that would act under public supervision for the development of Palestine, and he would call upon his friends and acquaintances in America to contribute and invest in construction projects.

Brandeis's vision of the appropriate Zionist strategy in Palestine did not coincide with that of Weizmann. Brandeis opposed transferring all of the funds for reconstruction to Keren Hayesod, the fund established by Weizmann's followers, and he criticized the wastefulness and lack of oversight in the institutions administered by the "Eastern Europeans." Brandeis believed that his own people, if put in charge, would implement the norms of supervision and transparency that he sought. Weizmann rejected Brandeis's position. The differences between the two leaders were not limited to matters of ideology and strategy. A hidden rivalry developed between them for the leadership of the Zionist Organization—a rivalry that would intensify over the coming years, with disastrous results for the organization.

Louis Lipsky sought to reform the organizational structure of the Zionist Organization of America (ZOA) and, beginning in the summer of 1918, set about doing just that. His inspiration, he said, came from Brandeis, who was dismayed by the dozens of organizations, associations, and clubs identifying as Zionist, each acting on its own. Lipsky decided to bring them all under the aegis of a single authority—to create a single, united Zionist organization. He called upon all of the Zionist associations and organizations in the United States—including Hadassah—to dismantle their independent organizational structures and join the ZOA as ordinary members.

Szold, who was painfully aware of the divisions and rifts within the Zionist movement, and the accompanying organizational and ideological failures, was not against the idea of reorganization per se. She argued, however, that Hadassah—a large organization with thousands of members actively engaged in furthering its goals—could hardly be compared to the dozens of small and insignificant Zionist associations. Szold felt that Lipsky was seeking the dissolution of Hadassah simply to incorporate its structure and large membership into the ZOA. She found Lipsky's personality somewhat disconcerting. Even Emanuel Neumann, a Zionist activist and a personal friend of Lipsky's, noted that the tall, gaunt, and unsmiling Lipsky was a dry and insensitive man.

No one disputed Szold's honored place among the Zionist leadership in America. Lipsky was not a particularly important figure in the movement, but his attacks against Hadassah were relentless. At a certain point, Szold had no choice but to respond to his demand that Hadassah join the ZOA, although she saw it as little more than a formal declaration. She was determined to maintain Hadassah's organizational and financial independence, and argued that all of Hadassah's funds were committed to supporting the medical unit in Palestine. Lipsky did not give up, and immediately began annexing Hadassah, abolishing its central committee and discontinuing its bulletin. Yet Lipsky expected the Hadassah chapters throughout the country to continue operating as before. "How this miracle is going to be brought about Mr. Lipsky understands, I do not," Szold remarked.[85] She was very wary of the effect of Lipsky's actions on the future of Hadassah, but never imagined the extent of the struggles that awaited her.

As part of Lipsky's structural reform of the Zionist Organization of America, various departments were established, such as the organization department, the finance department, and the education department—the last of these headed by Szold, who was also a member of the executive committee. Szold believed that the education department had a crucial role to play in conveying the Zionist idea to large numbers of American Jews. She planned to establish schools and youth clubs, train young leaders, publish Zionist literature, and more. Szold, who knew the Jewish communities in America and was well aware of the fact that most Jews had little affinity for Zionism, was a great believer in the power of Zionist propaganda. Considering the enormous size of the task, however, she was of two minds about accepting the position: "I acknowledge its supreme value, but I have no affinity for it. I am to have a great deal of help, but I find that the more help I have, the more I shall be reduced to doing routine work, and the routine work will be so enormous that I shall probably, even with the best organization, spend all the hours of the day on them."[86]

Szold had a particular aversion to excessive bureaucracy, which she believed complicated work, increased costs, and wasted her time. Despite her initial misgivings, Szold decided to take the job. As always, she found it hard to turn down roles she considered important. She was joined at the education department by the young educator Alexander Dushkin; the poet Jessie Sampter; Amy Schechter (Solomon Schechter's daughter); Rose Zeitlin, a Zionist activist and one of the founders of Hadassah; and Emanuel Neumann. Lipsky had little regard for educational activity among American Jews and did not support Szold's plans. He was obsessive in his struggle against Szold, and hoped that the younger members of her staff, such as Dushkin and Neumann, would answer to him. Nevertheless, Szold immediately set to work developing and expanding the organization's educational programs. She was greatly admired by her staff, for her personal qualities and for her work. Her authority was accepted without question. Neumann recounted that when he first came to work as educational director at the department headed by Szold, he was in awe of her: "Everybody treated her with enormous respect . . . and [she] seemed stern, rather distant and forbidding."[87] Working with her, however, he found her to be a pleasant woman, who gave him a free hand in the department. He and all the other members of the staff enjoyed working with her and admired her abilities.

Lipsky constantly sought to diminish Szold's power and standing within the ZOA and her control of Hadassah, which were a source of considerable irritation to him. He decided to discontinue the education department's propaganda efforts, claiming that they were too expensive. Szold refused, arguing that Zionist propaganda was the most powerful tool they had for spreading the Zionist idea among Jews. Lipsky rejected her explanations and continued to seek Szold's removal from the leadership of Hadassah. Szold was anxious about Hadassah's future, and feared that its name would be obliterated; even the medical unit she had organized was called the "American Zionist Medical Unit," with no mention of the name Hadassah. She shared her fears with Alice Seligsberg, who was in Palestine at the time, and asked her to look into the possibility of naming the children's hospital Dr. Kagan had founded, Hadassah, in order to memorialize the name of the organization behind the medical unit and the rehabilitation of the healthcare system in the Yishuv.[88]

Szold was uncertain whom to approach for help in her conflict with Lispky. Brandeis had greatly admired Szold and her accomplishments at Hadassah, but he was in Washington, on the Supreme Court, and Szold was in New York, at a loss as to how to handle Lipsky. She had devoted her life to building and fostering things that were important to her, and found herself unable to contend with Lipsky's scheming—although she had no intention of giving in to his dictates. Seeing no other alternative, however, she resigned from her position as head of the ZOA education department. The aggravation affected Szold's health. She was exhausted, and the doctor told her to take time off. "Quit tomorrow!" he said, explaining that her heart was in poor condition and needed rest. Recounting the doctor's advice in a letter to Alice Seligsberg, she added, "I need not tell you why it is in bad condition and why it needs rest. Perhaps the machinery is worn out."[89] Szold went to Maine in the summer of 1919, where she hoped to relax and regain her strength. She spent three months there.

Years later, in his memoirs, Lipsky implied that the decision to suspend the educational propaganda program came from above. "The work continued until 1919 when Zionist policy was diverted to accord with Mr. Brandeis' views as to the future of the organization. Education was to be directed exclusively to [the] service of specific projects. Political propaganda was to be discontinued."[90] This was a cynical exploitation of Brandeis's name. Not only was Brandeis a great admirer of Szold and her work, but at the heart of Lipsky's animus toward Szold was her friendship with Brandeis and Julian Mack. Lipsky feared that she would support them against Weizmann, and therefore he wished to get rid of her. Szold herself had no desire to fight with Lipsky, and even considered resigning from the executive committee of the ZOA because of him, but found it hard to leave the Zionist movement in which she had been active for so many years. As she considered her options, the solution she settled on was to go work in Palestine—something she had long wanted to do, and where she would not have to participate in ZOA meetings and not have to resign from the organization.

Another incentive to go to Palestine was provided by the reports she received from Alice Seligsberg on the state of the medical unit. Szold was concerned about the difficulties the unit was experiencing and the internal conflicts affecting its work. She hoped her presence would contribute to relieving some of the tension between the unit's head, Dr. Isaac M. Rubinow, and the doctors, and prevent further damage to the medical unit's essential work. Szold began her preparations for the trip, with the intention of remaining in Palestine for a period of two years. At that point she had not yet decided to settle there permanently. Her immediate aim was to avoid conflict with Lipsky. She never imagined that the bitter disputes with him would persist, even in Palestine.

10

IN PALESTINE

*S*ZOLD'S JOURNEY to Palestine got off to a rough start. On February 23, 1920, she set sail for Naples aboard the *Giuseppe Verdi,* hoping to reach Jerusalem within three weeks. She arrived in Italy on March 8, having been promised that her visa for Palestine would be waiting for her at the British consulate. Julia Aronson, with whom she had been traveling, received her permit and proceeded to Palestine as planned, but Szold's visa was not there. She checked with the consulate every day, to no avail. Frustrated by the long wait, she wrote to her sisters: "I wonder whether you realize how isolated I feel. There is not a soul to talk to."[1] Days turned into weeks, and Passover was fast approaching. Szold, who longed for the warmth of a Jewish home and the holiday atmosphere, traveled to Florence, to spend Passover at the home of Rabbi Samuel Hirsch Margulies, whom she had met on her trip to Palestine a decade earlier. She was warmly received by the rabbi and his family.

At Rabbi Margulies's home, she found a newspaper from Palestine, *Doar Hayom,* in which she read about the Arab riots on the holiday of Nebi Musa (April 4, 1920), which coincided with Passover that year. The week-long religious festival among Palestine's Muslims included a pilgrimage from Jerusalem to the site near Jericho of what was believed to be the tomb of Moses (Musa). This year, a young pilgrim, Amin al-Husayni, inflamed passions among the Muslim worshipers with hate-filled harangues against the Jews, after which an incensed crowd descended on the Jewish

A Nebi Musa festival

Quarter in the Old City of Jerusalem, shouting "Kill the Jews!" Arabs broke into Jewish homes, killing and wounding Jews and damaging property. British army units failed to protect the Jews, and some Arab policemen even helped the rioters. Ze'ev Jabotinsky arrived in Egypt in 1915 and held negotiations with the British government to create Jewish legions within the British army. In 1920 he arrived in Jerusalem with his family. He had foreseen the riots in Jerusalem and organized groups of volunteers to defend the Jewish Quarter, but they were greatly outnumbered. The riots raged for three days in Jerusalem and the surrounding area. Six Jews were killed and 200 were injured; property was looted and synagogues were damaged. The British neither prevented the riots nor tried to stop them. Szold was shocked by what she read.

From the newspapers she found in Rabbi Margulies's home, Szold learned that after the defeat of the Turks, the British had established a military administration in Palestine, pending an internationally approved decision regarding the future of the territory. Those appointed to head the military administration held pro-Arab views, had opposed the Balfour Declaration, and actively encouraged nationalist tendencies among the Arabs in Palestine. The Arabs were well aware of the military administration's positions, and at demonstrations protesters often called out "Al-dawla ma'ana" (The government is with us). This attitude contributed to the Arab attacks on the Jewish village of Tel Hai and the kibbutzim Kfar Giladi and Ayelet Hashahar, culminating in the Battle of Tel Hai (March 1, 1920), in which eight of the village's defenders, including the commander Joseph Trumpeldor, fell. Thus, even before she arrived in Palestine, Szold was exposed to the Jewish-Arab conflict.

Szold thoroughly enjoyed Passover at the home of Rabbi Margulies—a traditional Passover celebration, like the kind she had always known. There were twenty-one guests, speaking six different languages. Among them were Beatrice Samuel and her son Edwin. They were in Florence awaiting the arrival of her husband, Herbert, who had just spent three months in Palestine on behalf of the British government. Szold became friends with Beatrice and was especially pleased to meet Herbert a short while later; she found him a very impressive man who resembled a British aristocrat in his dress and bearing. Herbert Samuel was on his way to San Remo at the behest of British prime minister David Lloyd George, where he would attend the conference (convened on April 18, 1920) at which representatives of the Entente Powers would divide the former territories of the Ottoman Empire between them. Szold asked Herbert Samuel for his opinion on the conflict between Arabs and Jews in Palestine. Samuel was optimistic but admitted that the Arab problem was complicated, and he seemed concerned.[2] The connection between Szold and the Samuels continued over the coming years, after Herbert's appointment to the position of High Commissioner for Palestine.

After Passover, Szold returned to Naples to await her permit. When her friends Judge Julian Mack and Rabbi Stephen Wise heard of her delay in Italy, they came to her aid, using their contacts in the American administration. They sent Szold a telegram telling her to continue on her journey and that she would be issued a permit in Cairo. After seven weeks in Italy, she set sail for Alexandria on April 20, 1920, aboard the *Umbria*. On the ship, she met Dr. Montague David Eder, a British psychiatrist and member of the Zionist Commission, which had been established with the consent of the British government after the promulgation of the Balfour Declaration; headed by Chaim Weizmann, the commission had been tasked with furthering the recovery and development of the Yishuv.[3] Szold discussed the riots in Palestine with Eder, and he told her that the British had arrested Ze'ev Jabotinsky and twenty-one members of the Jewish self-defense group he had organized. The British made no distinction between attackers and defenders, and Jabotinsky and the members of his group were sent to prison in Acre. Szold was disgusted by the charges against Jabotinsky and his subsequent imprisonment. She remembered him from the time of the

1905 revolution in Odessa, when he had organized Jewish self-defense against the pogroms that followed in the wake of the failed revolt, and she hoped to meet him in Palestine.

Upon her arrival in Cairo, Szold finally obtained the permit she had been waiting for. Three days later, she left for Palestine by train. Szold was fascinated by the desert landscape she observed on the trip northward, inspired by the encounter between sand and sea and by the carpets of wild-flowers she saw as the train approached the southern Negev, and delighted by the fragrant spring air. As the train pulled into Lydda station, Szold was thrilled to finally be in Palestine once again. The station was noisy and chaotic: hundreds of soldiers and civilians looked for their luggage, which had been dumped haphazardly on the platform. The confusion of the station and her fatigue from a long journey with many delays threatened to overwhelm her. All her cares disappeared, however, the moment she set eyes on her friend Alice Seligsberg, who was accompanied by another of Szold's friends, a young woman named Nellie Straus, and by the medical unit's head, Dr. Rubinow, who had come to greet her. In their company, she set out for Jerusalem.[4]

Upon their arrival in the city, they went to the home of Dr. Helena Kagan, who had invited Szold to stay with her until she could find a permanent place to stay.[5] Kagan lived with her mother on the Street of the Prophets (Ha-Neveem Street), alongside consulates and the spacious homes of prominent Jews and Christians. Kagan, who had expected Szold weeks earlier, was away in Europe, and her mother showed Szold to the room that had been prepared for her. The welcome she received was a warm one. On the table at the center of the room, covered with a flowered cloth, stood a vase of flowers, a samovar with hot water for tea, and a basket of cookies and fresh bread. Alice Seligsberg and another of Szold's friends, Libby Oppenheim, added a jar of jam and a cake. Later in the day, other friends from the United States came to visit her, and she began to feel at home. The next day, Szold went to the offices of the medical unit in the Hôtel de France building, where she met with Rubinow; she had asked him to gather the entire staff so she could get to know each of them personally.

IN HER MEETINGS with leaders of the Yishuv, Szold felt the atmosphere of hope that had been kindled by the San Remo Conference weeks earlier. At the conference, it had been decided to assign the Palestine mandate to Britain, which was charged with implementing the Balfour Declaration. The decisions taken at the San Remo Conference were no longer simply a British promise to further the establishment of a national home for the Jewish

The American Zionist medical unit initiated by Hadassah, 1918

people, but a signed agreement between the victorious powers, with political implications. The British, who had feared the Arab reaction after the riots in Jerusalem and in light of the tense atmosphere, suppressed publication of the conference decisions pertaining to Palestine, but they could not hide them; reports of the decisions made at San Remo spread throughout the Yishuv, and soon the newspapers were full of articles about them.

On the front page of *Doar Hayom,* there was an article on the decisions made at San Remo and their significance,⁶ reporting Lloyd George's assertion that the San Remo Conference would be remembered as one of the shining moments on the path to world peace.⁷ There was an outburst of joy throughout the country. Wherever the news was heard, people hugged in the streets, celebratory prayers were conducted in the synagogues, and hopes soared. One account read as follows: "Late Monday night, the news of San Remo reached our colony [Rishon LeZion]. . . . The news spread like wildfire throughout the colonies. The colony's men and daughters ran through the streets drunk with joy, and at night, by the light of the moon, they read the telegram printed as a supplement to the newspaper *Doar Hayom,* which had been posted on all the walls."⁸

Eliezer Ben-Yehuda wrote a long essay, published in *Doar Hayom,* on the "miraculous wonder" that had happened to the Jewish people: "For two thousand years our people did not have, on the face of this broad earth, even one square foot they could call their own. Now, in a single leap, we will be a people like all others—one that is accorded the land of its fathers, the wondrous land of its great past, legally, internationally, with the acknowledgement of all of the powers, their agreement and political decision. This is the great wonder we have already witnessed!"[9]

Hope blossomed among Zionists in America as well. An extraordinary convention of the ZOA, held at the Lexington Avenue Opera House, attracted 1,500 delegates, and was chaired by Judge Julian Mack. The convention raised $206,000, including a pledge for $100,000 by the philanthropist Nathan Straus.[10]

Even before the mandate was officially assigned by the League of Nations, the British decided to replace the military administration in Palestine, the Occupied Enemy Territory Administration (OETA), with a civilian administration. This development was met with jubilation in the Yishuv, as the period of British military administration had been a dark one for the Yishuv and for Zionism, as restrictions had been imposed on Jewish immigration and settlement, and hopes for a Jewish-Arab agreement had been shattered. The excitement only grew when the League of Nations formally granted Britain the mandate over Palestine. A source of further elation in the Yishuv was the appointment of Sir Herbert Samuel as the first British High Commissioner for Palestine. High hopes were pinned on Samuel's ability to stabilize British rule and restore the peace throughout the country.

Samuel was a Zionist Jew who had studied at Oxford University, where he befriended Winston Churchill, future prime minister of the United Kingdom. Samuel had been elected to Parliament and had served as a cabinet minister. He joined the British army during the First World War and was sent to Egypt, where General Allenby was preparing for the Palestine campaign. Samuel was assigned to a communications unit on Allenby's staff. In Egypt, he gained firsthand knowledge of events in the Middle East, and after the war he used that knowledge to try to influence members of Parliament to allow the Jews to establish an independent political entity in Palestine.[11]

THERE WAS A CONSTANT STREAM of visitors and old friends who came to see Szold in Jerusalem: the educator Alexander Dushkin, with whom she had worked at the ZOA department of education; Professor Richard Gottheil; Norman

Bentwich, who was the attorney general of Mandatory Palestine and wore the uniform of a British officer; her friends Alice Seligsberg and Jessie Sampter; and Nellie Straus, the only daughter of Dr. Rosa Welt Straus, who had studied medicine in Vienna and subsequently immigrated to the United States, and Louis Straus, a wealthy businessman.[12] Nellie and Szold had first met in the United States, and Nellie greatly admired Szold; the two became friends, despite the age difference between them. Nellie's mother, Dr. Rosa Welt Straus, was active in the suffragist movement in the United States. She had met Henrietta Szold through her daughter, and through Szold's influence developed an interest in Zionism, under Szold's influence. When Nellie decided to go to Palestine in 1919, Rosa joined her—among other reasons, so that she could look after her daughter, who had a congenital heart condition. Nellie was delighted by Szold's arrival, and became a frequent visitor. Jessie Sampter had also decided to immigrate to Palestine from New York, having become a Zionist under Szold's influence. Szold made new friends in Jerusalem as well, and her circle in Palestine continued to grow.

After a few weeks as a guest in Dr. Kagan's home, Szold began to look for a place to rent, and found one near the Arab neighborhood known as the American Colony, on the outskirts of the city. She rented a house together with Sophia Berger, a social worker who had been in Palestine since the time of the British military administration and worked with the American Red Cross, and whom Szold had known in New York. Szold was delighted with the house, telling her sisters that it was "surrounded by a big garden, with olive trees, figs, oranges, and vines, not to mention flowers."[13] The house and its garden quickly became a meeting point for Szold and her friends. Berger loved to entertain, baking for their guests and making sure the samovar was always full.

One of the first places Szold visited outside Jerusalem was the Aaronsohn family home in Zichron Ya'akov. Before her arrival in Palestine she had heard of Aaron Aaronsohn's tragic death in 1919 in a mysterious plane crash while crossing the English Channel. To this day, the circumstances of the crash remain unknown. Szold mourned the loss of such a talented and accomplished man, whom she had called a friend and who she believed had been destined for great things.

Soon after Szold's arrival in Palestine, however, many people had approached her with complaints about Aaronsohn's experiment station in Atlit. They claimed that he had borrowed money from them that he had not returned. They presented documents attesting to Aaronsohn's debts and demanded the liquidation of the station's assets, which included land near Zichron Ya'akov and in the vicinity of Haifa. Szold, who had intended to pay the Aaronsohns a condolence call, found herself dragged into the struggle between the Aaronsohns and their creditors. Aaron's father hoped Szold might help them preserve what remained of Aaron's collection at the station, in memory of the son who was his pride; he feared that the station and its contents would be dismantled in the struggle surrounding its assets.[14]

Aaronsohn's father told her that before the station was taken by the Turks in October 1917, he had rushed over, gathered all of the documents, books, and collections, and packed them in crates bearing the seal of the American consul, in an attempt to protect them from looting. The Turks seized the crates and scattered them throughout the country. The mineral collection disappeared entirely, and the chemistry laboratory was destroyed. Only about a quarter of the books remained, and less than a third of the botanical collection. Upon Aaron's return to Palestine following the British victory, he gathered together whatever he could find, including crates of documents, accounts, receipts, and financial obligations that had been in Haifa at the time of the Turkish raid. After Aaron's death, his creditors placed their hopes in the station's assets.

The creditors had also approached Aaronsohn's American backers, including Julius Rosenwald, a member of the experiment station's American board of trustees. Now Rosenwald contacted Szold, who had organized the board of trustees and was the driving force behind it. Szold did not want to become personally involved in the dispute, and wrote to Rosenwald that Judge Julian Mack was planning to travel to London with Brandeis to attend the Zionist Organization conference, and if he came to Palestine, she would accompany him to Atlit so that he could look into the situation there. She suggested that Mack would then be able to discuss the matter with the board of trustees upon his return to the United States, and Rosenwald could decide how to proceed.[15]

Though she felt for Aaron's elderly and grief-stricken father, Szold wished to avoid getting involved in matters that might distract her from her main goal. After the long delay in Italy, she was eager to begin evaluating the work of the medical unit. She traveled around the country visiting the unit's clinics. Her first stop was the clinic in Jaffa. She remembered the terrible situation in the city on her previous visit, ten years earlier, and now noted the changes for the better, although a great deal of work still remained to be done.

She visited all the hospitals and clinics that Hadassah had established throughout Palestine. During these trips she met hundreds of workers, all of whom were dissatisfied with their salaries. The patients too had their grievances. The complaints weighed on her. "While from every quarter, colony, city, and settlement, demands come that we take over the medical service and furnish physicians, nurses, druggists, and automobiles, we are sneered at because we have automobiles. In short, we are damned if we do and damned if we don't."[16]

Though on these visits she had to deal with many problems and conflicts, the places and landscapes she saw on her trips inspired her. Of the two-and-a-half-hour journey from Jaffa back to Jerusalem, she wrote: "Such coloring never was on land or sea. The hills, the sky, the Arabs behind or on their donkeys or on camels, or on top of a hay wagon, the fields yellow and green, the moon rising over the hills as large as a wagon wheel."[17] She marveled at the pleasant coolness in the evening, even at the end of a hot day. On other excursions, Szold visited Nablus, Jenin, Nazareth, Tiberias, and Safed, and between accounts of her meetings with medical unit staff and patients, she described the land itself: "The land is treeless, largely waterless, at this season the green has largely disappeared, and the dry thornbushes almost crackle under the hot sun—and yet it is beautiful, so beautiful that I almost resent our intention to make it blossom and bear fruit. The stones are soft with colorfulness and between them spring up blossoms so curiously adapted to the peculiarity of the land that one cannot wonder enough."[18]

FACE-TO-FACE WITH THE JEWISH-ARAB CONFLICT

During the course of her visits to the Hadassah medical services around the country, Szold also encountered a tense political reality. "That is the way we had to travel," she recounted to her sisters. "Indeed for three days we had to have the protection of an armed gendarme. At least they said we had to. Wherever we came, the Jewish colonists in the fields were armed. Their little settlements were surrounded by trenches and protected by sandbags. The fear of the Bedouin is upon the whole land. In several colonies there has been violence, loss of life, and loss of all movable property."[19] Szold feared that the tension between Jews and Arabs would intensify and lead to further violent outbursts. She noted that the word *kibush* (conquest), taken from the Book of Joshua, was embraced by the Yishuv in various contexts, including "conquering the wilderness" and "conquering labor" (by hiring Jewish workers to farm, build roads, and drain swamps). To Szold, the word brought to mind war, and she realized that war was constantly raging in Palestine, both openly and beneath the surface, in all areas of life.

She wanted to hear a firsthand account of the Passover riots in Jerusalem, and so she went to visit Jabotinsky and his men in Acre prison, located in a medieval Crusader fortress. Allenby had just denied them a pardon, and they were planning a hunger strike. In London, the Zionist leadership pressed the British government to pardon Jabotinsky, who had been among the defenders in Jerusalem, not the attackers. Szold was impressed by him, and she remarked, "I have never sympathized with his ideas—he is militant and aggressive—but when one listens to him, they assume charm as well as cogency. My visit to him will be a memory I shall always want to recur to."[20]

The tension in Jerusalem was palpable. From her window, Szold could see soldiers training at the Russian compound. She wrote to her sisters that there had been another scare the day before: rumors were spreading that violence would erupt once again with the beginning of the Muslim holy month of Ramadan. Handbills had been distributed with the heading "Down with the Jews."[21] The strain in Arab-Jewish relations was manifest, and dominated every aspect of public life. The imminent arrival of the new high commissioner, Herbert Samuel, further exacerbated matters: his appointment had aroused Arab anger against the British and growing hostility against the Jews.

On July 1, 1920, the Royal Navy cruiser HMS *Centaur* entered the port of Jaffa, and Sir Herbert Samuel, wearing a white uniform and a sword, came ashore—"the twentieth-century Nehemiah," as Szold described him. There was little fanfare at the first high commissioner's arrival. Samuel and his entourage immediately left for Jerusalem by train, under heavy guard. The route from Jaffa to Jerusalem was lined with soldiers, as were the streets of Jerusalem itself, due to rumors that the Arabs were organizing unrest, although in the end nothing happened.[22] This reception gave Samuel a taste of what the country had in store for him. Like many in the Yishuv, Szold hoped that Samuel's arrival marked a change in British policy with regard to the conflict between Jews and Arabs. It was widely believed that Samuel would put a stop to the blatantly pro-Arab policies of the military administration, and that treatment of the Jews would improve under his tenure, restoring the peace.

Samuel took up residence in the Augusta Victoria compound on Mount Scopus, expropriated by the British when they took control of the city. The compound served as British military headquarters and the seat of the government of Palestine, as well as the high commissioner's residence. Samuel immediately set about addressing the Jewish-Arab conflict, which dominated all of his activities from the very beginning of his tenure. He believed that reconciliation between Jews and Arabs was possible, and he made every effort to bring it about. Soon after his arrival, he convened a meeting of Jewish, Muslim, and Christian leaders to discuss the measures he intended to introduce in the country. He sought to create an atmosphere of cooperation and mutual respect, which he believed would serve as a foundation for achieving an understanding between them and defusing tensions. At the meeting, Samuel read a message from the king, promising that the mandatory government would treat members of all communities with equal respect. He told the leaders that he intended to establish an advisory council under his own leadership, the members of which would select candidates from the various segments of the population for government positions. All ordinances would be presented to the council, and members would have the opportunity to raise issues for government attention. He announced that a law regulating immigration had been passed, and that an immigrant absorption department had been established. The law stipulated that 1,000 Jews would be permitted to immigrate to Palestine each year—well below Zionist Organization expectations.[23]

One of the first issues that came before the council was the name of the territory assigned to the British mandate. The name Palestine had been given to the land by the Greeks, and was subsequently adopted by the Romans and the Byzantines. Muslims considered it a part of southern Syria, and under Ottoman rule it had been divided into two administrative districts: Jerusalem and Beirut. The name Palestine had been adopted by the Christian world, and it was the name that appeared both in the Balfour Declaration and in the League of Nations document assigning the mandate to Britain. The Jews did not embrace the name Palestine, preferring to call the land Eretz Israel (Land of Israel), as it had been designated in rabbinic literature for centuries. Samuel wished to restore the Jewish name Eretz Isra'el and, employing his considerable diplomatic skills, managed to obtain the council's approval. It was decided that on official documents and postage stamps, the Hebrew initials "E.I." would appear alongside the name Palestine in English. The decision did not go uncontested. A group of Arab nationalists appealed to the court, arguing that the mandate required the use of all three official languages—English, Hebrew, and Arabic on all official documents. They therefore demanded that the name of the country appear in Arabic as well. The British court rejected the appeal, on the grounds that the court would not interfere in administrative matters.

Lady Beatrice Samuel, the high commissioner's wife, also took part in efforts to promote peace and understanding. Together with Helen Bentwich—who was the wife of Palestine's legal secretary and attorney general, Norman Bentwich, and Herbert Samuel's niece—she organized a women's council, comprising Jewish, Muslim, and Christian representatives. The purpose of the council was to address problems of the day and seek understandings between the communities, strengthening relations between them.[24]

Lady Samuel herself headed the council, while the other Jewish members were Szold, who enjoyed considerable prestige in the United States and in the Yishuv, Helen Bentwich, and Sophia Berger. One of the Christian members of the council was Effie Newton of Haifa, a "masculine" woman who smoked a pipe. Newton was hostile toward the Jews, highly critical of the British, and supported the Arabs. According to Helen Bentwich, Newton used her intelligence and considerable wealth to inflict a good deal of harm on the Jewish immigrants. Another representative of the Christian community was Bertha Spafford Vester, daughter of the founders of the American Colony—a group of Chicago natives who had come to Palestine to engage in philanthropic and missionary work. Spafford had lived most of her life in Jerusalem, knew the Arab women well, and helped them. After the arrival of the British, she became active in the country's social life. Spafford was outwardly friendly, but she did not support the idea of a Jewish national home. Two Muslim women later joined the council as well.[25]

Helen Bentwich recalled an episode from a session of the high commissioner's advisory council she had attended. Among the members of the council was a Bedouin sheikh "from the desert" (in her characterization) south of Beersheba, who wore traditional robes and never spoke a word. When Norman Bentwich read a bill that would allow women to practice law in Palestine, and his words were translated into Arabic, the sheikh stood up. Eyes glowing with rage, he placed his hand on his sword and declared, "Over my dead body." The bill did not pass.[26]

Helen realized that the women's council meetings would not achieve the goal of mitigating conflict between the communities. She therefore decided to start a ladies' club in Jerusalem, together with Mrs. Garstang (wife of Professor John Garstang, an archeologist), open to "women of all nationalities and communities." In the British tradition, the club was housed in elegant premises, and there was a housemother who looked after the building and served refreshments. The club was to host discussions, lectures, and parties, in order to afford women from different communities the opportunity to overcome the sense of alienation between them and encourage them to become friends. Lecturers were invited to address the women on topics pertaining to the country's development. Bentwich brought in Pinhas Rutenberg to present his plan to build a hydroelectric plant at the point where the Yarmuk meets the Jordan River, just below the Sea of Galilee, to demonstrate that efforts were being made to develop the country for all its inhabitants.

Pinhas Rutenberg was born in Ukraine, trained as an engineer, and studied the generation of electricity from flowing water. In his youth, he was one of the leaders of the 1905 Russian Revolution. In 1917, his revolutionary rivals gained the upper hand, and he was sent to prison. He was released about a year later, and in 1919 he left Russia and immigrated to Palestine.[27] The charismatic Rutenberg told the members of the ladies' club how he had come up with the idea of building a power plant. He had observed the severe shortage of water in the country, and believed the situation could be improved by building a hydroelectric plant at Naharayim that would be capable of pumping water from the Sea of Galilee to areas of the country where water was lacking. He described the difficulties he had encountered, because his plan seemed unrealistic and many doubted its feasibility. He was determined, however, and convinced the high commissioner to approve his project, raised the necessary funds, and started work on the plant.

Rutenberg invited the members of the club to visit the plant while it was still under construction. They accepted his invitation and were extremely impressed. They saw the difficult conditions in which the workers lived— in an area rife with malaria—as they constructed a plant that would improve health throughout the country. Helen Bentwich was pleased that they had made the visit.[28]

It soon became clear, however, that the club was unable to fulfill its mission of promoting understanding between the parties to the conflict. The missionary women persisted in their support for the Arabs, and there seemed to be no way to change or soften their position. The efforts of Herbert Samuel and his colleagues to ease tensions were equally unsuccessful. Szold was disheartened by the difficulty in finding a solution to the Jewish-Arab conflict, which she saw as a necessary condition for the expansion of the Yishuv and development of the country.

SZOLD HAD BARELY had time to acclimatize herself to life in Palestine before Rubinow informed her he would be returning to the United States. She remarked, "I dreaded it from the first moment I knew I was coming to Palestine. Dr. Rubinow is leaving for America on vacation. When I asked him if he is going with the intention of returning . . . [he did not know]. He is a tired nervous man."[29] Rumor had it that he was desperately in love with a young woman in Jerusalem, while he had a wife and children waiting for him in New York; in the end, he decided to return to his family. Szold, who was averse to gossip, makes no mention of this. Her general impression of Rubinow had been good. She was aware of the conflicts within the unit and the criticisms some had directed against Rubinow, but she gave him the benefit of the doubt, for the medical unit had been running smoothly under his direction.

Nurses and doctors pose for a photo in front of Hadassah Hospital in Safed.
Henrietta Szold stands in the center.

Rubinow's departure forced Szold to take over the administration of the unit herself until a replacement could be found, and she was daunted by the enormous size of the task: "Isn't it ridiculous that I should be directing hospitals, nurses' training school, laboratories, clinics, school hygiene, and most medical services? And isn't it sad that I should be fighting forty-five doctors?"[30] Her anxiety was exacerbated by the fact that she did not know whether Rubinow would be returning. She had planned to travel to London, to attend the Zionist Executive Conference, but had to cancel, knowing that she would be too busy running and supervising the medical unit.[31]

Szold was particularly troubled by the disputes within the unit. When she first arrived in Palestine, she realized that the staff hoped she would put an end to the conflicts between the doctors and the community, and between the medical staff and the unit's administration. "At the end of two weeks I was a wreck," she admitted. "I was ready to flee back to America. I wondered bitterly whether I had devoted twenty years of my life to an ideal that had turned out to be a will-o'-the-wisp. . . . In those first days after my arrival a voice kept shouting inside of myself: 'These are not your people. You have no part and parcel in them.'"[32] She complained to Harry Friedenwald that his colleagues in the medical unit were selfish and undisciplined. Instead of remembering that they had a special obligation to face the greatest of dangers in Palestine, they made excessive and outrageous pay demands. They all demanded the highest pay grade (there were twenty pay grades in the unit)—acting like a trade union, even as malaria raged throughout the summer. Szold was especially concerned after Rubinow's departure, as she was unfamiliar with the administrative details of the unit's medical work.

Szold's assumption of the role of director of the medical unit was not received well by the doctors, who refused to accept her authority on professional matters on the grounds that she had no medical background. She could not bear the doctors' demands and constant complaining. She wrote to Friedenwald that the fault was due to those who had organized the unit and selected its physicians. In Palestine, Szold found herself at the head of a complex project that faced financial, social, professional, and political problems on a daily basis.[33] In the fall, matters only got worse. Malaria reached epidemic proportions, claiming more victims than at any other time in living memory. Delegations from various parts of the country, including representatives of all of the workers' groups in both the north and the south, came to the unit's office to ask for help. When the wartime suspension of immigration ended and large numbers of immigrants began to pour in, the situation became unbearable.[34]

IMMIGRATION AND ITS TRAVAILS

The arrival of the SS *Ruslan* in Jaffa on December 18, 1919, marked the beginning of the Third Aliyah. Although small groups of Jewish immigrants had arrived in Palestine since the end of the war, the *Ruslan* was different. The ship, which had departed from Odessa on a voyage organized by the Zionist movement, carried 670 passengers. Some saw it as kind of a Zionist *Mayflower*.

Moshe Goldin-Zahavi, one of the passengers aboard the *Ruslan*, later recalled: "The welcome we received as we disembarked, wet from the rain, was extremely heartwarming. A public committee, headed by Menachem Ussishkin, worked hard to make things easier for us."[35] The excitement in the Yishuv at the *Ruslan*'s arrival reflected the hope that it would be followed by tens of thousands of pioneers from Russia, Poland, and Central Europe, allowing the building of the promised national home to begin in earnest.

On her visits around the country, Szold saw the terrible conditions in which the growing number of new immigrants lived. Some three hundred immigrants arrived each week, and not all of them were ideologically motivated pioneers. Worst off, however, were the pioneers. They had no money and were forced to wander the country in search of work. Those who managed to find a day or two of work per week considered themselves lucky, and most went hungry.

Help arrived from an unexpected quarter. Pinhas Rutenberg, who had begun construction of his power plant at Naharayim, south of the Sea of Galilee, needed workers. He convinced the mandatory government, through the department of public works, to commission a road from Tiberias to Tzemah. The contract was awarded to the Agricultural Laborers Union, affiliated with the Ahdut Ha'avodah party. Rumors of the construction of a road attracted many of the pioneers. They joined the crew working on the Tiberias–Tzemah road, and then went on to build additional roads: between Tabgha and Tiberias, between Haifa and Nazareth, and others. The work was exhausting, and the workers were unused to hard physical labor. Rocks had to be broken into gravel by hand with sledgehammers under the blistering sun. Injuries were common, and the combination of backbreaking work and malnutrition took its toll. One of the workers, Natan Haruvi, later recalled: "A few weeks after our arrival at the camp, there was a terrible heatwave in the Jordan Valley, and many of the camp's workers fell ill. Our entire group was sick. There was no room in the hospital in Tiberias for all of us."[36]

Szold was horrified at the sight of young people lying ill in tents, without medical attention. She appealed to Colonel George Heron, director of the mandatory health department, asking him to employ Jewish workers to provide care for the immigrants. Her request was rejected outright. She understood then that she had been naive to believe that the British, who were opposed to Jewish immigration, would help the immigrants. Szold went to visit the workers on the Haifa–Nazareth road, and she asked one of the doctors from the medical unit clinic in Haifa to join her.

She found that the immigrants working on the road crews lived in large camps of 300–500 workers each, six to a tent, and slept on sacks on the ground. The sanitary conditions were awful, with clouds of flies swarming around open latrines and an all-pervasive stench. Midges were yet another scourge—"a plague not in the Bible," wrote David Maletz, a member of Kibbutz Ein Harod and a writer. "Biting midges are a kind of tiny fly that, around the time of the barley harvest, fills the void of the world in countless swarms, droning and buzzing, attacking man and beast, flying into ears, mouth, nose, eyes, any hole or crack it can. It bites fiercely and harasses man and beast incessantly, driving them crazy. . . . Some strike wildly to the right and left, but to no avail. They, the midges, are unimpressed and continue their biting and maddening buzzing. Their swarms fill the void of the sweltering world, scorched by the blazing sun."[37]

In the tents, Szold and the doctor who had come with her found men suffering from malaria, burning with fever, with no one to help them. The workers asked Szold to provide them with medical care, and she agreed. The medical unit began to practice "road medicine." A field hospital was established at the workers' camp near Tiberias. Tents and beds were provided, and Szold sent doctors, nurses, and orderlies, though she simply did not have enough personnel to meet the needs of such a large number of patients.

Szold was particularly struck by a medical unit nurse named Tanya, who worked in the immigrant camp. Szold watched as Tanya moved with ease and grace through the mud between the clinic and the hospital tents.[38] Szold admired Tanya, as she did all of the pioneers, or *halutzim,* in whom she saw the fulfillment of her own Zionist dream: living simple, almost ascetic lives, grappling with the basic problems of living. "I have a strong desire to join them," she wrote.

She compared the pioneers to the inhabitants of the towns and colonies of the Yishuv, for whom she had considerably less respect. Not all of the immigrants to Palestine had come for ideological reasons; many had believed that they would be given good positions and a comfortable living in the city, and they were unwilling to do manual labor for low wages. Frustrated, many of them left the country in despair.

Even among the most committed pioneers, there were those who were unable to adjust to the austere lifestyle and backbreaking work. Szold sympathized with the pioneers who were unable to cope and wished to leave the country. She did not blame them; rather, she blamed the lack of sufficient resources for their absorption. More broadly, she blamed the Jewish people in the diaspora for their inability to recognize the opportunity they had waited for so long. Chaim Weizmann gave voice to this disappointment at the refusal of wealthy Jews to contribute to the building of the Jewish homeland in Palestine, exclaiming at the Zionist Organization conference in London, "Where are you Jewish people?" Weizmann warned that the shortage of funds was obstructing the development of the Jewish national home in Palestine, hindering the absorption of the large number of Jews willing and prepared to immigrate, and hampering those immigrants who were disappointed with Palestine and even desperate to leave from being able to depart.

Indirect criticism was leveled at Weizmann, for it was the Zionist Commission for Palestine, which he headed, that represented the Zionist movement and was supposed to further the development of the Yishuv and the realization of the vision of a national home. The commission was accused of being one of the causes of Zionism's failure at a time when hopes were soaring. It was criticized for having failed to rise to the political occasion and to provide the kind of bold leadership required at such a crucial juncture. Weizmann rejected such criticism of the commission, arguing instead that had the wealthy Jews truly dedicated themselves to the task, half a million Jewish immigrants could have been brought to Palestine.[39] Weizmann's words were a veiled criticism of the American delegation, headed by Brandeis, which took part in the London conference and had considerable influence on wealthy American Jews.

Szold was distressed by the lack of funds, as she believed that was impeding development in Palestine. She was also aware, however, of the role played by the military administration that had governed the country from the beginning of British rule through the installation of a civil administration until the appointment of a high commissioner. The commanders in charge of the military administration during the course of those two years had been pro-Arab, and were the primary cause of the missed opportunity to develop the country and lay the groundwork for the arrival of large numbers of Jewish immigrants. The military commanders had allocated most of the funds at their disposal to the Arab population, withholding assistance not only from the new immigrants, but also from the Old Yishuv. With the appointment of Herbert Samuel, the Jews demanded the dismissal of Ronald Storrs, who had served as military governor of Jerusalem. Herbert Samuel did not dismiss him, however, and Storrs remained in his position for a number of years more.[40] Szold had the opportunity to meet with Storrs, and she formed her own opinion of his character, his aversion to the Jews, and his defense of the Arabs. She described him as "a dilettante-littérateur, archeologist, [and] excellent music critic," who "handles the English language as a virtuoso does his fondled instrument," and "knows all of the prominent men and women in Britain, and their descent." Irony tinged his voice when he spoke of the expectations of the Jews to be granted peerages: "My head whirled—my poor democratic, uncolonial head, which never was good on genealogies." Furthermore, "he despises the Jews," she added, indignant at Storrs's disdain for the Jews, whom he accused of being materialists, incapable of withstanding the hardships in Palestine: "The pioneers? Oh! That is Zionism for the poor brother Jew. . . . The dilettante idealist's demands, as he sits on soft oriental cushions and looks upon brasses and rugs and rich hangings gathered in all parts of the east. The truth of the matter is that the Jew is not a 'native,' the Arab is. Kiplingesque!" Storrs made absolutely no effort to hide his antisemitism, but Szold remarked that she had at least "forced him to have a kosher lunch for me."[41]

THE FEDERATION OF HEBREW WOMEN

Szold was still burdened with the administration of the medical unit when another challenge presented itself. She received a visit from Bathsheba Kesselman, who was in the process of establishing a Jewish women's federation in Palestine. Kesselman, a native of Odessa, had gone to the United States with her husband to pursue a higher education, as Jews were barred from such institutions in Russia. Kesselman, who was a Zionist, became an active member of Hadassah, and was eventually elected chairwoman of the organization's large Brooklyn chapter. After she and her husband discovered that there was antisemitism in the United States as well, they decided to immigrate to Palestine, and in 1919 they settled in Jerusalem. One day, Kesselman was asked by a neighbor to help a woman in childbirth. She found the woman in a dark, damp basement, lying on the floor, without a mattress, moaning in pain. Kesselman was horrified. She had also seen women who could not afford to buy diapers and instead had to swaddle their babies in rags—filthy ones, due to the shortage of water in Jerusalem. The poverty and deprivation suffered by these women shocked her deeply. She also heard of the high rate of infant mortality, and decided to find a way to improve the lives of women and infants in the city. From her experience in Hadassah in New York, she understood the value of a large organization, and so decided to establish a women's federation in Palestine.

Kesselman was familiar with Szold and her work from the United States, and when she heard that Szold was in Jerusalem, she went to see her. She told Szold that she, together with some of her friends, had held a meeting on May 21, 1920, with the purpose of establishing a women's federation to provide assistance to mothers and pregnant women. Most of the women involved in establishing the federation were recent immigrants who had arrived as part of the Third Aliyah—the wave of Jewish immigration that followed the First World War. Kesselman asked Szold to serve as president of the federation, in order to lend greater weight to the new organization and to overcome any opposition.[42]

Szold was certain, in light of the severe shortage of nurses, that a corps of volunteers could make a vital contribution to Hadassah's healthcare system—for example, in teaching mothers the principles of hygiene and nutrition. When Kesselman offered Szold the title of president, Szold accepted, on the condition that she had no intention of being a figurehead, but would play an active role in the women's federation. Despite her weighty responsibilities as Rubinow's replacement, she took the role she had accepted very seriously, and her involvement was quickly felt in the federation.

Preparations were soon under way for the founding assembly of the women's federation, and two days before the assembly, posters were put up around the city, inviting women to a meeting "for the benefit of mothers and children in Jerusalem." The assembly took place on June 14 at the Amdursky Hotel and was attended by more than a hundred women. Kesselman greeted everyone and then introduced Szold.

Szold explained the importance of teaching hygiene and proper nutrition to pregnant women and to women with infants and children to look after. She praised volunteer work, which she called "holy work," capable of improving the condition of women and children, and she cited a few concrete examples. Her words made an impression, and it was decided to establish the Federation of Hebrew Women. Szold was elected president, and a committee was formed. Two months later, a second assembly, chaired by Szold, was held at the Lämel School. The assembly was attended by women of various backgrounds: Ashkenazi, Sephardi, Bukharan, and others. At that assembly Szold sought to set out the federation's goals and to adopt an organizational charter. She proposed that each neighborhood create its own framework, comprising a committee of three to five members, one of whom would serve as chairwoman. This was to ensure that the volunteers in each neighborhood would know who was in need in their area and could maintain direct and ongoing contact with them. Szold also upheld the principle that she had established at the school for immigrants in Baltimore and at Hadassah in the United States—that each member had to pay the organization something, in this case the sum of at least ten *grush*, to cover various expenses. So that members would feel a connection to and personal responsibility for the organization and its activities, it was decided that each neighborhood committee would send a representative to the executive committee of the federation.[43]

This structure was similar to the one adopted by Hadassah in the United States—an organization that had proven its efficiency. Subsequently, a number of specific committees were formed, such as the Committee for Mothers, responsible for encouraging pregnant women to avail themselves of the medical care provided by the Hadassah physicians. The volunteers visited women's homes and, when needed, gave them financial assistance as well. Other committees were established to provide mothers with guidance on how to care for their infants and to refer them to the Hadassah nurses and doctors for regular checkups. Another committee took care of orphans and abandoned children, and it was decided to establish an infants' home, where they could stay up to the age of two. These programs did not develop all at once, but were implemented gradually over the course of the early 1920s. Szold followed the work of the federation volunteers and offered them advice and support. Efforts were coordinated between Hadassah, which provided the medical services, and the federation, which offered guidance and social services. The project, which began in Jerusalem, soon spread to other cities: Haifa, Tiberias, Safed, and others. The women's achievements in the field of preventive care were truly remarkable. The joint effort between Hadassah and the Federation of Hebrew Women produced significant results, helping to reduce infant and child mortality.

Alongside the Federation of Hebrew Women, which focused on social issues, another group, the Union of Hebrew Women for Equal Rights in Erez Israel, led the struggle for women's suffrage. The union was headed by Sara Azaryahu, and counted Dr. Rosa Welt Straus among its members. Initially targeting local elections, the suffrage movement gained momentum with the establishment of the Yishuv's first assembly of elected representatives, in 1920.[44] The Federation of Hebrew Women and the Union of Hebrew Women for Equal Rights joined forces and in the next election, in 1925, they would present a joint women's list, headed by Szold and including Azaryahu and Kagan.

Szold breathed a sigh of relief when Rubinow returned in November 1920, after having been gone for three months. Finally released from the burden of the day-to-day running of the medical unit, she was able to get on with her life in Jerusalem. Her home had become a meeting place for eminent Jerusalemites and chance visitors alike. Pinhas Rutenberg told her of the many obstacles he faced as he sought to build a hydroelectric plant on the Jordan River, and of his plan to hire more pioneers to work on the road to the plant. Szold was impressed by his vision and by his plan to organize road building groups (*binuyot*) for the pioneers. "He is a real personage, a little too optimistic for my taste, but nevertheless interesting, and spirited," she noted.[45]

Szold seemed to be adjusting to life in Palestine, but she missed the United States. She celebrated the Fourth of July, singing and humming patriotic songs around the house. In the evening, she organized a picnic for the thirty students of the nursing school on the slopes of Mount Scopus, "exactly at full moon."[46] Friends she had known in the United States came to her house, along with new friends she had made in Jerusalem. She wrote to her sisters that she enjoyed her guests, and Sophia Berger ran the house, cooking for and entertaining everyone who came to visit them. She recalled that when they first rented the house, she and Sophia had agreed to share all of the housekeeping and cooking, but Sophia had not lived up to the agreement, turning down her help and doing everything herself. Weather permitting, Szold liked to sit with her guests in the garden, which gave her immense pleasure. Every Saturday, Alexander Dushkin, Norman Bentwich and his two sisters, Jessie Sampter, and others would come to see her, and they would talk, read, and study the Bible together.[47]

Szold was also invited to all the city's important society events. One such occasion was the wedding of the high commissioner's son, Edwin Samuel, who married a local woman named Hadassah Grasovsky, daughter of the linguist Yehuda Goor-Grasovsky. They met in Tel Aviv, when the Samuels and the Grasovskys lived in the same building. Beatrice Samuel had told Henrietta Szold about the engagement when they first met in Florence, en route to Palestine. Now she invited her to the wedding. Szold described the unusual wedding in a letter to her sisters. The wedding took place at the high commissioner's residence, on the Mount of Olives. The numerous guests included representatives of all of the country's many different communities: "sheiks and Dominican priests and Chacham Bashis and Russian popes and Abyssinian clergy," each in their traditional garb, "and military men," in their uniforms. The wedding canopy was placed at the center of the hall, with the guests "disposed on all four sides." The ceremony was to be performed by three rabbis, but all of a sudden everything came to a halt. One of the rabbis spoke to the master of ceremonies, who immediately rushed over to the high commissioner and had a whispered exchange with him. The guests were not informed of the reason for the delay, but Szold noticed that the fuss seemed to be over a bottle of wine. Later she learned that one of the rabbis had realized that the wine provided for the ceremony had no kosher certification, a sine qua non for a traditional Jewish wedding. The ceremony was held up for quite some time, and Szold imagined "a horseman having to gallop down to Jerusalem to fetch the wine" as Sir Herbert stood there in embarrassed silence. Eventually the wine was brought, and the ceremony continued.

A reception for the guests was held in another hall. "The wedding gifts were of truly Oriental splendor—carpets, and wines, and silver, and embroideries, and daggers, and chased revolvers. But the best and most Oriental of them were not displayed: thirty horses presented to the bride by the sheiks, and a whole village—houses, men, women, and children, and all their belongings."[48] At the end of her description of the wedding, Szold added wryly: "And then I rode down the hill to a meeting to discuss cutting down the budget."[49]

Szold's acquaintance with the Jerusalem elite continued to grow. Her sixtieth birthday, in December 1920, was celebrated on a grand scale, beginning with a gala dinner hosted by the medical unit's doctors and nurses at the Hôtel de France (where the unit had its headquarters) and attended by High Commissioner Herbert Samuel, Beatrice Samuel, and other important figures. The speakers expressed admiration for Szold, who had, in the space of a year, managed to bring order to the healthcare system. The criticism leveled against her by some of the medical unit staff had not completely vanished, but her personality, the respect she accorded to every person, and her willingness to listen and to help won her the admiration and love of many. After the dinner, a reception was held in Szold's honor, with 150 guests. The medical unit staff gave her a gift, an inscription in the Jewish National Fund's Golden Book, and they explained: "We have done this, not because you were the temporary director of Hadassah, not because you are a great Zionist or a well-known writer, but because you are a fellow-worker, a human being whom we love and honor." After the speeches, the chairs and tables were moved aside and everyone burst into an ecstatic hora—including Szold herself, who "wound in and out among the other dancers, rosy and brisk as a girl of sixteen." After the hora, there were waltzes and other dances, and they did not let Szold miss a single one. This went on until after midnight.[50]

VIOLENCE IN JAFFA

Szold experienced a number of difficulties and obstacles in Palestine, but she had not expected to find herself in the midst of an incident that almost cost her life. On May 1, 1921, a group of Jews held a parade from Tel Aviv to Jaffa, carrying red flags, to mark International Workers' Day. They were attacked by Arabs, and violence soon spread throughout Jaffa and the surrounding area, leaving many dead and injured.[51]

That morning, Szold had been visiting the medical unit clinic in Jaffa. When the driver who had brought her there realized that something was amiss, he suggested to Szold that they leave immediately. He quickly drove her to Tel Aviv, to the home of her friend Nellie Straus. As the two women were sitting down to lunch, they heard shots. Szold looked out the window and saw people running in the street. She went outside and asked someone about the shots. He told her that the Arabs in Jaffa were slaughtering the Jews.

Szold rushed to the hospital in Jaffa to help care for the injured. She was warned that she was risking her life, but she paid no heed to the warnings.

The hospital was full to capacity, and the injured who continued to arrive were forced to wait outside. The dead were laid in the courtyard because there was no more room inside the building. The Arabs were also rioting near Bet ha-Halutzim (Pioneer House), in the Ajami neighborhood, near the port. Bet ha-Halutzim had been established by Rubinow as an immigrant reception center and hostel, where immigrants were checked for contagious diseases and given vaccinations by medical unit physicians. Szold recounted: "In our hospital a boy of twelve came with his mother, both wounded, and they were looking for the father. They had been in Palestine two days, in the Bet Halutzim."[52]

Szold took down the names of the injured who arrived at the hospital, in order to inform their relatives. The seriously injured were immediately referred to the medical staff. There were not enough doctors and nurses to look after all of the injured, however. Medicine and bandages soon ran out as well, and there was a great deal of confusion. Someone at the hospital reported that the Arabs had attacked the Red House, a building that stood among the citrus groves between Jaffa and Mikve Yisrael and was home to the Yitzkar family and a number of lodgers, including the writer Yosef Haim Brenner.

The attacks against the Jews continued, and spread to other localities. Szold wrote: "Body after body was brought in, and it was a state! The little hospital looked like a shambles. The floor strewn with the wounded, and we had only the worst cases. Other hundreds were at the Gymnasium nearby, at the Immigrants' Reception House, at the French Hospital in the city, and in private homes. . . . The wounded in our hospital showed bullet wounds, knife wounds, and wounds from clubs and iron utensils. Some were actually battered."[53]

Szold telephoned the medical unit in Jerusalem, asking them to urgently send doctors and nurses to the hospital in Jaffa, as well as medicine and bandages. She remained in the hospital all that day and through the night. The following morning, she telephoned Jerusalem again, asking them to send bread and eggs for the wounded, as all the Jewish and Arab shops in Jaffa were closed and there was nowhere to buy food.[54]

The next day, news began to arrive regarding events at the Yitzkar family home. Reportedly, the Yitzkars and their lodgers had decided to leave the house during the night and make their way to Tel Aviv. However, a funeral procession for an Arab boy killed during the riots had just arrived at the Sheikh Murad cemetery, opposite the house. The angry mourners discovered the Yitzkars' group of six and attacked them. The writer Yosef Louisdor opened fire to fend off the attackers and killed one of them. Then the Arabs pounced on the six Jews, including Brenner, and killed them in a violent rage. Hours later, five bodies were found in the field. Louisdor's body was missing: the Arabs had mutilated, dismembered, and hidden it. Brenner had been a widely admired writer; according to a report in *Ha'aretz*, "The tragedy of Brenner's death caused profound grief throughout Tel Aviv and all over Palestine when the news reached it."[55]

Bechor Shitrit, an officer in the mandatory police force at the time, was put in charge of the investigation. He identified a number of suspects, including an Arab policeman from Jaffa and the brother and uncle of the Arab boy who had been killed, but all were acquitted due to lack of evidence. Szold was distraught, and all the more so when she heard that the British had not conducted an immediate investigation to discover who was responsible for the outbreak of violence against the Jews. When an investigation finally was launched, the conclusions they eventually reached were distorted.

Szold asked Colonel Heron of the health department to allocate funds to the medical unit to cover the high costs of treating the many wounded in the riots, but her request was not approved. Only a small fraction of the government budget was allocated to the Jews. There was also discrimination against the Jews in hiring at the health department, where there was a clear preference for Arabs.

The atmosphere Szold found in Jerusalem upon her return was tense. The Jews feared rioting in their own city, having heard of Arab attacks in Petach Tikva, Kfar Sava, Hadera, and Rehovot, but they lacked accurate information. As Szold wrote, "The Hebrew press is severely censored. Some days the editorial and no less the news columns are almost entirely white." Szold went to the police to give testimony of what she had seen in Jaffa, but no one could be found to take her statement. She noted that no Jew believed the Arab claim that the May Day parade in Tel Aviv had sparked the violence. Instead, the consensus among the Jews was that the violence had broken out as a result of Arab agitators, who claimed that the Balfour Declaration had been intended to dispossess the Arab population of Palestine. Szold rejected this argument outright: "Palestine is an empty land. The Jews need not and will not rob the Arabs of their rights or their property. Palestine could be made a land of immigration if the Christian and Moslem agitators were not thinking of their own advantage."[56]

Szold, who had gone to Palestine to evaluate the work of the medical unit and to help with its day-to-day administration, was swept up in the events gripping the country. The 1921 riots, to which she was an eyewitness, impressed upon her the complexity of the political situation in Palestine.

The medical staff in the office of Henrietta Szold in Jerusalem

Indeed, she viewed the Jewish-Arab conflict as the greatest obstacle to realizing the Zionist dream.

Though Szold was shaken by the clashes—there had not been a moment's peace since her arrival in Palestine—she continued her work at Hadassah, putting in ever longer hours. By her own account, her days began at 4:30 a.m. and ended at midnight. She would arrive in the office at 7:30 a.m. and leave at 6:00 p.m. Days on which she traveled outside Jerusalem were even longer. On a visit to Jaffa and Rehovot, she interviewed candidates for the nursing school.[57] She also told of her efforts to help eradicate malaria—to which cause Louis Brandeis, who had visited Palestine right after the war and remembered the difficult reality there and the high mortality from disease, personally donated $10,000.

Szold hoped that the Yishuv would continue to settle and develop the country, but the constant strife and violence undermined these hopes. The terrible and repeated clashes between Jews and Arabs tested Szold's belief in the conflict's resolvability and in the power of close personal relations between Arabs and Jews to defuse tensions. In light of the riots in Jaffa, Szold came to realize that the origins of the dispute were far deeper than she had previously imagined. She concluded that it was a struggle between two peoples clinging to the same piece of land, neither willing to renounce it, and that it was a war of life and death. In a letter she wrote late in 1921, she wondered: "Is there something particularly tragic in the circumstances that the Jews thought they were coming home to security—and leaving persecution outside?"[58]

Szold laid the blame squarely on the British administration and its pro-Arab leanings. She firmly believed that it was the Arabs who were insti-gating violence, while the Jews' hands were tied, since they were prohib-ited from carrying weapons—even for self-defense. Szold argued that in abdicating their duty to protect the Jewish population, the British were actually encouraging Arab violence. She hoped that even the high com-missioner was beginning to understand that he had been fooled by his British Christian advisors. Szold criticized British policy for retreating from support for the Jewish national home, promised in the Balfour Declaration.[59]

The leaders of the Zionist Organization were alarmed by the 1921 riots and decided to convene a meeting of the Zionist General Council (ZGC) to evaluate the situation and decide how to deal with Arab aggres-sion in Palestine. The meeting was set for July 1921 in Prague to discuss the establishment of a Jewish defense force in Palestine and efforts to stabilize relations with the Arabs. This meeting marked a noticeable shift in the type of subjects addressed by the ZGC, from the ideological and the organizational to the social and the political. The decision made by the leaders of the ZGC in Prague was to cooperate with the British authorities in Palestine while continuing to develop and expand the Yishuv. They hoped that British policy would change, but their hopes were short-lived. Violence again erupted on November 2 (Balfour Day), 1921, and Szold was once more an eyewitness. She wrote that Arabs had attacked Jews in Je-rusalem, with terrible results: five Jews were killed and some twenty wounded. There was considerable panic among the Jewish population, but Szold noted that they behaved impeccably, defending themselves to the best of their ability while obeying orders, so as not to give the Arabs any excuse for further violence. Great restraint was also shown at the funerals of the victims, although feelings among the Jews ran high.[60]

The newspapers reported that the riots were not spontaneous: the Arabs in Palestine, Egypt, and Syria had planned in advance to hold turbulent demonstrations on Balfour Day. The governors of Jaffa and Haifa, hearing about this, had summoned local Arab leaders and warned them against demonstrations and strikes. The result was that order was maintained throughout most of the country, with violence breaking out only in Jeru-salem. There, though, the rioters threw stones at Jewish homes and attacked

Jews in the alleyways with knives, sticks, and bombs. The violence raged for about six hours.[61]

The Jews of the city were furious with Jerusalem's governor, Ronald Storrs, whom they called "heir to Pontius Pilate"—a Roman governor of Jerusalem known for his cruelty and tyranny.[62] They wrote an outraged letter to the high commissioner, in which they voiced their distrust of Storrs: "As a result of these riots, the inhabitants of Jerusalem express an utter lack of confidence in the governor of the city, with regard to the security of the life and property of its inhabitants." They once again demanded Storrs's immediate dismissal, because he had broken his promise to protect them. An assembly of the city's Jewish merchants was convened, and its decisions were submitted to the high commissioner. The merchants blamed the government for having failed to protect them and for having failed to stop the riots. The government had not dispersed the demonstrators, and in fact allowed them to enter the Old City, resulting in bloodshed. The merchants wrote: "We hereby give public voice to our protest, in the strongest possible terms, against the illegal demonstration of 2 November, which took place under the eyes of the government, and we demand active security measures so that we may continue our work in complete tranquility."[63]

Storrs promised them that he would ensure their future safety, but the merchants did not believe him. They demanded a meeting with the high commissioner, with the governor and commandant of police in attendance. The high commissioner assured them that every measure would be taken to ensure public order.[64] The Jews also blamed Samuel for having pardoned the mufti of Jerusalem, Haj Amin al-Husayni, who had been sentenced to prison in absentia for his role in the Passover riots of 1920. Al-Husayni went on to become one of the most fanatic agitators against the Jews. Some called Samuel a traitor. David Ben-Gurion made a direct connection between al-Husayni's pardon and the riots in Jerusalem. His remarks appeared under the heading "Whose hands shed this blood?" "The wicked [military] administration was replaced by a Jewish high commissioner, and his first act was to pardon the rioters! Can it be that a Jewish ruler is abetting those who spill our blood?"[65]

Szold felt that the Yishuv's criticism of Storrs and their demand that Samuel dismiss a man who had done nothing to safeguard the Jews was justified. Still, Szold speculated that Storrs would not be replaced, despite the serious accusations against him, and she was right.[66] Storrs was not fired, and remained in his post for another five years. Yishuv leaders were angry with Samuel for having failed to take preventive measures to protect the Jews. Samuel, however, was not free to act as he pleased. He represented the British government, which had its own interests and did not wish to strain relations with the Arabs.

Szold found it hard to accept the idea that the Yishuv would be locked in a perpetual struggle, with no hope for the future. She firmly believed that a breach could be found in the wall of hatred, and that this would lead to reconciliation between the two peoples. She discussed the matter with her friends Norman Bentwich, Arthur Ruppin, educator Ernst Simon, and others. They too were troubled by the situation, and supported a peaceful arrangement with the Arabs. In these conversations, the seeds were sown that would eventually lead to the founding of Brith Shalom (literally "covenant of peace"), also known as the Jewish-Palestinian Peace Alliance—a group that actively sought solutions to the Jewish-Arab conflict.

Brith Shalom was established in 1925 not as a political party, but in order to offer a solution to the conflict between the two peoples struggling for control of Palestine. Although the group had few members, most were quite well known: intellectuals, writers, and public figures, originally from Central Europe and America. Among the members of Brith Shalom were Martin Buber, Gershom Scholem, Hugo Bergmann, Arthur Ruppin, Ernst Simon, and others. Their goal was "to pave the way to understanding between Hebrews and Arabs; to find ways to live together in Palestine, on the basis of complete political equality between the two peoples, with broad autonomy; and to find ways to work together for the development of the country."[67] The members of Brith Shalom believed that the longer they waited, the more entrenched Arab opposition to Zionism would become. It was therefore essential to reach a compromise and understanding with the Arabs as soon as possible.

Many of the members of Brith Shalom saw in Ahad Ha'am—who had written a great deal about relations between Jews and Arabs over the years—a spiritual leader and guide. In response to a Jewish boycott of Arab labor in Palestine, for example, Ahad Ha'am had written to Moshe Smilansky: "Political perils aside, I cannot abide the idea that our brothers are morally capable of treating the members of another people in this fashion, and I cannot help but think, if this is the way things are now, how will we treat others should we ever attain sovereign power in the Land of Israel? Indeed, if this is the 'Messiah,' let him come, but let me not see him."[68]

The members of Brith Shalom believed that the aspirations of Zionism should be realized in Palestine on the spiritual plane, in the creation of a new Jewish culture, and not in the attainment of political sovereignty and Jewish rule. They were willing to renounce the Zionist demand for unlimited Jewish immigration to Palestine, which had fueled Arab fears of a shift in the demographic balance. In so doing, they believed that they could win the hearts of the Palestinian Arabs and put an end to the conflict. At the time, Brith Shalom supported the establishment of a binational state where Jews and Arabs would have equal rights.[69]

Most of the Yishuv sharply condemned Brith Shalom's positions and accused its members of being blind to the reality in the country. Magnes, who was chancellor of the Hebrew University, angered many with an address in the spirit of Brith Shalom at the opening of the university's academic year (October 1929). Opposition to Brith Shalom would increase further following the riots of 1929.

At the time of Brith Shalom's founding and over the years, Ruppin and others considered Szold a member of their group. They knew how troubled she was by the conflict, and thought that she identified with their positions. Szold, however, did not believe that the solutions they proposed would be acceptable to either side. Like other friends and acquaintances, Szold was often invited to afternoon tea at Ruppin's home in the Jerusalem neighborhood of Rehavia. When he moved to a new home, he invited Szold over to see his beautiful garden, but the conversation focused primarily on the conflict with the Arabs. She admired Ruppin, his achievements as head of the Palestine Office, and his efforts to expand Jewish agricultural settlement. She was uneasy, however, with the idea of a binational state in Palestine, as she did not believe it would result in a peaceful solution with the Arabs. She thought that Brith Shalom's views were naive and unrealistic. Szold had no illusions: the riots of 1921, to which she had been a witness, led her to conclude that there was little chance of finding a solution to the Jewish-Arab conflict. From 1926 to 1928, Szold would spend most of her time in the United States, and so would not take part in Brith Shalom's discussions.

In late 1921, Szold's sister Adele wrote to her that she had met Brandeis and that he had been full of praise for Henrietta, her exceptional character and wisdom, and her remarkable achievements in Palestine. Szold was flattered by Brandeis's praise, but in her reply she dismissed it as stemming from "nothing more nor less than the fact that my monthly check comes to me from no one knows where" rather than weighing on the public purse, since she knew that Brandeis valued frugality and respect for public funds. She also observed, somewhat cynically, that the more idealistic men are in their profession, the greater their rivalry tends to be in chasing after "necessaries and luxuries." She added that she seemed to be the only one able to stand quietly by, without envy, while the rest crowded and jostled one another.[70]

Szold was disappointed by the moral atmosphere within the social and political system in Palestine. In that same letter to her sister she wrote, "I don't know whether I ever succeeded in making you understand the mixture of *idealism and materialism* which, to my mind, is the chief characteristic of Palestine life—of Jewish Palestine life. So far as I have the opportunity of judging, British life is compounded wholly of materialism. The British officials, I fancy, would hardly deny that they are here for a career. And as for the Arabs, they hardly know what public spirit means. Zionism has opened political vistas to them. Their political aspirations are the only manifestations of public spirit which I have noted. They have no voluntary associations of any kind for public purposes—no libraries, no hospitals, no schools of their own that amount to anything. They have only clubs, which, ostensibly social, serve political ends."[71]

Szold's mood was dark around this time. Her thoughts frequently went to Wisconsin, where her sister Rachel—the person dearest to her in the whole world—was terminally ill. She was also troubled by the problematic relations between Hadassah and the leaders of the Zionist Organization of America. In a letter she sent to her sister Adele, she told her that Rose Jacobs (one of the leaders of Hadassah) had been seeking to hasten Szold's return to America.[72] She was fully aware of the danger Hadassah faced, and feared that organization might fall victim to power struggles within the Zionist Organization. Before long, Henrietta found herself in the very thick of that struggle.

11

BETWEEN TWO WORLDS

"Until now the entire Zionist Organization has been fiddling while Jerusalem was burning," Chaim Weizmann complained, referring to his opponents in the ZOA and to Justice Louis Brandeis in particular.[1] The conflict between Weizmann and Brandeis had been in the air since 1919, and flared up again the following summer. The two disagreed on the correct approach to rehabilitation and future development in Palestine. Brandeis advocated the large-scale investment of private capital under public supervision, while Weizmann favored the Keren Hayesod—a public fund for the economic development of the Yishuv in Palestine, to be administered by the Zionist Organization under Weizmann's own leadership.

The decisions made at the San Remo Conference and the appointment of Herbert Samuel as the first high commissioner for Palestine seemed to present a rare opportunity for the realization of the Zionist dream of Jewish return to the Land of Israel and the immediate establishment of a sovereign political entity there. Weizmann spoke of the need to raise £25 million. To address this issue, the leaders of the international Zionist Organization had convened in London in July 1920—including, for the first time, representatives of the Zionist Organization of America. The American group numbered some forty delegates and was headed by Louis Brandeis. The delegates included ZOA president Julian Mack, Rabbi Stephen Wise, Felix Frankfurter, and other eminent American Zionists.

Brandeis was elected conference chairman, and his position regarding the development of infrastructure in Palestine was approved by majority decision. Weizmann was particularly offended because the decision had been made in London, his home ground. He later said, "I will never forget that meeting." The dispute between the two leaders delayed fundraising in the United States—the Yishuv's primary source of support. Weizmann appealed to Felix Frankfurter, who was close to Brandeis, for help: "You have the assurance of the Palestine administration, in principle. It is up to the [American] Jews to say what they are prepared to do."[2]

The rifts within the Zionist Organization deepened, and Szold followed the conflict between Weizmann and Brandeis with concern. She was fully immersed in her work in Palestine but kept an anxious eye on events in America. She feared that Hadassah would suffer the consequences of this turmoil—a fear that soon became an alarming reality.

Weizmann placed great stock in his ties with wealthy and influential figures in America, because they possessed the resources that the Zionist movement so desperately needed. In 1921, he traveled to the United States to try to placate Brandeis and find a way to the hearts of his wealthy supporters. Brandeis, however, refused to meet with Weizmann, and the American Jewish financial elite, including magnates like Jacob Schiff, stood by Brandeis. Most were not Zionists but would donate to the Zionist cause if asked to do so by Brandeis.

The divergence between the American-born Brandeis and the Russian-born Weizmann stemmed from differences in both outlook and upbringing. There was a marked difference in approach between Eastern European and American Jews. The Americans considered the Russians wasteful and inefficient in their management of the funds raised for Palestine, while Weizmann and his supporters asserted that they had no intention of submitting a detailed report for every dollar they spent, an assertion that was blasphemy to Brandeis and those around him. Szold identified with Brandeis's position and had always accounted for every dollar spent at the school for immigrants, Hadassah, and the other projects she had directed, meticulously registering all funds received and submitting detailed reports of all expenditures. Brandeis and Weizmann also differed in their respective commitments to the movement. Weizmann and other veteran leaders dedicated all of their time to Zionist affairs, while Brandeis and his associates also engaged in activities outside the movement.[3]

Lipsky, who had admired Brandeis a few years earlier, turned his back on him and aligned himself with Weizmann, as did a number of other American Zionist activists, including Abe Goldberg and Emanuel Neumann. The Weizmann camp carried the vote at the annual convention of the ZOA, defeating Brandeis on his home ground.[4] It was a pyrrhic victory, however. Brandeis submitted his resignation as honorary president, and his supporters, including Judge Mack, resigned from their positions in the ZOA and the international Zionist Organization. Brandeis and his associates began to focus their efforts on rehabilitation of the Yishuv through a new organization they established, the Palestine Economic Corporation (PEC).[5] The rift in the Zionist Organization and the resignations of Brandeis and his associates caused a sharp decline in ZOA membership and revenue.

Weizmann's supporters elected Lipsky general secretary of the ZOA, and he was placed in charge of fundraising for Keren Hayesod. Donations to Keren Hayesod failed to materialize, despite Lipsky's best efforts.[6] He decided to canvass the thousands of members of Hadassah, believing they would be an easy target, but he could not force them to donate. He did demand that the women who worked in the Hadassah office give to Keren Hayesod, threatening to fire them if they didn't. His efforts to raise money in other public circles floundered. The shortage of funds hampered efforts to increase immigration and exposed the weakness of the Zionist movement. The rivalry between the two camps intensified.

Szold was well aware of the urgent need to rehabilitate the Yishuv and to further its development, in order to facilitate the absorption of Jewish immigrants and promote the building of the national home. Nevertheless, she refrained from intervening, even at the height of the controversy. Many, however, knew of her ties to Brandeis, and especially of her relationship with Julian Mack, who was one of her closest friends. She feared that Lipsky would try to get back at her through Hadassah. She came up with a solution that managed, once again, to surprise her friends and family.

Szold informed the Hadassah central committee that she wished to resign as president of the organization—a position she had held since its founding, and continued to hold while in Palestine. She suggested that they elect a new president in her place. They chose Alice Seligsberg, who had recently returned to the United States, and Szold was elected honorary president. Her hope that her resignation would protect Hadassah proved false, however. The members of the central committee followed Szold's lead and tried to maintain neutrality in the dispute between Brandeis and Weizmann, seeking to sidestep the points of contention within the Zionist Organization. However, Szold's refusal to openly take sides was also liable to offend those who had expected her support, and trying to keep all options open was no simple task. Szold reached the drastic conclusion that Hadassah needed to seek independence from the ZOA.

The Hadassah leadership supported this position. Louis Lipsky, however, had no intention of losing the most important organization within the ZOA, and did all he could to prevent it. He believed that Brandeis and Mack were behind the whole thing.[7] Stubborn and unwilling to let go, Lipsky was determined to gain complete control over Hadassah, its revenues, and its assets. In June and July 1921, there was a tense exchange of letters between Lipsky and the Hadassah central committee. Lipsky informed the Hadassah committee members that should they refuse to accept the authority of the ZOA, they would be dismissed.[8] Szold argued that the ZOA had neither the legal nor moral authority to fire the directors of Hadassah, as they had been elected by thousands of Hadassah members throughout the country, in keeping with the organization's constitution. Hadassah informed Lipsky that its main concern at that time was the ongoing work of the medical unit in Palestine, which it had funded and would continue to fund. Lipsky again threatened to fire the Hadassah leaders and expel them from the ZOA. He notified the Hadassah central committee that he had decided to dismiss its members, for causing factional conflict, and sent letters of dismissal to all the committee members.[9]

Szold was no stranger to conflict, but this one—a battle for Hadassah's continued existence—was especially bitter, and she was determined to fight with all her might for the organization that was so dear to her heart. The members of the central committee embraced Szold's determination and decided to struggle alongside her with every means at their disposal. With this end in mind, they engaged the services of attorney L. Seligsberg.[10] Minnie Sobel and the other six members of the central committee decided to make a stand. They rented a new office at 31 Union Square, in Manhattan, and sent their new address to all of the Hadassah chapters. The letters were sent on official Hadassah stationery, on which the names of the members of the central committee were listed, along with that of Henrietta Szold as president. This led to a direct confrontation between the ZOA and the Hadassah leadership.

The members of the central committee knew that the thousands of Hadassah members, especially the chapter presidents, who were familiar with and admired Szold, would not cooperate with a leadership imposed from the outside. For a time Lipsky kept up his attacks, threatening legal action against Sobel and the other women.[11] But he suddenly changed his tone, becoming far less aggressive, although he had not changed his mind.

Then came the turning point. The members of the ZOA executive committee, who had been following the embarrassing exchange, decided it was time to put a stop to the fighting between Lipsky and Hadassah— fighting that was undignified and unworthy of the movement—and to reach an agreement with Hadassah. They proposed that Hadassah continue to operate as an independent organization and devote its efforts to supporting the medical unit, the nursing school, and its other projects. In return, they asked that Hadassah not openly challenge the ZOA. The proposal was signed not by Lipsky but by administrative committee member Morris Rothenberg. Since Hadassah's position had been accepted in its entirety, its central committee decided to approve the ZOA proposal. Rothenberg expressed satisfaction with the agreement and sent the central committee a polite and conciliatory letter thanking its members for their goodwill and for their willingness to cooperate with the ZOA, pledging that they would receive any assistance they might need. He concluded his letter by expressing his appreciation and admiration for Hadassah's important achievements, "for the sake of the goal we all hold dear."[12]

Throughout the summer in which the conflict between Hadassah and the ZOA took place, Szold, who was still in Palestine, was involved behind the scenes. Her associates in Hadassah consulted her every step of the way. When the agreement between Hadassah and the ZOA was finally concluded, Szold was relieved. She had gotten what she wanted: the independence to continue the organization's activities as before, under its original name, with full control of its funds and assets—crucial for the realization of its plans. Szold greatly appreciated her colleagues' actions in working together with her to fend off the attacks against Hadassah and the attempts to steal the organization from them. Beyond the achievement of preserving Hadassah's autonomy, Szold and the members of the central committee derived great satisfaction from the fact that they had not allowed themselves to be strong-armed. They had proved that they were not the weak side in the dispute and, in standing their ground, had achieved what they rightly deserved. Their success would have a significant impact on the challenges ahead, and it would also serve as an example for other women. Even as all of this unfolded, Szold continued to pursue all of her activities in Palestine—in the healthcare system, the hygiene department, and the nursing school—while attending weekly meetings of the medical unit administration, of which she was a member.[13]

Amid all of the turmoil, Szold also had moments of satisfaction. One such moment was the graduation ceremony of the Hadassah Nurses' Training School's first class, on December 3, 1921. Szold, who was in charge of the school and whose brainchild it had been, made every effort to attend to the students' needs. She knew each and every one of them personally, and they would come to her with their problems, which she would do her best to help resolve. Szold was moved by the sight of these young women, who had completed their studies and were about to

The first group of graduate nurses, with Henrietta Szold at center

go out into the world. The graduation was a festive event, attended by many illustrious figures. The wife of the high commissioner, Beatrice Samuel, presented the diplomas to the twenty-two graduates. Speeches were made by Anna Kaplan, director of the Nurses' Training School, and David Eider, on behalf of the Zionist Commission, while the keynote address was given by Szold herself. Most of the graduates found positions within Hadassah, after the nurses who had come to Palestine with the medical unit returned to the United States.

TRAPPED

To Szold's mind, the immediate challenge remained the struggle against severe disease, which she had observed on her first trip to Palestine, when four out of every five infants died. Szold wanted to turn things around, ensuring that four out of every five infants survived, and believed such a revolution was possible. "Great work could be done in Palestine, if only it had a leader," she wrote. She sought a physician of stature, someone capable of leading such a project and of dedicating the necessary time and energy to developing a prevention-based healthcare system for the Yishuv. Her efforts to find such a person, however, failed time after time, and she was forced to remain in Palestine to oversee the growing healthcare system. At the same time, Szold continued to keep an eye on Hadassah's affairs in America.

Some two years had passed since she had left the United States, and her plans to return were constantly postponed. She felt trapped. She knew from the start that the task she was undertaking was a very complex one, requiring simultaneous and concerted effort in two countries geographically distant from each other. She had initially thought that she would be able to return to the United States from time to time, as needed. To her dismay, she found herself unable to leave Palestine, and longed for the moment she would be able to set sail for America. She had to cancel her plan to attend the September 1921 Zionist Congress, held at Carlsbad, and to proceed from there to America. Rubinow went to the congress, and in his absence, responsibility for the medical unit fell once again to Szold, making it impossible for her to leave. The medical unit had just completed three years of activity, and most of the original doctors and nurses had returned to the United States. Rubinow too had decided to go back to America in 1922; Szold tried to convince him to stay, but he refused. On the eve of his departure, Rubinow remarked that he had made far more enemies than friends during his time in Palestine—both among the medical unit staff and among the Zionist leadership, for having put the needs of the patients above those of the unit's employees, and among the "outside medical men," for having insisted that the unit's physicians have no private practice. "So I have not made many friends, did not get much gratitude. . . . But I hope you will believe me if I say that my thoughts will always be with Palestine."[14]

A heavy burden of responsibility rested on Szold's shoulders: running Hadassah and all its operations—twelve institutions, hospitals, health centers, and clinics throughout the country—with a staff of six hundred people and a budget of over half a million dollars. Her days began at dawn, and when she returned home in the evening, the correspondence and reports that piled up on her desk kept her busy well into the night. Only after midnight was she able to write personal letters to friends and family. Szold had no choice but to remain in Palestine and impatiently await the arrival of a permanent replacement for Rubinow as director of the medical unit and relieve her of the onerous burden she carried.

BEYOND HER HEALTHCARE WORK, Szold was always open to new initiatives. One day, Yeshayahu Press, principal of a girls' school in the Old City of Jerusalem, came to her office.[15] He told her that many of the families of the girls at his school suffered from malnutrition, and the girls themselves experienced weakness and fatigue from hunger—at times even fainting in class—that affected their ability to concentrate on their studies. He asked Szold if she could provide the girls with nutritious lunches at school. There was no need to explain to Szold the importance of good childhood nutrition, a cause she supported with all her heart, but she could not accede to Press's request that she fund the project, as Hadassah's finances precluded allocating funds for this purpose. But she promised that she would try to help.

In a fortunate coincidence, Rabbi Dr. Maurice Harris, an educator at Temple Israel in New York, was visiting Palestine at the time, and came to see Szold. He told her that his students had collected "Chanukah *gelt*" (money of Chanukah) for the children in Palestine, without any specific goal or recipient in mind. Szold suggested that he give the money to help pay for lunches for the girls at Press's school. She explained to Harris that there were other schools in Jerusalem and elsewhere in the country where the children were also in need of nutritious lunches, as their families were very poor. Harris was enthusiastic about the idea and promised that upon his return to America, he would raise funds to help feed the schoolchildren in Palestine. True to his word, once back in the United States, he organized a committee that founded the Children's Palestine Fund, which aimed to raise money to feed the children of the Yishuv. Szold was pleased to see that this nutrition project was adopted by Jewish children in America. [16]

Szold had a reputation in America as a public figure who had dedicated her life to the Yishuv. She received appeals and requests of all kinds—including some rather odd ones. A woman from New York wrote to Szold asking her to find out whom her daughter Esther was spending her time with in Jerusalem. She had heard that her Esther, a strikingly beautiful eighteen-year-old, was seeing a man twenty years her senior, and asked Szold to try to convince the girl to end the relationship. Szold invited Esther to her home and asked her about the man she was seeing. Esther told her the man in question was the painter Reuven Rubin—the most famous artist in Palestine, and an acquaintance of Szold's. When she discovered that Esther was in love with him and wished to marry him, Szold told the young woman to follow her heart. [17] Most of the appeals Szold received, however, pertained to her own areas of activity. She was known not only for her actions in the field of healthcare, but also as a kind of patron for initiatives of various kinds. Those who approached her with proposals, asking for her blessing and her help, knew that she was unrivaled in her ability to get things done. She had become a one-person institution.

In the nutrition program, for example, Szold stressed the importance of teaching the children nutritional principles as well as cooking, setting the table, and table manners. Szold decided that the families would be asked to pay a nominal fee for the school lunches, in order to avoid the feeling that they were receiving charity. Those who could not afford even that small fee were exempted. She suggested that children as young as kindergarten age be taught to participate in preparing the meals they ate at school. A contribution from the ESCO Foundation allowed Szold to provide schools with kitchens, even on the agricultural settlements.[18] In these kitchens, locally grown vegetables, fruit, and other produce, such as eggs, milk, and cheese, were used to teach the children how to prepare nutritious meals. Some parents objected to the cooking classes, claiming that they were a waste of school time. Szold expected the teachers to explain to the children the importance of studying nutrition and cooking at school, in the hope that they might, in turn, convince their parents.[19]

The program got under way in 1923. A kitchen was inaugurated at Yeshayahu Press's school, where lunch was prepared for the girls and they were taught the principles of a healthy diet. Young Hadassah, an organization founded in November 1920 by Hadassah in the United States for its younger members, joined the effort to expand the initiative to many other schools throughout the country. As she had always done in its parent organization, Szold sought to engage the members of Young Hadassah in specific projects they could support and follow. She believed that this would strengthen the personal connection between American Jews and Palestine. Within a few years, the program came to encompass most of the schools in the Yishuv. Of course, a country-wide network of school cafeterias demanded a large and regular source of funding, in order to ensure the continuity of the program. On Hadassah's instigation, both the Jewish National Council (JNC, a body comprising representatives of the Jewish political parties in Palestine) and the mandatory government lent their support to the initiative. The program, including cooking and nutrition education, was integrated into the school curriculum, and teachers were trained accordingly.

Szold knew that no single person could oversee so many large-scale projects. She therefore sought to engage others in all of her undertakings, both to share the burden of responsibility and to expand the circle of volunteers. It was more than just an organizational strategy. She considered involving as many people as possible in social programs a value in itself, promoting popular engagement in voluntary activity for the good of society as a whole.

DESPITE HER EXTENSIVE ACTIVITIES in Palestine, her accomplishments, and the great admiration she enjoyed, Szold was uneasy. She had left the United

States, but she had failed to find a true home in Palestine. She had never been fully accepted by the members of the Yishuv, many of whom were of Eastern European origin. Her management style was unconventional, as was the very fact that she was a woman in a position of authority. Many in the Yishuv resented her efforts to impose rigid and unfamiliar American standards on the working conditions and financial administration of the healthcare system in Palestine. The leaders of the labor movement accused her of medical imperialism. A similar view was taken by the Palestinian doctors who replaced the medical unit physicians who had gone back to America. On top of that, Szold was continually frustrated by the Hadassah doctors' repeated requests for higher salaries. She explained to them, time and again, that Hadassah was in financial straits, but to no avail. Her patience ran out. At one meeting with the doctors, she exploded, banging on the table and stamping her feet in anger.

Worn out by the disputes and frustrated with the situation in Palestine, Szold decided to return to America. The separation from her family also weighed on her. Citing her age, Szold informed her sisters that she intended to retire from the taxing work that had sapped her strength.[20]

Szold's desire to return to New York also stemmed from the need to protect Hadassah, which remained under constant threat. The leaders of Hadassah in the United States were pressing her to return. They had successfully stood up to Lipsky's attempts to take control of Hadassah, but they feared the future: Lipsky's joining the Weizmann camp and the "Weizmannite" takeover of the ZOA did not bode well.

In the summer of 1922, she decided that the time was ripe for her to return to the United States. She asked Rubinow to return to Palestine for a short while, to run the Hadassah Medical Organization (HMO), as the medical unit was now called, and he agreed. After an absence of six months, Rubinow discovered, to his surprise, that a woman with no background in hospital administration or medicine had done an exemplary job running all of Hadassah's medical activities in the country.[21]

In August 1922, Szold left for Europe, to attend that year's conference of the Zionist General Council (ZGC), again held in Carlsbad. En route, she stopped in Vienna to visit with relatives. She saw her cousins, most of whom had been successful in their professions and were well-to-do. Some were assimilated and had married non-Jews, for which she was sorry.[22] After the ZGC conference, Szold had intended to continue directly to the United States, but she received a number of urgent telegrams from Rubinow describing Hadassah's grave financial situation and asking her to travel immediately to Paris to meet with Baron de Rothschild, to persuade him to support the HMO. After she arrived in Paris on September 30, she went to see Rothschild. She was struck by the opulence of his palace—the paintings by famous artists and the rich tapestries that hung in the entrance hall and along the stairs, the baron's mahogany-lined office and its art treasures, and the carefully tended gardens outside. The seventy-seven-year-old baron cut an impressive figure, and he received her with courtesy and respect. She presented her request, certain he would agree to help. Instead, he criticized Americans who came to him for money when there were magnates and bankers in the United States whose businesses spanned the American continent. Szold later wrote that he had told her "go to America and tell the Guggenheims and the Blumenthals and the Warburgs to do their duty."[23]

Szold had planned to proceed from Paris to New York, but Rubinow implored her to return to Palestine. He wrote that he had agreed to replace her for a short time only and was unwilling to extend his stay any further. With little choice, she left Paris and boarded a ship back to Palestine. During the voyage, she struggled to think of a way to resolve Hadassah's financial difficulties. She hoped that the Joint Distribution Committee would increase its contribution to Hadassah, and that other organizations would follow suit. Szold felt that it was beyond her capabilities to deal with fundraising as well as the administration of the medical unit: "It is too much for a woman of my age and disposition to face. I am not ashamed to admit that I am a coward about it. Perhaps I may still have to do what I felt like doing in Paris—decamp to America and you." Szold explained to her sisters that her ability to come to the United States on a short visit was also affected by the fact that she was unmarried and therefore not entitled to the benefits Hadassah afforded to married women serving in Palestine, including paid visits to the United States to see their husbands and children.[24] Szold did not have the money to pay for such a trip herself.

Szold returned to Palestine from Paris on November 1, 1922. She traveled around the country to evaluate the state of Hadassah and found a "sinking ship," as Rubinow put it: a healthcare system that had shrunk beyond recognition. Rubinow had made drastic cuts, closing the hospital in Tiberias and reducing the number of beds in the Jaffa hospital by 12 percent. Hadassah's vehicles were no longer being used, the clinic in the Old City of Jerusalem had been closed, and the doctors' salaries for the months of September and October had not been paid.[25] Szold managed to convince Nathan Straus to pledge $20,000 to help prevent Hadassah from collapsing, but it was not enough. She wished that Keren Hayesod would pay its debt to the organization; it had been stipulated at the time of its establishment as the ZOA's only fund that Hadassah would be given a share of any money it raised. Knowing how poorly Keren Hayesod was run, however, Szold understood that Hadassah would never see a cent from the fund. She described Keren Hayesod as an illusion. Szold hoped that salvation would come from the United States—to which end she needed to actively raise funds herself. But instead of setting about that task, she was forced to remain in Palestine.[26]

For Szold, there were gratifying moments as well, such as an invitation to help establish a welfare station in Haifa. The women behind the initiative sought to arouse public interest in the problems of poverty and disease and how they could be overcome. Szold promised the activists in Haifa that Hadassah would provide funding for lectures and would supply a nurse and a doctor for the welfare station. She was extremely pleased with the large number of people showing an interest in public medicine and welfare—as opposed to those who dismissed their importance.[27] The swelling ranks of volunteers willing to contribute to the public good warmed her heart. She also had the opportunity to enjoy the fruits of her labors, as the Nurses' Training School produced a second graduating class. But she was not always satisfied with the local-born nurses, meant to replace the American nurses who had returned to the United States. Influenced by the local doctors, they too demanded higher wages and improved working conditions. Over time, however, they came to appreciate Szold's work and her devotion to them. In any case, the graduation ceremony was a festive occasion, and many in attendance heaped praise on Szold. She in turn praised the nurses for their dedication to their work, remarking that they were particularly worthy of praise because they did not behave like the doctors.[28] Szold formed an association of graduates of the Nurses' Training School, including members of both graduating classes.

Judah Leib Magnes immigrated to Palestine with his family and settled in Jerusalem. Szold was happy to see her old friend and was among the first to visit his home. Magnes had heard of Szold's predicaments at work and offered his help. He would come to the office every day and discuss all of the problems she faced. Szold wrote that beyond the invaluable professional assistance he provided, she delighted in his company and in that of his wife and children.[29]

On her birthday, Szold's friends convinced her to take a break from work. She went to Jericho with a few friends, and Herbert Samuel offered them the use of his holiday residence there. They stayed for two days and toured the charming city. It was not easy for Szold to return to the routine of long and arduous workdays, but hardest of all was the news she had received that her sister Rachel was to be operated on. She was deeply worried and

Dr. Judah Leib Magnes,
chancellor of Hebrew
University 1925–1934

would very much have liked to be at Rachel's side, but she had to remain in Palestine, at the helm of Hadassah. She longed for the appointment of a new director of the HMO. Three years' absence seemed like an eternity to her.

In the United States, negotiations had been successfully concluded with Dr. Shimon Meshulam Tannenbaum, who had agreed to take Rubinow's place as director of the HMO. Szold, who wanted to see her sister Rachel as soon as possible, asked Magnes to replace her until Tannenbaum's arrival. Magnes agreed, and she left for America.

BETWEEN TWO WORLDS

Szold was eager to get to the United States as quickly as possible, but at that time, the trip from Palestine to America took three to four weeks. She documented the journey in her diary. On March 30, 1923, she left Jerusalem for Jaffa, where she boarded a train for Alexandria. On April 7, she set sail for Mauritania and then Cherbourg, and from there she boarded a ship to the United States, arriving in New York on April 23.[30] She would follow the same route on her return to Palestine.

In New York, she stayed at the Alexandria Hotel. No sooner did she arrive than she left her things at the hotel and rushed to Wisconsin to see Rachel. Her heart broke to see her sister suffering. The doctor had told Rachel that he hoped she would recover, but at the sight of her pale face and swollen body, Henrietta understood that her situation was grave. Henrietta tried to raise her sister's spirits but wept for her in her heart. Rachel and her husband, Joe, had been unable to have biological children, so they had adopted two children a number of years earlier, moved to a new house, and opened a new chapter in their lives. When her malignant illness struck, their world came crashing down around them.

Henrietta's other sisters had also experienced hardship in recent years. Bertha's husband, Louis, had passed away, leaving her with five children. Even Adele, who had always been a very private person, wrote to Henrietta of her failing marriage. She was clearly depressed, and looked to Henrietta for support. Henrietta, who was a sort of matriarch to her sisters, did not know whom to help first. She regretted not being able to do more for them. All she could offer was emotional support, and even that was difficult for her, due to the constraints on her time.

Szold's schedule in America was extremely demanding. The Hadassah leadership needed her to fend off opponents, strengthen the organization and its standing, and above all to raise money. The US economy was booming, and they wanted to increase the number of chapters, recruit new members, and raise more money for Hadassah's activities in Palestine, which faced rising costs and shrinking resources. They sought to strengthen Hadassah politically as well, and in particular to remove it from the authority of the ZOA, which was in deep crisis and eyed Hadassah with envy, once again plotting to incorporate it into the umbrella organization. The members of Hadassah's executive committee had faith in Szold's ability to deal with the complex tasks they faced. In that same year, Alice Seligsberg completed her term as Hadassah president, and in 1923 Szold was elected to the role for the second time. Her commitment and sense of responsibility toward the organization grew even further. Szold embarked on a nationwide campaign to boost both membership and fundraising. However, just as she worried about events in America when she was in Palestine, she was now troubled by the difficulties of the HMO in Palestine.

From this point on, Szold would go back and forth between America and Palestine. Every voyage—there were sometimes two or even three a year—meant spending a considerable amount of time on trains and ships. In some years, she spent up to five months at sea. It comes as no surprise that Szold once quipped, "For me apparently there will be no salvation but to live on the ocean between America and Palestine."[31]

Dr. Tannenbaum, who had replaced Rubinow as head of the HMO, did not adjust to life in Palestine and went back to America after only one year. The local doctor who replaced him also resigned before long, citing poor health. Both doctors were overwhelmed by the job. Szold followed these developments with great concern, as the organization's situation in Palestine continued to deteriorate. A long-term replacement was sought in America, but in the meantime, the HMO remained without a director. After seven long months of intensive efforts, Szold was forced to interrupt her work in the United States and return to Palestine. Every minute was precious, and she made no stops along the way, arriving in Jerusalem on December 19, 1923.[32]

During the course of her journeys back and forth, she decided to give up her house in Jerusalem and stay instead in a hotel. Sophia Berger had gotten married, and Szold could not afford to keep the house on her own, nor did she wish to live there alone. She also lacked the strength to look for an apartment, considering all of the other challenges she faced. She chose to stay at the Eden Hotel, at the corner of Hahistadrut and Hillel, until things quieted down a little. Meanwhile, Szold was happy to hear that a suitable candidate for the position of director had been found in New York: Dr. Ephraim Bluestone from Mount Sinai Hospital.

After the rapid succession of directors, Szold wanted to ensure that the new director of the HMO would show more perseverance. She left Jerusalem in April 1924 and met with Bluestone in New York. She was impressed by him and believed he would last in Palestine. It was agreed that he would leave for Palestine as soon as possible, and remain as director of Hadassah for at least three years. Bluestone, a committed Zionist, believed that the problems with the country's healthcare system could be resolved—and he made every effort to do so, despite the numerous obstacles he faced. He was particularly troubled by the constant disputes among the doctors and between the doctors and the Hadassah administration, but he remained at his post for three years, as he had promised.

There was no improvement in the ZOA's financial situation. Keren Hayesod's revenues were down, and the crisis only worsened in 1923. The fundraising campaign in Europe was also a complete failure. Arthur Ruppin, who visited America, could not believe that Keren Hayesod was incapable of meeting its obligations to its own partners. Repeated deficits were covered with bank loans. The fund did not even have enough money to pay for its own fundraising drive in New York, which was supposed to bring in half of its annual revenue.[33] Keren Hayesod was poorly run, its organizational apparatus bloated and inefficient, with high salaries and expenses swallowing much of its meager revenue.

Keren Hayesod's failure was blamed on Louis Lipsky, who was in charge of fundraising. The more he failed at this task, the greater became his desire to force Hadassah to submit to his authority. He tried again in 1923, as he had in 1921, to seize control of Hadassah's organizational apparatus (made up entirely of volunteers) and to appropriate its coffers for Keren Hayesod. The Hadassah leadership was compelled once again to defend the organization's independence. Szold was charged with the task of opposing Lipsky, who would stop at nothing to save his declining reputation and standing at the ZOA. Szold's renewed tenure as president of Hadassah required that she spend more time in the United States than she had previously done.

Weizmann met with Julian Mack, Louis Brandeis, Jacob Schiff, and others in an effort to reestablish rapport with them. A number of wealthy individuals had already begun to donate money to support the Yishuv, although they themselves did not identify as Zionists. Weizmann returned to America a few months later, to attend a joint conference in February 1924 of Zionist and non-Zionist Jews at the Astor Hotel in New York. Louis Marshall chaired the conference; Brandeis and Mack were absent. Also in attendance were rabbis who had previously refused to cooperate with the Zionists. The conference aimed to find ways in which the non-Zionists might agree to support the Yishuv in Palestine. Discussions would drag on for another five years.

While Szold was in the United States in 1925, a number of organizations changed their fundraising approach. The JDC launched a three-year fundraising plan, with a goal of $15 million. The ZOA, fearing that its own fundraising efforts would suffer as a result, proposed that the prominent Zionist organizations—the Jewish National Fund (JNF), the Hebrew University Fund, the Mizrachi Fund, and Hadassah—conduct a joint campaign with Keren Hayesod, to be called the United Palestine Appeal (UPA). All of the organizations agreed to the ZOA proposal, with the exception of Hadassah, which made its participation contingent upon certain guarantees. Neumann, who observed the developments, remarked that the women of Hadassah had been the hardest nut to crack, as they had been extremely cautious. They had demanded a guarantee that they would receive an amount equal to the sum their own campaign had raised the previous year, as a first charge on the revenue of the joint appeal. The members of the UPA had little choice in the matter, and thus agreed to Hadassah's conditions.[34] Hadassah also stipulated an addendum to the agreement demanding recognition as the sole Zionist women's organization in the United States, precluding any further attempts to sow discord within Hadassah or to establish another Zionist women's organization alongside it. Lipsky, who had been humiliated in his previous dealings with Hadassah, agreed to this demand, expressing his hope that the agreement would serve to further the friendly relationship existing between the two organizations.[35]

Szold went to Palestine in September 1925, to check on the HMO. Satisfied with Bluestone's administration, she returned to America two months later.[36] She was eager to get back to the United States in order to oversee implementation of the UPA agreement, in accordance with the arrangement reached with Hadassah. She traveled to Palestine once again in March 1926, but she was uneasy.[37] Her thoughts constantly strayed to America, where her sister Rachel was on her deathbed. Szold's friend Sophia Berger tried to distract her, suggesting they visit Ramallah on the holiday of Shavuot to see the wheat harvest. The Arab women in their traditional dress, carrying sheaves of wheat, evoked for Henrietta images of Ruth and Naomi, transporting her back through the millennia. Despite the welcome diversion, she could not stop thinking of her sister. After only three months in Palestine, she headed back to America. She arrived in New York in August and immediately went to see Rachel, whose condition had worsened considerably. As she sat by Rachel's bedside, she felt powerless, unable to help the dearest person to her in the whole world. A few weeks later, Rachel passed away.[38]

The death was traumatic for Henrietta. Rachel had been her strongest connection to America—a beloved sister and her most devoted friend, who had always encouraged her, supported her, advised her, and helped her through all of her difficulties and doubts over the years. Henrietta was also very attached to Adele and Bertha, but they were much younger than she was and had not been a part of her life since childhood, as Rachel had. Grieving deeply, she withdrew even from her closest friends. Everything seemed empty and pointless. When Alexander and Anna Marx invited her to a celebration in honor of their son Jacob, she sent her regrets: "I am not yet in the tranquil mood to rejoice in an assemblage even with you."[39] Szold decided to resign as president of Hadassah; Irma Lindheim was elected in her place.[40]

Szold's health deteriorated, and her doctor had her undergo a series of tests to find the source of her weakness. A few weeks later, although her health had not improved, she chose to return to Palestine. She found no rest during the voyage. When she arrived in Jerusalem, in late February

Szold speaks at the cornerstone-laying ceremony for the Straus Health Center in
Tel Aviv, 1927

1927, she felt a little better, but remained dispirited and anxious. She seemed
ready to conclude her life's work and withdraw from everything. She decided to write a will. Her possessions were few and modest: two bookcases
and a few personal items, which she left to her sisters.[41]

IT WAS NOT LONG, however, before Szold was recalled to action. Magnes asked
for her help, and she could not say no. He needed her help in planning the
cornerstone-laying ceremony for the Straus Health Center in Tel Aviv. He
had organized the ceremony himself but had encountered numerous obstacles. The high commissioner, who had been invited to speak, asked that
the ceremony be as brief as possible. Magnes therefore sought to limit the
number of speakers, but he felt he could not leave out any of the institutions and authorities. Apart from the high commissioner, he had asked the
mayor of Tel Aviv to speak, as well as the head of the mandatory health
department, the American consul, and Nathan Straus, who had donated
the money to build the center. Magnes asked Szold to preside over the ceremony, and she found herself in the eye of the storm. As the list of speakers
grew longer, Magnes decided that Szold, who was a member of the ZGC,
would also represent the Zionist Executive, but the Zionist Executive insisted on sending its own representative to the ceremony. Other officials

had also asked to speak, and in the interest of saving time, it was decided not to translate the speeches into English—a lacuna for which Szold would apologize at the beginning of the ceremony.[42] She was amazed at the mad rush for the slightest honor and at the pettiness of the various apparatchiks—two of the most appalling and frustrating phenomena she had encountered in Palestine.

While in Palestine, she observed the tensions between Hadassah and the directors of the Histadrut (General Federation of Jewish Workers in Palestine) sick fund, who demanded that Hadassah provide all of the funding for their clinics, even while insisting on maintaining complete autonomy with regard to planning and organization—a demand that was politically motivated. Though Szold had hoped to scale back her activities, she found herself on the front lines, unable to stand idly by, as a social and economic crisis that had been building in Palestine reached its height and threatened to destroy all of Hadassah's achievements.

PROSPERITY AND CRISIS

During the years in which Szold traveled back and forth to America, the Yishuv experienced a profound change. Prior to 1924, there was a severe economic crisis in Palestine: the Zionist movement's budget was at an all-time low and its institutions lacked the means to help the Yishuv, bringing the community's development to a standstill. Unemployment increased, and the general atmosphere was one of disappointment and despair. Immigration fell, and emigration rose. The situation changed dramatically in 1924, however, with the arrival of a new wave of immigrants: the Fourth Aliyah.

Most of these immigrants were from Poland, as a result of the policies enacted by the Polish prime minister and finance minister, Władysław Grabski, to stabilize the country's economy and currency. Urban commercial interests in Poland were affected by high taxes, the concentration of credit at the state banks, and the loss of Russian markets. Many Jews thus decided to emigrate and, in light of new restrictions on immigration to the United States enacted in 1924, looked to Palestine. Some called it the "Grabski Aliyah." Most of the immigrants were members of the lower middle class—shopkeepers, artisans, middlemen, and small-scale manufacturers. Only a small number were wealthy merchants or industrialists. The wave also included immigrants from Central Europe and other regions, but the Polish group was by far the largest and most influential.

In the years 1924–1925, 55,000 Jewish immigrants arrived in Palestine—34,000 in 1925 alone—and tens of thousands more were expected.

The atmosphere in the Yishuv was euphoric. At times it seemed like the entirety of the Jewish people was coming to Palestine en masse. There was a construction boom, and a number of factories—such as the Lodzia textile factory, named for the Polish city of Łódź—were established. Word of the Yishuv's fast-developing economy spread throughout Eastern Europe. The Jews in Poland were astounded by the news from Palestine: "Aliyah [Jewish immigration to Palestine] is a topic of conversation everywhere. The Jews of the region are beating a path to our Palestine Office, while prominent public figures are discussing the purchase of land and sending delegations to Palestine to that end."[43]

Most of the new immigrants settled in the cities, particularly in Tel Aviv. Contrary to previous waves of immigrants, these new arrivals were not interested in agricultural work. The demand for land in the city increased, as did the demand for construction workers, and Tel Aviv experienced a period of rapid growth. Factories, shops, and department stores were opened, and there was a sense of optimism and prosperity in the air. The Fourth Aliyah increased the population of Tel Aviv almost fourfold. According to census data, the city's inhabitants numbered 15,000 in 1922. From mid-1924 to early 1926, an unprecedented wave of over 40,000 immigrants arrived in the city. Investment in construction in Tel Aviv increased fivefold, as compared to the previous year, and the future looked bright.

Before long, however, everything ground to a halt. People with little capital of their own had taken out loans, often at high interest rates, to invest in construction and industry. When they were unable to meet their financial obligations, their workers and suppliers were dragged down with them. By late 1925, unemployment had begun to rise, and it quickly doubled. In 1926, the wave of immigration ended, and capital stopped flowing. The following year saw a full-blown crisis, which continued into 1928. Construction came to a standstill and the purchase of building lots slowed to a trickle, eventually ceasing altogether. Many of the workshops and factories failed, and commerce suffered. People withdrew their savings from the banks, and credit was restricted. A further deterioration of the situation in Poland made matters even worse: those who had counted on an influx of capital from that country were sorely disappointed. With the crisis in the construction industry, many workers—carpenters, glaziers, welders—lost their jobs. The Zionist movement as a whole had no cash reserves set aside for emergencies.

Misfortune seemed to come from all directions at once. In addition to the severe economic crisis, there was an outbreak of typhus in 1926, with nearly 30,000 people hospitalized in that year—and only a sixth of that number could be accommodated in government hospitals.[44] The prevailing mood among the recent immigrants was one of despair, and the number of immigrants in 1927–1928 plummeted to 2,000 per year, while the number of emigrants soared to 50,000.

The crisis was felt throughout the country. The education department was unable to pay its teachers, who consequently went on strike, shutting down all of the schools. Arthur Ruppin concluded: "Perhaps it needed this catastrophe, after a long period of illusion as to the absorptive capacity of Palestine, to teach us what Palestine can and can not do."[45] Weizmann remarked that "only heartless and irresponsible demagogues can, at this time, advocate unlimited immigration to Palestine."[46] Ironically, secretary of state for the colonies Winston Churchill's white paper of 1922, which had imposed restrictions on Jewish immigration to Palestine due to the country's limited absorptive capacity, arousing the Yishuv's ire, was now substantiated by the Zionist leaders themselves.

A desperate Weizmann wrote to Emanuel Neumann that teachers and other employees had not been paid for three months, that there were 8,000 unemployed, and that there was no money left to go on with the work. He explained that they were on the verge of bankruptcy, and that if the bills of the executive were not paid, there was no telling how far the disaster might go. "It is incredible that we should be broken," he wrote, "but I cannot see ahead at present," adding that he was "quite prepared to go down with the ship."[47]

AT ABOUT THE SAME TIME, Henrietta Szold was contacted by Siegfried Lehmann, a well-known physician and educator, asking for her help in transferring his orphanage from Berlin to Palestine. Szold had heard of Lehmann, the son of assimilated German Jews who had studied medicine and served as a doctor in the German army during the First World War. While in Eastern Europe, he encountered traditional Jews for the first time, and was introduced to Zionism.[48] He also observed dozens of orphans and abandoned children searching for food in the garbage and sleeping in stairwells. He founded a children's home for them, which he later moved to Berlin. Lehmann was praised for his educational methods and for his dedication to children. He had a circle of friends in Berlin who supported his work, providing the necessary funds for his orphanage. Szold agreed to help Lehmann and, through her connections with the British authorities in Palestine, obtained immigration certificates for him and for the children. They arrived in Palestine in 1927 and settled in the Lydda Valley, where Lehmann founded the Ben Shemen Youth Village.

Szold found little comfort in her public endeavors. She was no longer eager to travel to the United States, but she also failed to find her place in Palestine. After only three months in Jerusalem, she decided to return to America. She continued to work for the Zionist movement, stopping in London on her way to New York to attend a meeting of the executive committee of the Zionist Organization in April 1927, at which her fellow members of the Zionist Executive committee tried to convince her to take part in efforts to help the Yishuv overcome the crisis. She finally reached New York in mid-May.[49]

While Szold was back in New York, another unexpected disaster befell the Yishuv when in July 1927 a severe earthquake struck. The newspapers reported heavy losses in life and property: "Yesterday, at exactly seven minutes past three, the unsuspecting inhabitants of Jerusalem experienced a terrible earthquake the likes of which had not been felt in Jerusalem for many years. Even the oldest members of the community do not remember an earthquake as terrible and as strong as this, which lasted a number of seconds. The earthquake caused a great deal of damage in Jerusalem: houses were destroyed, people killed, and many injured. The earthquake also struck Safed and Tiberias and other places, causing extensive damage."[50]

Reports of the extent of the damage and the number of casualties reached Szold in New York. Her grief at the misfortunes that had befallen the Yishuv and its inhabitants combined with her profound personal grief for the death of her sister Rachel, and it was more than she could take. She felt unable to cope with all the challenges, and wished only to live out her days with her sisters in the United States. It never occurred to her that her greatest achievements still lay ahead, back in Palestine.

12

IN THE NATIONAL ARENA

*A*s SZOLD WAS CONSIDERING her next steps, she found herself courted by Weizmann's people, who sought to convince her to act in a new capacity. Weizmann himself asked her to join the Palestine Zionist Executive (also called the Jewish Agency Executive). She was wary of political activity, remarking, "My father raised me for Jewish scholarship. . . . I have often felt in all these years of Palestinian and Zionist work that my father would not have been satisfied with me."[1] Szold had been involved in Zionist activity for many years, but she had always focused on projects she considered essential at the time. When she thought of politics, she imagined endless discussions and arguments in smoke-filled rooms, and people who were stronger on speeches and meetings than on action. She knew that they wielded power, but she preferred to devote her own energy to meeting the real needs of society.

Above all, she felt that she must ensure the survival of the Hadassah Medical Organization in Palestine, at a time of severe economic crisis. She was thus compelled to resume her travels in order to secure the necessary funds for Hadassah. Paradoxically, this also meant that she had to appeal to those who held political power. Along the way, she became increasingly involved in the Zionist Organization, attending the meetings of its various institutional bodies.

In late April 1927, Szold took part in a meeting of the executive committee of the Zionist Organization, in London, after which she went on to New York. That summer, she returned to Europe to attend the Fifteenth Zionist Congress, in Basel.[2] At the congress, Szold was elected to the Palestine Zionist Executive, making her one of the international Zionist Organization's three representatives in Palestine. The other two were Harry Sacher and Colonel Frederick Kisch, both from Great Britain. Sacher was a solicitor and a Zionist leader close to Weizmann.[3] His wife, Miriam, was the daughter of Michael Marks and the sister of Lord Simon Marks, wealthy people prominent in the economic and social elite in Britain. Lord Israel Sieff was married to another one of Marks's daughters. Through his marriage to Miriam Marks, Sacher gained entry to the economic and social elite in Britain, many of whom were active Zionists. In 1918, Sacher had traveled to Palestine with the Zionist Commission, headed by Weizmann.

Kisch, a British officer and Cambridge graduate, had been born in India to a father who worked in the British colonial service. In his Zionist activities, Kisch was a Weizmann supporter. He was elected to the Palestine Zionist Executive (the Jewish Agency Executive) in 1922, and in the years 1929–1931 headed the political department of the Jewish Agency in Jerusalem.[4]

Szold was the first and only woman on the Zionist Executive. Unlike Sacher and Kisch, she was neither British nor a Weizmann supporter. Nevertheless, in light of her achievements and influence in the American Jewish community, Weizmann favored her appointment, in a bid to attract influential and wealthy members of Brandeis's camp. He knew that Brandeis's circle had the means to save the Zionist Organization from collapse, and Szold's friendship with Brandeis, Mack, and others was well known. After her appointment to the Zionist Executive, Szold wrote to her sisters: "The most disconcerting feature is that at this critical juncture the great Zionist movement had no one else to turn to but a tired, worn-out old woman of sixty-seven."[5]

In point of fact, she was not at all surprised, understanding full well why she had been chosen. Each of the three members of the executive was put in charge of one or two departments, and Szold was given education and health. The education system was in deep crisis. The coffers were empty, and there was no money to pay the teachers' salaries. An austerity plan had been drawn up, including the elimination of the eighth grade in all schools and the first year at teachers' colleges, as well as the closure of a number of schools. After not having been paid for seven months, teachers declared a national strike. Szold enjoyed a reputation as a successful fundraiser, and she knew the first task was to extricate the education department from its financial straits.

The teachers and principals did not welcome Szold's leadership. It was unusual for a woman to serve in a senior position in the Yishuv, and the men felt it was beneath their dignity to submit to her authority. Her accomplishments in the field of healthcare were relatively unknown among those who had not come into direct contact with her, and educators wondered what an American woman could do to further Hebrew education in Palestine. They saw her as a foreigner, unfamiliar with life in the Yishuv in general and its education system in particular. Szold ignored the atmosphere around her and got straight to work. She studied the proposals to reduce the deficit, such as closing schools and eliminating the eighth grade, and expressed firm opposition to them, believing that such cuts would be a fatal mistake for the future of education in the Yishuv.

Her first step was a fundraising trip to the United States, where she hoped to raise enough money to pay the teachers' salaries. She returned to Palestine three months later, in November 1927, with enough funds to save the education system from collapse. The teachers were paid and the strike ended. Szold did not like being treated simply as a fundraiser. She knew that the situation was difficult and money essential, but she did not see her role as limited to resolving the department's financial problems. The education system was dear to her heart, and she wished to strengthen and improve it. She invited Dr. Isaac Berkson, a well-known educator from the United States, to come to Palestine, and appointed him superintendent of the education department.[6] With Berkson's help, Szold hoped to reform the education system, improve administration and oversight, and formulate a coherent education policy for the coming years. She also planned to expand the types of educational programs offered. Harry Sacher wrote of Szold that "she squeezed forty-eight hours out of every day."[7]

Having resolved the most immediate financial crisis, that of the teachers' unpaid salaries, Szold was also responsible for safeguarding the stability of the education system in the future, ensuring that its financial needs—further increased by the reforms she sought to enact—would continue to be met. In her first year in charge of the department, she managed to obtain sufficient funds to balance the budget, with the help of Baron de Rothschild. In the following year, the department's deficit was covered by a donation from Young Hadassah in the United States. Szold was proud of what she had achieved. At a press conference in the offices of Keren Hayesod, Szold declared: "When the current Zionist Executive took office in October 1927, the teachers were owed four months' pay, in addition to an old debt from the Zionist executive in Palestine. They received their first salary in December and, to date [June 1928], all obligations toward them for the past five months [January–May] have been met. This has not been the situation for a number of years. Now we see that, despite various cuts effected here and there, the integrity of the education system has not been compromised, and the overall budget has increased from 112,000 to 115,000 Palestine pounds, as well as an additional budget of five thousand pounds for special roles."[8]

The education department budget for 1929 relied on a number of sources: the Zionist Executive in Palestine, the Jewish National Council, the mandatory government, and tuition paid by parents. Szold calculated that even if all of the bodies concerned were to live up to their commitments, the budget would still be 73,000 pounds short, simply to maintain the status quo. She was doubtful, however, that all of the promised sums would indeed arrive, as she was well aware of Keren Hayesod's shortcomings; in fact, Keren Hayesod had contributed absolutely nothing to the education budget in the preceding years, and she would be forced to find other sources of revenue. Ultimately, she managed to cover most of the operating costs for that year, amounting to 123,000 Palestine pounds, but she was not satisfied. The reforms she envisioned required thousands of pounds in additional resources.

Many marveled at Szold's fundraising abilities. She seemed to have a magic wand with which she was able to work wonders where others had failed. For those who knew her, it was no mystery. She enjoyed the trust and admiration of all her friends and acquaintances in America, including a number of very wealthy philanthropists. They knew that every dollar they contributed to a cause advocated by Szold would go directly to that cause, without cumbersome and wasteful bureaucracy. So when she asked for their help, they gave it willingly.

Szold continued to address the problems of the education system. In the name of efficient management, however, she unwittingly stepped on a landmine. She knew that she needed to reduce costs, but she did not want cuts to come at the expense of teaching hours, and thus looked for other solutions. Szold was unfamiliar with the Jewish education system in Palestine, which was divided into three separate streams: General, Religious (Mizrachi), and Labor. The latter two streams were controlled by political parties, and their curricula were developed in accordance with the parties' demands, in keeping with their respective ideologies. Szold visited schools throughout the country, and on one such visit to the town of Safed, she saw two small schools: a General school for girls, and a Mizrachi school for boys. The cost of maintaining these two schools was particularly high because of the small number of students in each school, while the tuition paid by the parents covered less than 10 percent of the total expenditure. Szold thought that combining the two schools would save money. Furthermore, she believed that a great deal of money could be saved by eliminating the separate streams entirely, and thus suggested that the Labor and Mizrachi streams merge with the General educational stream. The very idea provoked the ire of the entire religious camp, which was particularly sensitive to matters of education. Religious parents were fiercely opposed to having boys and girls in the same class, and did not trust non-religious teachers to teach their children. The backers of the Labor stream were also adamantly opposed to the idea, as they wished to educate their children in the spirit of their own ideology.[9]

The movements behind the various educational streams jealously guarded them, seeing the educational institutions in the Yishuv as central to the dissemination of their respective ideologies among the students and their parents. Consequently, they bore a grudge against Szold, which intensified over time, particularly on the part of the religious movements, which perceived her as a threat to their interests. In raising the idea of merging the educational streams, Szold demonstrated her extraneousness to the political reality in the Yishuv and her lack of awareness of the centrality of ideology in Jewish Palestinian society. The heads of the various educational streams accused Szold of trying to impose American values on the education system in Palestine.

In all her endeavors, Szold always sought the cooperation of those she worked with—something she considered essential to achieving her goals. When she realized the extent of the opposition to her proposal, she turned to other avenues. There was still ample room for improvement. She set about addressing administrative shortcomings that had become entrenched in the education system. The period leading up to the first of July was a time of terrible anxiety for teachers every year, because that was when letters of dismissal due to budgetary constraints were sent out. Szold viewed this threat hanging over the teachers' heads as morally unacceptable. At Szold's insistence, the Zionist Executive decided to discontinue the practice of sending letters of dismissal to the teachers. But the decision would remain a dead letter unless the necessary funds could be found. Since the executive itself was unable to provide these funds, Szold had to look elsewhere.

Szold also identified the need for urgent reform of the education system on an organizational level. She proposed the establishment of an office for the collection of tuition from parents. Such an arrangement would free teachers from having to collect the money, allowing them to focus on their pedagogical responsibilities. Szold also wanted to spare children from poor families the embarrassment of being handed notices to their parents in front of their classmates. She believed that a tuition collection office would heighten awareness in the Yishuv of the cost of education and the need to contribute toward its continued existence, with the ultimate goal of having the Yishuv assume the lion's share of responsibility for its own education system. Another area in which Szold felt improvement was needed was that of school oversight. There were schools that had not been inspected in years. She increased the number of inspectors, thereby boosting the general level of oversight. She also saw this as an important step toward obtaining more funding for Jewish public schools from the mandatory government, although the very fact that such support was contingent upon the efficiency of the Zionist Executive's administration of the school system was problematic.

WHEN SAMUEL COMPLETED HIS TERM as high commissioner in 1925, he was replaced by Herbert Charles Onslow, Lord Plumer, an army officer who had served with distinction in the First World War, after which he was made a field marshal and given a peerage.[10] In his role as high commissioner, he regularly invited Jewish, Muslim, and Christian leaders to his residence to get to know them personally. He was very impressed by Szold, and they met frequently. Her conversations with Lord Plumer and the head of the government department of education gave her some insight into the workings of the British administration, which she petitioned to contribute to the Zionist Executive education department budget. Szold was a meticulous administrator and gave the government no cause to withdraw its financial support. She sought to reinforce the autonomous structure of the Jewish schools under the direction of the Zionist Executive, in the hope of making the education department into a strong and stable administrative body.

Further opposition awaited Szold as she proceeded with her plans to reform the education system. She did not see her role as limited to fund raising and addressing organizational shortcomings, and she took a keen interest in educational content. She wanted to introduce a curriculum that would broaden the students' horizons and teach them values. The goal of the Zionist ideal in returning to the Land of Israel, as she saw it, was the creation of a spiritual center. Even those who emphasized the expansion of Jewish settlement did not imagine a Yishuv devoid of spiritual values.[11] Szold got into trouble once again, however, by underestimating the value that the educational streams placed on the absolute autonomy they enjoyed in determining the educational content and values they imparted to their students. Conflict ensued, with teachers and parents accusing Szold of trying to impose American views, ideas, and values on their children.

Szold learned her lesson and became more circumspect in her proposals, but she did not give up on her goal of improving the education system. She added further educational programs to meet the needs of the Yishuv. Many who came to Palestine during the large wave of immigration in the 1920s, including young adults, did not speak Hebrew. Szold proposed providing them with evening Hebrew classes, to facilitate their integration into the workforce and society. She hoped to repeat the success of the night school for immigrants she had founded in Baltimore some thirty years earlier as a bridge to integration in American society. Szold's plan to open schools for recent immigrants laid the cornerstone for the *ulpan* system (in Hebrew, a school for immigrants) that served large numbers of immigrants also after the establishment of the State of Israel. Another program greatly favored by Szold was vocational training, which would provide students with the skills they needed to find employment. She wished to impress upon the members of the Zionist Executive that there was more to education than simply balancing the budget, so she stressed the need to formulate and adopt a coherent education policy for the coming years—a five-year plan, at the very least—including a clear set of priorities, explaining, "The answer to all of these questions cannot be left to fate and chance."[12]

Szold sharply criticized the inefficiency of the education system, which she saw as the Achilles heel of this and other institutions within the Yishuv. Brandeis and his associates also criticized the inefficiency of public institutions in Palestine. Szold argued that administrative failings not only were a waste of time and energy, but ultimately cost money as well. She did not merely criticize the system's shortcomings, but prepared a detailed proposal for its improvement, which she hoped to present to the Zionist Congress.

THE SIXTEENTH ZIONIST CONGRESS, convened in Zurich in August 1929, did not get around to addressing Szold's reports and proposals. It had other issues to deal with. The structure of the Zionist Executive was changed, creating the "enlarged Jewish Agency," which would include Zionists and non-Zionists. This decision was the culmination of a long process initiated by Chaim Weizmann to recruit the non-Zionist philanthropists in America to his camp. Weizmann expected them to cooperate with him, open their wallets, and save the Zionist Organization from the deep financial crisis in which it found itself. He placed great hopes in Louis Marshall, a non-Zionist, to help him achieve his goals.

Marshall was born in Syracuse, New York, to an Orthodox family with German roots. He graduated with honors from Columbia Law School and became a successful lawyer. Jonathan Sarna called Brandeis and Marshall "two Jewish giants of the law." They were the same age but, unlike Brandeis, Marshall had a deep connection to Jewish tradition and Jewish community throughout his life. Marshall fought against racial and religious discrimination and was involved in various legal battles of a social nature. When he moved to New York, he joined Temple Emanu-El, where Jacob Schiff was also a member. Marshall did not identify as a Zionist, but he served as president of the American Jewish Committee and was sensitive to any attack on the Jewish community in the United States and around the world. Marshall was considered for a seat on the Supreme Court during the tenure of Chief Justice William Howard Taft but was passed over for political reasons.[13] Weizmann truly believed that Marshall was the key to bringing about a change in relations between the Zionist Organization and American Jewry's wealthiest and most prominent figures.

At the Zionist Congress, Weizmann gave Marshall a very warm introduction, and the delegates welcomed him with a standing ovation. Marshall, who was well known for his many years of public service in America and in Europe, thus came to serve in a new capacity, as a member of the executive of the Jewish Agency for Palestine. The statement establishing the enlarged Jewish Agency also stipulated that the head of the Zionist Organization would serve as its head as well—thereby extending Weizmann's presidency from one to two bodies. The Jewish Agency became synonymous with the Zionist Executive, which now had two centers of activity, London and Jerusalem. Weizmann was satisfied with the new members of the executive, and the congress closed on a festive and optimistic note.[14]

Szold was elected to the Jewish Agency executive, but would no longer head the education department. Instead she was offered the information department but declined, upset that her work at the education department had been cut short at the height of her reorganization efforts, after less than a year and a half in the education department. Szold submitted her resignation from the Jewish Agency. Her decision was welcomed by the leaders of Hadassah in the United States, who had been uncomfortable with her membership in the Jewish Agency Executive in Palestine in the first place. They wished to maintain Hadassah's status as an apolitical body.

The greatest opposition to Szold's departure from the education department came from the teachers and principals. The very same people who had initially resisted her leadership had come to admire the way in which she had revolutionized all aspects of the country's education system. In the midst of a grave financial crisis, she had managed to save the education system from collapse, placing it on a path to fiscal health and better administration. She left her mark on the department, improving its organizational administration and expanding its educational programs within a short time. She thus earned the teachers' respect and admiration—for her achievements, for her broad-mindedness and her integrity, and for the cooperation she fostered among the department's employees at every level.

The teachers' union journal published a special section, entitled "In Honor of Henrietta Szold," in which praise for Szold was interspersed with protests against her removal from the education department. Protests against Szold's departure also appeared in the general press. Union leaders and education department employees who had always complained that the political leadership did not take them seriously or value their work had finally found in Szold someone who listened to them, valued their work, and was devoted to them. "We feel that we have, once again, been slapped in the face."[15]

Shoshana Persitz, a Tel Aviv city councilor, heaped praise on Szold for her dedication and achievements, thereby expressing the thoughts and feelings of many of the country's educators:

> In these difficult times for the Yishuv, with money scarce and unemployment [high], I will never forget Miss Szold: her attention to every detail, even the most trivial of matters; her earnestness, ability, and tenacity in resolving the most important problems of our lives; her efficiency, professionalism, stamina, and modesty. I and many like me will remember these things for the rest of our lives. For years, the Zionist Executive treated education like a stepchild—until Miss Szold came along, brought education out in the open, and increased its prestige. It is hard to understand how the Zionist General Council agreed to let Miss Szold go—a person trusted by most of the Yishuv. During her tenure, we were freed from the Damoclean sword of budget cuts that destroy our work, and most of the Yishuv is unhappy and refuses to come to terms with Miss Szold's departure from the administration of the education system, which it considers it a severe blow.[16]

Employees at the education department highlighted another aspect of her work:

> Szold's work at the office is the stuff of poetry and art. There is indeed beauty and poetry in such work, and just like we say that the hoe of the workers in the [Jezreel] Valley and in the Galilee sings, so we can rightly say that Szold's pen sings with her wonderful critical sense and refinement of language and style. She is among the first to come to work every day, and the last to leave

the office, and she always goes home with a briefcase full of memos, plans, proposals, and studies. Those of us who are much younger admire and envy her energy, the way she treats the clerks who work with her, which is po- etry in itself. At this time, we have but [four] words in our mouths: "We will miss you."[17]

In her work at the education department, Szold gained public recognition in Palestine. When she first started, she was perceived as a representative of American Jewry, and her efforts to introduce American administrative concepts and practices were unpopular among the Eastern Europeans. As head of the education department, she came into contact with many teachers, principals, inspectors, and parents. She thus became a familiar public figure, and came to be held in high esteem—even within the labor movement, which had previously resisted her initiatives in the healthcare system, including oversight of its own healthcare institutions and general sick fund. The labor movement admired the progressive American approach she brought to the education department, which became more sensitive to the needs of the poor—something that coincided with the movement's own ideological principles.

The General Zionists stressed another side of her work. Shoshana Per- sitz described Szold as an educational innovator who had helped to es- tablish the legitimacy and importance of education in the cities, while the ethos of the Yishuv and especially of the labor movement viewed manual labor and agricultural settlement as the ideal. Szold became a well-known figure in the Yishuv and was mentioned from time to time in the local press. For example, A. Globman, writing in the Histadrut daily *Davar,* described Szold as unassuming and sincere, always willing to listen, diligent, modest in her personal life, and ambitious in her aspira- tions for the public good. Furthermore, Globman noted Szold's dedica- tion to the poor—in contrast to the indifference of his colleagues in the Histadrut: "During the economic crisis, when hundreds of the unem- ployed stood in long lines at Histadrut House in Tel Aviv, how many di- rectors of the Yishuv's institutions and politicians had the decency to descend from the mountain to this vale of tears? Yet she came, in person, to witness the relief efforts with her own eyes and to empathize, with feeling and heart."[18]

WHILE AT THE EDUCATION DEPARTMENT, she continued her work in the healthcare system, where there was never a shortage of conflict either. Tensions within Hadassah in Palestine persisted, and its director, Dr. Bluestone, who had

Dr. Chaim Yassky

made every effort to address the organization's problems, went the way of his predecessors and in 1928 decided to return to the United States at the end of his agreed-upon three-year term. Bluestone's assistant, Dr. Chaim Yassky, was appointed acting director of the Hadassah Medical Organization.[19] Yassky was an ophthalmologist who had taken part in the battle to eradicate trachoma and now headed the ophthalmology department at the Hadassah Hospital in Jerusalem. Szold was satisfied with his work as acting director, and three years later, he was appointed permanent director of Hadassah—a position he held with success for many years. Yassky was also among the founders of the Hadassah Hospital on Mount Scopus and the Hadassah School of Medicine.

Yassky's lifetime of dedication and achievements would come to a tragic end, however, in the spring of 1948. At the height of the Arab-Israeli War, on the morning of April 13, a convoy carrying a hundred doctors, nurses, and other personnel set out for the hospital on Mount Scopus. While passing through the Arab neighborhood of Sheikh Jarrah, the convoy came under heavy fire. A number of vehicles managed to get away, but two buses, an ambulance, and an armored escort car were caught in the ambush. The fighting went on for many hours, with the members of the convoy trying to keep the attackers from approaching the vehicles. Nevertheless, the Arabs managed to set the two buses on fire. Seventy-eight doctors, nurses, and other Hadassah Hospital staff were killed in the attack. The British only intervened in the evening, rescuing the survivors from the trapped vehicles. Yassky was among the killed.

DURING THE TIME in which Szold was busy with healthcare and the education crisis in the Yishuv, Hadassah in the United States was experiencing a different kind of crisis. Louis Lipsky, who was in charge of Keren Hayesod, tried once again to bring Hadassah under ZOA control, in order to draw attention away from his own failure in raising funds. At the time, Hadassah was a large organization, with some 37,000 members.[20] The ZOA's membership was only a third of that, and would continue to decline over the course of the following four years.

Lipsky was angry with the Hadassah leadership for its decision to remain independent of the ZOA and retain control over the donations it received—amounting to some $50,000. He described Irma Lindheim, who served as Hadassah president after Szold's resignation, describing her as a rich, self-confident woman and a tough fighter. Lipsky suspected that Lindheim and her colleagues not only were concerned with maintaining control of Hadassah funds, but were secretly seeking to overthrow the current ZOA leaders in order to replace them with supporters of Brandeis and Mack, who had resigned from their positions within the organization. Hadassah had clashed with Lipsky before, and its leaders did not hesitate to fight back this time either. Echoes of the conflict even reached the general press. The *New York Times* reported at length on the revolt against the ZOA leadership—including the resignation of Stephen Wise and other members of the administrative committee of the ZOA, the struggle of Hadassah ("the women's Zionist organization with a membership of 50,000 women"), and Hadassah president Irma Lindheim's opposition "to the regime of Louis Lipsky," which she accused of "political machinations."[21] All of these clashes stood in the shadow of the crises in Palestine and the great financial crash in America.

THE 1929 RIOTS

The riots of 1929 were the culmination of nearly a decade of conflict between Arabs and Jews in Palestine. There was relative calm during the tenure of Lord Plumer as high commissioner, but he resigned in 1928, after having held the position for only three years. Plumer's successor, Sir John Robert Chancellor, had previously been a colonial officer in British Africa, and failed to understand the nature of the tensions in Palestine. His role, as he perceived it, was to serve the native Arab population of the land. He disapproved of the terms of the mandate instrument, which promised to establish a Jewish national home in Palestine and facilitate Jewish immigration to the country. He served as high commissioner from 1928 to 1931, and his negative approach to the Jews exacerbated the Arab-Jewish conflict. His tenure brought an end to years of relative calm, ushering in a period of violent clashes.

In September 1928, a dispute over the right of Jews to pray at the Wailing Wall set in motion a series of tragic events. The space near the Wall belonged to the Supreme Muslim Council, which sought to limit Jewish activities there. On Yom Kippur, September 24, 1928, hundreds of Jews came to pray at the Wall, and a screen was set up to separate male and female worshipers. Jewish prayer at the Wailing Wall was a sensitive issue. Jews were allowed to pray there, but they were not allowed to bring benches or set up screens—acts perceived by the Arabs as an attempt to lay claim to the site, which they considered exclusive Arab property, as the Wall and the area in front of it were part of the Haram al-Sharif, the Muslims' territory. Any change in prayer arrangements was seen as a violation of the conditions on which Jews were accorded the right to pray there. The Arabs protested the placement of the screen, and the British police forced their way through the worshipers during the Yom Kippur prayer service and removed it.[22] In response, a group of young Jews organized a march to the Wall, carrying the blue and white Zionist flag. The Arabs responded by throwing stones at Jewish worshipers.

The next stage of the conflict unfolded in August 1929, when the mufti of Jerusalem, Haj Amin al-Husayni—an extreme nationalist who had been involved in the riots in Jerusalem in 1920—urged Muslims to attack the Jews, who he claimed were plotting to seize control of the Haram al-Sharif mosques. On the morning of Friday, August 23, 1929, Muslims poured into the Haram area, wielding clubs, knives, and daggers. They were joined by Arabs from nearby villages, armed with guns. The Arab mob attacked Jews within the Old City and then proceeded beyond the city walls to attack outlying Jewish neighborhoods. They attacked and gained control of Kibbutz Ramat Rachel, south of the city, setting fire to its buildings and uprooting its orchards, destroyed the neighborhood of Talpiot, and attacked other neighborhoods in the western and northern parts of the city. The Haganah, a Jewish self-defense force established earlier, took control of the city center and sent its men to other parts of the city, but the defenders were few, and the British police lacked sufficient forces to stop the attackers.[23]

Arab rioters also struck in Petach Tikva and in other Jewish towns and villages, looting and wreaking destruction wherever they went. Ruppin was

Jewish families flee the Old City in Jerusalem during the 1929 riots

horrified at the devastation he witnessed at Kibbutz Hulda: "On Tuesday, I went from Tel Aviv to visit Huldah, most of which was destroyed and burnt to ashes during the disturbances. Many of the trees have also been burnt. There is nobody there. The place makes a terrible impression."[24]

The violence reached its peak in Hebron and Safed. In Hebron, more than sixty men, women, and children were brutally murdered, and their homes looted. Some 500 Jews took refuge in the Hebron police station, from where they were eventually evacuated to Jerusalem. In Safed, rioters killed twenty Jews, including children and the elderly, looted their homes, and set the buildings on fire. The fire spread to the Arab quarter and was quickly put out, saving the lives of the remaining Jews. Military reinforcements finally arrived after five days of rioting throughout the country, in which 133 Jews had been killed and 400 injured. There were casualties among the Arabs as well, mostly killed by the British as they sought to stop the rioters.

Szold was not in the country during the riots. After attending the Zionist Congress in Basel, she went on to the United States, arriving in New York in September 1929. She learned of the violence in Palestine from letters she received from friends. She was shocked by the force of the riots and the brutality of the massacres. She recalled the riots of 1921, which she herself had witnessed; at the time she had been critical of the restraint shown by the British in the face of Arab aggression, nor had she believed

Synagogue in
Hebron, destroyed
by Arab rioters in
1929

that Arab aggression would diminish with the pardoning of Haj Amin al-
Husayni after he had been sentenced to prison for his role in the riots of
1920. She later learned that al-Husayni had played a central role in the
riots of 1929 as well. The British colonial secretary, Sidney James Webb,
Lord Passfield, appointed a commission to "enquire into the immediate
causes which led to the recent outbreak in Palestine and to make recommendations as to the steps necessary to avoid a recurrence." The members
of the commission—commonly known as the Shaw Commission, after its
chairman, Sir Walter Shaw—arrived in Jerusalem at the end of October
1929.[25] They sought to determine the degree to which Jews, Muslims, and
the government were responsible for the disturbances, and to that end they
met with representatives of all three parties. The Arabs blamed the Jews,
accusing them of trying to take over the entire country, including the
Wailing Wall, and of purchasing land and evicting Arab tenants. The rep-

resentatives of the Palestine government claimed that they were unaware of the events, although they had in fact witnessed them. Yishuv representatives Arthur Ruppin and Harry Sacher rejected the Arab accusations, claiming that they had asked only that Jewish immigration and settlement be allowed to continue. In its report, published in late March 1930, the commission concluded that the riots were due to Arab animosity toward the Jews, disappointment at having failed to achieve their political and national aspirations, and fears for their economic future. Jewish immigration and land purchases were cited as the primary cause of these feelings.[26]

At around the same time as the report was released, Lord Balfour passed away. Weizmann delivered a tearful eulogy at the Zionist General Council. Balfour's death symbolized the end of an age of great hopes for the Yishuv and for the establishment of a Jewish national home in Palestine with British support.

The Jews submitted a memorandum to the British government, protesting the Shaw Commission's one-sided, pro-Arab conclusions. Lord Passfield decided to send Sir John Hope Simpson to investigate the issues of land settlement, immigration, and development policy, said to lie at the heart of tensions between Arabs and Jews. Arthur Ruppin met a number of times with Hope Simpson to try to explain the events in Palestine to him, arguing that the violence was entirely due to Arab aggression. Ruppin presented him with figures demonstrating the feasibility of settling tens of thousands of Jews on the land without harming the Arabs in any way. Hope Simpson was polite and heard Ruppin out, and Ruppin was under the impression that his arguments had been well received and that a friendship was developing between them. He wrote that he was on the best possible terms with Hope Simpson, who had spoken favorably of him to the high commissioner.[27] Hope Simpson's report, published some two months later, came as a shock to Ruppin and the Yishuv. It failed to recognize the potential for industrial growth in Palestine, advised restricting Jewish land purchases, and determined that immigration should be contingent upon the country's economic absorptive capacity.

In October 1930, Lord Passfield published a white paper based on Hope Simpson's report. The Passfield white paper imposed restrictions on Jewish immigration and land purchases, and sought to promote the establishment of a popularly elected legislative council, which would effectively hand control to the Arab majority. This white paper illustrated the dramatic shift in British policy, which had abandoned its commitment to further the establishment of a Jewish national home in favor of appeasement of the Arabs. The white paper sparked Jewish protests in Palestine and in Jewish communities around the world. Legal experts argued that the white paper stood in contradiction to the mandate instrument, and demanded that it be withdrawn.

Szold learned of these developments upon her return from the United States in late May 1931, after having been away from Palestine for a number of months. She immediately felt the tense political atmosphere in the country, and expressed her dismay: "I must confess that I cannot follow all its involutions intelligently. But I do know that the officials handling all such legislation, in Jerusalem and in London as well, are violently opposed to Jewish aspirations. . . . The opposition to us [is] basely unjust."[28]

The Passfield white paper represented a crossroads for the Yishuv. The Zionist leadership had been operating on the premise that there was enough time to increase the number of Jews and develop the land. The white paper proved them wrong. They had lost the race, because they had failed to foresee the growth of fanatic Arab nationalism and the appearance of radical political forces that would demand control of the country. The plan to establish a legislative council—supported even by High Commissioner Arthur Grenfell Wauchope, who assumed his post in 1931 and was considered sympathetic to the Jewish cause—was seen as de facto recognition of the right of the Arab majority to rule, raising concerns for the political future of the Yishuv.

The 1929 riots and their aftermath left the entire Yishuv reeling, and the members of Brith Shalom were no exception. Ruppin resigned as chairman of the association, concluding: "The situation is paradoxical: what we can get [from the Arabs] is of no use to us, and what we need we cannot get from them. At most, the Arabs would agree to grant national rights to the Jews in an Arab state."[29] Ruppin understood full well the fate that awaited a Jewish minority dependent on the goodwill of the Arab majority. What was more, he argued, "such a settlement . . . would kill . . . enthusiasm for the cause of Zionism in Palestine. A Zionism which would agree to such a compromise with the Arabs would not have the support of the East European Jews and would very soon become a Zionism without Zionists."[30] The belief of many of the members of Brith Shalom that an understanding could be reached with the Arabs for peaceful coexistence in Palestine was shaken. Those who felt as Ruppin did left the association, while there were significant differences of opinion among those who remained, and within a few short years the group disbanded entirely.

Szold had reached the same conclusion as Ruppin years earlier. She believed that the Jews stood little chance of flourishing in a binational state. A national minority living under hostile Arab rule, trapped in a suffocating and vulnerable ghetto, would never attain the kind of spiritual rebirth so dear to the hearts of the members of Brith Shalom. The issue troubled her greatly. "I am sure you will read between the lines that the weight of the Arab question hangs upon me," she wrote to a friend, adding that "it grows more menacing every day."[31] Szold sought answers in the experiences of other nations. She read the published letters of Gertrude Margaret Bell, an English writer, traveler, and political officer, which she wrote in Syria and Arabia, and Szold was very impressed by them: "Her letters . . . demonstrate what a lively, active, intelligent, and energetic woman can do in the field of politics. I am convinced that she did more than Lawrence for the Arabs. And she served her government well, especially in that she influenced them to deal uprightly with the native population."[32]

Szold also read Sir John Simon's report on India and Gandhi, as well as a work by Dr. Hans Kohn (a lecturer at Hebrew University in Jerusalem) on nationalism in the Middle East. None of these books, however, was able to provide a solution to the questions that troubled her. "We Jews and our Zionist movement are but a speck of dust on these huge scales. There is the possibility that the League of Nations will understand the highest demands of world justice and will have the power to enforce those demands. . . . As for the situation right here, it is difficult, difficult beyond words, and promises to become more difficult as the year wears on."[33]

A FEW WEEKS AFTER the 1929 riots in Palestine, severe economic crisis struck in America. The 1920s had been a time of exceptional prosperity in the United States. Suddenly, though, the stock market crashed, and in a single day—Black Thursday, October 24, 1929—millions of people lost everything they owned. Hundreds of banks failed and their customers lost all their savings. Factories closed, agriculture suffered, and millions became unemployed. Many were unable to repay their loans and mortgages and lost their homes. Great fortunes were also wiped out. Herbert Hoover, the president at the time of the crash, was not reelected in 1932; the new president, Franklin Delano Roosevelt, promised to pull America out of the crisis.

Weizmann struggled to save the Zionist Organization from collapse. The hopes he had placed in the establishment of the enlarged Jewish Agency were not realized. A short time after the Zionist Congress, Louis Marshall passed away, due to complications from surgery he had undergone in Switzerland.[34] With his death, Weizmann lost his primary source of support in the enlarged Jewish Agency. Weizmann had succeeded in bringing about the election of Felix Warburg, the most prominent of the non-Zionist leaders in America, to the chairmanship of the agency's administrative committee. Warburg, who was Jacob Schiff's son-in-law, supported the

Hebrew University and other institutions (the Israeli moshav Kfar War-burg is named after him). Warburg soon resigned, however, dashing all of Weizmann's hopes for cooperation with the non-Zionist faction. The economic crisis delivered a further blow to the Zionist Organization, as the American philanthropists on whom Weizmann had been counting were concerned with their own losses and in no mood to make charitable donations. The economic crisis in the United States was also felt in Europe, which had not yet recovered from the First World War, so assistance from that quarter was not forthcoming either. The Yishuv was deeply concerned about the future of Jewish immigration and settlement in Palestine.

A VICIOUS CIRCLE

After resigning from the Jewish Agency, Szold spent nearly ten months in the United States. On her seventieth birthday, in 1930, her friends organized a series of parties and celebrations. She received hundreds of letters, telegrams, and gifts from friends and from the members of Hadassah. The members of the Histadrut teachers' union in Palestine did not forget Szold, and when they heard that she was turning seventy, a number of articles were published in the union's journal, singing her praises and congratulating her in honor of the occasion. The many celebrations were not to Szold's taste. She found the endless speeches hard to bear. Then she received word that she had been elected to the executive of the Jewish National Council (JNC), a body comprising representatives of the Jewish parties in Palestine. The members of Hadassah wanted Szold to stay in America, and were not happy to see her join the JNC. Her sisters also tried to convince her to retire and stay in America.

Szold was surprised at her election to the JNC. The Federation of Hebrew Women, which had named Szold head of their electoral list, took part in the council elections, but lacked the numbers to win representation on the executive. Szold had no idea who had supported her election. She decided to return to Palestine, where she discovered, to her surprise, that she owed her election to Mapai (Mifleget Po'ale Eretz Israel—the Workers' Party of the Land of Israel). "They gave up one of the seats to which they were entitled, in order that I might be assured a place. Their intention was that I should be the seventh member of the Executive, the member holding the balance."[35]

Szold had already learned that in Palestine she was seen as a kind of firefighter, someone they could call upon at times of severe financial crisis, as they did when they appointed her to head the education department.

The executive members of the Jewish Agency attend a birthday party for Henrietta
Szold in 1930. Szold is at center, with David Ben-Gurion on her right.

Her help was especially crucial in light of the economic crisis in the United
States, which made fundraising all the more difficult. There was more to
her election, however, than her fundraising abilities. She was also seen as
someone who could soften the teachers' adamant opposition to the transfer
of the education department from the Zionist Executive to the JNC. In
fact, they hoped that she might be able to lead such a move, in view of the
esteem in which the teachers had held her ever since her tenure as head of
the education department.

The decision of the leaders of Mapai to support Szold's election to the
JNC executive met with opposition from the party's members. They did
not understand why one of the three seats reserved for Mapai was given
to Szold. Szold's election was particularly favored by Mapai leader David
Ben-Gurion, however. He saw the JNC as a powerful tool for action within
the Yishuv. Ben-Gurion explained his choice of Szold as follows: "There
are few among us who are suited to such constructive organizational work.
Miss Szold is suited." It was not Ben-Gurion's only explanation. Under his
leadership, Mapai wanted to further consolidate its position and silence
its opponents. Bringing Szold into his camp's orbit was important to him
for a number of reasons: "To gather around the workers all who might be
close to them. Although Szold is not a socialist, she is one of those decent
Zionists who are fast disappearing. She is a woman and she is an American, and by bringing Szold in, we are bringing her closer to us, along with
an important circle of Americans, who hear baseless things about us, and
whom she will bring closer to us."[36]

David Ben-Gurion, chair of the
Jewish Agency executive

The last reason was of particular importance to Ben-Gurion. He recognized the growing importance of American Jewry—the largest Jewish
community in the world, with the Jews of the Soviet Union cut off from
the West. Ben-Gurion was aware of Szold's influence in America and,
through her, hoped to bring the American Jewish leadership closer to the
labor movement in Palestine. Another advantage that did not escape Ben-
Gurion was Szold's close ties to the mandatory government: "It is crucial
that we have someone on the executive who is able to meet with the government and speak to them in their own language." The leaders of the
Yishuv were mostly Eastern European and were unfamiliar with Western
mores and political culture.

Szold was unsure about returning to Palestine, remaining undecided for
a period of weeks. "My mind is blank on my future. . . . I am finding it
difficult beyond words to decide to go back, but I am finding it equally
difficult to adjust myself to contemporary life in America. I can't see myself
at work here fruitfully."[37]

SZOLD'S FRIENDS in Palestine were surprised to hear of her return to Jerusalem
from New York. She had been away for so long that many thought she
had decided to stay in America. When she finally arrived in Palestine, she
was welcomed with great enthusiasm: "I had what may be called a 'Mes-

sianic' reception. My coming meant, according to some, the beginning of real work; according to others the completion of the work; some expected me to solve all public problems; others to find a solution for their private woes and troubles. After subtracting all these 'interested' parties, there remained, I cannot but say, a large group of friends who were just glad to welcome me back. Some of them came down from Jerusalem and all the way to the vessel lying at anchor outside Jaffa; some met me as I disembarked at Jaffa, many crowded into my room at the hotel when I reached Jerusalem, and there has been a steady flow of them since."[38]

After her lengthy absence, Szold was surprised to see the difference between the mood in Palestine and that in America. In America, the economic depression dominated conversation, while in Palestine, she noted, "all the articulate talk [is about] politics. . . . The preoccupation with the government and Ramsay James MacDonald (a British politician who was the first Labour Party member to become Prime Minister of the United Kingdom, in 1924) and Passfield and Hope Simpson and Sir John Chancellor and the lesser officials . . . that is what is paralyzing the forces that should devote themselves to organization."[39]

Szold immediately set to work at the JNC. "Twenty-four hours after my arrival, I traveled to Tel Aviv for a meeting, and since then I have been there three times for the same purpose. The meetings in Tel Aviv do not exempt me from the meetings in Jerusalem. Palestine is as meeting-beridden as the United States."[40] The first task she was charged with was the transfer of the education and health departments from the Zionist Executive to the JNC.

The JNC, which represented the Yishuv, was unprepared to assume responsibility for tasks that required a regular budget. There was no existing system of organization or tax collection on which at least part of the health and education budgets could be based. Teachers familiar with the situation in the JNC strongly opposed the transfer of the education department. Szold herself was against the move, believing there was no justification for it. Her position was not a matter of principle; she simply understood that the JNC was structurally and administratively incapable of running the department. "It is suspended in mid-air so long as the *kehillot* [local Jewish communities in Palestine] are not organized in such a manner as to levy taxes upon their constituencies and collect them," she wrote.

The JNC also neglected to institute basic organizational practices. It was thus left unprepared and unable to assume any essential public roles. It was clear to Szold, who was an inveterate realist, that nothing could be achieved under these circumstances. Frustrated, she wrote to her sisters:

"We . . . are caught in a vicious circle—no money, hence no organization of the local communities, hence no tax levy, hence no money. I feel like a squirrel in one of those barbarous cages they used to have."[41] Despondent, she wrote to Alice Seligsberg, "We Jews seem to have an unconquerable penchant for the political aspects of life. The Asefat Ha-Nivharim, the annual National Assembly of the Knesset Israel, arouses great interest; so does the choice of the members of the Vaad Leumi [the JNC]. But when it comes to brick-laying, the enthusiasm wanes." As Szold would later put it, "Everything is chaotic and the chaos is static."[42]

SOCIAL WORK

Szold longed to establish a professional social work system—so important for the Yishuv in general and for the most vulnerable in particular. She believed that "the old Lady Bountiful system, based on hysteria and not on justice to the unfortunate," must be replaced.[43] During the course of her work at the education department, Szold became aware of the existence of hundreds of abandoned children, orphaned or from broken homes, who were not in school and, in some cases, had turned to crime. These children slept in the streets, on city benches, in doorways, or in empty crates.[44] Szold was horrified by the phenomenon and sought to eradicate it. She also met with many refugees who had survived the 1929 riots, escaping from Hebron and Jerusalem after having lost family members, their homes, and everything they owned. More than a year later, they were still helpless, including children who had lost their parents in the massacres, and the Yishuv was unable to care for them and rehabilitate them.

When Szold agreed to join the JNC executive, she resolved to establish a social service department, although she was well aware of the difficulties that entailed. The severe lack of funds was perhaps the most obvious difficulty, but it was by no means the only one. In fact, she faced a far more difficult task: changing the prevailing view that charity needed to be a spontaneous act. Few in the Yishuv recognized the need for professional social services.

In previous generations, Jewish communities boasted a variety of charitable institutions, such as funds for poor brides, soup kitchens, shelters, burial societies, collection boxes, and free loan societies. Such institutions also operated in the Old Yishuv in Palestine. Assistance was generally intracommunal, granted to members of a given religious community, Hasidic or immigrant group. Some funds were established by individual donors or by members of the community to meet specific needs, such as an orphanage, institutions for the elderly or the chronically ill, schools for the blind, and so forth. These funds and institutions were generally run without oversight or financial transparency. There were also religious endowments, such as homes bequeathed to the community for the use of poor Torah scholars, which were equally free of any kind of scrutiny. Community leaders would sometimes use such properties for their own needs.

Szold criticized the prevailing approach in the Yishuv, which favored uncoordinated charity. People believed that volunteers could do the job, and that there was no need for professionally trained social workers. She knew that changing such entrenched views was like moving a mountain: "The resistance to technically trained forces is as outspoken as ever. . . . Shall we have to suffer and suffer still more before we realize that we can't kick the world's experience aside?"[45]

The Ashkenazi and Sephardi leaders of the Old Yishuv sought to maintain control over their communities and had no interest in cooperating with the JNC. They opposed Zionist administration or oversight of their charitable institutions, just as they had opposed the work of the American nurses when they first arrived. They also feared that social workers would introduce social values and ideas at odds with their own beliefs. It was thus clear to Szold that bringing experienced social workers into the Old Yishuv under these circumstances would be an arduous task. If only she had the funding, she would have hired social workers who, over time, would have changed popular perceptions of their profession, just as the nurses had. As long as there was no money even to hire a single social worker for each of the three big cities, however, she stood no chance of success.[46]

Szold was particularly convinced of the efficacy of family casework in providing relief to those in need. "People must beg," she complained. "There is no center in any community to which to refer them with the assurance that their case will be lovingly investigated and dealt with."[47] Szold also had trouble convincing the community of the importance of professional administration of social services: "But even if money were available . . . we shall never get anywhere in Palestine if we invite experts with the promise of large emoluments. I think the attitude is all wrong, but one cannot run counter to a determined public opinion, especially not in these days of economic crisis in America and in Germany."[48]

The education and health departments were not transferred to the JNC in 1931. The biggest obstacle was the opposition mounted by the teachers. The Zionist Executive was determined, however, to eventually transfer the two departments to the JNC and rid itself of the economic burden they entailed. Those opposed to the move held assemblies, at which well-known figures expressed their support for the teachers' position. The revered labor leader Berl Katznelson spoke passionately against the move: "He who speaks out on this matter [i.e., against the transfer] does not resemble a judge, but rather one who goes to the gallows. . . . There is poison in this proposal!" Despite the protests, the Zionist Executive decided to go ahead with the move, and in 1932, the education department was transferred to the JNC. Szold remarked, "The gift is accompanied by a deficit of £8,000."[49]

A NEW ERA in British rule began at the end of November 1931, when Sir Arthur Grenfell Wauchope replaced John Chancellor as high commissioner.[50] During Wauchope's tenure as high commissioner (November 1931 to February 1938), the country underwent far-reaching change. The Jewish population more than doubled, from 170,000 in 1929 to 400,000. Worldwide, the great economic crisis of 1929 brought about political change that led to the rise of fascist regimes in several places, including the Nazi Party, which paved the way for Hitler's ascension to power in Germany. Jews fled for their lives—many of them to Palestine. Wauchope allowed the immigration of German Jews, and they were joined by tens of thousands of Jews from Poland, Romania, and other countries.

When Wauchope took up his post in Palestine, he was fifty-seven years old. After the completion of the high commissioner's residence in Talpiot, with its grand halls, he threw parties and balls to which he invited Jewish, Muslim, and Christian leaders, as well as leading members of the country's various communities. He hoped that bringing them together would help to defuse the tension and hostility between them. In his first years as high commissioner, Wauchope was a breath of fresh air for the Yishuv, particularly when compared to his predecessors. Some in the Yishuv considered him the best of all the high commissioners. He visited Jewish towns and villages throughout the country and was especially impressed by the kibbutzim. He attended cultural performances and festive events in the Yishuv, and was on friendly terms with Jewish leaders: Ben-Gurion, Chaim Arlosoroff (head of the Jewish Agency's political department), and Moshe Shertok (Sharet), head of the Political Department in the Jewish Agency after Haim Arlosoroff was murdered and later the foreign minister of the State of Israel.[51] Henrietta Szold was among those who frequented Wauchope's home, and they soon became friends. She told Wauchope of her plans, and he agreed to help her improve the condition of the poor in the Yishuv, especially youth.

Szold had already begun to identify and help needy families through Hadassah's hygiene department. Working through the education system, however, she was unable to reach the abandoned children and juvenile offenders who were not in school. Szold was outraged by the way in which the mandatory authorities dealt with juvenile offenders apprehended by the police. In 1928, while still at the education department, she was asked by the mandatory government to help deal with young offenders. She continued to do so in 1931–1932, and was appalled by the way in which the police handled juvenile offenders and by their lack of understanding of the children's needs. "The Palestine government took a great step forward . . . in the appointment of a probation officer. He is a Britisher and was in despair as to how he was to deal with the Jewish boys, whose language or languages he cannot understand. The result is that I became his deputy for Jewish cases," she recorded. She opposed holding abandoned children together with juvenile offenders, because of the adverse effect the violent behavior of the latter had on the former, "who are very juvenile and not offenders at all, but sick, defective, undernourished, mentally and physically starved children."[52] She was shocked to discover that "the first punishment decreed by the court according to the statute book is—flogging." She also protested against the fact that the Jewish children were not provided with kosher food while in custody.

Szold agreed to serve as a probation officer for juvenile offenders. She met with the government official in charge of juvenile offenders and suggested introducing the "big brother" mentoring approach. The government repeatedly proposed sending the Jewish offenders to boarding schools such as Shefayim and the Ben Shemen Youth Village, and to the kibbutzim, but Dr. Berkson and Szold were not in favor of the idea. Szold held meetings with physicians and educators to find appropriate ways of dealing with these children: "My chief occupation at the moment is dealing with the juvenile offender. He is so much less an offender than the people who want to reform him. They talk from start to finish in terms of reformatory institutions, when all that the little wretches need is larger opportunity for recreation and for education of the hand."[53]

Szold persisted in her efforts to establish a central agency within the JNC that would provide social services for the entire country. In the meantime, she sought to explain the nature and importance of social work to decision-makers at the various institutions, stressing the fact that she was referring to professional social workers, not volunteers. In a letter to Alice Seligsberg, she remarked: "What do you think of my temerity in undertaking such a task? When I came to Palestine, I acted as though I were an expert on medical affairs. Fate made me pretend to be an expert on educational affairs in 1927. And now, in 1931, having passed the Psalmist's term of years [i.e., age seventy], I dare go into another field in which expertise is imperative. But what am I to do if experts . . . refuse to tackle the job, and tackled it must be?"[54]

Having seen her place in Palestine for the foreseeable future, Szold threw herself into work at the JNC. She left her room at the Eden Hotel and rented a small ground-floor apartment in a two-story building at 16 Ramban Street. The apartment opened on a small garden in which Szold took great pleasure. It was her oasis of calm after long, hard days at work: "My room and my bookcase continue a delight, and . . . I have been enjoying my garden, consisting of a pink hydrangea and a pot of varied cacti. . . . I found myself growing very fond of it. . . . It claimed my attention morning and evening. If I didn't water it abundantly—more than the Jerusalem water supply permits—it drooped so pathetically that I had to devote myself to it. . . . You see, I am getting to be as domesticated as Adele's cats."[55]

Szold had little time for leisure, however. She attended JNC meetings in Tel Aviv and Haifa, and visited the Ben Shemen Youth Village from time to time. Since her two colleagues on the Zionist Executive, Sacher and Kisch, were out of the country, she also dealt with labor disputes in the orange-growing regions as well as other matters that required her presence in Tel Aviv.

The JNC coffers were empty, but Szold's personal finances improved: "In various ways—two cash birthday presents, a gift of cash from Mr. Straus, and my fee as executrix of Mrs. Kantrowicz's will—I accumulated about $2200."[56] Szold did not spend the money on herself—even money given to her as a personal gift. The sum was too small to improve matters at the JNC, so Szold used the money to further projects close to her heart. She felt a particular affinity with the young pioneers and decided to establish a Rural Clinic Building Loan Fund. The first sum allocated by the fund went to the building of a clinic in Nahalal, and the members of the moshav invited her and her friends to the dedication ceremony. Szold received a further $5,000 from her friend Mrs. Rosenwald, with which she established a Rural School Building Loan Fund. The first school built with assistance from the fund was in Kibbutz Deganiah, in the Jordan Valley. When she read of the plight of Jews in Soviet Russia, she also became a regular contributor to Magen, a fund established in Palestine to help the Jews in that country. On learning of her generosity, her sister Adele joked that she had never imagined that someone in their family would become a wealthy philanthropist.

Despite her disappointment at the delays in establishing a social service department, Szold was determined to press forward. She received help from the mandatory government and managed to raise money among her friends in the United States, and in 1934 she opened social service offices in Jerusalem, Tel Aviv, Haifa, and Petach Tikva, hiring social workers trained in

Germany. The wave of immigration from Germany that followed Hitler's rise to power presented a further challenge. Szold drew upon funds from the Jewish Agency's newly created department for the settlement of German immigrants, as well as other sources. She established the social service department in the JNC and, a year later, founded a school of social work, eventually incorporated into the Hebrew University. Immigration increased over the course of the 1930s, and Szold was able to call upon experienced social workers among the immigrants themselves. Her contribution to the development of social services in the Yishuv failed to win public recognition at the time, unlike political or economic developments that caught the popular imagination. Appreciation of the importance of social services grew over the years, however, with the arrival of immigrants from developed countries, who recognized the value of such services in their countries of origin.

Szold remained at the head of the social service department for a number of years, until she resigned in order to devote all of her time and energy to another project she had been working on for some time—a project that would become the greatest of all her endeavors.

13

THE MOTHER OF YOUTH ALIYAH

HE ECONOMIC CRISIS of 1929 had a devastating effect in Germany. The economy collapsed and millions were left without work. Inflation, unemployment, and political turmoil oiled the wheels of Adolf Hitler's ambition and increased the popularity of the National Socialist Party he headed. The Nazi leader conducted a vicious campaign against the Jews, whom he designated "enemies of the German people," calling upon the masses who attended his rallies to drive them out.

Szold was greatly troubled by the surge of antisemitism in Germany. Hitler's appointment as German chancellor on January 30, 1933, only intensified her trepidation. Other Zionist leaders shared her concerns. The German-born Arthur Ruppin wrote, "In Germany, Hitler has become chancellor! That a demagogue like Hitler has become the leader of the German people is definitely a sign of the country's decline. From a moral point of view, the situation of the Jews in Germany is frightful. A catastrophic collapse of all the hopes of the liberal Jews to assimilate among the German people."[1]

Ruppin found the idea that a bitter fate awaited German Jewry hard to accept. Even after the National Socialist electoral victory on March 5, 1933, he was skeptical about the shocking rumors he had heard regarding the disappearance of Jewish communists. "Most likely, much of this is untrue; but how much?" he wrote.[2] Most of the Jews in Germany found it hard to cope with the threats they now faced, and their responses varied. Those who had converted to Christianity were certain they would not be affected. Their numbers had risen rapidly since the turn of the century, and by the time the Nazis came to power, such converts represented some 44 percent of the country's entire Jewish population. Victor Klemperer, who had converted to Christianity as a young man, married a Protestant woman, and identified as a German, wrote: "I am German forever, German 'nationalist.' . . . The Nazis are un-German."[3] A short while later, he was dismissed from his position as professor of Romance languages at the Technische Hochschule in Dresden. Assimilated Jews who had not converted but had married non-Jews and were estranged from their people also believed that they would be spared.

Many young Jews had served in the German army during the First World War, some of them decorated for bravery and distinguished service. They believed that their loyalty to their country would protect them. A Jewish woman appealed to German president Paul von Hindenburg, writing that her fiancé had been killed on the battlefield, as had two of her brothers, while her only surviving brother had returned blind from the war. All three brothers had been awarded the Iron Cross for their service. "But now," she wrote, "it has gone so far that in our country . . . there are open calls for pogroms and acts of violence against Jews." Hindenburg acknowledged receipt of the letter and informed the woman that he strongly opposed violence against Jews. The president's reply was passed on to Hitler, who added in the margin, "This lady's claims are a swindle! Obviously there has been no incitement to a pogrom."[4]

Many intellectuals did not believe that a wild man like Hitler would remain in power for very long in a civilized country like Germany. They thought the Nazi incitement would stop once the party came to power. Professor Karl Mannheim, a well-known sociologist at Frankfurt University, did not believe he would be affected—until he was dismissed from his post. Martin Buber and Arnold Zweig also believed that the threat would pass. Buber wrote, "Anti-Semitic legislation would be possible only if the balance of power shifted in favor of the National Socialists, but . . . this is hardly to be expected."[5] Similarly, Henrietta Szold saw the Nazi persecution of the Jews as yet another chapter in the long history of antisemitism. Although the methods employed by the Nazis were unprecedented, Szold, like many others, tended to believe that Hitler would become more moderate once in power, and the ill wind would eventually subside.

Not all Jews in Germany shared this view. With the rise of the Nazis to power, some Jewish intellectuals, artists, writers, and scientists understood that a fundamental change had come over the country, and they decided to leave. Albert Einstein, who was visiting the United States, chose not to return to Germany. He was expelled from the Prussian Academy of Sciences, his citizenship was revoked, and he was reviled in Germany. Biochemist Fritz Albert Lipmann, who would later win the Nobel Prize in Physiology or Medicine, went with his wife first to Sweden and then to the United States.[6] World-famous conductors Otto Klemperer and Bruno Walter were also forced to flee, as were many Jewish writers and philosophers. Arnold Zweig went to Palestine, while Walter Benjamin went to Paris. When the Nazis occupied France, Benjamin fled to Spain, where he died from suicide in 1940. Hannah Arendt went to Paris and then to the United States. Not all opponents of the Nazi regime were able to leave Germany. At the age of eighty-six, the famous painter Max Liebermann was too old to emigrate. Liebermann was a past president of the Prussian Academy of the Arts and a recipient of Germany's highest order of merit (Pour le Mérite), yet his resignation from the academy elicited no response from his colleagues.[7] Wealthy Jews who had foreseen the danger and were able to obtain visas for themselves and their families departed Germany for Britain, the United States, or Switzerland. Some, like Salman Schocken, emigrated to Palestine.

Those who remained in Germany and expected Hitler to ameliorate his positions were to discover just how wrong they were. The Nazis wasted no time in introducing a series of anti-Jewish measures. On April 1, 1933, they imposed a boycott of Jewish shops and department stores throughout Germany. More than half of Germany's Jews earned their livelihood in commerce—including department store owners such as the Israel and Schocken families, whose stores were among the largest in Berlin. Panic spread among the Jewish shop owners. A week later, on April 7, the Law for the Restoration of the Professional Civil Service was promulgated, effectively removing Jews from all public positions. Some 22,000 Jews worked in the professions, including 8,000 physicians, as well as lawyers, artists, writers, actors, and musicians employed at publicly funded cultural institutions. All were dismissed at a stroke, and many were reduced to poverty. The Jewish community was flooded with requests for assistance but was unable to cope with the situation. On hearing the news, Arthur Ruppin wrote, "It is almost unbelievable that the proud German Jewry of 1920 should, within such a short time, have to face such a terribly degrading situation. Jewish doctors have been dismissed from the hospitals and Jewish judges from the courts. A general feeling of terror and legal insecurity reminiscent of the Middle Ages pervades German Jewry. The press is subject to strict censorship, and is extremely cautious about what it publishes."[8]

The Jews had barely begun to grasp the significance of the anti-Jewish measures when another law was passed on April 25, restricting the number of Jews admitted to schools and universities. Two weeks later, in the square in front of the opera house in Berlin and in cities and towns throughout Germany, Nazi students burned tens of thousands of books by Jewish authors, including Heinrich Heine, Albert Einstein, Arnold Zweig, Raymond Aron, Stefan Zweig, and many others. The book burnings were particularly traumatic for German Jews: beyond their economic impoverishment and exclusion from the public sphere, this was a further slap in the face to Jewish writers and thinkers who had contributed so much to German culture.

Ruppin understood the seriousness of the Nazi threat and was quick to help his brothers and sisters escape from Germany. Other Zionist leaders also helped their families get out of Germany. In 1933, 50,000 Jews left Germany, followed by a similar number over the course of the next two years, and many more wished to do the same. Szold believed that urgent assistance should be extended to German Jews. She knew that many families lacked the financial means to emigrate, while others had relatives who were too old to leave their homes and go to a foreign country. They also stood little chance of obtaining an entry visa to any country. She understood that the situation would not improve anytime in the near future, but it was hard to figure out exactly how to help the Jews under the Nazi threat.

UNDERPRIVILEGED CHILDREN

Poorer Jews had no choice but to remain in Germany, while others were conflicted about leaving. Parents who stayed in Germany saw their children tormented by classmates and teachers alike. Marta Appel described how her children would cry when they came home from school, as a result of the treatment to which they were subjected. They were forced to listen as the teachers denounced all Jews "as scoundrels and as the most destructive force in every country where they were living," while their classmates fixed their gazes on them, "examples of an outcast race."[9] The humiliation continued on the playground as well, as Jewish children were taunted and physically assaulted. German Jewish educator Joseph Walk wrote of "the suffering of a Jewish child forced to go to school day after day, to face derision, humiliation and even bodily harm."[10] Parents could not bear to see their children suffer. Marta Appel feared for her children: "'If only I could take my children out of here!' That thought was occupying my mind more and more. I no longer hoped for any change as did my husband. Besides, even a changed Germany could not make me forget that all our friends, the whole nation, had abandoned us in our need. It was no longer the same country for me."[11] Appel was not alone in her desire to get her children out of Nazi Germany. Many parents sought temporary havens for their children until the danger had passed.

Even before Hitler became chancellor, Recha Freier came up with an idea to help Jewish children. Freier lived near Alexanderplatz in a working-class area home to many Jewish immigrants from Eastern Europe. One summer's day, six teenage boys came to ask for her help. Not in school and unable to find work, they had no way of supporting themselves. Freier had no idea why they had come to her—she was not a well-known public figure—but she tried to help them anyway. She thought they could be sent to Palestine, but when she approached leaders of the Jewish community for assistance, she was met with scorn and derision.[12] She had no immigration certificates, no money to pay the boys' travel expenses, and no arrangements for them once they got to Palestine. Without these, there was no way to send them to Palestine. Freier had heard of Henrietta Szold and wrote to her, asking for help in obtaining immigration certificates for the boys who had come to her.

Szold was all too familiar with the bitter reality in Palestine, where so many abandoned children and orphans were left to their own devices, as the Yishuv had neither resources nor social workers to help them. She wondered how these boys from Germany would manage on their own, without any means of support, particularly at a time of high unemployment in Palestine. Szold was uncertain about how to respond to Freier's request and consulted with Dr. Arthur Biram, principal of the Reali School in Haifa, and Dr. Ernst Simon, who taught there. Both men thought it unwise to bring the boys to Palestine without the means to support them or allow them to study.[13] Dr. Siegfried Lehmann was visiting Berlin at the time, and when Freier asked him to take the six boys into the Ben Shemen Youth Village he directed, he agreed. The mandatory government had provided him with immigration certificates to bring Jewish orphans to Palestine, and his reputation as a brilliant and dedicated educator helped him secure the financial support of wealthy donors for his youth village.

After Hitler's rise to power, Freier established the Jüdische Jugendhilfe committee. She approached the envoys of the various Zionist movements involved in organizing the immigration of youth movement graduates to Palestine, suggesting they take underprivileged minors as well. The envoys rejected the suggestion, however, because they knew what had happened on previous occasions when groups of unaccompanied children had been brought to Palestine. A case in point was the experience of Israel Belkind, a pioneer in the field of education in Palestine, who brought a group of fifty-one Jewish orphans, survivors of the Kishinev pogrom, to Palestine. Unable to find an institution that would take the children or to raise sufficient funds to provide for their care, he was eventually forced to close the temporary institution he had created.[14]

Some parents in Germany applied directly to educational institutions and youth villages in Palestine, such as the Reali School, Mikveh Israel, and the girls' agricultural training farm in Nahalal, and enrolled their children. The parents arranged to cover all the costs of their children's education and living expenses. Szold agreed to help them. She met with Albert Hyamson, head of the mandatory government department of immigration, and asked him to issue immigration certificates for these children—of which there were only a few dozen at the time. Circumstances changed, however, following the barrage of anti-Jewish measures enacted by the Nazis during their first months in power.

In May 1933, Chaim Arlosoroff, head of the Jewish Agency's political department, visited Germany and witnessed the situation there: "I was constantly besieged by acquaintances, relatives, and friends, wanting help to immigrate to Palestine."[15] Arlosoroff estimated at more than 40,000 the number of Jews who had come to the Palestine Office to look into the possibility of immigrating to Palestine with their children. In the fall, the number of families seeking to immigrate swelled further. Many parents who were unable themselves to immigrate wanted to send their children to Palestine, just to get them out of Germany. Arlosoroff believed that the Yishuv could absorb large numbers of Jewish children from Germany, contingent upon the establishment of dozens of new youth villages along the lines of Ben Shemen, while others could be sent to schools on the kibbutzim and agricultural settlements.

Middle-class parents were prepared to pay for their children's schooling and upkeep in Palestine but were wary of handing their children over to unfamiliar institutions. They were, however, willing to entrust them to Zionist Organization leaders, in return for assurances that they would be provided with suitable schooling and living conditions. Weizmann, Ruppin, and other leaders supported efforts to bring these children from Germany to Palestine, and hoped that their parents would follow. While still in Germany, Arlosoroff arranged for a meeting with the British high commissioner in Palestine, Arthur Wauchope, to convince him to issue the necessary immigration certificates for the children.

Upon his return to Palestine, Arlosoroff invited Wauchope to visit the Ben Shemen Youth Village so that he might witness firsthand the quality of education offered there. Wauchope was duly impressed with the institution and with its director, Dr. Lehmann, and promised to provide immigration certificates for the children from Germany. Arlosoroff immediately sat down to devise a course of action to bring the plan to fruition. That very evening, however, June 16, 1933, as he was walking on the beach in Tel Aviv with his wife, Sima, he was shot and killed. Arlosoroff's murder heightened tensions within the Yishuv. It was unclear who was responsible, but blame was laid on his political rivals. Szold was shocked. She knew Arlosoroff and had been impressed with him. She deeply regretted the loss of such a talented and promising young man.

Arlosoroff's initiative, however, lived on. At the Eighteenth World Zionist Congress, held in Prague in August 1933, it was decided to establish a department within the Jewish Agency "for the settlement of German Jews," to oversee the absorption of German Jewish families in Palestine. Arthur Ruppin was chosen to head the department. It was also decided to establish a bureau within the department for unaccompanied immigrant youth. Weizmann and Ruppin, who recognized Szold's educational and organizational abilities, pressed her to take charge of youth immigration. They believed that Szold was the best and possibly the only person capable of dealing with this difficult and complex task. She turned them down.

Szold was seventy-three years old and had planned to return to the United States to be with her family. She was concerned about the Jewish children in Germany and, as head of the JNC social service department, was well acquainted with the difficulties experienced by children who had immigrated to Palestine from Germany with their parents: "The tide of German immigrants is constantly swelling. In Tel Aviv, the goal of eighty percent of them, the housing problem has assumed gigantic proportions. Whole families are sleeping on the beach for want of vacant rooms. . . . On the first of October Tel Aviv begins a local collection for the erection of barracks to meet immediate needs, and cheap dwellings in view of the large volume of immigrants announced for October."[16]

Under the circumstances, Szold did not see how the Yishuv could cope with unaccompanied children. Far from indifferent to the plight of German Jewry, she joined the committee for the settlement of German Jews in Palestine and was elected committee chair. She was also active in other organizations dedicated to the same cause. In October 1933, Szold traveled to London on behalf of the JNC to meet with representatives of the Central British Fund for German Jewry, in order to discuss the fund's ability to support the absorption of German Jewish immigrants in Palestine. Szold was well known in Jewish circles around the world, and received a warm welcome in London. She was invited to dine with Weizmann, and a reception was held in her honor at the elegant Palace Hotel on Kingston Road, attended by leading members of the local Jewish community. At a dinner hosted by Harry Sacher at his home, Szold met Simon Marks and Israel Sieff, members of the Jewish moneyed aristocracy in Britain. She was also invited to dine with Rabbi Joseph Herman Hertz, Britain's chief rabbi and an old friend of Szold's.[17]

Ruppin convinced Szold to travel on to Germany from London, in order to see the situation there for herself. He hoped she would be persuaded to found an organization for youth immigration to Palestine. Szold set sail for Germany aboard the SS *Naldera*. In Berlin, she heard part of Hitler's pre-election speech on the radio: "He referred to the emigrants who had left and were leaving the Third Reich as gypsies—*Zigeuner.* The interpretation is that he referred to all fugitives—Jews, liberals, pacifists and socialists. The audience in his hall . . . referred it expressly to the Jews alone. They cried: 'The Jews, the Jews!' The city is placarded with every sort of propaganda poster that imagination can devise. In the hotels, in the restaurants, in the synagogues, in the office buildings, on the streets, poster after poster. . . . The streets of Berlin are dead, empty. The shops are empty."[18]

In Berlin, Szold met with dozens of people, from morning to night: Jewish community representatives; the directors of the Palestine Office in Germany, Wilfred Israel and Dr. Ascher; members of the Jewish Youth Aid association; and envoys of the Jewish youth movements. She also met many frightened parents who told her of their children's suffering and wished to explore the possibility of sending them to Palestine. Szold was especially touched by her conversations with parents, which swayed her to accede to Ruppin's request. Years later, she described how those meetings with parents in Berlin made her feel a personal commitment to each and every one of the children.

On her way back to Palestine, Szold sat on the deck of the ship and wrote down ideas for the swift organization of an apparatus to bring the children, prepare places for them, and raise the necessary funds. As soon as she arrived, she informed Ruppin of her willingness to assume responsibility for youth immigration. Ruppin immediately convened a meeting, at which Szold was appointed head of Youth Aliyah—an organization that would work in conjunction with the Zionist Organization in Germany to bring German Jewish children to Palestine. A committee was established, comprising representatives of various organizations, to help Szold find suitable places for the young immigrants in Palestine. The meeting's concluding statement stipulated, among other things, that "no budget shall be allocated for this operation at the present time."[19] The task of raising funds for this ambitious project was left entirely to Szold.

Neither Szold nor the Zionist Organization was free to plan the youth immigration project as they saw fit. Authority regarding the immigration and absorption of the children rested with the mandatory government. The first hurdle Szold faced was to persuade the government to issue immigration certificates for hundreds of children. She met with High Commissioner Wauchope and with Albert Hyamson, head of the mandatory government's department of immigration, in order to convince them of the necessity of the project. Weizmann and his associates exerted pressure on the government in London, pointing out that certificates had previously been granted to students enrolled at the Hebrew University and the Technion, and to teenagers who wished to attend high schools in Palestine. The British agreed to issue immigration certificates in limited numbers, with the program to be reviewed every six months. They also impeded the work of Youth Aliyah with a variety of onerous restrictions. The certificates were limited to German citizens ages fifteen to seventeen who had been accepted to recognized educational institutions in Palestine. Housing had to be prearranged, and parents were required to pay in advance for all school and living expenses for the first year, and guarantee payment of all further expenses until their children turned eighteen. The visas were personal and non-transferable, and those that were not used were simply lost.

It soon became clear, however, that many parents who had previously been willing to pay for their children's education and upkeep were no longer able to do so, as they had since lost their jobs and suffered economic persecution. Funding therefore fell to the Zionist Organization, which gave the British a commitment that it would guarantee the education and upkeep of these children. In practice, responsibility for funding was laid squarely on Szold's shoulders. Szold herself added a further condition: a medical examination. She wanted to ensure that those with chronic illnesses did not become a burden on Youth Aliyah, which did not have the resources to care for sick children. She also wanted to prevent children with infectious diseases, such as tuberculosis, from coming to Palestine, so as not to infect others. Every Youth Aliyah candidate had to fill out a form with personal details, as well as a preference for religious or other type of education. Szold wanted to ensure that all of the children received the kind of education to which they were accustomed.

Youth Aliyah was a unique and unprecedented undertaking. For the first time, the Zionist Organization took upon itself to bring unaccompanied children to Palestine and to care for and educate them until they reached the age of majority. The task grew even harder after the outbreak of the war, as much younger children—orphaned in the Holocaust—were brought to Palestine, settled, and taken care of for longer periods by the institutions of Youth Aliyah.

YOUTH ALIYAH

"The organization of the transfer of the children from Germany to Palestine . . . deals with children—it is not child's play," Szold wrote.[20] She had been involved in many projects in the past but recognized that Youth Aliyah was unique in its complexity and in the degree of responsibility it entailed at every step. The children were coming to a foreign and unfamiliar country, without their parents, and all of the roles ordinarily played by parents in the raising of a child had to be filled. Szold felt responsible to each and every parent to meet the needs of the children in the best possible fashion and deal with the difficulties they faced.

Szold poured all of her strength into the meticulous planning of every detail. Arrangements had to be made on two fronts: in Germany and in Palestine. In Germany, a group of envoys of the Zionist youth movements gathered children from around the country, while others, such as Adam Simonsohn, Georg Lubinsky, Franz Ollendorf, Erich Rosenblit, and Eva Stern, worked together in Berlin to organize the children's passage. They took care of everything—from selecting the candidates in keeping with the British requirements to preparing the children themselves in order to mitigate the culture shock and difficulties in adjusting to life in Palestine. At the preparatory (*hakhsharah*) camps they established, counselors told the children about Zionism and life in Palestine, and taught them songs and a little Hebrew. Every boy and girl whose immigration was approved was given a list of clothing and other items suitable for the Palestinian climate. The *hakhsharah* camps helped to create a sense of group cohesion among children who did not know each other before. Each group of children was assigned a counselor at the camp, who accompanied them on their journey to Palestine. Szold sought to keep the *hakhsharah* counselors with their respective groups in Palestine as well, at the various schools and youth villages.

The most difficult part of the operation was the integration of the children in Palestine. The British certificates were contingent upon the creation of suitable educational institutions and boarding schools prior to the arrival of each group. This included hiring teams of teachers, counselors, and support staff to provide the necessary services for hundreds of immigrant children. The existing institutions were unable to cope with such large numbers. Szold looked into the possibility of bringing the children to the cities, as most had come from large cities in Germany. Building schools and dormitories from scratch, however, would have been time-consuming and costly. Beyond buildings, administrators, teachers, and counselors, they also had to provide for the children's accommodations and every other need. The agricultural colonies presented the same difficulties as the cities.

The only real option open to Szold was to appeal to the kibbutzim, which already had the basic infrastructure—schools, kitchens, dining rooms, clinics, and laundries. The agricultural work done on the kibbutzim also held out the possibility of vocational training, which Szold had decided would be part of the education given to the immigrant children, in order to allow them to earn a living after completing their schooling. Another consideration was the fact that settling the children on kibbutzim was far cheaper than in urban institutions. The economic circumstances of the younger kibbutzim were precarious, however, and had gotten considerably worse in the wake of the crisis of 1929. Kibbutz members lived in barracks, or even tents. Szold refused to house the children in tents, and she promised the kibbutzim loans for construction and payment for the children's education and upkeep. The kibbutzim thus became a central element in the absorption of youth immigration, by virtue of circumstances rather than design (as many would later claim).

The Youth Aliyah Office and youth movement envoys in Berlin wasted no time and immediately began to organize groups of children from all over Germany for immigration to Palestine. Szold spent a good deal of time obtaining the necessary immigration certificates. She met with the high commissioner and the head of the immigration department, to whom she submitted all of the candidates' personal information, but the mandatory authorities were slow to respond. Finally, the British allocated 350 certificates for the first half of 1934, and Youth Aliyah got under way. The first group, headed for Kibbutz Ein Harod, was supposed to comprise sixty-three candidates, ages fifteen to seventeen. Upon closer examination, however, it was discovered that some of the candidates did not meet the British criteria—whether because of their age or because they did not hold German citizenship—and only forty-three were approved. The strict enforcement of the rules imposed by the British caused considerable hardship and distress to those who had been on the verge of departing for Palestine but were disqualified at the last minute. The phenomenon repeated itself in the groups that followed. Szold was aware of the disappointment experienced by the children who were turned back, and she made every effort to convince the British to make some allowances—generally to no avail.[21] The delays in Germany meant that the departure of the first Youth Aliyah group was postponed by a few weeks.

ON A COLD WINTER'S DAY in February 1934, forty-three boys and girls stood with their luggage on the platform at the Anhalter Bahnhof in Berlin. Their parents bade them a tearful farewell, waving as the train pulled out of the station, unaware this would be the last time they would see their children.

On February 19, the SS *Martha Washington* docked at Haifa. Onboard was the group of children from Germany and their counselor, Chanoch Reinhold. Henrietta Szold left Jerusalem early that morning in order to meet them and was waiting on the dock when they arrived. The children spent the night in Haifa, traveling to Kibbutz Ein Harod the following day. Szold accompanied them to the kibbutz and stayed there with them for two days. She wanted to inspect their housing arrangements, aware that the permanent structures were not yet ready and that no temporary barracks had been built either. The kibbutz had proposed housing them temporarily in a building that had previously served as a cowshed or, alternatively, in tents. Szold had rejected both proposals. The kibbutz members thus agreed to vacate their own barracks for the children's use, while they themselves moved into tents. Szold also inspected the kitchen and the food the children were served, in order to ensure that everything was in order. She subsequently did the same for each and every Youth Aliyah group—meeting them at the harbor and accompanying them to the kibbutz or institution to which they had been directed. Even before the first group had left Germany, preparations were already under way to organize the next groups. In the winter of 1934, two more groups were prepared for immigration to Palestine: a group of girls, sent to the training farm established by Rahel Yanait Ben-Zvi in Jerusalem, and a group of religious boys, sent to Kvutzat Rodges.

Finding places for the religious children was a particularly arduous task. While the secular kibbutzim served as the primary destination for immigrant youth, there were hardly any religious kibbutzim. In the early 1930s, Rodges—named for the German locale where its founding members underwent their *hakhsharah* training—was the only religious kibbutz in the country, and was still in its infancy. The Rodges group did not have a moment's peace from the time they set foot in Palestine in 1929. First came four years of disagreements, departures, and arrivals. By 1933, little remained of the original group, and most of the members were recent immigrants who had arrived that very year. It was only in 1934 that the group moved to a location that had been assigned to them, near Petach Tikva. They suffered economic hardship, making a living as day laborers in the surrounding villages. The decision to cooperate with Youth Aliyah was not an easy one, not least because the number of child immigrants they had been asked to take was double their own membership. The arguments in favor of accepting the children were pragmatic as well as ideological: it was hoped that the payment they would receive from Youth Aliyah would help reduce their deficit somewhat.[22]

Youth Aliyah children in a kibbutz, dancing in front of their new houses

In June 1934, the first group of religious youth from Germany arrived at Kvutzat Rodges, and its members were stunned by what they saw. Shlomo Dan described it as follows: "Tents scattered in a barren landscape, without electricity or running water. The bathrooms were far away from the tents. The structure that had been built for us was ready, while the members of the kibbutz themselves lived in tents."[23] Shulamit Nahalliel, who was part of the first Youth Aliyah group to come to Rodges, recalled: "To welcome us, the members had prepared a nice gate. We looked around us and all we saw was sand, sand, and more sand. We had come from big cities in Germany. They made us cocoa, but by the time we got there, a few flies had already committed suicide in it. . . . Kibbutz member Leah showed us our rooms, but we were not alone in the rooms; we had boarders—fleas. A short time after our arrival, there was an outbreak of typhus. Many of the kibbutz members got sick, and three died."[24] Kvutzat Rodges member Meshulam Windreich (Margalit): "We suffered harsh conditions, many fell ill, and some died, like our friend Eli Michaelis. I also got typhus and was in the hospital for three months, unconscious for one."[25]

Although disturbed by the harsh conditions at Rodges, Szold had no choice but to send the children there, due to heavy pressure from religious groups and the constant accusation that she was excluding religious youth from the immigration program. It was difficult to find suitable places for them, since few religious educational institutions had dormitories and those that did were unable to take in large numbers of immigrant students. Szold provided the members of Kvutzat Rodges with a loan to build adequate housing for the children, and pressed them to complete construction before the children's arrival. The structure they built had running water and acceptable hygienic conditions, but Szold was troubled by the fact that the children were exposed to contagious diseases that endangered their lives. Due to the shortage of appropriate institutions, groups of religious children were delayed in Germany until places could be found for them in Palestine. The religious leadership repeatedly accused Szold of discrimination against the religious children. They said she herself was a Reform Jew and therefore favored non-religious children over Orthodox children. Szold was not, in fact, a Reform Jew; her father was one of the founders of Conservative Judaism in the United States. All of her explanations fell on deaf ears.[26]

The accusations were a slap in the face for Szold. Anyone who knew her knew that she was religiously observant, and her accusers were well aware of the difficulty in finding appropriate institutions for religious children. Szold rejected the notion that her job consisted of moving the children from place to place, as if they were objects. She recalled the frightened faces of the children in Germany as they said goodbye to their parents and left hearth and home for the unknown. The children's faces reflected the terrible tragedy that had befallen German Jewry. Szold strove to give them the feeling that they were welcomed with open arms in Palestine and deserved the very best, and was deeply wounded by the unfair accusations leveled against her.

THE YOUTH ALIYAH OFFICE

The Youth Aliyah Office oversaw all of the planning and arrangements for the children's arrival, education, upkeep, and follow-up. Szold worked closely with the Jewish Agency's Central Bureau for the Settlement of German Jews. The Youth Aliyah Office itself had only one employee: the secretary, Emma Ehrlich. Szold did not want a large staff. She preferred to be on top of things, to do things herself, and to ensure that everything was done in the best possible fashion. She also feared that a large

Szold speaks at the cornerstone-laying ceremony for Hadassah Hospital on
Mount Scopus, Jerusalem, 1934

apparatus would entail considerable employee training and supervision
that would take up a great deal of her time, and she was generally of the
opinion that bureaucracy does more harm than good. She conducted
the office's extensive correspondence herself, in English, German, and
Hebrew.

At the same time, Szold continued to fulfill her other roles. In October 1934, there was a cornerstone-laying ceremony for the Hadassah
Hospital on Mount Scopus, near the Hebrew University, and Szold served
as ceremony chair. She delivered the opening address, in which she recalled
the immense efforts over the years that had gone into making this moment
possible. She promised that the projected institution would be the largest
and most modern hospital in the entire Near East. The speeches were
broadcast via radio to New York and London.[27] After the ceremony, Szold
rushed back to the Youth Aliyah Office and the task of preparing for the
arrival of the next groups from Germany. In mid-December another eighty-
six children arrived and were taken to the Jordan Valley settlements.
Szold herself met them at the harbor and escorted them to the kibbutzim.
She stayed with them for two days, to ensure that they had everything they
needed, including mosquito nets. The members of the host kibbutzim all
gathered at Kvutzat Deganiah Aleph, where they held a "charming recep-

tion," which included singing and dancing. Szold wrote: "My pessimism regularly vanishes when I spend a few hours in a *kvuza*."[28]

BEYOND THE ABSORPTION of the children in the Yishuv and all that entailed, Szold was charged with a further task—raising funds to cover Youth Aliyah's ever-expanding costs. Within a year and a half of Youth Aliyah's founding, some 700 children had been settled in dozens of kibbutzim and educational institutions. The number of candidates rose quickly, and thousands of child immigrants were expected. The project's budgetary requirements increased accordingly. The coffers of the JNC and the Jewish Agency were empty and the revenue of Keren Hayesod negligible.

Szold was troubled by the lack of reliable funding for Youth Aliyah. She contacted her friends and acquaintances in Jewish communities around the world, explaining that Youth Aliyah was preparing for the settlement of 2,500 children in Palestine and needed their help. Szold enjoyed a sterling reputation, and the response was overwhelming. She founded Friends of Youth Aliyah associations in Europe—Britain, Holland, Denmark, Sweden, Norway, Italy, Bulgaria—South Africa, and Canada. Jews the world over were touched by the fate of their co-religionists in Germany, especially that of the children. They opened their hearts and wallets, and their contributions would provide Youth Aliyah with underlying financial support. Szold avoided raising funds in the United States, because she knew that it would have aroused the ire of Keren Hayesod. The money raised in other countries far outstripped donations to Keren Hayesod, eliciting vociferous complaints from its leaders, who attempted to curtail Szold's activities.

The sums raised by the various Friends of Youth Aliyah associations were considerable but still failed to meet the organization's constantly growing needs. Szold wrote to Hadassah president Rose Jacobs and the Hadassah executive committee, asking for their support. Hadassah had more than 30,000 members in the United States at the time and was still growing. They acceded to Szold's request and were able to provide around half of Youth Aliyah's operating budget. The sums provided by Hadassah increased as the situation for Jews under the Nazi regime worsened, allowing the project to bring many children to Palestine. The funding from Hadassah was central to Youth Aliyah's operation and growth, but it was still not enough. Additional resources were required, and Szold had to find them.

In the summer of 1935, Szold traveled to Amsterdam to attend a meeting of the associations that had raised money for Youth Aliyah. Her aim was to highlight the complexity and countless challenges posed by the task of settling the children in Palestine, and to present some of the educational institutions at which they were enrolled. She wished to thank Youth Aliyah's European supporters for their contributions and to encourage them in their efforts. Szold knew that there is nothing more motivating than direct, personal contact. En route to Holland, she stopped in Lucerne, Switzerland, to attend the Nineteenth World Zionist Congress.[29] She was of two minds about attending, as she wanted to avoid conflict with religious leaders who had accused her of discriminating against religious children. Ultimately, however, she decided that it was best to impress upon the delegates the tremendous difficulties faced by Youth Aliyah, the complexity of the task it had undertaken, and the heroic efforts it had made—even as it prepared for the arrival of many more children.

To Szold's surprise, she received a warm welcome at the congress, including greetings for her seventy-fifth birthday. At the session she attended, she was showered with praise for her many achievements—not least for her youth immigration work. Szold, who had been asked to address the congress, reviewed Youth Aliyah's work, the obstacles it faced, and the preparations under way for the absorption of thousands of children in the coming years. Chaim Weizmann, who was the session chair, announced that it had been decided to establish an agricultural settlement in her honor, as an expression of the gratitude felt by thousands of supporters and parents whose children she had saved from the clutches of the Nazis. What Weizmann and the others could not have known was that this was only the beginning for Youth Aliyah, which over the coming years would save tens of thousands of children from the bitter fate that awaited them under the Nazis. The kibbutz, which was named Kfar Szold, was established in the foothills of the Golan Heights, on the edge of the Hula Valley. Its fields were dotted with basalt stones, and a number of springs bubbled to the surface in the vicinity.

On September 15, 1935, a week after the congress ended, the Reichstag—in session at the Nazi Party convention in Nuremberg—enacted racial laws prohibiting sexual relations between Aryans and Jews, and restricting German citizenship to those of "German blood." The tens of thousands of Jews who had assimilated into German society and those who had converted to Christianity were disabused of the notion that their adopted identity would protect them. Even those who had served in the army and proven their patriotism and loyalty to Germany on the battlefield were completely defenseless. Although conditions in Germany continued to deteriorate, some continued to believe that the situation was serious but not hopeless. They were concerned, of course, but remained convinced that things were still tolerable and would soon change. However, the atmosphere of fear and anxiety in which they lived was clearly visible to outside observers. Ruppin described acquaintances he met at a hotel in a small German town: "Every time the Erlangers conversed with other German Jews at the hotel, they looked around in fear and spoke in hushed tones. A terrible feeling came over me, as if the days of the Inquisition and the Marranos had returned."[30]

The pressure on Youth Aliyah skyrocketed. Frightened parents were anxious to get their children out of Germany. German Jews were not alone, however. Poland's 3 million Jews suffered economic hardship as a result of the discriminatory policies of the Polish government. Antisemitism was rife and violence against Jews commonplace in many of the country's cities and towns. Urgent appeals were made to Youth Aliyah for the transfer of Jewish children from Poland to Palestine. David Ben-Gurion, who visited Poland at the time, remarked, "The nightmarish state of Polish Jewry—a state of perpetual political, physical, and moral pogroms—may be much worse than in Germany. The poverty is shocking; black despair and helplessness."[31]

Weizmann too demanded that the children from Poland be allowed to immigrate to Palestine, noting that "the German tragedy is . . . in size, much smaller than the Polish," and quoted the Polish foreign minister: "'There are a million Jews too many in Poland.' What does it mean? Where can they go?"[32] Other Zionist leaders also highlighted the plight of Polish Jews and their children, who suffered discrimination and violence at school. Jewish leaders in Poland pleaded with Szold to take Polish Jewish children to Palestine. Appeals also came from Romanian Jews to enroll their children in Youth Aliyah. Szold understood their situation, but their immigration was out of her hands. The British had agreed to issue immigration certificates only to children from Germany. There were millions of Jews in Eastern Europe, and the British did not want to come under pressure to allow the immigration of tens of thousands of children from that region.

HANS BEYTH: THE TRUSTED ASSISTANT

At this point, a new figure joined the administration of Youth Aliyah. Henrietta Szold met Hans Beyth by chance at the Bureau for the Settlement of German Jews. She noticed a shy young man standing in the hallway, engaged him in conversation, and invited him to come to her office.

Hans Beyth was born in 1901, in the German town of Bleicherode, to an assimilated Jewish family. At an early age, he became acquainted with a number of young Zionists and was impressed by them. He kept in touch

Hans Beyth, Henrietta
Szold's assistant at Youth
Aliyah

with them even after he moved to Berlin, where he worked at a bank, rising rapidly through the ranks and living a life of luxury. He continued to correspond with his Zionist friends and went to visit them at a *hakh-sharah* camp, where they were preparing for their imminent immigration to Palestine. He decided to join them, but wanted to visit Palestine first. In 1926, Beyth went to see his friends at Kibbutz Ein Harod. He looked into the various economic activities at the kibbutz, spoke to members, and came to the conclusion that the kibbutz would do well to open a cannery. As he planned to work in the cannery himself, he decided to gain experience working at a German cannery first. Having done that, he raised a large sum of money and also contributed some of his own, bought the necessary machinery, and shipped it to Ein Harod. He was certain the kibbutz would welcome the machinery, and was surprised to hear that the kibbutz was not interested in opening a cannery at all. Beyth was unfamiliar with the prevailing spirit and ideology of the kibbutz movement at the time. At this early stage in the movement's development, the kibbutz members were committed to agriculture rather than industry, which they identified with bourgeois society. The expensive machines that Beyth purchased were simply left to rust. In 1935, Beyth left Germany and immigrated to Palestine. He hoped to make use of his expertise in the field of finance, and went to the Bureau for the Settlement of German Jews, where he met Szold.

Szold was impressed with the enthusiastic young man and asked him to work at the Youth Aliyah Office. Two years after the organization's founding, Szold was preparing for the arrival of hundreds more children from Germany, and needed another staff member. Beyth turned out to be an unusually dedicated worker, above and beyond Szold's expectations. He began to work with her, accompanying her on her visits to Youth Aliyah institutions, and became her trusted assistant. He quickly acquainted himself with all of the difficulties the job presented, and spoke readily with the children and counselors. In many photos, Szold appears seated in the center, a solemn look on her face, surrounded by children and counselors all listening attentively. Beyth appears at her side, gazing at the children, his face beaming and eyes smiling. He had a phenomenal memory and, years later, remembered the names of hundreds of former Youth Aliyah children and the difficulties they faced. In Beyth, they saw an older brother. They admired Szold, but they loved Hans Beyth.

When he first arrived in Palestine, Beyth spoke no Hebrew, and Szold spoke to him in German—the language spoken at the Bureau for the Settlement of German Jews. His visits provided the children with a welcome opportunity to communicate in their mother tongue. At the kibbutzim and educational institutions where they lived and studied, they were encouraged to learn, read, and speak Hebrew rather than German. The conversations with Beyth thus came as a relief.

The days spent at the Youth Aliyah Office stretched from early morning to night, and Beyth did not go home as long as Szold was still there. He even came to work on his wedding day, leaving the office in the afternoon to go to the ceremony, which was held nearby. The ceremony was brief and attended by family members and a close circle of friends. Two hours later, Beyth returned to the office, and only then told Szold of his marriage.

Szold and Beyth became close friends outside of office hours. When his children were born, Szold would appear with a gift. When he had a daughter, after two sons, he named her Miriam Henrietta. On Miriam Henrietta's first birthday, Szold sent her a letter to read when she grew up.[33] Beyth's eldest, Michael, studied at the Hebrew *gymnasia* in Rehavia and would pass by the Youth Aliyah Office on his way home. On days when his father was there, he would come in and sit near him. The Beyth children saw very little of their father during the week. He would leave home early in the morning, before they woke up, and return late in the evening, after they had gone to bed.

Szold was not one to spend all of her time behind a desk. Every week, she dedicated two or three days to visiting Youth Aliyah institutions, in order to gain a better grasp of how she might help the children. She and

Hans Beyth and Henrietta Szold talk with Youth Aliyah counselors

Beyth would leave Jerusalem before dawn and would immediately get to work. Szold wanted to meet the teachers and counselors and speak with them, but mostly she wanted to talk to the children themselves. She spoke to them in their language, asking whether they were satisfied with the institution and with their studies, and whether they had any requests. Szold understood how hard it was for them to be separated from their parents and to adjust to a foreign country and a new language. Beyth was involved in all of Szold's plans and decisions, and admired her and her vast experience. More staff was hired over the course of the following years, as Youth Aliyah placed thousands of children in dozens of kibbutzim and educational institutions. Beyth was the most senior staff member and Szold's assistant director, assuming the role of director of Youth Aliyah after her death.

HENRIETTA SZOLD: "THE MOTHER OF YOUTH ALIYAH"

Szold worked hard to create favorable physical and educational conditions for the children, without losing sight of their personal and emotional needs. When unexpected difficulties arose, she hastened to address them personally. She instructed the counselors at the schools and kibbutzim to notify her of any illness or other source of concern. In one such case, Rahel Yanait Ben-Zvi informed Szold that one of the girls at her training farm

Henrietta Szold speaks with Youth Aliyah children

had been unwell and, on the doctor's advice, had been taken to the hospital, where she was examined and it was decided that surgery was required. Szold hurried to the hospital, spoke to the doctors there, and asked them to postpone the operation. She then contacted the girl's parents in Germany, told them about their daughter's condition and the doctors' recommendation, and asked for their consent. They told Szold that they trusted her judgment. After the operation, she went to visit the girl, and when she was discharged from the hospital, Szold found a place for her at a convalescent home.

The girls at Yanait Ben-Zvi's training farm had trouble adjusting to their new lives. Yanait Ben-Zvi, who had come to Palestine with the Second Aliyah and was imbued with the pioneering spirit, sought to wean the girls from their attachment to Germany and German culture.[34] She forbade them to speak or read German, and made every effort to instill in them the value of manual labor and the avoidance of luxury. The girls, who had come from bourgeois homes in large cities, found it hard to adapt to the ascetic lifestyle and hard physical work at the farm. Yanait Ben-Zvi would not relent, however, and the conflict eventually came to Szold's attention. She went to visit the farm and spoke with the girls. Sympathetic to their situation, she agreed to their request to be transferred to a different institution. Yanait Ben-Zvi was deeply offended, and the incident cast a shadow over her relations with Szold for years to come.

On another occasion, a kibbutz complained to Szold of improper behavior on the part of one of the Youth Aliyah girls. They accused the girl of having tried to seduce a number of men on the kibbutz, and asked Szold to send her elsewhere. Szold went to investigate, speaking with the kibbutz members and with the girl herself; she came to the conclusion that the girl was not cut out for kibbutz life, and transferred her to another institution.

A further case brought to Szold's attention involved a seventeen-year-old girl who had decided to marry and leave Youth Aliyah. Szold asked the girl to come see her, and tried to persuade her that she was too young for marriage and should finish high school and learn a trade first. The girl was adamant and rejected all of Szold's arguments. Szold inquired about the young man she wanted to marry and whether he had the means to support a family. She asked to meet the young man, in order to form her own impression of him, and notified the girl's mother in Germany of her daughter's intention to marry so young. To her surprise, the mother did not oppose her daughter's decision. When Szold saw that it was pointless to try to deter the girl, she invited her to come and see her again, spoke with her at length, and offered congratulations on her forthcoming marriage. Before they parted, Szold told her that if she ever found herself in trouble of any kind, she should not hesitate to come to her, and she would do whatever she could to help.

Shimon Sachs of Ein Harod recalled the following episode:

During the summer break, three of us boys decided to go on a trip together, and we hitchhiked to Jerusalem. We were given a small amount of money, but it was not enough. We had no relatives or acquaintances in the city. We walked around until we were exhausted. It was a long, hot day. We ate pita with falafel and enjoyed the smells of spices and coffee in the Old City. When we got tired, we decided to sleep at the train station. We lay down on the wooden benches and fell asleep, but were woken up by a blinding light. Standing over us was an Arab policeman, who ordered us to leave the premises immediately. Wretched and crushed we got up. Where should we go? Then one of us suggested that we go to Miss Szold's. After all, she had explicitly invited us and told us that her home is always open. We cast lots to decide who would ring the bell. She was still awake; the light was on in her room. She remembered us: "Boys from Ein Harod," she said. She made up beds for us and, in the morning, got up before us to make us breakfast.[35]

Like a devoted mother, Szold did not stop caring for "her children" after they had grown up and left Youth Aliyah, but tried to help them deal with all the challenges they faced in the adult world.

Yitzhak Olshan, a distinguished jurist who served on the Israeli Supreme Court, recalled how in 1939, as a young lawyer, he was assigned to defend a young man who had been caught in possession of a pistol—an offense that carried a five-year prison sentence. Olshan spoke to the young man and discovered that he was a member of the Haganah, which was why he was carrying a gun. He told Olshan that he was a Youth Aliyah graduate and, of his entire family, only he and his mother remained, and she was due to arrive in Palestine in a few days' time. Olshan called Szold, who was head of Youth Aliyah, and asked her to testify as a character witness on the young man's behalf. She came to court, took the witness stand, and in flawless English told the judge about the children of Youth Aliyah, the terrible tragedy they had experienced in their homeland, and their forced separation from their parents. She asked the court to show leniency. Szold made an impression on the military judge, and the young man was given a token sentence of one month in prison. Olshan told the judge that the young man's mother was due to arrive in a few days and would be shocked to find her son in prison. The judge agreed to release the accused without punishment, and he was able to meet his mother at the dock.[36]

At eighteen, some of the graduates of Youth Aliyah joined kibbutzim, while others went to the city. It was not easy for them to find work or a place to live, and they had no parents or other relatives in the country to whom they could turn. Hans Beyth recalled how one evening a graduate of Youth Aliyah knocked on his door and told him that she had been unable to find work and was desperate. He promised to arrange a loan that she could pay back after she found work, and he made sure she got the money the very next day. Szold knew of several similar cases and decided to set up a special fund for Youth Aliyah graduates, to support them until they found work. Some of the graduates chose to go on to university or to pursue studies in music or art, and Szold wanted to encourage them in their aspirations, providing them with scholarships. She contacted the famous American Jewish singer and actor Eddie Cantor, told him about her plan to establish a fund for Youth Aliyah graduates, and asked him to contribute. After a lengthy correspondence, in which Szold explained the nature of Youth Aliyah, Cantor made a large donation and the fund was named in his honor: the Eddie Cantor Fund for Graduates.[37] Many Youth Aliyah graduates relied on the fund's assistance as they began their adult lives in the country.

Szold came to be known as "the mother of Youth Aliyah." Twelve-year-old Nahum, for example, wrote to her from Kibbutz Hulda:

> Shmuel, our counselor, told us that you are the mother of all the children. I want to ask you, how is it possible to be the mother of so many children? I wanted to ask you, if you are everyone's mother, could you be my mother too. It is true that Hannah [the mother of his adoptive family on the kib-butz] is good to me. I go to her room every day, where she plays with her children, and I play with them too. But Uzi and Rachel call her both "Hannah" and "Mother," and I can call her only "Hannah." I once called her "Mother" too, and Uzi said that she is not my mother. Now that Shmuel has told us that you are everyone's mother, I want you to be my mother too. Then all the children would say, "That's Nahum's mother." And I would play with you, and you would take walks with me on Shabbat, just the two of us, and you would tell me about flowers and dreams and other things.[38]

Years later, when Mother's Day was instituted in the State of Israel, the date chosen was the anniversary of Henrietta Szold's death, February 13.

Szold was aware of the trauma the children had suffered as a result of the sudden, forced separation from their families. The transition from a home environment to a dormitory was not an easy one, but adapting to kibbutz life was even harder, as the concept of communal living was completely foreign to them. They had to hand their clothes in to the common storeroom and the money their parents had given them to the communal treasury. Moreover, most came from large cities and bourgeois families and found it hard to adjust to austere country life and agricultural labor. The pangs of homesickness were a constant presence.

One of the essential features of Youth Aliyah as devised by Szold was the close bond between the counselors and their respective groups. The counselors were with the children from the end of the school day through the evening and night, acting, to some extent, as surrogate parents. The counselors at religious institutions were themselves religiously observant. Counselors who had come with the groups from Germany remained with them at the various host kibbutzim and institutions. The counselors spoke German and were familiar with the culture and lifestyle in which the children had grown up, and thus they acted as a sort of bridge between the children's past and present. They were attuned to the children's feelings and needs and sensitive to any unusual behavior on their part, often enabling them to discover its cause.

Szold held the counselors in the highest esteem. She asked them for regular reports on the children's health and any significant behavioral problems. She maintained constant contact with them and encouraged them in their work. When she visited the kibbutzim and Youth Aliyah institutions, she would meet with the counselors and listen to what they had to say. She encouraged them to establish an association and to hold regular meetings where they could exchange views and discuss the difficulties they encountered. Szold suggested that Chanoch Reinhold (Rinott)—the outstanding counselor who had come from Germany with the first Youth Aliyah group—organize and head the association. The counselors published a bulletin and held frequent meetings, which Szold attended whenever she could.

Members of the participating kibbutzim "adopted" the Youth Aliyah children, in order to make the difficult process of acclimatization a little easier for them. While some kibbutz members encouraged the children to speak Hebrew and renounce their German language and culture, others—immigrants from Germany themselves—tried to make them feel at home. When they first arrived and were not yet fluent in Hebrew, the German-speaking kibbutz members were a great comfort to them. They would invite the children to their homes and tried to help them as much as possible. Shimon Sachs remembered the members of Ein Harod long after he had left Youth Aliyah: "There were people at Ein Harod who gave us so much and we wanted to be like them. One of these was Sara Yetzker, whose world revolved around the fruit trees at the foot of Mount Gilboa. I will never forget the ice-cold water she offered me from a clay pitcher [on a hot summer's day]. I also remember the writer David Maletz, who discussed world literature with us. He knew German and I remember the conversations we had with him about Franz Kafka and Thomas Mann."[39]

The counselors and educational directors in the city were no less attentive to the children's needs than their kibbutz counterparts. Ten-year-old Dolly Greenberg—future Israeli Supreme Court justice Dalia Dorner—was sent to the Neve Hayeled boarding school near Nahariya, run by a German-born couple, Herman Hirsch and his wife, Bertha Daniel Hirsch. There were some fifty boys and girls from various countries at the institution, most of them orphans, living six to a room. The funding provided by Youth Aliyah was scant. Dorner recalled that, nevertheless, "our *yekke* [German] counselors taught us universal values, love of humanity, and respect for all human beings. Careful attention was paid to our education. We were taught table manners and music appreciation, urged to engage in athletic activity, and encouraged to adapt to life in Palestine. The time I spent in Youth Aliyah was the happiest and most formative period of my life. The values instilled in me there have been a model for my entire life."[40]

Szold also had the highest regard for the social workers who cared for the children, many of whom had come to Palestine from Germany in the 1930s. They were extremely dedicated and worked long hours in order to help as many children as possible. The social worker Dora Strauss-Weigert, who was herself from Germany, spoke to the children in their own language and got them to open up to her, helping those who suffered from loneliness or homesickness or who were having trouble adjusting to their new home. Dvora Eliner (Dora Fraenkel), a German-born social worker, worked in the religious sector. As the number of Youth Aliyah children increased, so did the number of social workers employed by the organization. They treated children who suffered from anxiety disorders and other conditions reported by the counselors.

THE NEED TO GUARANTEE the children's safety at a time of increased violence in Palestine posed a serious problem. The Arab Revolt, which broke out in 1936 and included attacks against Jewish targets throughout the country, was a source of great concern to Szold. The Jewish population of Palestine had nearly doubled in the early 1930s (from 175,000 in 1931 to 335,000 in 1935), due to the arrival of large numbers of Jews from Germany and Poland, and the Arabs were determined to put a stop to it. They declared a general strike, hoping to destabilize the economy of the Yishuv, and informed the British that the strike would continue until their demands to halt Jewish immigration were met. At the same time, Arabs began attacking Jews, forcing Jewish passengers off buses and beating and stabbing them to death. Two Jews were murdered on the Tulkarm Road, and another three were slaughtered on the way from Safed to Tiberias. Jewish settlements around the country suffered attacks—fields and orchards were burned, property damaged, and casualties inflicted. Sixteen Jews were killed in Jaffa, with no end in sight.[41]

Szold instructed counselors at Youth Aliyah institutions to suspend field trips and keep the children inside kibbutz or school grounds at all times. When travel was unavoidable, adult accompaniment was required. The children resented these restrictions, but Szold was adamant and stressed how important they were. As a result of Szold's efforts, very few Youth Aliyah children came to harm during the disturbances. One boy was lightly injured but did not require hospitalization, while another sustained a leg injury and had to undergo surgery.

Szold's own travels around the country—whether meeting arriving Youth Aliyah groups at the port or visiting schools and kibbutzim—continued unabated. She had several near misses, including the following harrowing experience:

I am writing at the end of what has been perhaps the most murderous week since the beginning of the disturbances all but two years ago. I have lost count of the victims, young men, old men, women, and children, with practically not a word of condemnation of the outrages in the Arab press. Last Sunday I felt closer to the ruffianism than ever before. I traveled up to Haifa in a taxi. At less than twenty minutes' distance from the end of our journey, we had a puncture. It delayed us by over a half-hour. Less than an hour later—at five-thirty—two taxis were attacked by armed bands on that very spot. It happened that one of the cars was driven by an Arab chauffeur. All the passengers were wounded, the chauffeur was killed. It's gruesome. And there seems to be no end to it . . . and all this is happening in a country poignantly beautiful and peaceful-looking. Such a riot of bloom, such verdure, such blue skies . . . such rich promise of crops, with oranges gleaming from the trees. . . . Today cables came from Hadassah: Eddie Cantor collected $32,000 for the Austrian Youth Aliyah. Meantime it seems certain that we shall have to tackle Rumania, too. There should be many Eddie Cantors unless the Hitlers and Francos can be made innocuous.[42]

Regarding other events, she wrote:

On Friday a bomb exploded in the Jaffa marketplace killing [many people]. . . . In the afternoon my associate in the Aliyah, Mr. Hans Beyth, met a friend of his in the streets of Jerusalem. The friend had just arrived in town, his taxi having managed to escape from Ramleh. . . . As soon as the news of the bomb explosion in Jaffa reached Ramleh, the hoodlums there jumped to the conclusion that the dastardly deed was perpetrated by the Jews; and they stoned and shot at every taxi carrying Jews. Mr. Beyth's friend was covered with blood from top to toe, but not his own. He escaped unhurt, but the woman who sat next to him in the taxi was wounded in the cheek and her blood ran profusely.

And who was the woman? One of the Burgenlanders, the Austrians, seventy in number, who for months had been living on a raft in the Danube, not permitted to land in Austria (their home for centuries) or to take refuge in Czechoslovakia or Hungary on which their Danubian perch abutted, scourged daily by the Nazis who boarded the raft for the purpose, stung by swarms of mosquitoes by day and plagued by rats at night, their clothing dropping from them, undernourished by the food other Jews managed to get to them. For months all sorts of efforts were made to secure for them United States affidavits or Palestinian certificates. Two weeks ago some certificates were obtained; and she, this bleeding woman in the taxi, had been among the first to be released from her Danubian open-air prison, and promptly she dropped from the frying pan of the Nazis into the fire of the Arabs.[43]

BEFORE THE STORM

The British decided to revisit their policies in Palestine, and King Edward VIII appointed a royal commission headed by Lord William Peel—the Palestine Royal Commission, later popularly called the Peel Commission. Members of the commission were charged with the task of ascertaining the causes of the disturbances. Furthermore, they were asked to recommend a course of action to put an end to the Arab strike and to the disturbances. The commission members traveled throughout the country, visiting both Arab and Jewish centers and settlements, in order to gain a firsthand impression of the respective communities. To their surprise, as they entered an old shack on the edge of one of the kibbutzim, they discovered a grand piano, taking up most of the room. At the piano sat a famous musician from Germany. One of the members of the commission, Sir Horace Rumbold, a former British ambassador to Germany, remembered the pianist from Berlin, where he had heard him play. Rumbold turned to him and said, "This must be quite a change for you," to which the pianist replied, "Yes, it certainly is a change. I went from hell to heaven."[44]

The commission met with Arab and Jewish leaders, including Szold. Fearing that the British would stop youth immigration, she described Youth Aliyah's important work and achievements. She also told the commission members about the healthcare system, including the clinics and hospitals that Hadassah had established throughout the country to serve both the Jewish and Arab populations. She had hoped that the members would be impressed by the Yishuv's efforts to better the lives of all of the country's inhabitants, and was disappointed by their reactions. They were not prepared to listen, and told her that they already knew all about Hadassah.

Szold felt offended by and disappointed in the Peel Commission. She knew that no good would come of it for the Yishuv. Upon returning to London, the commission submitted its report to the government on July 7, 1937. The report's primary recommendation was to partition western Palestine into two states—one Jewish and one Arab.[45] The Arabs rejected the proposal outright. Among the Jews it provoked heated debate and was a source of considerable contention. The area designated by the commission for the Jewish state was small, and those who opposed the idea argued

The Jewish delegation to the Peel Commission, 1937

that the establishment of a state on such a small portion of the entire territory was unconscionable. Those who favored accepting the proposal believed in the immense value of an independent Jewish state, even within reduced borders.[16] The debate raged at the 1937 Zionist Congress, overshadowing all other issues. Hardest of all was the Peel Commission's recommendation to limit Jewish immigration to 15,000 per year for the coming five years. The Jews protested against such restrictions, but to no avail. Although disappointed in the Peel Commission, Szold took comfort in the fact that the restrictions did not affect Youth Aliyah, as its children were issued certificates as students, and their numbers continued to grow.

The political developments that followed in the wake of the Peel Commission's recommendations agitated the Yishuv. The colonial secretary, William Ormsby-Gore, supported the partition plan, as did High Commissioner Wauchope, who sought to convince Jewish and Arab leaders of its necessity. In order to win over the Arabs, he adopted the commission's recommendation for severe restrictions on Jewish immigration. The Arab countries intervened, however, taking a pan-Arab position against the establishment of a Jewish state of any kind in Palestine. Arab pressure worked, and the British abandoned the partition plan. Wauchope, who had been sympathetic to the Yishuv, was replaced as high commissioner in an unexpected way: while he was on holiday in London, it was decided that he would not be returning to Palestine, although his tenure had just been extended in 1936, by a further five years. In his place, the British government appointed Harold MacMichael, and Ormsby-Gore was replaced by Malcolm MacDonald. The new appointments were indicative of the way the wind was blowing: the men's pro-Arab sympathies were clear. The most severe and immediate measure was the adoption of the Peel Commission's recommendation to restrict Jewish immigration.

The mandatory government also sought to limit the expansion of Youth Aliyah to countries other than Germany. In light of pressure to allow the immigration of vulnerable youth from Poland and other countries, new restrictions were imposed in order to restrict their numbers. For example, it was decided that children who were not from Germany could not be sent to kibbutzim, which were the primary and most readily available destination. In the fall of 1937, Youth Aliyah planned to bring hundreds of children from Austria, Poland, and other countries. Due to the lack of available places for them, however, their immigration was postponed. Yitzhak Gruenbaum and other leaders in the Yishuv blamed Szold, and demanded an immediate increase in the number of children brought from Poland and other eastern Europe countries.

In 1937, Szold took part in the Twentieth Zionist Congress in Zurich. From Zurich she went to Germany to attend a farewell party for 112 children about to leave for Palestine. She was shocked by what she saw. In the two years since the enactment of the Nuremberg Laws, the situation in Germany had deteriorated significantly. Szold described the Jews there as "living corpses . . . capable of only one emotion—fear. . . . Those over forty-five or fifty have resigned themselves to their fate—they will rot in Germany." "Besides the parents of the young people now on their way to Palestine," she added "there came to the farewell 'party' many parents whose children have long been in Palestine in the Youth Immigration groups. They crowded round me, many of them with photographs of their children, which they thrust at me wanting to know whether I recognized them. While most of them expressed their happiness at their children's experiences in Palestine, some of them had petitions. I was nearly torn to pieces. . . . I am tired, very tired. I hope to get some rest on the boat, the *Marco Polo*. I shall need it, for I have five strenuous weeks ahead of me in Palestine before I set out for America to attend the Hadassah Convention."[47]

Szold was seventy-seven years old, but her travels continued apace. She agreed to come to the Hadassah Convention in Atlantic City, on the condition that she not be made the center of it. At the convention, she was surrounded with affection. The climax for Szold was when Hadassah voted a $25,000 donation, in memory of Felix Warburg, to her Central Children's Fund. She also received a $5,000 birthday gift. It was clear to everyone that she did not keep such gifts for herself, instead using them to further the cause to which she was dedicated. Szold was very pleased. "Hadassah," she wrote, "is a marvelous, flexible, well-oiled machine."[48]

After the Hadassah Convention, Szold remained in the United States for about two months. She visited her sisters: Bertha in Baltimore, and Adele and her husband, Thomas Seltzer, in Connecticut. They tried to convince her to stay in America. She would have liked to, but felt she had to return to Palestine: "Personally, a mountain of accumulated problems awaits me. Isn't it clear that it would be easier to remain in America? But one has a conscience."[49]

THE MAP OF EUROPE CHANGED in a matter of weeks. On March 12, 1938, Wehrmacht troops entered Austria and were welcomed by cheering crowds in Vienna. On the following day, Austria was annexed to the German Reich, and two days later, Hitler stood on the balcony of the Hofburg, the former imperial palace, and addressed hundreds of thousands of euphoric Viennese, declaring in a thundering voice: "As Führer and Chancellor of the German nation and Reich, I now report to history that my homeland has joined the German Reich."[50] The annexation of Austria to Germany (the Anschluss) brought some 200,000 Austrian Jews, mostly in Vienna, under Nazi control. Nazi persecution of the Jews began immediately, under the direction of SS officer Adolf Eichmann. "What the Germans learnt in the Reich in the course of five years, they have applied with Satanic efficiency in Vienna in the course of as many days," Szold wrote to her sisters, adding: "I can't think of anything but Hitler's hellish efficiency in the matter of Austria. As a matter of fact, I am depressed by what has happened, not first and foremost by reason of the fate of the Jews, but by what it forebodes for humanity. Is it possible to avoid the bloodiest war of history after what this week brought the world? And Czechoslovakia cannot but be the next victim."[51]

In Austria, Jewish businesses were confiscated, state employees dismissed, and licenses to practice medicine and the law revoked. Looting, expulsions, and public humiliation were commonplace, and Jewish homes were robbed with impunity. Money, jewelry, furniture, cars, homes, and businesses were taken by force from their Jewish owners. Jews who could not bear the humiliation died from suicide. Jewish communal institutions were shut down, and thousands of Jews flocked to the embassies of the United States and other countries, in the hope of obtaining a visa. More than 100,000 Austrian Jews were forced to leave the country during the first year of Nazi rule. There was a flood of requests from Austria for immigration certificates to Palestine, which the mandatory government denied. Even the wealthiest Austrian Jews had become impoverished and were thus unable to qualify for certificates as "capitalists."[52] Thousands of telegrams were sent by Austrian as well as Czechoslovak and German Jews to their relatives in Palestine, pleading for help in obtaining immigration certificates. Szold herself received such requests, as she wrote to her sisters: "The Austrian situation is overwhelming me. Practically daily I get a letter from one of our relatives in Vienna—some of them want certificates, some inquire whether I can secure affidavits for them for America."[53] Szold could not help her relatives, and did not want to use her connections with the heads of the Jewish Agency to get them certificates at the expense of other Jews. All of her relatives in Europe perished.

Szold was informed that the Nazis were allowing the Youth Aliyah Offices in Austria to continue to operate, and she demanded that the mandatory government issue the necessary certificates as soon as possible. The counselors in Vienna immediately began preparing groups of children for immigration to Palestine. In Vienna, Jewish children ages fourteen to seventeen were rescued before the outbreak of the war. Some were taken to Palestine, others to Britain and other countries. Jews in Prague followed the developments in Austria with trepidation, knowing that their country would be the next to come under Nazi control. Preparations were already under way to get the children out of Czechoslovakia. Everything depended on obtaining sufficient immigration certificates for Palestine.

Many parents from Austria and Czechoslovakia wrote to their children in Youth Aliyah, desperately seeking their help in arranging their own immigration to Palestine. Some wrote of the poverty and hardship they were experiencing. Disturbed by the news from home, many sought to leave Youth Aliyah and go to work, in order to send money to their parents. Szold and the counselors did their best to dissuade them. With unemployment high, they stood little chance of finding work anyway. Some, however, were adamant in their decision.[54] Over the course of the following two years, matters only got worse, and Jewish parents throughout the Reich were desperate for solutions. Szold found herself in a race against time.

KRISTALLNACHT WAS a turning point in the history of German Jewry. On the night of November 9–10, 1938, anti-Jewish pogroms broke out throughout Germany. Synagogue windows were smashed and the synagogues themselves set on fire. Police and firefighters intervened only to prevent the flames from spreading to neighboring buildings. Organized groups attacked Jews in their homes, hurling their possessions from the windows. According to an eyewitness in Cologne, "gramophones, sewing machines, and typewriters tumbled down into the streets. One of my colleagues even saw a piano being thrown out of a second-floor window. Even today one can still see bedding hanging from trees and bushes."[55] The destruction and looting continued for days. The Nazis arrested thousands of Jews, whom they detained for weeks, subjecting them to constant humiliation and torture. When they were finally released, they were shadows of their former selves. Many of those arrested never returned. According to the figures released by the Germans, 191 synagogues were destroyed and ninety-six Jews killed. Research has shown, however, that the number of synagogues destroyed and the number of Jews who were killed or died from suicide was in fact much higher.[56] The shock among German Jews was immense. The violence also spread throughout Austria. SS units destroyed synagogues, and Torah scrolls were thrown on bonfires. Thousands of Jewish homes and shops were looted. In Jewish cemeteries, tombstones were smashed. The elderly and the sick, as well as children, were caught and beaten by mobs. The November pogroms shook the Jews of the Reich to the core.

Kristallnacht was also a turning point in the history of Youth Aliyah. The dramatic events in Europe led Szold to change the policies that had served the organization since its establishment five years earlier. She decided to get the groups of children waiting in Germany and Austria out of those countries as soon as possible—even without certificates, *hakhsharah,* or medical examinations. The idea was to move them to Western European countries, to await immigration certificates there.

At the same time, Britain continued to pursue its policy of restricting Jewish immigration to Palestine, and immigration certificates became even harder to obtain.[57] Jewish Agency leaders suggested bringing 2,000 young Jews to Palestine, partly in the guise of students at the Hebrew University

and the Technion, as student permits were not included in the general immigration quota. The British, however, required proof of enrollment and
payment of tuition in advance. The students were unable to meet these
requirements, and the Jewish Agency's coffers were empty. Alternatively,
they sought to exploit the certificates granted through Youth Aliyah, demanding that the organization present those over eighteen as if they were
younger. The British were wary of any attempt to circumvent the rules and
threatened to reconsider the Youth Aliyah permits altogether. Edwin
Samuel (Herbert Samuel's son), who worked for the mandatory government, cautioned the Jewish Agency leaders that any attempt to deceive
the British could jeopardize the entire Youth Aliyah project.

Szold faced a dilemma. She wanted to allow the many young people
waiting to come to Palestine to do so as quickly as possible, but she feared
putting the entire project at risk. She saw violating or circumventing the
agreements with the mandatory government as a dangerous gamble that
could destroy all of the arrangements so painstakingly reached with the
British. She was especially concerned about the thousands of boys and girls
awaiting immigration certificates in transit countries. The Jewish Agency
leadership disagreed with Szold, arguing that the British position was im-
moral and unjust, guided by cynical motives and selfish interest, with the
sole objective of placating the Arabs. They also accused British officials of
antisemitism, and felt justified in trying to sidestep their regulations. Szold
was determined not to allow Youth Aliyah to be transformed from a project
for the immigration of students into a conduit for the immigration of
workers. It was one of the most bitter conflicts Szold had to contend with.
Years later, she was still accused of having shown shortsightedness in insisting on upholding agreements that her detractors saw as obstacles costing
the lives of many young people.

In September 1938, Szold was hospitalized for angina. Her hectic lifestyle, constant anxiety, and stress from the many conflicts in which she
found herself involved took their toll. Her doctors ordered a few weeks'
rest, but as soon as she felt a little better, she returned to work.

With the German invasion of Czechoslovakia and the occupation of
Prague in March 1939, a further 120,000 Jews came under Nazi control,
suffering the same fate as the Jews of Vienna. Jewish-owned property was
confiscated, businesses were looted, and restrictions were imposed, as in
Austria. The Jews of Czechoslovakia had been on edge ever since the Munich Agreement, aware of the dangers they faced. Nevertheless, many were
in no hurry to leave their homeland. They were at a loss as to how to deal
with the reality in which they now found themselves. Two days after the
beginning of the German occupation, all of the Zionist offices and social

institutions were shut down. Only Youth Aliyah was allowed to continue
to operate, since its declared goal was the expatriation of Jewish children—
an endeavor favored by the Germans, who wished to see every last Jew
removed from European soil. Parents pressed Youth Aliyah to take their
children out of Czechoslovakia, and the organization worked around the
clock to get them ready to leave. Within a short time, they were able to
move a group of 300 children to neighboring countries not under Nazi control, even as they continued to prepare additional groups.

Alongside Youth Aliyah, other organizations and Jewish community
leaders in countries under German control acted to get as many children
out as possible, without age restrictions—including children as young as
three or four. The children were quickly moved to various Western European countries, where they were to await permanent visas or Palestine immigration certificates. Greta Kraus, who was sent to Denmark, recalled:
"We were allowed to take one suitcase, one bag, one photograph, and ten
German marks."[58]

The countries of Western Europe refused to accept unlimited numbers
of refugee children, and imposed quotas. Denmark agreed to accept 300
children from the Reich, Sweden 500, and France 300; the Netherlands
fixed an overall quota of 7,000, including non-Jewish as well as Jewish
refugees. Norway and Belgium also established quotas, as did other countries. All of the countries in question granted permission only on condition that the children remain within their respective borders for a limited
period. Further conditions included guarantees from local Jewish communities that they would house and feed the children. In 1939, thousands
of children were sent to transit countries in the hope of saving their lives.
Only a portion were with Youth Aliyah. In each of the countries, groups
of volunteers from local Jewish communities attended to the children's
needs. The Youth Aliyah children were accompanied by counselors, who
looked after them as they awaited their certificates for Palestine.[59]

Szold appealed to all of her contacts in the mandatory government,
while the Jewish leadership in London exerted pressure on the British
government to increase the quotas for Youth Aliyah—and they succeeded.
In 1939, Youth Aliyah was granted 2,500 certificates, the largest number
ever allocated to the organization from its inception in 1934 to the end of
the war. Szold worked tirelessly to raise the funds to support the children—
who had doubled in number—at the various Youth Aliyah institutions and
kibbutzim. Within only a few months, she managed to raise over 400,000
Palestine pounds.

In Britain, growing public pressure on the government to lift the restrictions on Jewish immigration to Palestine at such a difficult hour met with

Jewish protest demonstration against Palestine white paper, May 1939

failure. The British feared renewed Arab violence. Instead, they decided to allow tens of thousands of Jewish children to come to Britain, where they would be allowed to remain until they could return home. The operation, known as the Kindertransport, was run by volunteers who organized groups of children in countries under German control for transfer to Britain. Among those sent to Britain were 2,000 non-Jewish children. About a thousand Youth Aliyah children were also taken to Britain, together with their counselors.[60]

At the height of the panicked flight of Jews from the lands of the Reich, in May 1939, the British Foreign Office issued a white paper reflecting the government's pro-Arab policy. Jewish immigration to Palestine was limited to 75,000 people over five years, and the Jewish purchase of land from Arabs was restricted.[61] Closing the gates to Palestine as the Nazi persecution of the Jews was escalating provoked outrage in the Yishuv. Large rallies and protests were held throughout the country, at which anti-British signs and banners were raised.

Youth Aliyah children arriving at Jaffa Port

Szold's sisters, Bertha and Adele, went to Palestine to see her in April 1939, because she was too busy to go to America. They accompanied her on visits to Youth Aliyah institutions and kibbutzim but, for the most part, toured the country on their own, because she was unable to get away from work. Bertha and Adele were particularly struck by the tension between Jews and Arabs. "There were barricades along most of the roads leading into the city," Adele wrote to her husband, along with curfews and searches for arms. Even non-prohibited spots were unsafe. The curator of the Rockefeller Museum, an Englishman, had been shot as he was putting his car into his garage in a supposedly safe section of the city.[62] Henrietta was extremely busy and could not spend much time with her sisters during their visit. She never imagined that it would be the last time she would see them. After their return to the United States, Bertha and Adele pleaded with her to retire, as she was nearly eighty years old. She replied that she wanted to take their advice, but found herself unable to do so: "I always knew it was hard to get a job, but I never knew it was so hard to get out of a job, as I am finding it."[63]

During the summer months, the winds of war were already blowing. Szold, who remembered the horrors of the First World War, was extremely worried. In August 1939, the Zionist Congress met in Geneva, in the shadow of the approaching war. Emanuel Neumann recalled the delegates speculating whether and when the international frontiers would be closed and how they would return home. He remarked that "the congress was hurrying through its business before the lights went out in Europe."[64]

In the final days of August 1939, as the war fast approached, a ship docked at the Jaffa port, carrying a group of Youth Aliyah children. As was her custom, Szold left Jerusalem early in the morning to go meet the children at the port. The ship was unable to enter the harbor, as the water was not deep enough, and stood hundreds of meters from the coast. The passengers were ferried ashore in small boats. The children were frightened as the boats tossed back and forth on the waves. When they reached shore, the Arab boatmen lifted each of the children safely onto the dock.

On one of the boats was fifteen-year-old Naftali Bezem. He recalled how he felt sick in the boat and apparently fainted when he was lifted ashore. When he opened his eyes, he found himself in the arms of a woman with white hair, who he later discovered was Henrietta Szold.[65] The experience of the pitching boat was traumatic for the boy and symbolized leaving behind everything he had ever known, but also reaching a safe harbor. Bezem went on to become a famous painter in Israel, and many of his works feature boats. Even when painting entirely different subjects, he would paint a small boat, as a kind of signature, in the corner of the canvas.

14

WAR AND CALAMITY

HE WORLD WAR BROKE OUT with the Nazi invasion of Poland on September 1, 1939. Wehrmacht ground troops, supported by over a thousand aircraft, encircled the Polish army and occupied the country with lightning speed. The Jews who fled eastward found themselves trapped in Soviet-controlled territory. The Red Army invaded Poland, in accordance with a secret pact with the Germans for the partition of the country. Polish leaders established a government in exile. The leaders of the Yishuv decided to lend their support to the British in the war against the Nazis, despite anger over the recent white paper restricting Jewish immigration to Palestine. David Ben-Gurion's view was that the Yishuv should support the British war effort as if there were no white paper and oppose the white paper as if there were no war.

In London, Chaim Weizmann made a last-minute attempt to save Jewish children in Poland. As soon as the war broke out, Weizmann put his scientific abilities at the service of the War Office, as he had during the First World War, to great effect. He asked the British government, in light of the tragic situation in Europe, to grant 25,000 Jewish children from Poland, ages ten to fifteen, immediate entry to Palestine. Weizmann stressed that this would not constitute a breach of the white paper, as the paper itself included a provision for the admission of 25,000 refugees, promising special consideration to refugee children. Weizmann hoped the British would keep their promise. He also obtained the consent of Witold Hulanicki, the Polish consul in Palestine.

Officials in the Colonial and Foreign Offices, however, did everything they could to block the initiative. In internal communications, the move was dismissed as a trick of the Zionists and a transparent attempt to exploit the war to further their political aims. The memos were peppered with antisemitic remarks.[1] Weizmann approached the colonial secretary, Malcolm MacDonald, imploring him to grant entry to the refugee children as promised, going as far as to say that denying them entry was tantamount to sentencing them to death. He warned that the Jews of Poland were in immediate danger and that it was imperative to grant the permits he had requested, at the very least, to save the lives of 25,000 children. He promised that all the costs would be borne by the Jews in Palestine and in other countries. He appealed to MacDonald's conscience, telling him that it was a matter of life and death and that the children's fate lay entirely in his hands.[2] MacDonald spoke to the foreign secretary, Lord Halifax, and they resolved to bring the matter to the rest of the government before reaching a final decision. Letters were sent to High Commissioner Harold MacMichael, to John Shuckburgh of the Colonial Office, and to the Foreign Office. The urgent need for action was clear to everyone, but MacDonald, like his colleagues, feared an Arab reaction and avoided taking immediate action. The Colonial Office dragged its feet. By late September, the Nazis already controlled central and western Poland, and with the fall of the Polish government, the British informed Weizmann that the plan was no longer feasible.[3] The fate of the children, like that of all of the Jews in Nazi-occupied Poland, was sealed. Had Weizmann's plan not been thwarted, it would have been one of the Second World War's greatest rescue operations.

With the outbreak of the war, all Jewish organizations in countries under German control ceased activities, with the exception of Youth Aliyah, which the Nazis allowed to continue to operate because its declared goal was the transfer of Jewish children out of Europe. This coincided with the Nazi goal of "cleansing" Europe of its Jewish population, adults and children alike. The Youth Aliyah counselors in Europe continued to work quickly and selflessly to organize the children and get them out of harm's way.

At the same time as Jewish leaders were frantically working to get children out of Europe, Szold was also overwhelmed with personal grief. In March 1940, she learned that her sister Adele had passed away in New York after a prolonged illness. Her heart went out to her youngest sister—an educated, talented, and creative woman, who died childless and alone—

and deeply regretted that she had been unable to be by her side. Of her entire family, only her sister Bertha remained.

FROM THE EASTERN FRONT, the Nazis turned to Western Europe and, within a short time, conquered one country after another. In May 1940, German tanks crossed the border into the Netherlands, and frightened Jews urgently sought to reach the country's North Sea ports to escape to England. Among them were seventy-five Youth Aliyah children, helped by a Dutch woman, Geertruida Wijsmuller. She took the children from an Amsterdam orphanage to the port of Ijmuiden and convinced the captain of a Dutch ship about to sail for England to take them aboard, thereby saving their lives. Not all the groups waiting in Holland managed to leave the country, however. Within days, the Germans were advancing on The Hague, and following the heavy bombardment of Rotterdam, the Dutch surrendered. The Germans then went on to conquer the countries of Western Europe in rapid succession, from Norway to France.

Szold was shocked by the news. The worse Nazi treatment of the Jews in the occupied countries became, the more Szold worried about the children who had been sent to transit countries and had fallen into German hands. In group photographs taken near Youth Aliyah centers before the Nazi occupation, the children appear well dressed, chatting or laughing in front of the camera, as if at summer camp. In 1941, the Nazis prohibited all Jewish emigration from countries under their control. The fate of the Youth Aliyah children, like that of many local Jews who had sought to escape but failed, was sealed.

Benito Mussolini, leader of the ruling Fascist movement in Italy, joined the war alongside Germany in June 1940. Mediterranean shipping routes were blocked and immigration to Palestine via Italy was suspended. In light of the situation in the Mediterranean, Szold appealed to the countries of Eastern Europe in a desperate attempt to get the groups of children awaiting transport out as quickly as possible by land.

Meanwhile, Britain was growing alarmed at the rapid German advance in Western Europe. Neville Chamberlain was forced to step down as prime minister and was replaced by Winston Churchill, who formed a national coalition government. After conquering the western part of the continent, German forces turned their attention to Britain, the only remaining threat to their hegemony. German aircraft began an extensive bombing campaign of British cities—London in particular. Thousands were killed in the bombings, and large areas of London, including many historic buildings, lay in ruins. Churchill urged Britons to remain strong in the face of the killing and destruction wrought by the Nazis. In a stirring speech, he told the British people: "I have nothing to offer but blood, toil, tears and sweat. . . . You ask, what is our aim? . . . It is victory, victory at all costs . . . for without victory, there is no survival."⁴

The Battle of Britain continued until mid-September 1940. The British army fought bravely, and although the Royal Air Force suffered heavy losses, the Germans were defeated and their plan to invade Britain thwarted. The Youth Aliyah children in Britain were spared the terrible fate that awaited Jewish children in countries under Nazi occupation. During the heavy German bombing of London, Manchester, and other cities, large numbers of women and children were evacuated to the countryside. Many of the Jewish refugee children who were evacuated were placed in non-Jewish homes and cut off from the Jewish community. The Youth Aliyah counselors kept in constant touch with the children entrusted to them. A number of *hakhsharah* groups were formed, where the children were given agricultural training. Many of the Youth Aliyah children who had been transferred to England emigrated to Palestine after the war, with some joining existing kibbutzim and others founding kibbutzim of their own.

The British further tightened their immigration policy in Palestine, denying entry to Jews escaping from Europe. Left with little choice, groups of Jews began to prepare for clandestine emigration to Palestine. To that end, 1,771 people set sail from Central Europe to Palestine aboard two ships. The British discovered and arrested them before they could come ashore, and transferred them—along with 1,800 illegal immigrants—to another ship, the SS *Patria,* hired to take them to Mauritius. "[Then] a tragedy occurred. . . . [The *Patria*] blew up and sank within fifteen minutes in Haifa Bay. Around 260 persons lost their lives; 209 bodies were eventually recovered. . . . The survivors of the *Patria* were permitted by the British to remain in Palestine . . . and were interned for some time at a detention camp at Athlit."⁵

Szold set up an emergency organization to help the illegal immigrants, collecting funds from various groups, including Hadassah, and got immediately to work. She tried to help those who were interned at Atlit, sending them clothing and food, but primarily she exerted pressure on the British to release the children and transfer them to Youth Aliyah institutions.

DESPITE THE DIRE SITUATION, Szold's eightieth birthday in December 1940 did not pass unnoticed. Youth Aliyah members past and present, representing some 10,000 of their peers, gathered to honor Szold at the Ben Shemen Youth Village. The doctors and nurses at Hadassah Hospital also organized a

Henrietta Szold with Youth Aliyah children in a kibbutz

celebration in her honor. Events were held in 500 cities around the United States.

Hadassah, which had some 95,000 members at the time, sent Szold a gift of $25,000, which she donated to an educational program under the auspices of Youth Aliyah—the Child and Youth Welfare Organization—to provide assistance to children from Arab and Muslim countries. Szold received hundreds of congratulatory letters, many from people she did not know. For the most part, however, her attention was focused on the arrival of 235 children from Romania and Sweden, who had been granted transit visas by Turkey, allowing the group to pass into Syria and then to Palestine. Efforts continued to try to save as many Youth Aliyah groups as possible.

In the middle of this work, Szold was once again struck by grief, this time at the passing of her friend Louis Brandeis, a man she admired greatly.[6] She was invited to pay tribute to him at Ein Hashofet (the kibbutz named in his honor) and at a meeting of the Zionist Executive. She also learned, with great sadness, of the personal tragedy suffered by Chaim Weizmann, whose son Michael—a British fighter pilot—had been reported missing in action while flying a mission against German submarines. Chaim and Vera

Weizmann hoped he would be found alive, but were informed a few days later that he had been killed. In addition, their elder son, Benjamin (Benjie), suffered combat fatigue during the war. The Weizmanns thus had direct experience of the tragedy of war.

WITH THE OUTBREAK OF THE WAR, a sense of restlessness came over the Yishuv. Young people had no desire to sit by and do nothing while their counterparts in other countries were going to war. Youth Aliyah graduates too wished to enlist and were all the more motivated to fight the satanic forces of darkness seeking to destroy their own families. From the beginning of the war, the Zionist leadership had acted, both in Palestine and in London, for the establishment of Jewish battalions in order to create a fighting Jewish brigade within the British army. Weizmann used his influence with Churchill and others. His intention was not only to help the British in the war against the Nazis, but also to further the establishment of an independent Jewish state. Some 95,000 men and 46,000 women answered the Jewish Agency's call at the beginning of the war to enlist, with most expressing their desire to serve in the British army. The British, however, agreed to enlist only 10,000 Jews in the first two years of the war, because the number of Arab volunteers was small, and they did not want a pronounced Jewish majority among the Palestinian recruits. They were also wary of creating an independent Jewish military force, and therefore they ensured that command remained in the hands of British officers. The Palestine volunteers included many Youth Aliyah graduates. Even boys who had not yet turned eighteen lied about their age in order to enlist.

Szold recognized the importance of joining the fight against the Nazis, but she felt responsible for the welfare of the boys and girls of Youth Aliyah—especially those who were the sole surviving members of their families. She understood why they were so eager to fight the Germans, who had destroyed their lives and threatened the lives of their parents and relatives. By this time, they had also lost contact with their families and did not know what had happened to them. Hans Beyth, who had left many relatives and close friends behind, understood them all too well, but he agreed with Szold. Szold and Beyth went to the kibbutzim and schools to speak to the counselors and the students. They did not want to criticize enlistment per se, but merely to dampen the enthusiasm to join the fighting forces, especially among those who were still underage. Szold asked them, "What would your parents say? Would they want you to risk your lives in the war?" Many years later, Shimon Sachs, who was a member of Youth Aliyah at Kibbutz Ein Harod at the time, recalled the encounter with Szold:

"We were tense before the meeting. When she stood before us and spoke, each of us felt she was speaking to them personally. She gave voice to the anguish in our hearts and to our fears for our parents in the diaspora. She hinted at the light in our lives in our new world . . . and filled us with renewed faith."[7] They were also receptive to Beyth, in whom they saw an older brother, but many remained steadfast in their determination to fight. The recruits from the Yishuv during the war numbered about 26,000, including a disproportionate number—thousands of boys and 200 girls—from Youth Aliyah.

In early 1942, reports began to appear in the press in Palestine about the deportation of Jewish adults and children to concentration camps from which they never returned. These were followed, later in the year, by reports that Jews were being murdered en masse. The Yishuv was in a state of shock. Nearly everyone had relatives in Europe, and the idea that they had all been condemned to death was beyond comprehension. No one could have imagined that entire communities, men, women, and children, would be consumed in the flames of the crematoria, disappearing off the face of the earth.

THE YISHUV IN THE SHADOW OF THE HOLOCAUST

In the years 1941–1942, the number of immigrants from war-torn Europe diminished significantly, as did the number of children brought to Palestine by Youth Aliyah. At the same time, earlier groups were completing their course of study at the various kibbutzim and Youth Aliyah institutions. Szold decided to use the places that opened up for local underprivileged, abandoned children, whose plight she remembered well from her struggle as a member of the Jewish National Council for the establishment of a social service department. She hoped that providing them with the opportunity to continue their studies and learn a trade would help them integrate into society. She also sought to create greater social cohesion between Jews from Arab and Muslim countries (Edot ha-Mizrah) and those of European (Ashkenazi) heritage. A few kibbutzim were selected for the project, including Kibbutz Tirat Tzvi, for religious children.

In selecting the children, she was assisted by her colleagues at the social service offices operated by the JNC social service department she had founded. The social workers were pleased at the chance to improve the prospects of these unfortunate children. They visited the families and offered parents the opportunity of enrolling their children in the program at various kibbutzim and Youth Aliyah institutions. The conditions in which these families lived, mostly in poor neighborhoods in Jerusalem, Tel Aviv, and the other cities, were harsh. The social workers who visited their homes encountered extreme poverty. One social worker told of a family of ten that lived in a small tin-roofed shack, sleeping on mattresses laid out on the floor of a single room. Most of the fathers worked as low-paid occasional laborers. In some of the families, a parent had died, and the children were sent out to work at a young age. Most of the girls worked cleaning houses. When the social workers suggested to parents that they enroll their children in the youth community program, some declined because they needed them to help support the family. Ninety children were selected for the program's first cycle, and Szold continued to enroll underprivileged children in subsequent cycles. By the end of the war, about 1,000 local children had joined the Youth Aliyah program, mostly on kibbutzim.[8]

CHILDREN FROM ARAB AND MUSLIM COUNTRIES

In 1941, thousands of Jews fleeing persecution in Yemen, including many children, sought refuge in the British protectorate of Aden. Szold contacted the Jewish Agency emissary in Aden and asked him to send the children to Youth Aliyah in Palestine. Sixty-four children were accepted, with no health or age requirements; the group included a number of children under fourteen. They were housed at the Meir Shfeyah Youth Village, where they were guaranteed a traditional environment. Immigration from Yemen continued, and of the hundreds of children who arrived in Palestine, fifty more were sent to Shfeyah. Due to the shortage of places at religious institutions, some of them were sent to foster families in Rehovot.

In the summer of 1941, reports reached Palestine of the Farhud—a violent pogrom against the Jews of Baghdad. In light of the dangers they faced in Iraq, Ben-Gurion called for their immediate immigration to Palestine, adding that immigration from Europe was no longer possible due to the maritime blockade, leaving only overland immigration from neighboring countries.[9] Eliyahu Dobkin, head of the Jewish Agency's immigration department, also called for youth immigration from Turkey via Syria. Emissaries sent to Iraq helped organize the immigration of children from that country, and small groups of children from Syria were sent to the youth community (*hevrat no'ar*) at Kibbutz Afikim and to other institutions. A group of fifteen- to seventeen-year-old girls from Syria and Lebanon was sent to the Ayanot women's farm. Over the course of the following two years, Youth Aliyah placed and looked after some 850 children from Turkey. Jewish immigration from Arab countries was illegal, which is why they were smuggled into Palestine in small groups. From 1941 to 1943, some 10,000 children immigrated to Palestine, including about 1,000 from

Mediterranean countries, as well as Holocaust survivors placed and cared for by Youth Aliyah.[10]

In the summer of 1942, the Yishuv itself came under threat, as German forces advanced toward Palestine. General Erwin Rommel's Afrika Korps pushed into Egypt and, in July 1942, reached El Alamein, where the British managed to halt his eastward drive. The British had prepared for the possibility that they might have to withdraw from Palestine. The fate of the Yishuv lay in the balance, and the Jewish inhabitants of Palestine were gripped by fear. Some in the Haganah considered preparing for a desperate, Masada-like last stand. When the British defeated the Germans at El Alamein on November 4, 1942, the entire Yishuv breathed a deep sigh of relief.

THE TEHRAN CHILDREN

That same summer, at European Jewry's darkest hour, word reached the Yishuv that tens of thousands of Jews, adults and children, who had fled Poland and found refuge in the Soviet Union at the beginning of the war had survived and were on their way to Palestine. This raised hopes that many more Jews might have managed to escape the clutches of the Nazis and that they too might make their way to Palestine. The excitement was palpable.

The Soviets acceded to a request by the Polish army in exile, under the command of General Władysław Anders, allowing it to leave the Soviet Union. Anders's forces numbered about 30,000, including some 600 Jews and 300 Polish civilians. The Soviets granted permission to the soldiers' families and to children from Polish orphanages on Soviet soil to go with them. Anders's intention was to transfer the Polish recruits to Iran, then under British control, and to join the war against Germany. There were many Jewish refugees in the Soviet Union, who had fled Poland at the time of the German invasion. When they learned that the Polish soldiers and civilians would be leaving the country, many tried to take advantage of the opportunity to reach Iran. Jewish mothers who heard that the Polish orphanages were to be evacuated sought to place their children in those institutions, in order to save them from the ravages of hunger and disease that had already taken a deadly toll. Infants were laid on the orphanages' doorsteps, and older children were snuck in with crosses around their necks, pretending to be Christians. The children left for Tehran, with the soldiers, in the summer of 1942.

The Jewish Agency sent emissaries to Tehran to help the Jewish refugees as they arrived in Iran. One of these emissaries, Reuven Shefer, described his first encounter with the refugees: "I stood in Pahlavi [today Bandar e-Anzali], near the port, as a group of eight hundred refugees, including some fifty Jews, disembarked. Never before have I seen such a heart-wrenching sight. . . . [They were] swollen with hunger, clad in rags, broken in spirit and utterly without hope."[11]

In the Yishuv, it was estimated that up to 1 million Jews had escaped to Iran. Many had died of hunger, exposure, and disease, and it was clear that the surviving refugees were in need of urgent assistance. The Jewish Agency asked members of the Yishuv to send parcels of food and clothing. The goal was to resettle them in Palestine as soon as possible. Many children were expected, and Szold was stirred to action. She saw these children as harbingers of a great wave of immigration, which she believed the Yishuv had the capacity to absorb.[12] Certain that the children would be entrusted to Youth Aliyah, she began to prepare for their arrival.

All of the children who arrived in Tehran were housed in a large camp. The Jewish Agency emissaries were charged with the task of identifying the Jewish children and moving them to a separate camp, known as the Jewish orphanage, established for that purpose by operatives of the Mossad le-Aliyah Bet.[13] When word of the separate camp got around, some children ran away from the main camp and came to the Jewish orphanage of their own accord. In August 1942, there were 612 children in the Jewish camp, about 100 of whom were between six months and ten years. A month later, their number rose by a further 80. Zipporah Shertok, wife of Moshe Shertok (Sharett), then head of the Jewish Agency's political department, volunteered to work at the Jewish orphanage, and she described the living conditions and the state of the children in the camp. "A hundred children up to age eight lived together in the barracks. They slept on thin mattresses on the floor, and only some of them had sheets. The children older than eight were housed in tents. They slept on mats on the floor, without mattresses, and covered themselves with blankets. Some of the tents were incomplete and let in the rain and the cold, and the children got sick. Two hundred children are barefoot, while the others have worn out shoes. Not all of them have an overshirt, and none have a coat."[14]

Zipporah Shertok asked for clothing, shoes, and coats to be sent from Palestine. The food, distributed three times a day, was poor. "The children finish their daily portion of bread in the morning," Shertok wrote, "and have none left for the rest of the day. They eat on the ground or on the blankets they use at night, without tables or cloths. There are flies everywhere here, and no amount of Flit [insecticide spray] will solve the problem."[15]

Sickness was rife. The children arrived in Tehran already thin and wasted by hunger and disease. Thirty-six of them had to be hospitalized

Tehran children look out of the train window

immediately. The camp hospital admitted children for eye diseases, infectious skin conditions, and other ailments. Fourteen children died in the first month. The children worried about their parents, whom they had left behind in the Soviet Union. They wrote letters but received no answers, and feared the worst. Their anxiety reached a fevered pitch during the prayer for the dead, recited on Yom Kippur, the Day of Atonement. Szold wrote to the Jewish Agency executive that "on Yom Kippur, the entire camp was gripped by tremendous weeping. The educators [who were there] still speak of that day with sorrow and pain."[16]

Szold convened a meeting with Beyth and the counselors, to coordinate care for the younger children—a new area for Youth Aliyah, which had thus far served only older children. The organization also needed to prepare financially to support children who would not attain majority for many years, and would thus remain at Youth Aliyah institutions for longer periods.

Many in the Yishuv believed that the children who had reached Tehran were merely the beginning, and that tens of thousands of children would follow in their footsteps. They were reluctant to entrust them to Youth Aliyah, as the various political movements in the Yishuv all wanted control of the children's absorption, in order to swell their own ranks. Youth Aliyah thus found itself at odds with much of the Yishuv. Some, like Ben-Gurion, were willing to enlist Szold's help but were not prepared to give her control over the children's education. Szold was very offended by the treatment she received. She believed it was better to entrust the children to Youth Aliyah—a non-partisan organization with considerable experience in caring for immigrant children—than to those whose interests were primarily political. Ultimately, a compromise was found whereby Youth Aliyah would be subject to the authority of the Jewish Agency executive. The compromise limited Szold's autonomy, although she still exercised significant control over the children's absorption.

The children's departure from Tehran was delayed by a number of months. The shortest possible route from Iran to Palestine was sought, in order to spare the children, who were already debilitated, the hardship of a protracted journey. Iraq refused to allow them to pass through its territory, so with no alternative, a longer route was chosen. On November 2, 1943, the first group, numbering 600 children, left Tehran. A group of 200 children followed a few days later. They were taken to Abadan, where they boarded a ship for British India. They waited in Karachi for two weeks for a ship to Aden, proceeding from there to the port of Suez.

A heartwarming experience awaited the children even before their arrival in Palestine. They were met at Port Said by Hans Beyth and a group of Youth Aliyah graduates serving with the British forces in Egypt. The soldiers prepared packages of sweets for the children, and anxiously scanned the arrivals in the hope of finding a familiar face, perhaps a lost member of their own families. From Port Said, the children continued their journey by rail, arriving in Palestine on February 18, 1943. News of their

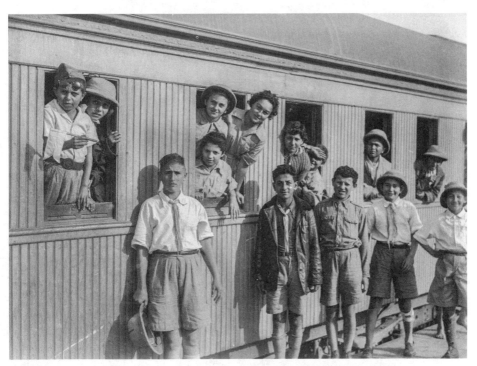

The Tehran children arrive in Palestine, 1943

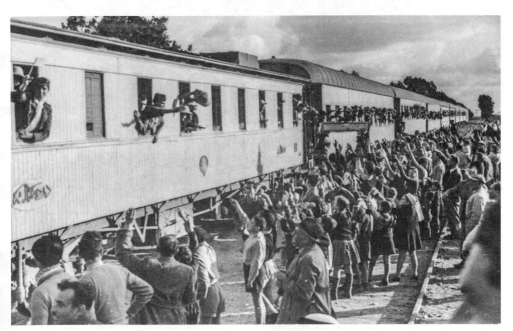

People in the train station welcome the Tehran children

Szold and her secretary Emma Ehrlich (*at right*) wait for the Tehran children at the
train station

arrival spread like wildfire. Hundreds of people came to the train station
to welcome them with oranges and sweets. The newspapers announced
their arrival with rousing headlines, such as "The Homeland Welcomes
the Tehran Children with Open Arms" and "And Your Children Will Return to Their Own Land." Articles described the harrowing sight the
children presented: "Old before their time, their outward appearance is
grim. Most are emaciated and gaunt. Their faces are drawn, their eyes dull
from sleeplessness and cold. . . . It is a heart-rending sight."[17]

With the arrival of the children, the debate regarding their absorption
heated up. Szold proposed establishing temporary camps at which the
children could be interviewed and assigned to the various institutions.
These camps would be staffed by doctors, psychologists, and social
workers, as well as counselors and teachers. As public institutions, Szold
determined, the camps would adhere to religious tradition—observing
the dietary laws and the Sabbath, and conducting weekday and Sabbath
prayers, with the proviso that children who did not wish to attend the
prayer services would not be forced to do so. Despite her frail health,
the eighty-three-year-old Szold traveled to Atlit, where the temporary

camp for the Tehran children was located, and personally oversaw their absorption.

ROMANIA, KINGDOM OF DEATH

Romania had one of the largest Jewish populations in Europe. The country was not occupied by the Nazis, but it had formed an alliance with Germany and adopted its murderous policies against the Jews. In Romania, Jews were not sent to concentration camps; they were murdered in brutal pogroms.

One of the most horrifying episodes of the Holocaust in Romania was the massacre in Transnistria—an area between the Dniester and Bug Rivers that had previously been part of Ukraine but was awarded to the government of Romanian prime minister Ion Antonescu in recognition of Romania's participation in the war against the Soviet Union. Some 150,000 Jews were deported to Transnistria, where, in the winter of 1941–1942, temperatures dropped to forty degrees below zero. Yonah Melaron, a twelve-year-old survivor, described the events that followed: "They [the Jews] were left in the fields without food or water, in freezing temperatures for days, and thousands died of hunger and cold."[18] Of the 150,000 Jews deported to Transnistria, only 50,000 survived. "It was a holocaust in every way, but the Romanians were not as sophisticated as the Nazis. They did not tattoo numbers on the arms of the Jews," recalled Aharon Schechter, born in Bukovina, the youngest of six and the only member of his family to survive. His parents, brothers, and sisters perished, along with tens of thousands of other Jews, from disease, hunger, and cold.[19] Jean Ancel, a historian of Romanian Jewry, referred to Transnistria as the Kingdom of Death.[20]

By 1944, some 450,000 Jews had perished in Romania, while 300,000 Jews were still alive—including 17,000 children. Most of the children had lost at least one parent; 5,000 had lost both parents. They survived thanks to the assistance they were given by the ghetto committees, a number of leading figures in the Romanian Jewish community, and dedicated physicians who cared for the sick children. Many were taken to Bucharest, where they were housed at orphanages supported by Romanian Jewry and the JDC. The Zionist leadership sought to send them to Palestine, and efforts were made to get them out of Romania through the Red Cross. Negotiations dragged on for over a year, and it was only in April 1944 that the Romanian authorities allowed them to depart. The British promised them immigration certificates. On May 2, 1944, 120 children, including some as young as four, reached Palestine. Further groups successfully followed them. Upon their arrival, the children were placed in the care of Youth Aliyah.

A dramatic change occurred in August 1944, when Romania's King Mihai cut his country's ties with Germany and joined the Allies. Soviet forces entered Bucharest, marking the beginning of communist rule in Romania. Jewish immigration to Palestine resumed in October, and by the end of 1944, a further 2,000 child survivors reached Palestinian shores, where they were received by Youth Aliyah. After the war, most of the remaining child survivors from Romania were also taken to Palestine.

YOUTH ALIYAH, under Henrietta Szold's leadership, was widely praised but also severely criticized. She was accused of having been too selective before the war—in imposing medical requirements, for example. After the war, the Yishuv leadership came under increasing criticism for not having saved more children from the Nazis. This criticism ignored the severe limitations on immigration imposed by the British in the 1930s, and was largely the product of a profound sense of frustration at the destruction of European Jewry. Szold, like so many others, was convinced that, given time, they would have been able to bring many more immigrants. The Nazis, in fact, pursued a policy of actively deceiving the Jews in countries under their control, as well as the political leaders of those countries, hiding their true intentions from them. Research has shown that even those (both Zionists and non-Zionists) who recognized the inevitable necessity of emigration from Europe mistakenly believed that there was enough time for orderly immigration to Palestine. Regarding the question of whether the Holocaust could have been foreseen, Holocaust scholar Saul Friedländer wrote of the victims that "theirs were the only voices that conveyed both the clarity of insight and the total blindness of human beings confronted with an entirely new and utterly horrifying reality."[21] Who could indeed have imagined the horrors of the Holocaust? As it was, Youth Aliyah provided a rescue operation unparalleled anywhere in the 1930s and during the Holocaust. The organization directed by Henrietta Szold offered children whose entire world had been destroyed a new home and a bridge to a new life in Palestine.

In February 1944, Youth Aliyah celebrated its tenth anniversary. The festivities in Palestine were subdued due to the war, but in the United States, the women of Hadassah organized events in many different cities to mark the special occasion. Boston University decided to award Henrietta Szold an honorary doctorate in recognition of her achievements, but there was a snag. The university's practice had always been to confer such degrees in the presence of the recipient, who would be invited to speak at a special ceremony in her or his honor. A trip to Boston was, of course, out of the question for Szold, due to the perils of wartime travel and to her own frail health. In light of the unusual circumstances, the university decided to forgo Szold's presence, but asked that she address the ceremony via radio from Jerusalem. This raised another problem, however. An intercontinental broadcast at the height of the war required permission from the highest echelons in Washington and London. Szold's friends in London appealed to Sir Isaiah Berlin of Oxford University, who was close to Winston Churchill and was his personal envoy in Washington. Berlin was only too glad to help. He managed to obtain the necessary permits from both sides, and arrangements were made to transmit Szold's address from the studios of the government broadcasting service in Jerusalem to Boston University. The ceremony at Boston University was reported in the press, but the efforts behind the scenes that made it possible were never revealed.

IN THE SUMMER OF 1944, Szold came down with pneumonia and was hospitalized a number of times at Hadassah Hospital. A few weeks later, her condition improved and she returned to work. Hans Beyth came to see her every day, reporting on the continuing work to bring child survivors from Europe. Szold was frustrated; she felt responsible for the absorption of the thousands of child survivors but was no longer able to play an active role. To her regret, she never managed to complete the task of placing and caring for all the children who had survived the Holocaust and were waiting in Cyprus and other European countries. She relied on Beyth to continue her work. No one expected Beyth to die as well, before completing the task.

Beyth continued Szold's work at Youth Aliyah after her death, running the organization in the spirit of the values and principles she had established. He spent weeks on end at the temporary camp in Atlit, where the children were interviewed and assigned to the various kibbutzim and institutions. He worked around the clock, alongside the rest of the Youth Aliyah staff, to keep the children's stay at the temporary camp to a minimum. After a few weeks of concerted effort, permanent arrangements had been found for most of the children, and Beyth decided to go home to his wife and young children for the weekend, after a prolonged absence. On Friday, December 26, 1947, he left for Jerusalem, intending to return to Atlit on Sunday. When he reached Tel Aviv, his friends tried to dissuade him from continuing to Jerusalem, explaining that the road was dangerous, plagued by Arab snipers. Beyth, however, was determined to go home. Near al-Qastal, in the Jerusalem hills, his

Henrietta Szold addresses the ceremony at Boston University via radio upon
receiving an honorary doctorate on the tenth anniversary of Youth Aliyah, 1944

bus came under attack, and he was shot and killed. He was survived by his
wife, Lotte, and four young children: Michael, the eldest son, eight years old;
Yoram; Miriam Henrietta; and one-year-old Ruth.

Beyth's funeral was attended by large numbers of Jerusalemites and by
dozens of delegations of teachers and principals and hundreds of Youth
Aliyah students from institutions around the country, as well as Youth
Aliyah graduates who grieved for him and came to pay their last respects.
The mourning that descended on the Yishuv at Beyth's death reflected the
deep affection the Youth Aliyah students had for him and the esteem in
which the teachers and counselors held him. Beyth's death symbolically
represented the end of Youth Aliyah's formative period, in which he had
played a central role.

From its beginnings in Germany through the dark years of the Holocaust, Youth Aliyah saw nearly 30,000 children educated at hundreds of
its institutions on kibbutzim and agricultural settlements as well as in cities.
The organization continued to operate for decades, even after the establishment of the State of Israel, serving over 300,000 children. In its later
years, there was greater diversity among the children it helped, but Youth
Aliyah continued to uphold the values and pedagogical principles established by Henrietta Szold at the project's inception.

EPILOGUE
From Mount Scopus to the Mount of Olives

*I*N LATE 1944, Szold's health took a turn for the worse. At the beginning of December, she had difficulty breathing and was admitted to the hospital. A few weeks later, her condition improved slightly, and she was moved to the nursing school, where she remained under observation. She had many visitors at the hospital, including members of the Zionist Executive and the Jewish National Council. When David Ben-Gurion showed up late one night, the nurse looking after Szold hesitated about letting him into her room; Ben-Gurion apologized and explained that he had been held up at an urgent meeting. Magnes came to visit her every day and, on one occasion, encountered Weizmann. Magnes accompanied Weizmann to Szold's room and waited at the doorway. When Szold noticed him standing there, she asked the nurse to tell him to come in. She then took his hand and told him that she had just been telling Weizmann that of all the things he, Weizmann, had done throughout his life for the Zionist movement, the greatest was his coming to Palestine at this time to show his support for the Yishuv, despite previous disagreements regarding the best way to influence British policy to further the Zionist cause.[1] She added that it made her happy to see Weizmann and Magnes together. Weizmann took Szold's other hand and Magnes remarked on the fact that they were both holding her hands, to which she replied that they must put their differences aside. When they left the room, Weizmann said to Magnes that indeed they must put their differences aside.[2] Szold had good reason to be pleased to see the two men together. They had long been at odds over Magnes's role as leader of the Ihud movement, which advocated compromise with the Arabs—even at the cost of renouncing mass immigration to Palestine. It was a position that Weizmann, as president of the Zionist Organization, and his colleagues on the Zionist Executive strenuously opposed.

In early February 1945, Szold's condition worsened. She remained under observation at the nursing school, where she received the best of care. Hans Beyth and Szold's secretary, Emma Ehrlich, came to see her every evening. They kept her abreast of Youth Aliyah affairs, and she continued to develop new ideas. She suggested that Beyth establish a large transit camp at Kibbutz Alonim to house the thousands of child survivors expected to arrive after the war, pending their permanent assignment to the various institutions. She also suggested that they create a regular training program for Youth Aliyah counselors, to meet the growing need for counselors to care for the child survivors. Szold continued to encourage the Youth Aliyah staff to maintain a high standard of education without losing sight of children's individual needs, even when they arrived in large numbers. Szold was concerned about her inability to return to work at Youth Aliyah just as thousands of child survivors, orphaned and traumatized, were expected.[3]

She hoped that she would recover again, as she had in the past, but her health only deteriorated further. Dr. Kleinberg, Szold's personal physician, tried to cheer her up. "It will be spring soon," he said, "and with it, you too will be reinvigorated, Miss Szold."

She did not have the strength to reply. The doctors issued a daily update on Szold's condition to the press.

On February 13, 1945 (30 Shevat 5705), at 10:00 a.m., Szold lost consciousness. A group of student nurses kept a vigil at her bedside and recited psalms.[4] At 7:40 p.m., she passed away at the nursing school that bore her name. Upon hearing the news of her death, Judah Magnes, Moshe Shertok, Eliezer Kaplan (members in the Jewish Agency Executive), Dr. Avraham Katznelson (director of the health department of the Zionist executive), Justice Gad Frumkin, members of the Youth Immigration Bureau, and others, made their way to the nursing school on Mount Scopus. The leaders of the Zionist institutions met to discuss the funeral arrangements and decided that a cortege from the nursing school to the cemetery on the Mount of Olives would depart at 2:00 p.m. the following afternoon.

The next morning, news of her death was reported in large headlines on the front pages of all of the newspapers, accompanied by a large photo-

graph of Szold and emotional eulogies.⁵ The war was raging in Europe
and the Red Army was advancing toward Berlin, but the main articles in
all of the papers were about Szold. Details of the funeral arrangements
were released to the press and pushed aside news of the war. In *Davar*,
Szold's funeral was given considerable prominence, with a large headline
at the top of the page. Two large bereavement notices were published in
all of the papers—one by the Child and Youth Immigration Bureau and
the other by the counselors' association, which read "Henrietta Szold,
bearer of the youth's dreams project and its guide."

On February 14, the first day of the Hebrew month of Adar, hundreds
of people from every part of the country braved the cold and the rain to
come to the nursing school on Mount Scopus to pay their last respects to
Henrietta Szold. Her bier was placed in a large hall, with candles at its
head. An honor guard of nurses stood by as a long line of women and men,
young and old, filed past, many with tears in their eyes. There were representatives of the International Red Cross, and soldiers in British uniforms—
graduates of Youth Aliyah—stopped to salute her. Before the procession
got under way, Magnes recited the Kaddish prayer.

The funeral procession departed at 2:00 p.m. The bier was carried by
Chaim Weizmann, Labor Zionist leader Yitzhak Ben Zvi, David Remez
(secretary of the Histadrut; later minister of education of the State of Israel),
Rabbi Moshe Ostrovsky, Judah Magnes, and Daniel Auster (acting mayor
of Jerusalem), and accompanied on both sides by the students of the Alice
Seligsberg School of Social Work. At the building's exit stood an honor
guard of nurses in white uniforms. Following the bier were the Sephardi
chief rabbi, Meir Hai Uziel; the president of the Zionist Organization,
Chaim Weizmann; the chairman of the Jewish Agency executive, David
Ben-Gurion; members of the Zionist Executive, and many members of other
Zionist institutions. Representatives of the entire political and ideological
spectrum came to pay their last respects to Henrietta Szold, as did the employees of Hadassah Hospital and the Histadrut, social workers, and members of women's organizations. When the bier passed the hospital, the doctors and nurses came out and stood, heads bowed, by the side of the road.

Szold's funeral resembled a state funeral. At the head of the procession
walked British officials in their dress uniforms. The high commissioner,
Field Marshal John Standish Viscount Gort, was represented by Brigadier
Cumming-Bruce, while the high commissioner's secretary, accompanied by
an aide in decorated uniform, carried a large wreath. Justice Bernard Shaw
represented William Fitzgerald, chief justice of the Supreme Court of Palestine, and Chief Secretary John Shaw. Also in attendance were the heads
of the various Palestine government departments and other high-ranking

Szold's bier, with candles at her head, at the nursing school on Mount Scopus, with an honor guard of nurses in white uniforms, February 14, 1945

British officials: the head of the immigration department, the head of the health department, a representative of the financial secretary's office, the Jerusalem district commissioner, a representative of the British forces in Palestine, and members of the consular corps in Jerusalem. Religious leaders stood out in their traditional garb, including the Anglican bishop of Jerusalem, Dr. Weston Henry Stewart, and representatives of the various churches, alongside Muslim sheikhs.

The funeral, one of the biggest Jerusalem had ever seen, was attended by thousands of people from all walks of life. Hadassah nurses, led by the nursing school director, Shulamith Cantor, marched in their white uniforms. There were Hebrew University professors, writers, teachers and school principals, mayors, and kibbutz and agricultural settlement members. Hundreds of Youth Aliyah teachers and counselors who had worked with Szold, and thousands of Youth Aliyah students and graduates who remembered Szold from her many visits and had come from all over the country to pay their respects, all walked in silence.

There was a group of Youth Aliyah children carrying a large wreath with the words "To our dear mother, who saved us from the valley of death.

The funeral procession of Henrietta Szold passing by Hadassah Hospital on
Mount Scopus on its way to the Mount of Olives

Immigrant youth from Transnistria" written on it. Other Youth Aliyah delegations—among them the Tehran children, immigrants from Yemen and
Turkey, and many others—carried signs with the names of their respective institutions. They walked with bowed heads, filling the streets of Jerusalem.[6] Among the thousands of mourners, there was not a single
member of Szold's family.

The sky cleared and a strong wind blew down from the hills as the
mourners walked slowly along the Mount Scopus road to the national library building, where the procession stopped and Chief Rabbi Uziel recited Kaddish. They then proceeded in buses and cars to the cemetery at
the Mount of Olives.

All were transfixed by the stunning view of the Temple Mount and the
city of Jerusalem stretching out below. There Henrietta Szold was buried
next to Professor Israel Kligler, one of the pioneers in the battle to eradicate
malaria in Palestine. In accordance with her wishes, no eulogies were given
at the graveside. Flowers and wreaths were laid, and as the sun was about to
set, the final Kaddish was recited by fifteen-year-old Shimon Kritz, one of
the Tehran children, whose voice was choked with tears. Many others wept.

Cantor Israel Bardiki of the Hurvah Synagogue intoned the El Male prayer as strong winds blew. The mourners stood around the grave with bowed heads for a while longer before making their way out of the cemetery.

Flags on Zionist institutions throughout the country flew at half-mast, and the newspapers continued to publish bereavement notices and articles about Szold for weeks to come. The *New York Times* wrote: "Jew, Moslem and Christian may well bless her memory for what she was and what she did."[7] The Hadassah National Council in the United States convened memorial meetings in all of its chapters, in 700 Jewish communities throughout the country. A month later, a memorial meeting was held at Carnegie Hall, in New York.

In the days following her death, the newspapers in Palestine published countless bereavement notices, placed by institutions and organizations and by all of the kibbutzim where Youth Aliyah children resided. In the religious daily Ha-Tzofeh, a notice placed by Kibbutz Sde Eliyahu stuck out. It read, "Shrouded in grief, we stand by the grave of the mother of Youth Aliyah, Miss Henrietta Szold, We will sanctify her memory among us forever." The notice was signed, "Sde Eliyahu, religious immigrant youth's first Kibbutz." Kibbutz Hafetz Hayim, affiliated with the ultra-Orthodox workers' movement (Poale Agudat Israel), also published a bereavement notice in Szold's memory. The religious circles in the Yishuv that had been critical of Szold in her lifetime came together after her death to express sincere admiration for her work.

Her funeral reflected her life's work—the relationships she had built with members of all of the communities in Palestine, of all faiths and political views. A long and active life, marked by dramatic events, thus came to an end.

Henrietta Szold did not rest in peace, however. The Jewish-Arab conflict that was such a source of concern to her over the years continued to plague her even after her death. In the war of 1948, the Old City of Jerusalem and the surrounding neighborhoods and hills, including Mount Scopus and the Mount of Olives, fell to Jordan's Arab Legion. A number of years later, the Jordanians paved a road through the Jewish cemetery on the Mount of Olives, smashing the headstones in its path and covering them with asphalt. Among the damaged graves was that of Henrietta Szold.

In 1967, in the Six-Day War, the Old City, Mount Scopus, and the Mount of Olives came under Israeli control. The damaged graves were identified and restored. In 1968, a new headstone was erected at the grave of Henrietta Szold, and the women of Hadassah held a memorial service for her on the anniversary of her death. They laid olive branches, a symbol of the Hadassah organization, around the grave. Former Hadassah presi-

Hadassah women attend a memorial service at the restored grave of Henrietta
Szold, with a new headstone, in 1968

dent Tamar de Sola Pool spoke at the emotional gathering, and two Youth
Aliyah students laid a wreath.[8]

The new headstone was similar to the original one erected at the time
of Szold's death: a simple stone, without titles or praise, bearing only her
name, her father's name, the dates of her birth and her death, and the traditional inscription "May her soul be bound up in the bond of life."

Henrietta Szold's funeral gave expression to the high esteem in which
she was held by people of all walks of life in Palestine. It was also a demonstration of the tremendous changes that had occurred in the status of
women from the mid-nineteenth century through the twentieth century,[9]
as reflected in the life of Henrietta Szold—a change similarly reflected
in the prestige she enjoyed in the United States in the last two decades of
her life.

FROM EXCLUSION TO ACCLAIM

In a ceremony held at City Hall in Manhattan in 1936, Mayor Fiorello La Guardia gave Henrietta Szold the key to the city, in recognition of her initiative to establish a night school for immigrants. La Guardia recognized the institution's importance in helping immigrants find their way in American society and culture. His esteem for Szold was also related to his own background as the child of immigrants:

> If I, the child of poor immigrant parents, am today Mayor of New York, giving you the freedom of our city, it is because of you. Half a century ago you initiated that instrument of American democracy, the evening night school for the immigrant. . . . Were it not for such programs of education and Americanization at the time of our largest immigrant waves, a new slavery would have arisen in American society perhaps worse than the first.[10]

The ceremony took place when Szold was seventy-five years old, decades after she had founded and run the school for immigrants in Baltimore. Despite the school's importance as an invaluable instrument for the integration of immigrants into American society, she had received no public recognition at the time.

It was only in the final decades of her life that Szold received recognition for her many achievements. The key to the city of New York was but one of numerous awards and honors bestowed on her. In 1930, she received an honorary doctorate from the Jewish Institute of Religion, the first woman to be so honored. Upon conferring the degree, the institute's founder and president, Rabbi Stephen S. Wise, offered the following words of praise:

> Henrietta Szold, great among women, and an example of uncompromising nobleness among the immortal rebuilders of her people's life in the land of Israel; inspiring bringer of multitudes of Jewish women, Hadassah, to the altar of high service to their people and their people's Homeland.[11]

On the occasion of the tenth anniversary of Youth Aliyah, Boston University decided to confer an honorary doctorate on Henrietta Szold, in recognition of her achievements. At the ceremony, which took place in Boston on March 13, 1944, University president Daniel L. Marsh offered the following characterization of Szold:

> Distinguished for social settlement work in America and in Palestine . . . accomplisher of unparalleled reclamation and rehabilitation work in Palestine . . . You have spent your years as a tale that is told, and the tale is one of a life devoted to the pursuit of the beautiful, the true, and the good.[12]

Szold's portrait on a banknote of the Bank of Israel

President Franklin D. Roosevelt sent personal greetings:

> Since 1889, when you organized the first English and Americanization classes in your native Baltimore, you have devoted yourself to the best social and educational ideals, both here and in Palestine. Your direction of Youth Aliyah has been characteristic of the qualities that have won you such respect and affection. . . . The coming liberation of Europe will present us all with unparalleled problems. We must heal broken bodies, rebuild shattered lives and faith. I am sure that in this task Youth Aliyah with your guidance will take its place to the forefront, as in the past.[13]

Henrietta Szold's unique qualities shone through in the projects she conceived and developed in light of the values she held dear. The night school for immigrants that she established was open to every immigrant regardless of faith, gender, or age. When founding Hadassah, Szold sought not only to empower women and to encourage them in the struggle for equal rights, but also to foster a spirit of social cohesion and equality between members.

The values that guided Szold in her public activities received expression in her personal life as well. Although she raised enormous sums of money for the projects she founded, she took no payment whatsoever from the public purse, in the United States or in Palestine. Her lifestyle bordered on the ascetic, to the point that her friends wondered how she managed to live at all. She never owned her own home, living in a series of small rentals throughout her life. Even when she was given sums of money as personal gifts—on her birthday, for example—she never used them for her own needs, but started funds to build kibbutz and village clinics and schools for underprivileged children.

There was a discrepancy, however, between Szold's public life—filled with admiration and acclaim, especially in her later years—and her self-perception. The regret she felt at her personal disappointments lent Henrietta a visible aura of sadness, yet her intimate life remained unknown to the public. In the eyes of hundreds of thousands of members of Hadassah and many others, in the United States and in Palestine, Szold was and still is a model leader: always confident, focused, and determined, a woman of principle, and a guiding light.

AS I WRITE THESE LINES, we find ourselves in the grip of the coronavirus pandemic, our faith in human scientific and technological prowess deeply shaken. Suddenly, we are helpless against a virus that has spread throughout the world, causing more than a million deaths among people of all walks of life, as well as far-reaching social, economic, and cultural damage. At the same time, widespread protests challenge society to address the ills of racism and discrimination. Many intellectuals and scientists are asking themselves whether these crises will result in a change in our way of thinking, and how they will affect the future development of society. Writing about Henrietta Szold, I cannot help but wonder how she would have dealt with the current crises. As an original and creative thinker, what insights would she have had to offer, and how would she have striven to repair a broken world?

NOTES

ACKNOWLEDGMENTS

CREDITS

INDEX

NOTES

INTRODUCTION

1. As Szold was born only a few days before the end of 1860, the year of her
    birth is often given as 1861.

2. Dvora Hacohen, *Yaldei ha-zman: Aliyat ha-no'ar 1933–1948* [Children of the time: Youth Aliyah 1933–1948] (Jerusalem: Yad Vashem, Ben Zvi Institute, and Ben Gurion University, 2011).

3. Eli Lederhendler, "Classless: On the Social Status of Jews in Russia and Eastern Europe in the Late Nineteenth Century," *Comparative Studies in Society and History* 50 (2008): 509–534; Eli Lederhendler, *Jewish Immigrants and American Capitalism, 1880–1920: From Caste to Class* (Cambridge: Cambridge University Press, 2009).

4. Szold to her sister Rachel, October 31, 1891, HADA, RG 13/25, 6. See Chapter 3.

5. Nancy F. Cott, ed., *No Small Courage: History of Women in the United States* (New York: Oxford University Press, 2000), vii.

6. Quoted in Marvin Lowenthal, *Henrietta Szold: Life and Letters* (New York: Viking Press, 1942), 65.

7. Jill Reynolds and Stephanie Taylor, "Narrating Singleness: Life Stories and Deficit Identities," *Narrative Inquiry* 15, no. 2 (2005): 197–215.

8. Kathryn E. Bojczyk et al., "Mothers' and Their Adult Daughters' Perceptions of Their Relationship," *Journal of Family Issues* 32, no. 4 (2011): 452–481; Pamela S. Nadell, *America's Jewish Women: A History from Colonial Times to Today* (New York: W. W. Norton, 2019), 98–99.

9. Shalom Ratzabi, *Between Zionism and Judaism: The Radical Circle in Brith Shalom, 1925–1933* (Leiden: Brill, 2002).

10. A number of biographies of Henrietta Szold have been published over the years. Marvin Lowenthal's *Henrietta Szold: Life and Letters* was commissioned by the Szold family, who had final say over what was written. It is missing a number of important aspects of Szold's life, as well as the historical background of the events it describes. Irving Fineman's *Woman of Valor: The Life of Henrietta Szold 1860–1945* was commissioned by the Hadassah Women's Organization. The most recent biography, Joan Dash's *Summoned to Jerusalem: The Life of Henrietta Szold,* is more than forty years old and incomplete in its coverage. In all three of these biographies, discussion of the historical context of Szold's many endeavors is sparse, particularly with regard to her life in Palestine and her work there.

11. Jonathan D. Sarna, "America's Most Memorable Leaders," in *The Individual in History: Essays in Honor of Jehuda Reinharz,* ed. ChaeRan Y. Freeze, Sylvia Fuks Fried, and Eugene R. Sheppard (Waltham, MA: Brandeis University Press, 2015), 129–142.

12. Henrietta Szold to Judah Magnes, December 8, 1944, Judah Magnes Archive, National Library of Israel, Jerusalem.

1 BEGINNINGS

1. Alexandra Lee Levin, *The Szolds of Lombard Street: A Baltimore Family, 1859–1909* (Philadelphia: Jewish Publication Society, 1960), 7–8.

2. Shulamit Volkov, *Germans, Jews and Antisemites: Trials in Emancipation* (Cambridge: Cambridge University Press, 2006), 49–51.

3. Levin, *The Szolds of Lombard Street,* 385–386. The Schaar boys were Moritz, Michael, Heinrich, Paul, Eduard, and Naftali, and the girls were Julie, Josephine (Pepi), Minna, and Sophie.

4. Zacharias Frankel (1801–1875) was born in Prague and studied philosophy and ancient languages at the University of Pest in Budapest, where he was awarded a doctorate. In 1854, he became head of the Jewish Theological Seminary in Breslau, which he had co-founded, and served as professor of Talmudic studies. Esther Seidel, *Zacharias Frankel und das Jüdisch-Theologische Seminar/and the Jewish-Theological Seminary* (Berlin: Hentrich & Hentrich, 2013).

5. Isaac M. Fein, *The Making of an American Jewish Community: The History of Baltimore Jewry from 1773 to 1920* (Philadelphia: Jewish Publication Society, 1971), 89–93.

6. David Einhorn was born in Bavaria in 1809, studied at the Würzburg yeshiva, and was ordained as a rabbi. He developed a radical Reform stance, immigrated to the United States when he was forty-six, and was invited to serve as the rabbi at Har Sinai Congregation in Baltimore in 1855. Fein, *The Making of an American Jewish Community,* 82–83.

7. Jonathan D. Sarna and Benjamin Shapell, *Lincoln and the Jews: A History* (New York: St. Martin's Press, 2015).

8. Isaac M. Fein, "Baltimore Rabbis during the Civil War," in *Jews and the Civil War,* ed. Jonathan D. Sarna and Adam Mendelsohn (New York: New York University Press, 2010), 181–196.

9. David Herbert Donald, *Lincoln* (Cambridge, MA: Harvard University Press, 1995).

10. Sarna and Shapell, *Lincoln and the Jews,* 154–155.

11. Levin, *The Szolds of Lombard Street,* 40.

12. Sarna and Shapell, *Lincoln and the Jews,* 214.

13. Walt Whitman, "This Dust Was Once the Man," in *Leaves of Grass* (New York: Modern Library, 1921), 287.

14. Fein, *The Making of an American Jewish Community,* 121–122; Shari Rabin, *Jews on the Frontier: Religion and Mobility in Nineteenth-Century America* (New York: New York University Press, 2017).

15. Sophie to her mother, May 30, 1869; quoted in Levin, *The Szolds of Lombard Street,* 63.

16. Betsy and Sally Levin, granddaughters of Bertha Levin, interview with the author, August 19, 2009, Baltimore.

17. Henrietta was born in 1860, Rachel in 1865, Sadie in 1868, Bertha in 1873, and Adele in 1876. Levin, *The Szolds of Lombard Street,* 386–387.

18. Alexandra Lee Levin, *Vision: A Biography of Harry Friedenwald* (Philadelphia: Jewish Publication Society, 1964).

19. Fein, *The Making of an American Jewish Community,* 149, 181–196; Eric L. Goldstein and Deborah R. Weiner, *On Middle Ground: A History of the Jews of Baltimore* (Baltimore, MD: Johns Hopkins University Press, 2018); John Klier, *Russian Jews and the Pogroms of 1881–1882* (Cambridge: Cambridge University Press, 2011).

2 NEW HORIZONS

1. Marion A. Kaplan, *The Making of the Jewish Middle Class: Women, Family, and Identity in Imperial Germany* (New York: Oxford University Press, 1991), 63.

2. Henrietta Szold (as Sulamith), "Our Baltimore Letter," *Jewish Messenger,* March 1878.

3. Marvin Lowenthal, *Henrietta Szold: Life and Letters* (New York: Viking Press, 1942), 17.

4. Szold, "Our Baltimore Letter," August 6, 1880; Alexandra Lee Levin, *Henrietta Szold: Baltimorean* (Baltimore: Jewish Historical Society of Maryland, 1976), 1–19.

5. Levin, *Henrietta Szold: Baltimorean,* 1–19.

6. Lowenthal, *Henrietta Szold,* 14.

7. Levin, *Henrietta Szold: Baltimorean,* 1–19.

8. Levin, *Henrietta Szold: Baltimorean,* 1–19.

9. On the pogroms in Russia at the time, see John Klier, *Russians, Jews, and the Pogroms of 1881–1882* (Cambridge: Cambridge University Press, 2011).

10. Isaac M. Fein, *The Making of an American Jewish Community: The History of Baltimore Jewry from 1773 to 1920* (Philadelphia: Jewish Publication Society, 1971).

11. Levin, *Henrietta Szold: Baltimorean,* 1–19.

12. Lowenthal, *Henrietta Szold,* 22.

13. Lowenthal, *Henrietta Szold,* 22–23.

14. Alexandra Lee Levin, *The Szolds of Lombard Street: A Baltimore Family, 1859–1909* (Philadelphia: Jewish Publication Society, 1960), 140.

15. See Chapter 8.

16. Levin, *The Szolds of Lombard Street,* 140. See Chapter 8.

17. Henrietta Szold, "Johns Hopkins University," *Education: An International Magazine* 3 (September 1882–July 1883): 543–544; Levin, *Henrietta Szold: Baltimorean,* 2.

18. Levin, *Henrietta Szold: Baltimorean,* 1–19.

19. Levin, *Henrietta Szold: Baltimorean,* 4.

20. Lance J. Sussman, "The Myth of the Trefa Banquet: American Culinary Culture and the Radicalization of Food Policy in American Reform Judaism," *American Jewish Archives Journal* 57 (2005): 29–52.

21. *Jewish Messenger,* July 27, 1883.

22. Jonathan D. Sarna, *American Judaism: A History* (New Haven, CT: Yale University Press, 2004), 144–151.

23. On the distinction between Orthodox, Traditional, and Conservative Jews in the twentieth century, see Chaim I. Waxman, *Social Change and Halakhic Evolution in American Orthodoxy* (Liverpool: Littman Library of Jewish Civilization, 2017).

24. "Declaration of Principles: The Pittsburgh Platform (1885)," quoted in Richard N. Levy, *A Vision of Holiness: The Future of Reform Judaism* (New York: URJ Press, 2005), 259–262.

25. JTS was established in 1886 but did not develop as expected. It later gained momentum with the arrival of Rabbi Solomon Schechter. See Hasia Diner, "Like the Antelope and the Badger: The Founding and Early Years of the Jewish Theological Seminary, 1886–1902," in *Tradition Renewed: A History of the Jewish Theological Seminary,* ed. Jack Wertheimer (New York: Jewish Theological Seminary, 1997), 1:1–42.

26. Shari Rabin, *Jews on the Frontier: Religion and Mobility in Nineteenth-Century America* (New York: New York University Press, 2017).

27. Sarna, *American Judaism;* Diner, "Like the Antelope and the Badger."

28. Friedenwald studied in Berlin from 1887 to 1890.

29. Alexandra Lee Levin, *Vision: A Biography of Harry Friedenwald* (Philadelphia: Jewish Publication Society, 1964), 97.

30. Henrietta to Harry, December 31, 1889; Lowenthal, *Henrietta Szold,* 34.

31. Levin, *Vision,* 97.

32. Levin, *Vision,* 116–117.

33. Levin, *Vision,* 119.

34. Levin, *Vision,* 140.

35. Austin Corbin (1827–1896), quoted in "Reviving a Prejudice," *New York Herald,* July 22, 1879, 5.

36. The Seligman incident occurred in 1877. See Salo Wittmayer Baron, *Steeled by Adversity,* ed. Jeannette Meisel Baron (Philadelphia: Jewish Publication Society, 1971), 323–324.

37. John Higham, "Ideological Antisemitism in the Gilded Age," in *Send These to Me: Immigrants in Urban America* (Baltimore: Johns Hopkins University Press, 1984), 95–116; Sarna, *American Judaism.*

38. Klier, *Russians, Jews, and the Pogroms,* 2011.

39. Judah Leib (Leo) Pinsker was born in Tomaszow, Poland, in 1821. When he was five years old, his family moved to Odessa, in southern Russia.

40. Leo Pinsker, *Auto-Emancipation,* trans. D. S. Blondheim (New York: Maccabean, 1906), 3, 6. See Shlomo Avineri, *Herzl's Vision: Theodor Herzl and the Foundation of the Jewish State* (New York: Katonah, 2014).

41. Baron, *Steeled by Adversity,* 286.

42. Emma Lazarus, "The New Colossus," in *The Oxford Book of American Poetry,* ed. David Lehman (New York: Oxford University Press, 2006), 184.

43. "The Emma Lazarus Memorial Number," *American Hebrew,* December 9, 1887; Levin, *The Szolds of Lombard Street.*

♪ THE IMMIGRANTS ARE COMING

1. Eric L. Goldstein and Deborah R. Weiner, *On Middle Ground: A History of the Jews of Baltimore* (Baltimore: Johns Hopkins University Press, 2018).

2. About 25,000 immigrants, mostly members of the Hibat Zion and BILU movements, arrived in Palestine during the First Aliyah (1882–1903), and about 35,000 arrived during the Second Aliyah (1903–1914). See Moshe Sicron, *Immigration to Israel, 1948–1953* (Jerusalem: Central Bureau of Statistics, 1957); Derek Penslar, *Zionism and Technology: The Engineering of Jewish Settlement in Palestine, 1870–1918* (Bloomington: Indiana University Press, 1991).

3. Isaac M. Fein, *The Making of an American Jewish Community: The History of Baltimore Jewry from 1773 to 1920* (Philadelphia: Jewish Publication Society, 1971), 147–150; George E. Barnett, "The Jewish Population of Maryland," in *The American Jewish Year Book, 5663,* ed. Cyrus Adler (Philadelphia: Jewish Publication Society, 1902), 46–62; Goldstein and Weiner, *On Middle Ground.*

4. The I.B.L. Hebrew Literary Society of Baltimore was established in 1888, and the Baltimore Zion Association (Hevrat Zion) in 1893.

5. Correspondence between Henrietta Szold and Saul Bernstein, Szold Papers, JMMA. See Jobi Zink, "Saul Bernstein: Baltimore Artist," *Generations,* Winter 2001, 36–42.

6. Szold to Rabbi Joseph Herman Hertz, October 5, 1889, AJA, H. Szold Correspondence.

7. Szold to Rachel, October 31, 1891, HADA, RG 13/25, 6.

8. Szold to Rachel, November 8, 1891, CZA, A125/17.

9. Baron Maurice de Hirsch was born in 1831 and died in 1896. See Theodore Norman, *An Outstretched Arm: A History of the Jewish Colonization Association* (London: Routledge and Kegan Paul, 1985); Gur Alroey, "Zionism without Zion? The Territorial Ideology and the Zionist Movement, 1882–1956," *Jewish Social Studies* 18, no. 1 (2011): 1–32.

10. Szold to Baron de Hirsch Fund, April 26, 1891, JMMA, H. Szold Correspondence.

11. Szold to Rachel, November 8, 1891, HADA, RG 13/25, 6.

12. *Darkest Russia* was published on July 17, 1891, as a supplement to the *Jewish Chronicle.* See Sam Johnson, "Confronting the East: *Darkest Russia,* British Opinion and Tsarism's 'Jewish Question,' 1890–1914," *East European Jewish Affairs* 36, no. 2 (2006): 199–211.

13. Szold to Rachel, October 31, 1891, HADA, RG 13/25, 6.

14. Szold to Benjamin Hartogensis, July 14, 1890, HADA, RG 13/25, 6.

15. Henrietta Szold, "The Night School of the Hebrew Literary Society," 1893, JMMA, H. Szold Correspondence.

16. Alexandra Lee Levin, "Henrietta Szold and the Russian Immigrant School," *Maryland Historical Magazine* 57 (1962): 1–15.

⚶ THE INTELLECTUAL WORLD

1. The Chicago World's Fair was held between May 1 and October 31, 1893.

2. Henrietta Szold to Rachel, August 5, 1888, JMMA, H. Szold Correspondence.

3. Faith Rogow, *Gone to Another Meeting: The National Council of Jewish Women, 1893–1993* (Tuscaloosa: University of Alabama Press, 1993).

4. Genesis 21:12.

5. Henrietta Szold, "What Judaism Has Done for Women," in *The World's Congress of Religions: The Addresses and Papers Delivered before the Parliament. And an Abstract of the Congresses Held in the Art Institute. Chicago, Illinois, U.S.A., August 25 to October 15, 1893, under the Auspices of the World's Columbian Exhibition*, ed. J. W. Hanson (Chicago: Monarch Book Company, 1894), 587–593.

6. Felicia Herman, "From Priestess to Hostess: Sisterhoods of Personal Service in New York City, 1887–1936," in *Women and American Judaism: Historical Perspectives*, ed. Pamela S. Nadell and Jonathan D. Sarna (Hanover, NH: University Press of New England, 2001), 148–181; Nancy F. Cott, *The Grounding of Modern Feminism* (New Haven, CT: Yale University Press, 1987); Anne Firor Scott, *Natural Allies: Women's Associations in American History* (Urbana: University of Illinois Press, 1993).

7. Jonathan D. Sarna, *JPS: The Americanization of Jewish Culture, 1888–1988: A Centennial History of the Jewish Publication Society* (Philadelphia: Jewish Publication Society, 1989), 1–12.

8. Hasia Diner, "Like the Antelope and the Badger: The Founding and Early Years of the Jewish Theological Seminary, 1886–1902," in *Tradition Renewed: A History of the Jewish Theological Seminary*, ed. Jack Wertheimer (New York: Jewish Theological Seminary, 1997), 1:1–42.

9. Sarna, *JPS*, 10.

10. Barry E. Supple, "A Business Elite: German-Jewish Financiers in Nineteenth-Century New York," *Business History Review* 31, no. 2 (1957): 143–178.

11. Mayer Sulzberger (1843–1922) was born in Heidelsheim, Germany, where his father served as cantor. He received a traditional Jewish education.

12. Isaac Leeser (1806–1868) was born in Prussia. On his arrival in the United States, he was appointed cantor and preacher at the Spanish-Portuguese Congregation Mikveh Israel in Philadelphia, acting as the synagogue's de

facto rabbi. He had the idea of establishing a Jewish publishing house, but it did not come to fruition. See Jonathan D. Sarna, *American Judaism: A History* (New Haven, CT: Yale University Press, 2004), 76–79.

13. Sarna, *American Judaism,* 7–8.

14. Sulzberger to Szold, November 18, 1891, JMMA. Szold's article on the *tkhines* was published in the *Hebrew Standard.*

15. Szold to Rabbi Hertz, October 5, 1887, AJA, H. Szold Correspondence.

16. Sarna, *JPS,* 48.

17. Cyrus Adler (1863–1940) graduated from Johns Hopkins and was awarded a PhD in Semitics in 1887. After completing his studies, he embarked on a fifteen-month tour of the Mediterranean and the Levant, including a visit to Palestine in 1891.

18. Adler was appointed president of Dropsie College in Philadelphia in 1907. Following the death of Solomon Schechter in 1915, he was appointed interim leader of the Jewish Theological Seminary, and later served as the elected president of that prestigious institution through 1940. Adler also wrote about his friend Jacob Schiff: Cyrus Adler, *Jacob Schiff: His Life and Letters* (Garden City, NY: Doubleday, Doran, 1928).

19. Sarna, *JPS,* 48; Irving Fineman, *Woman of Valor: The Life of Henrietta Szold, 1860–1945* (New York: Simon and Schuster, 1961), 52.

20. Szold to her parents, quoted in Sarna, *JPS,* 49.

21. Sarna, *JPS,* 48.

22. *Die Ethik des Judenthums* was published in 1889 and, in its English translation, *The Ethics of Judaism,* in 1900 and 1901.

23. Szold to her parents, Sarna, *JPS,* 49.

24. Szold to Rabbi Hertz, 1895, AJA, H. Szold Correspondence.

25. Szold to Cyrus Adler, May 26, 1895, and Cyrus Adler to Szold, May 27, 1895, JMMA.

26. Sarna, *JPS,* 49.

27. Szold to her parents, May 23, 1898, quoted in Sarna, *JPS,* 49.

28. Shlomo Avineri refutes the claim that Herzl was inspired by the Dreyfus Affair to write *The Jewish State.* See Shlomo Avineri, *Herzl's Vision: Theodor Herzl and the Foundation of the Jewish State* (New York: Katonah, 2014).

29. Léon Blum (1872–1950), *Souvenirs sur l'Affaire* (Paris: Gallimard, 1993), 34–49; Pierre Birnbaum, *Léon Blum: Prime Minister, Socialist,* trans. Arthur Goldhammer (New Haven, CT: Yale University Press, 2015), 18–31. On the Dreyfus Affair in general, see Ruth Harris, *Politics, Emotion, and the Scandal of the Century* (New York: Metropolitan Books, 2010).

30. Henrietta Szold, "The Year 5660," in *The American Jewish Year Book, 5661,* ed. Cyrus Adler (Philadelphia: Jewish Publication Society, 1900), 14–39.

31. Szold, "The Year 5660," 17–18.

32. Ritchie Robertson, "The New Ghetto and the Perplexities of Assimilation," in *Theodor Herzl: Visionary of the Jewish State,* ed. Gideon Shimoni and Robert S. Wistrich (Jerusalem: Magnes Press, 1999), 39–51.

33. Szold, "The Year 5660," 16.

34. Szold, "The Year 5660," 16–17, 38.

35. Szold, "The Year 5660," 38–39, 37–38. The Fourth Zionist Congress was held in London August 13–16, 1900. The JCA was founded by Baron Maurice de Hirsch in 1891 in order to offer aid to Russian Jewish refugees in Argentina, America, and Palestine. See Theodore Norman, *An Outstretched Arm: A History of the Jewish Colonization Association* (London: Routledge and Kegan Paul, 1985).

36. Szold, "The Year 5660," 14.

37. Szold, "The Year 5660," 38–39.

38. Szold, "The Year 5660," 638.

39. *The American Jewish Year Book, 5662,* ed. Cyrus Adler (Philadelphia: Jewish Publication Society, 1901), 191–308.

40. Henrietta Szold, "From Kishineff to Bialystok," in *The American Jewish Year Book, 5667* (Philadelphia: Jewish Publication Society, 1906), 34–89.

5 TRANSITIONS

1. They moved to Callow Avenue in 1896. Alexandra Lee Levin, *The Szolds of Lombard Street: A Baltimore Family, 1859–1909* (Philadelphia: Jewish Publication Society, 1960), 346.

2. Joseph Herman Hertz (1872–1946) was born in Rebrin, in the Kingdom of Hungary (now the Slovak Republic). His parents' financial situation forced them to immigrate to the United States in 1885, when Hertz was thirteen.

3. Rabbi Hertz was appointed chief rabbi of the United Kingdom in 1912, an office he held until his death in 1946.

4. H. Szold to Rabbi Hertz, August 8, 1902, AJA, II. Szold correspondence.

5. "Necrology," in *The American Jewish Year Book, 5663,* ed. Cyrus Adler (Philadelphia: Jewish Publication Society, 1902), 197.

6. Szold to her family, July 8, 1922, quoted in Marvin Lowenthal, *Henrietta Szold: Life and Letters* (New York: Viking Press, 1942), 58.

7. Alexandra Lee Levin, *Henrietta Szold: Baltimorean* (Baltimore: Jewish Historical Society of Maryland, 1976). On the agricultural colonies, see Ellen M. Eisenberg, *Jewish Agricultural Colonies in New Jersey, 1882–1920* (Syracuse, NY: Syracuse University Press, 1995).

8. A report in the *Baltimore Sun,* March 14, 1903, praises Szold for her lecture to the members of the Woman's Literary Club, given at the home of Bessie Smyth; Levin, *Szolds of Lombard Street,* 367.

9. Szold wrote about the state of the Zionist movement in America in volumes 2 and 4 of *The American Jewish Year Book.*

10. Evyatar Friesel, "American Zionism and American Jewry: An Ideological and Communal Encounter," *American Jewish Archives* 40, no. 1 (1988): 5–23.

11. Joyce Antler, *The Journey Home: How Jewish Women Shaped Modern America* (New York: Free Press, 1997), 98.

12. Szold's thoughts on the Zionist movement appeared in *The American Jewish Year Book, 5661,* ed. Cyrus Adler (Philadelphia: Jewish Publication Society, 1900).

13. Louis Marshall was born in 1856 and died in 1929. On Reform Jews turning to Zionism, see Michael A. Meyer, *Response to Modernity: A History of the Reform Movement in Judaism* (New York: Oxford University Press, 1988).

14. Steven J. Zipperstein, *Elusive Prophet: Ahad Ha'am and the Origins of Zionism* (London: P. Halban, 1993).

15. The FAZ was founded on July 4–5, 1898. The assembly elected Richard Gottheil as president, Stephen Wise as secretary, and seven delegates to the Second Zionist Congress. Wise, who was nearing the end of his academic studies at the time, served as secretary for only a year. Evyatar Friesel, *Ha-tnuah ha-Tziyonit be-Artzot ha-brit ba-shanim 1897–1914* [The Zionist movement in the United States, 1897–1914] (Tel Aviv: Tel Aviv University and Hakibbutz Hameuchad, 1970), 29–32.

16. Friesel, *Ha-tnuah ha-Tziyonit,* 29.

17. Steven J. Zipperstein, *Pogrom: Kishinev and the Tilt of History* (New York: Liveright, 2018); Eli Lederhendler, "Classless: On the Social Status of Jews in Russia and Eastern Europe in the Late Nineteenth Century," *Comparative Studies in Society and History* 50 (2008): 509–534.

18. Hayim Nahman Bialik, "On the Slaughter," in *Chaim Nachman Bialik: Selected Poems,* trans. Ruth Nevo (Jerusalem: Dvir/Jerusalem Post, 1981), 34–37.

19. Quoted in Monty Noam Penkower, *Twentieth Century Jews: Forging Identity in the Land of Promise and in the Promised Land* (Boston: Academic Studies Press, 2010), 8.

20. "In the City of Slaughter" was published in English in 1906. Hayim Nahman Bialik, "'Al HaShechitah," trans. Helena Frank, *Jewish Quarterly Review* 19, no. 1 (1906): 127–135.

21. Henrietta Szold, "A List of Leading Events in 5663," in *The American Jewish Year Book, 5664,* ed. Cyrus Adler (Philadelphia: Jewish Publication Society, 1903), 218–219.

22. Alexandra Lee Levin, *Vision: A Biography of Harry Friedenwald* (Philadelphia: Jewish Publication Society, 1964), 168–169.

23. Cyrus Adler, ed., *The Voice of America on Kishineff* (Philadelphia: Jewish Publication Society, 1904).

24. Henrietta Szold, "From Kishineff to Bialystok," in *The American Jewish Year Book, 5667* (Philadelphia: Jewish Publication Society, 1906), 34–89.

25. American Jewish population estimates: 1880, 230,000–300,000; 1920, 3,300,000–3,600,000. Jonathan D. Sarna, *American Judaism: A History* (New Haven, CT: Yale University Press, 2004), 375.

26. Derek Penslar, *Theodor Herzl: The Charismatic Leader* (New Haven, CT: Yale University Press, 2020).

27. Harry Friedenwald to Bertha Friedenwald, August 27, 1903, quoted in Levin, *Vision*, 172–173.

28. There were 295 votes in favor of sending the survey team, and 175 against. See Shmuel Almog, *Zionism and History: The Rise of a New Jewish Consciousness* (New York: St. Martin's Press, 1987), 238–304; Robert G. Weisbord, *African Zion: The Attempt to Establish a Jewish Colony in the East Africa Protectorate, 1903–1905* (Philadelphia: Jewish Publication Society of America, 1968).

29. Harry Friedenwald to Bertha Friedenwald, quoted in Levin, *Vision*, 173.

30. Ernst Pawel, *The Labyrinth of Exile: A Life of Theodor Herzl* (New York: Farrar, Straus & Giroux, 1989), 366–368.

31. Zipperstein, *Elusive Prophet*; Shlomo Avinery, *The Making of Modern Zionism: The Intellectual Origins of the Jewish State* (New York: Basic Books, 2017).

32. Szold, "A List of Leading Events in 5663," 220.

33. Sarna, *American Judaism*, 187.

34. The couple married in 1887.

35. Shuly Rubin Schwartz, *The Rabbi's Wife: The Rebbetzin in American Jewish Life* (New York: New York University Press, 2006), 32–42; Ismar Schorsch, "Schechter's Seminary: Polarities in Balance," introduction to Solomon Schechter, *Studies in Judaism* (Piscataway, NJ: Gorgias Press, 2003), v–xxxii.

36. Adina Hoffman and Peter Cole, *Sacred Trash: The Lost and Found World of the Cairo Geniza* (New York: Notebook, 2011), 6–7.

37. Hasia Diner, "Like the Antelope and the Badger: The Founding and Early Years of the Jewish Theological Seminary, 1886–1902," in *Tradition Renewed: A History of the Jewish Theological Seminary*, ed. Jack Wertheimer (New York: Jewish Theological Seminary, 1997), 1:3–42.

38. Martha Washington Levy, "The Year 5662," in *The American Jewish Year Book, 5663*, ed. Cyrus Adler (Philadelphia: Jewish Publication Society of America, 1902), 15–17; Henrietta Szold, "National Organizations," subsection "The Jewish Theological Seminary of America," in *The American Jewish Year Book, 5663*, ed. Cyrus Adler (Philadelphia: Jewish Publication Society of America, 1902), 122–124.

39. Schorsch, "Schechter's Seminary," v–vi; Jonathan D. Sarna, "Two Traditions of Seminary Scholarship," in *Tradition Renewed: A History of the Jewish Theological Seminary*, ed. Jack Wertheimer (New York: Jewish Theological Seminary of America, 1997), 2:55–80.

40. Exodus 3:2.

41. Rubin Schwartz, *The Rabbi's Wife*, 36.

42. Rubin Schwartz, *The Rabbi's Wife,* 36.

43. Schorsch, "Schechter's Seminary," xi.

44. Solomon Schechter, "Women in the Temple and Synagogue," in *Studies in Judaism,* First Series (Philadelphia: Jewish Publication Society, 1896), 313–325; "The Memoirs of a Jewess of the Seventeenth Century," in *Studies in Judaism,* Second Series (Philadelphia: Jewish Publication Society, 1908), 126–147; Schorsch, "Schechter's Seminary," xx–xxii. See also Glückel of Hameln, *Glikl: Zikhronot 1691–1719* [Glückel: Memoirs, 1691–1719], trans. and ed. Chava Turniansky (Jerusalem: Zalman Shazar Center, Ben-Zion Dinur Center, and Hebrew University, 2006).

45. Alexander Marx (1878–1953) was one of Moritz Steinschneider's outstanding students.

46. Israel Friedlaender (1876–1920) was born in Kovel, Volhynia (today in Ukraine). At age twenty he moved to Berlin to study at the university there. He earned his PhD at the University of Strasbourg, where he was subsequently appointed lecturer in Semitic languages.

47. Friedlaender was the first president of the Bureau of Jewish Education in New York, the first president of Young Judea, and a trustee of the Educational Alliance, founded on New York's Lower East Side.

48. Louis (Levy) Ginzberg was born in 1873 and died in 1953.

49. Jonathan D. Sarna, *JPS: The Americanization of Jewish Culture, 1888–1988: A Centennial History of the Jewish Publication Society* (Philadelphia: Jewish Publication Society, 1989), 130–131.

50. David Golinkin, introduction to Louis Ginzberg, *Legends of the Jews,* trans. Henrietta Szold, 2nd ed. (Philadelphia: Jewish Publication Society, 2003).

51. Ginzberg to JPS, October 9, 1903, quoted in Sarna, *JPS,* 390.

52. Sulzberger to Ginzberg, October 9, 1903, quoted in Sarna, *JPS,* 390.

53. Sarna, *JPS,* 390. The first volume was published in 1909, and the sixth in 1928.

54. Herzl continued meeting with statesmen and world leaders, such as Pope Pius X, King Victor Emmanuel of Italy, and others.

55. Quoted in Dan Kurzman, *Ben-Gurion: Prophet of Fire* (New York: Simon and Schuster, 1963), 63. On Ben-Gurion's reaction to Herzl's death, see also Shabtai Teveth, *Ben-Gurion: The Burning Ground* (Boston: Houghton Mifflin, 1987), 19.

56. Quoted in Pawel, *Labyrinth of Exile,* 528.

57. Quoted in Pawel, *Labyrinth of Exile,* 530.

6 · LOVE AND MISERY

1. Szold to Alexander Marx, September 12, 1904, JMMA, H. Szold Correspondence.

2. Marcus Jastrow passed away on October 13, 1903.

3.   Quoted in Baila Round Shargel, *Lost Love: The Untold Story of Henrietta Szold: Unpublished Diary and Letters* (Philadelphia: Jewish Publication Society, 1997), 47–48.

4.   Shargel, *Lost Love,* 48.

5.   Moses Dropsie (1821–1905), publisher of the *Jewish Quarterly Review,* was the son of a Jewish father and a non-Jewish mother who converted to Judaism. He devoted his fortune to the advancement of Jewish studies.

6.   Ginzberg to Szold, August 17, 1905, quoted in Eli Ginzberg, *Keeper of the Law: Louis Ginzberg* (Philadelphia: Jewish Publication Society of America, 1966), 114.

7.   Shargel, *Lost Love,* 49.

8.   Evyatar Friesel, "American Zionism and American Jewry: An Ideological and Communal Encounter," *American Jewish Archives* 40, no. 1 (1988), 13–15.

9.   Szold to Friedenwald, February 13, 1906, JMMA, H. Szold Correspondence.

10. Evyatar Friesel, *Ha-tnuah ha-Tziyonit be-Artzot ha-brit ba-shanim 1897–1914* [The Zionist movement in the United States, 1897–1914] (Tel Aviv: Tel Aviv University and Hakibbutz Hameuchad, 1970), 174.

11. *The American Jewish Year Book, 5667,* 1906.

12. Henrietta Szold, ed., "From Kishineff to Bialystok: A Table of Pogroms from 1903 to 1906," in *The American Jewish Year Book, 5667* (Philadelphia: Jewish Publication Society, 1906), 34–89.

13. Henrietta Szold, "The Government of the United States and Affairs of Interest to the Jews, 1905–1906," in *American Jewish Year Book, 5667,* 90–102; "Jews in the Congress of the United States, Fifty-Ninth Congress," in *American Jewish Year Book, 5667,* 103. The members were Henry Mayer Goldfogle of New York, in the House of Representatives; Julius Kahn of California, in the House of Representatives; Lucius Nathan Littauer of New York, in the House of Representatives; Adolph Meyer of Louisiana, in the House of Representatives; and Isidor Rayner of Maryland, in the Senate.

14. Ginzberg to Szold, August 10, 1906, quoted in Shargel, *Lost Love,* 56–58.

15. Ginzberg to Szold, August 10, 1906; Eli Ginzberg, *Keeper of the Law,* 114–115.

16. Szold to Ginzberg, June 10, 1907, JTSA, L. Ginzberg correspondence file.

17. Ginzberg to Szold, August 2, 1907, Ginzberg to Szold, June 10, 1907, JMMA, H. Szold Correspondence.

18. Szold to Anna Marx, July 24, 1908, and August 15, 1908, JMMA, H. Szold Correspondence.

19. Irving Fineman, *Woman of Valor: The Life of Henrietta Szold, 1860–1945* (New York: Simon and Schuster, 1961), 160.

20. Ginzberg to Szold, September 15, 1908, and September 24, 1908, quoted in Fineman, *Woman of Valor,* 160.

21. Ginzberg to Szold, September 26, 1908, quoted in Fineman, *Woman of Valor,* 160.

22. Fineman, *Woman of Valor,* 163.

23. Szold Diary, November 12, 1908, JMMA.

24. November 17, 1908, quoted in Fineman, *Woman of Valor,* 173.

25. Szold to Adele Katzenstein, October 20, 1908, quoted in Ginzberg, *Keeper of the Law,* 128–129.

26. Jonathan D. Sarna, *JPS: The Americanization of Jewish Culture, 1888–1988: A Centennial History of the Jewish Publication Society* (Philadelphia: Jewish Publication Society, 1989), 65.

27. Ginzberg to Szold, February 21, 1909, quoted in Ginzberg, *Keeper of the Law,* 129.

28. Schechter to Szold, mentioned in Szold's Diary, January 21, 1909, JMMA, H. Szold Correspondence.

29. Marx to Szold, January 23, 1909, JMMA, H. Szold Correspondence.

30. Marx to Szold, February 8, 1909, JMMA, H. Szold Correspondence.

31. Ginzberg, *Keeper of the Law,* 105–129.

32. Ginzberg, *Keeper of the Law,* 107.

33. Ginzberg, *Keeper of the Law,* 107–108.

34. Ginzberg, *Keeper of the Law,* 108–109.

35. Alexandra Lee Levin, *The Szolds of Lombard Street: A Baltimore Family, 1859–1909* (Philadelphia: Jewish Publication Society, 1960), 374.

36. Ginzberg, *Keeper of the Law,* 105–113.

37. On July 15, 1909; see Sarna, *JPS,* 132.

38. Szold Diary, July 15, 1909, and July 20, 1909, quoted in Shargel, *Lost Love,* 302–303.

39. Szold Diary, July 21, 1909, quoted in Shargel, *Lost Love,* 302–303.

⁊ THE LAND OF DREAMS

1. Szold Diary, August 2, 1909, CZA, A125/276.

2. Szold Diary, August 13, 1909, CZA, A125/276. On Emma Goldman, see Vivian Gornick, *Emma Goldman: Revolution as a Way of Life* (New Haven, CT: Yale University Press, 2013).

3. Maurice Hewlett, *The Queen's Quair, or, The Six Years' Tragedy* (Leipzig: Tauchnitz, 1904).

4. Szold to her family, August 13, 1909, CZA, A125/276.

5. Szold to her family, August 15, 1909, CZA, A125/276.

6. Norman Bentwich, *Philo-Judæus of Alexandria* (Philadelphia: Jewish Publication Society, 1910).

7. Szold to Mathilde Schechter, August 17, 1909, JTSA.

8. Elkan Nathan Adler was born in 1861. After his death in 1946, he willed a large portion of his manuscripts to the Jewish Theological Seminary in New York.

9. Szold to Mathilde Schechter, August 17, 1909, JTSA.

10. Szold to her sisters, August 20, 1909, August 24, 1909, CZA, A125/276; Szold to Marx, undated, JMMA, H. Szold Correspondence.

11. They arrived on September 3, 1909. Szold Diary, CZA, A125/276.

12. Szold Diary, September 3, 1909, CZA, A125/276.

13. Szold to Mathilde Schechter, September 15, 1909, CZA, A125/276.

14. Szold to Marx, September 12, 1909, CZA, A125/276.

15. Szold to her sisters, October 27, 1909, CZA, A125/276.

16. Cecil Bloom, "The Institution of *Halukkah*: A Historical Review," *Jewish Historical Studies* 36 (1999–2001): 1–30; Szold to her sisters, November 3, 1909, CZA, A125/276.

17. Mania Shochat 1879–1961, https://jwa.org/encyclopedia/article/shochat-mania-wilbushewitch.

18. Derek J. Penslar, *Zionism and Technocracy: The Engineering of Jewish Settlement in Palestine, 1870–1918* (Bloomington: Indiana University Press, 1991).

19. Zvi Saliternik, *Korot ha-milhamah ba-kadahat be-Eretz Yisra'el ve-hadbaratah* [The history of the war against malaria in the Land of Israel and its eradication] (Jerusalem: Israel Institute of the History of Medicine, 1979). Thanks to Mrs. Shulamit Gibbent in Jerusalem, who drew my attention to this work written by her father.

20. John Murray, *Handbook for Travellers in Syria and Palestine* (London: J. Murray, 1868).

21. Avraham Moshe Luncz, *Moreh derekh be-Eretz Yisra'el ve-Suriyah* [Guide to Palestine and Syria] (Jerusalem: A. M. Luncz, 1908), 51.

22. Luncz, *Moreh*, 52–68; for a description of the road from Jaffa to Jerusalem, see Luncz, *Moreh*, 82–87.

23. Luncz, *Moreh*, 68–77.

24. Szold Diary, November 17, 1909, CZA, A125/276.

25. Szold Diary, November 17, 1909, CZA, A125/276.

26. Mark Twain, *The Innocents Abroad, or, The New Pilgrim's Progress* (Hartford: American Publishing Company, 1870), 559.

27. Shlomo Avineri, *Herzl's Vision: Theodor Herzl and the Foundation of the Jewish State* (New York: Katonah, 2014), 18.

28. For a brief survey on the subject of the European consulates in Jerusalem, see Yehoshua Ben-Arieh, *Jerusalem in the 19th Century*, vol. 1, *The Old City* (Jerusalem: Yad Izhak Ben-Zvi, 1984), 184–189.

29. Alexandra Lee Levin, *Vision: A Biography of Harry Friedenwald* (Philadelphia: Jewish Publication Society, 1964), 189–190.

30. Szold to Elfreda Solis-Cohen, December 12, 1909, CZA, A125/276.

31. Szold Diary, November 16, 1909, CZA, A125/276.

32. Szold to her sisters and to Dr. Marx, December 12, 1909, CZA, A125/276.

33. Szold to her sisters, December 12, 1909, JMMA; Szold to Dr. Marx, December 12, 1909, JMMA, H. Szold Correspondence.

34. Szold to her sisters, November 29, 1909, CZA, A125/276.

35. Szold Diary, December 12, 1909, CZA, A125/276.

36. Szold to Mathilde Schechter, September 26, 1909; Szold to Marx, January 2, 1910, JMMA, H. Szold Correspondence.

8 THE DEPTHS OF MISERY

1. February 10, 1910. The invitation is in JMMA, H. Szold Correspondence.

2. Szold Diary, March 2, 1910, CZA, A125/989.

3. Szold Diary, March 17, 1910, CZA, A125/989.

4. Szold Diary, March 3, 20, 24, and 25, 1910, JMMA.

5. Szold Diary, April 4, 1910, JMMA.

6. Aaron Aaronsohn to Julian Mack, quoted in Shmuel Katz, *The Aaronsohn Saga* (Jerusalem: Gefen, 2007), 109.

7. Szold Diary, March 28 and 29 and April 4, 2010, JMMA.

8. Szold Diary, April 6, 1910, CZA, A125/989.

9. Szold Diary, March 7, 1910, JMMA.

10. Szold Diary, March 7, 1910, JMMA.

11. Szold Diary, March 5, 1910, JMMA.

12. Szold Diary, April 10, 1910, CZA, A125/989.

13. Szold Diary, March 17, 1910, CZA, A125/989.

14. Szold Diary, March 17, 1910, CZA, A125/989.

15. Szold Diary, April 18, 1910, CZA, A125/989.

16. Szold Diary, March 7, 1910, JH.

17. *Report of the Executive Committee, Presented at the Second Annual Convention of the Jewish Community (Kehillah), New York, February 25 and 26, 1911.* On the establishment of the Kehillah, see Arthur A. Goren, *New York Jews and the Quest for Community: The Kehillah Experiment, 1908–1922* (New York: Columbia University Press, 1970).

18. Szold Diary, April 18, 1910, CZA, A125/989.

19. Szold Diary, March 7, 1910, JMMA.

20. Jonathan Bruce Krasner, *The Benderly Boys and American Jewish Education* (Waltham, MA: Brandeis University Press, 2011).

21. Szold Diary, March 17, 1910, JMMA.

22. Szold Diary, June 8, 1910, CZA, A125/989; also quoted in Jonathan D. Sarna, *JPS: The Americanization of Jewish Culture, 1888–1988: A Centennial History of the Jewish Publication Society* (Philadelphia: Jewish Publication Society, 1989), 133.

23. Szold Diary, June 10, 1910, and Szold to Sulzberger, June 12, 1910, both quoted in Sarna, *JPS*, 133.

24. Israel Davidson (1870–1940) was born in Lithuania but brought up in America. An expert in medieval Jewish literature, he began teaching at the seminary in 1905.

25. Szold Diary, June 12, 1910, JMMA.

26. Szold Diary, June 12, 1910, JMMA.

27. Szold Diary, June 19, 1910, JMMA.

28. Szold Diary, July 20, 1910, JMMA.

29. Szold to Mathilde Schechter, November 10, 1910, JTSA.

30. Szold Diary, March 28, 1910, CZA, A125/989.

31. Thank-you letter from Bertha Szold Levin to Cyrus Adler, 1911 (exact date illegible), CZA, A125/248.

32. Szold to Miss Felsenthal, August 14, 1911, HAD.

33. Szold to Marx, September 3, 1911, HAD.

34. Szold to Alice Seligsberg, September 28, 1911, HAD.

35. On Sampter, see Joyce Antler, *The Journey Home: Jewish Women and the American Century* (New York: Free Press, 1997), 98–135; Bertha Badt-Strauss, *White Fire: The Life and Works of Jessie Sampter* (New York: Reconstructionist Press, 1956).

9 THE HEALING OF MY PEOPLE

1. Joyce Antler, *The Journey Home: Jewish Women and the American Century* (New York: Free Press, 1997), 104.

2. Steven J. Zipperstein, *Elusive Prophet: Ahad Ha'am and the Origins of Zionism* (London: P. Halban, 1993).

3. Mira Katzburg-Yungman, *Hadassah: American Women Zionists and the Rebirth of Israel* (Oxford: Littman Library of Jewish Civilization, 2012).

4. See Esther 2:7.

5. The name Hadassah was adopted by the national organization at its second national convention, held in Rochester, New York, in June 1914. See Evyatar Friesel, *Ha-tnuah ha-Tziyonit be-Artzot ha-brit ba-shanim 1897–1914* [The Zionist movement in the United States, 1897–1914] (Tel Aviv: Tel Aviv University and Hakibbutz Hameuchad, 1970), 175.

6. Rose Zeitlin, *Henrietta Szold: Record of a Life* (New York: Dial Press, 1952), 37–48.

7. Michael Brown, "Henrietta Szold's Progressive American Vision of the Yishuv," in *Envisioning Israel: The Changing Ideals and Images of North American Jews,* ed. Allon Gal (Jerusalem: Magnes Press, 1996), 60–80.

8. Szold to Julia Felsenthal, November 7, 1914, as well as members of other chapters, AJA, H. Szold Correspondence.

9. Light had convinced Szold to sit for a portrait. See Zeitlin, *Henrietta Szold,* 49.

10. In 1909, the centennial year of Abraham Lincoln's birth, Victor David Brenner designed a 1¢ coin bearing the late president's image.

11. Louis Lipsky (1876–1963), the son of Polish immigrants, was born in Rochester, New York. He was elected chairman of the board of the Federation of American Zionists in 1911. His papers are in the collection of the American Jewish Historical Society.

12. On Lillian Wald (1867–1917), see Marjorie N. Feld, *Lillian Wald, A Biography* (Chapel Hill: University of North Carolina Press, 2008); Arthur Hertzberg, *The Jews in America: Four Centuries of an Uneasy Encounter: A History* (New York: Simon and Schuster, 1989), 150; Doris G. Daniels, *Always a Sister: The Feminism of Lillian D. Wald* (New York: Feminist Press, 1989).

13. Antler, *Journey Home,* 105.

14. Zeitlin, *Henrietta Szold,* 51.

15. Rachel Landy was born in 1884 and died in 1952.

16. See Eric L. Goldstein, "Rose Kaplan," *Jewish Women: A Comprehensive Historical Encyclopedia,* March 1, 2009, Jewish Women's Archive, https://jwa.org/encyclopedia/article/Kaplan-Rose.

17. Nathan Straus was born in 1848 and died in 1931.

18. See Ionel Rosenthal, "Nathan Straus' Contribution to the Dairy Industry in Palestine," *Journal of Israeli History* 15, no. 2 (1994): 91–99.

19. In response to a request by Aaron Aaronsohn, Straus opened a health station outside of Jerusalem as well, primarily to deal with the malaria epidemic.

20. Zeitlin, *Henrietta Szold,* 50–53.

21. Antler, *Journey Home,* 141.

22. Alice Seligsberg, "Chronicles of Hadassah 1912–1914," HAD; Antler, *Journey Home,* 5.

23. Antler, *Journey Home,* 105.

24. Hull House was a settlement house founded by Jane Addams and Ellen Gates Starr, named after the building's original owner, Charles Jerald Hull. The settlement expanded rapidly, and by 1911 it comprised thirteen buildings.

25. Alice Seligsberg, "Chronicles of Hadassah," *Hadassah Newsletter,* May 1927, HAD.

26. Helena Kagan, *Reshit darki bi-Yerushalayim* [My first steps in Jerusalem] (Tel Aviv: WIZO, 1983), 45. Dr. Helena Kagan (1888–1978) was the first pediatrician in Palestine.

27. For the same reason, educator and women's activist Sara Azaryahu also studied in Bern, Switzerland. Sara Azaryahu, *Pirke hayim* [Chapters of life] (Tel Aviv: M. Newman, 1957), 43.

28. Kagan, *Reshit darki,* 48–49. Kagan lived to the age of eighty-nine, and continued her work for nearly three decades after the establishment of the State of Israel in 1948. In 1975, she was awarded the Israel Prize.

29. Kagan, *Reshit darki,* 46–48; Ephraim Sinai, *Bi-melo ha-ayin: Me'olamo shel rofe* [An eyeful: From the world of a doctor] (Tel Aviv: Cherikover, 1984), 119.

30. Szold to Dr. Biskind, September 9, 1914, AJA, H. Szold Correspondence.

31. Szold to Elvira Solis, August 25, 1915, quoted in Marvin Lowenthal, *Henrietta Szold: Life and Letters* (New York: Viking Press, 1942), 84.

32. Emanuel Neumann, *In the Arena: An Autobiographical Memoir* (New York: Herzl Press, 1976), 34.

33. Philipa Strum, *Louis D. Brandeis, Justice for the People* (Cambridge, MA: Harvard University Press, 2013); Jeffrey Rosen, *Louis D. Brandeis: American Prophet* (New Haven, CT: Yale University Press, 2016); Jonathan D. Sarna, "The Greatest Jew in the World since Jesus Christ," *American Jewish History* 81, nos. 3–4 (1994): 346–364.

34. Louis D. Brandeis, *Brandeis on Zionism: A Collection of Addresses and Statements* (Washington, DC: Zionist Organization of America, 1942).

35. Sidney Ratner, "Kallen and Cultural Pluralism," *Modern Judaism* 4, no. 2 (1984): 185–200; William Toll, "Horace M. Kallen: Pluralism and American Identity," *American Jewish History* 85, no. 1 (1997): 57–74.

36. Brandeis, *Brandeis on Zionism,* 28–29.

37. Brandeis, *Brandeis on Zionism,* 33.

38. Neumann, *In the Arena,* 33.

39. Dr. Shmarya Levin (1867–1935) was a Zionist leader, writer, and essayist who played an active role in a number of Zionist congresses.

40. Szold to Dr. Biskind, September 9, 1914, AJA, H. Szold Correspondence. See also Mary McCune, *The Whole Wide World without Limits: International Relief, Gender Politics, and American Jewish Women, 1893–1930* (Detroit: Wayne State University Press, 2005), 51.

41. Julian Mack (1866–1943) was a federal judge, a Jewish and Zionist leader, and the first chairman of the Jewish delegation to the Versailles Peace Conference (1919). Kibbutz Ramat Hashofet was named in his honor. See Harry Barnard, *The Forging of an American Jew: The Life and Times of Judge Julian W. Mack* (New York: Herzl Press, 1974).

42. Julius Rosenwald (1862–1932) was a businessman and philanthropist, best known as part owner of Sears, Roebuck and Company. Mary Fels (1863–

1953) was an editor, activist, and philanthropist. See Hasia Diner, *Julius Rosenwald: Repairing the World* (New Haven, CT: Yale University Press, 2017).

43. Szold to Adler, Szold to Sulzberger, December 1, 1915, quoted in Jonathan D. Sarna, *JPS: The Americanization of Jewish Culture, 1888–1988: A Centennial History of the Jewish Publication Society* (Philadelphia: Jewish Publication Society, 1989), 134.

44. Sarna, *JPS*, 137–138.

45. "List of Books Issued by the Jewish Publication Society of America," in *The American Jewish Year Book, 5677*, ed. Cyrus Adler (Philadelphia: JPS, 1916): 588–592.

46. Sarna, *JPS*, 137.

47. Henrietta Szold, "Recent Jewish Progress in Palestine," in *The American Jewish Year Book, 5676*, ed. Joseph Jacobs (Philadelphia: JPS, 1915), 25–158.

48. Simon Miller, "President's Address," in *The American Jewish Year Book, 5677*, ed. Cyrus Adler (Philadelphia: JPS, 1916), 416.

49. Szold to Elvira Solis, August 22, 1916, quoted in Lowenthal, *Henrietta Szold*, 91.

50. Szold to Cyrus Adler, December 1, 1915, and Szold to Elvira Solis, August 22, 1916, quoted in Lowenthal, *Henrietta Szold*, 90–92.

51. Szold to Haym Peretz, September 16, 1916, quoted in Lowenthal, *Henrietta Szold*, 92–93.

52. Moshe Smilansky (1874–1953), *Perakim be-toldot ha-Yishuv* [Chapters in the history of the Yishuv] (Tel Aviv: Dvir, 1978), 177.

53. Eran Dolev, Yigal Sheffy, and Haim Goren, eds., *Palestine and World War I: Grand Strategy, Military Tactics and Culture in War* (London: I. B. Tauris, 2014).

54. Chaim I. Waxman, *America's Jews in Transition* (Philadelphia: Temple University Press, 1983).

55. Shoshana Halevy, *Parshiyot bereshit be-toldot ha-Yishuv* [Early affairs in the history of the Yishuv] (Jerusalem: Ben Zvi Institute, 1989), 194–195.

56. Kagan, *Reshit darki*, 41.

57. Nathan Efrati, *Mi-mashber le-tikvah: Ha-Yishuv ha-Yehudi be-Eretz Yisra'el be-Milhemet ha-Olam ha-Rishonah* [From crisis to hope: The Yishuv in the First World War] (Jerusalem: Ben Zvi Institute, 1991); Isaiah Friedman, *Germany, Turkey and Zionism 1897–1918* (Oxford: Clarendon Press, 1977), 345–373.

58. Kagan, *Reshit darki*, 42.

59. Smilansky, *Perakim*, 176.

60. Kagan, *Reshit darki*, 54.

61. Szold to Elvira Solis, August 25, 1915, quoted in Lowenthal, *Henrietta Szold*, 90–91; Antler, *The Journey*, 105.

62. The American Joint Distribution Committee was established in November 1914, and was headed by Jacob Schiff and his son-in-law and business partner Felix M. Warburg, with the help of Nathan Straus and others.

63. *Hadassah Bulletin,* March 1918.

64. Letters from Szold to her friends Jessie Sampter, Alice Seligsberg, Elvira Solis, and others, AJA, H. Szold correspondence.

65. Szold to Alice Seligsberg, March 27, 1917, quoted in Lowenthal, *Henrietta Szold,* 96–97.

66. Szold to Elvira Solis, April 12, 1917, quoted in Lowenthal, *Henrietta Szold,* 98.

67. Szold to Alice Seligsberg, March 27, 1917, quoted in Lowenthal, *Henrietta Szold,* 97.

68. Mordechai Ben-Hillel Hacohen, *Milhemet ha-amim: Yoman* [War of the nations: An Eretz Israel diary 1914–1918] (Jerusalem: Ben Zvi Institute, 1981).

69. Rabbi Moses Kliers to Meir Dizengoff. April 23, 1917. In the author's possession.

70. M. B. Hacohen, *Milhemet ha-amim.*

71. Kagan to Szold, October 1917, CZA, A125.

72. Szold to Jacob Schiff, March 12, 1918; *Hadassah Bulletin,* March 1918, included a copy of Dr. Kagan's report on the medical unit expenditures.

73. Norman and Helen Bentwich, *Mandate Memories, 1918–1948* (London: Hogarth Press, 1965); Jehuda Reinharz, *Chaim Weizmann: The Making of a Statesman* (New York: Oxford University Press, 1993), 2:172–212; Norman A. Rose, *Chaim Weizmann: A Biography* (London: Weidenfeld and Nicolson, 1986); Leonard Stein, *The Balfour Declaration* (London: Vallentine-Mitchell, 1961), chap. 8; Aaronsohn to Szold, January 4, 1918, HADA, RG 13.

74. Azaryahu, *Pirke hayim,* 145.

75. Szold to Jessie Sampter, January 21, 1918, quoted in Lowenthal, *Henrietta Szold,* 101 104.

76. Szold to Jessie Sampter, January 21, 1918, quoted in Lowenthal, *Henrietta Szold,* 101–104.

77. Joshua Yellin, *Zikhronot le-ven Yerushalayim* [Memoirs of a Jerusalemite] (Jerusalem: Zion Press, 1924), 202.

78. Kagan to Szold, December 25, 1917, HADA, RG 13 / 5.

79. Azaryahu, *Pirke hayim,* 148–149.

80. Szold to Seligsberg, November 20, 1918, HADA, RG 13 / 5.

81. Julian Leavitt, "American Jews in the World War," in *The American Jewish Year Book, 5680,* ed. Harry Schneiderman (Philadelphia: JPS, 1919), 141–155.

82. Eran Dolev, *Allenby's Military Medicine: Life and Death in World War I Palestine* (London: I. B. Tauris, 2007), 157.

83. Weizmann was not the only one to do so. A number of prominent figures exerted influence on the British foreign secretary. Brandeis used his friendship with Woodrow Wilson to persuade the president to support the issuance of the British declaration. See Reinharz, *Chaim Weizmann,* 2:172–212.

84. Brandeis, address at the second annual conference of the Palestine Land Development Council, New York, May 27–28, 1923.

85. Szold to Alice Seligsberg, August 4, 1918, quoted in Lowenthal, *Henrietta Szold,* 110.

86. Szold to Alice Seligsberg, August 4, 1918, quoted in Lowenthal, *Henrietta Szold,* 109.

87. Neumann, *In the Arena,* 42–44.

88. Szold to Seligsberg, January 24, 1919, quoted in Lowenthal, *Henrietta Szold,* 114.

89. Szold to Seligsberg, July 13, 1919, quoted in Lowenthal, *Henrietta Szold,* 114–115.

90. Louis Lipsky, *A Gallery of Zionist Profiles* (New York: Farrar, Straus and Cudahy, 1956), 141.

10 IN PALESTINE

1. Szold to her sisters, March 23, 1920, HADA, RG 13/5 H. Szold.

2. Szold to her sisters, April 7, 1920, quoted in Marvin Lowenthal, *Henrietta Szold: Life and Letters* (New York: Viking Press, 1942), 124.

3. The Zionist Commission for Palestine was established to work in conjunction with Jewish leaders in Palestine and the British authorities to help the Yishuv recover from the damage it had sustained during the war and to promote its development, particularly in the fields of healthcare, education, welfare, and Jewish settlement. The commission (active 1918–1921) included prominent Zionist leaders such as Menachem Ussishkin, Aaron Aaronsohn, Zalman David Levontin, and Israel Sieff, as well as representatives of non-Zionist groups such as David Eder of the Jewish Territorial Organization (ITO), Major William Ormsby-Gore (a British officer and politician who sympathized with the Zionist cause), James de Rothschild, and others. See Naomi Sheperd, *Ploughing Sand: British Rule in Palestine, 1917–1948* (New Brunswick, NJ: Rutgers University Press, 2000).

4. Szold to her sisters, May 11, 1920, quoted in Lowenthal, *Henrietta Szold,* 131–136.

5. Helena Kagan, *Reshit darki bi-Yerushalayim* [My first steps in Jerusalem] (Tel Aviv: WIZO, 1983); Zippora Sehory-Rubin, *Doktor Helena Kagan: Ha-rof'ah shehafkhah le-agadah* [Dr. Helena Kagan: The doctor who became a legend], *Cathedra* 118 (2006): 89–114.

6. *Doar Hayom,* May 9, 1920.

7. *Doar Hayom,* May 14, 1920; Sheperd, *Ploughing Sand.*

8. S. Wilinetz in *Doar Hayom,* May 10, 1920.

9. Eliezer Ben-Yehuda in *Doar Hayom,* May 21, 1920.

10. "Zionists Outline Palestine's Future," *New York Times,* May 10, 1920; *Doar Hayom,* May 28, 1920.

11. Leonard Stein, *The Balfour Declaration* (London: Vallentine Mitchell, 1961), 135–137; Bernard Wasserstein, *Herbert Samuel: A Political Life* (Oxford: Oxford University Press, 1992), 198–199.

12. Nellie Straus-Mochenson, *Our Palestine* (Tel Aviv: n.p., 1939); H. Safran, "Rosa Welt Straus," *Encyclopedia of Jewish Women,* Jewish Women's Archives, https://jwa.org/encyclopedia/article/welt-straus-rosa.

13. Szold to her sisters, July 4, 1920, JMMA, H. Szold Correspondence.

14. Efraim Fischel Aaronsohn to Henrietta Szold, June 13, 1920, HADA, RG 13 / 5; Shmuel Katz, *The Aaronsohn Saga* (Jerusalem: Gefen, 2007).

15. Szold to Julius Rosenwald, June 14, 1920, CZA, A125 / 989.

16. Szold to her sisters, July 19, 1921, quoted in Lowenthal, *Henrietta Szold,* 139.

17. Szold to her sisters, May 26, 1920, quoted in Lowenthal, *Henrietta Szold,* 138.

18. Szold to her sisters, June 21, 1920, quoted in Lowenthal, *Henrietta Szold,* 141.

19. Szold to her sisters, June 21, 1920, quoted in Lowenthal, *Henrietta Szold,* 141.

20. Szold to her sisters, June 21, 1920, quoted in Lowenthal, *Henrietta Szold,* 142; Joseph B. Schechtman, *Fighter and Prophet: The Vladimir Jabotinsky Story,* vol. 1 (New York: Yoseloff, 1956); Brian Horowitz and Leonid Katsis, eds., *Vladimir Jabotinsky's Story of My Life* (Detroit: Wayne State University Press, 2016).

21. Szold to her sisters, June 21, 1920, quoted in Lowenthal, *Henrietta Szold,* 142.

22. Szold to her sisters, July 4, 1920, quoted in Lowenthal, *Henrietta Szold,* 143.

23. Bernard Wasserstein, *The British in Palestine: The Mandatory Government and the Arab–Jewish Conflict, 1917–1929* (London: Blackwell, 1991).

24. Norman and Helen Bentwich, *Mandate Memories, 1918–1948* (London: Hogarth Press, 1965); Bertha Spafford Vester, *Our Jerusalem: An American Family in the Holy City, 1881–1949* (Garden City, NY: Doubleday, 1950).

25. Norman Bentwich and Helen Bentwich, *Mandate Memories,* 63–67; Jane Fletcher Geniesse, *American Priestess: The Extraordinary Story of Anna Spafford and the American Colony in Jerusalem* (New York: Doubleday, 2008), 282.

26. Bentwich and Bentwich, *Mandate Memories,* 66.

27. Sara Reguer, "Rutenberg and the Jordan River: A Revolution in Hydro-Electricity," *Middle Eastern Studies* 31, no. 4 (October 1995): 691–729.

28. Bentwich and Bentwich, *Mandate Memories,* 67.

29. Szold to her sisters, May 26, 1920, HADA, RG 13/5.

30. Szold to her sisters, June 21, 1920, quoted in Lowenthal, *Henrietta Szold,* 140.

31. Szold to her sisters, June 3, 1920, CZA, A125/989.

32. Szold to Harry Friedenwald, March 16, 1921, JMMA, H. Szold Correspondence.

33. Szold to Harry Friedenwald, March 16, 1921, JMMA, H. Szold Correspondence.

34. Szold to Seligsberg, January 3, 1921, quoted in Lowenthal, *Henrietta Szold,* 158; Harry Sacher, *Zionist Portraits and Other Essays* (London: Anthony Blond, 1959).

35. Moshe Goldin-Zahavi, "Aliyat 'Ruslan,'" in *Sefer ha-aliyah ha-shelishit* [The Third Aliyah book], ed. Yehuda Erez (Tel Aviv: Am Oved, 1964), 1:137.

36. Natan Haruvi, "Kvish Teveryah Tzemah," in *Sefer ha-aliyah ha-shelishit,* 1:247; David Ophir, "Al Hof Kinneret," in *Sefer ha-aliyah ha-shelishit,* 1:256. See also Natan Haruvi, "Tiberias-Tzemach Road," http://www.haruvi .co.il/road_en.html.

37. David Maletz, *Young Hearts: A Novel of Modern Israel,* trans. Solomon N. Richards (New York: Schocken, 1950). Maletz was a member of Kibbutz Ein Harod and a writer.

38. Szold to her sisters, November 7, 1920, HADA, RG 13/5 H.

39. *Haaretz,* July 28, 1920; Rose, *Chaim Weizmann,* 271–272.

40. Ronald Storrs, *The Memoirs of Sir Ronald Storrs* (New York: G. P. Putnam's Sons, 1937), 385, 413, 462; Wasserstein, *Herbert Samuel,* 198–199.

41. Szold to her sisters, August 4, 1921, quoted in Lowenthal, *Henrietta Szold,* 186–187.

42. Szold Diary, April 30, 1920–July 2, 1920, JMMA.

43. Shifra Shvarts and Zipora Shehory-Rubin, *Hadassah for the Health of the People: The Health-Education Mission of Hadassah: The American Zionist Women in the Holy Land* (Tel Aviv: Dekel, 2012).

44. Margalit Shilo, *Girls of Liberty: The Struggle for Suffrage in Mandatory Palestine,* trans. Haim Watzman (Waltham, MA: Brandeis University Press, 2016).

45. Szold to her sisters, November 22, 1920, HADA, RG 13/26, folder 2.

46. Szold to her sisters, July 4, 1920, quoted in Lowenthal, *Henrietta Szold,* 143.

47. Szold to her sisters, December 8, 1920; quoted in Lowenthal, *Henrietta Szold,* 157.

48. Edwin H. Samuel, *A Lifetime in Jerusalem: The Memoirs of the Second Viscount Samuel* (Jerusalem: Israel Universities Press, 1970), 54–55.

49. Szold to her sisters, December 8, 1920, quoted in Lowenthal, *Henrietta Szold,* 157–158.

50. Szold to Seligsberg, January 3, 1921, quoted in Lowenthal, *Henrietta Szold,* 162.

51. Wasserstein, *The British in Palestine,* 89–107.

52. Szold to her sisters, May 18, 1921, quoted in Lowenthal, *Henrietta Szold,* 175–180.

53. Szold to her sisters, May 18, 1921, HADA, RG 13/5 H. Szold.

54. Szold to her sisters, May 18, 1921, HADA, RG 13/5 H. Szold.

55. *Ha'aretz,* May 4, 1921; Anita Shapira, *Yosef Haim Brenner: A Life,* trans. Anthony Berris (Stanford, CA: Stanford University Press, 2015), 360–366. The men killed in the incident were Yosef Haim Brenner (age forty), Zvi Gugig (age twenty-five), Yehuda Yitzkar and his son Avraham Yitzkar (age nineteen), the writer Yosef Louisdor (twenty-eight), and the writer Zvi Shatz (age thirty-one).

56. Szold to her sisters, June 22, 1921, HADA, RZ 13/25.

57. Szold to her sisters, July 13, 1921, HADA, RZ 13/25.

58. Szold to Mrs. Emil Weinham (exact date illegible), HADA, RZ 13/25.

59. Szold to her sisters, July 13, 1921; Szold to Mrs. Weinheim, November 9, 1921, HADA, RZ 13/25.

60. Szold to her sisters, July 13, 1921, HADA, RZ 13/25.

61. *Hamizrachi,* November 4, 1921.

62. Pontius Pilate, Roman governor of Judaea (26–36 CE), erected statues of the emperor in the city of Jerusalem, looted the Temple treasury, and murdered those who protested against him. He served as governor at the time of the crucifixion of Jesus.

63. *Doar Hayom,* November 6, 1921.

64. *Hamizrahi,* November 4, 1921.

65. David Ben-Gurion, *Zikhronot* [Memoirs] (Tel Aviv: Am Oved, 1971), 1:177–178.

66. Szold to Mrs. Weinheim, November 9, 1921, HADA, RZ 13/25.

67. *Jewish-Arab Affairs: Occasional Papers Published by the "Brit-Shalom" Society* (Jerusalem, 1931), 59–60; Shalom Ratzabi, *Between Zionism and Judaism: The Radical Circle in Brith Shalom, 1925–1933* (Leiden: Brill, 2002), ix–xiii; "Brit Shalom," http://www.zionistarchives.org.il/en/AttheCZA /AdditionalArticles/Pages/BritShalom.aspx.

68. Ahad Ha'am to Moshe Smilansky, November 18, 1913, in *Igrot Ahad ha'am* [The letters of Ahad Ha'am] (Tel Aviv: Dvir, 1960), 5:113; Steven J. Zipperstein, *Elusive Prophet: Ahad Ha'am and the Origins of Zionism* (London: P. Halban, 1993).

69. Joseph Heller, *Mi-Brit Shalom le-Ihud: Yehudah Leib Magnes ve-ha-ma'avak li-mdinah du-le'umit* [From Brith Shalom to Ichud: Judah Leib Magnes and the struggle for a binational state in Palestine] (Jerusalem: Magnes Press, 2003).

70. Szold to her sisters, December 3, 1921, quoted in Lowenthal, *Henrietta Szold,* 197–198.

71. Szold to her sisters, December 3, 1921, quoted in Lowenthal, *Henrietta Szold,* 198.

72. Rose G. Jacobs (1888–1975) was president of Hadassah in the years 1930–1932 and 1934–1937.

11 BETWEEN TWO WORLDS

1. Chaim Weizmann, *The Letters and Papers of Chaim Weizmann,* vol. 10, Series A, *July 1920–December 1921,* ed. Bernard Wasserstein (New Brunswick, NJ: Transaction Books, 1977), 105.

2. Weizmann, *Letters and Papers,* vol. 10, Series A, 105.

3. George L. Berlin, "The Brandeis-Weizmann Dispute," in *Essential Papers on Zionism,* ed. Jehuda Reinharz and Anita Shapira (New York: New York University Press, 1996), 337–368; Ben Halpern, *A Clash of Heroes: Brandeis, Weizmann, and American Zionism* (New York: Oxford University Press, 1987); Jehuda Reinharz, *Chaim Weizmann: The Making of a Statesman* (New York: Oxford University Press, 1993), 2:172–212.

4. Emanuel Neumann, *In the Arena: An Autobiographical Memoir* (New York: Herzl Press, 1976), 56.

5. Melvin I. Urofsky, *American Zionism from Herzl to the Holocaust* (Garden City, NY: Anchor Press, 1975), 340.

6. Deborah E. Lipstadt, *The Zionist Career of Louis Lipsky, 1900–1921* (New York: Arno Press, 1982).

7. Urofsky, *American Zionism,* 341–345.

8. Lipsky to Hadassah, July 8, 1921, HADA, RG 13/5.

9. Lipsky to Levensohn, June 22, 1921, HADA, RG 13/5.

10. Att. L. Seligsberg to Minnie Sobel, June 30, 1921, HADA, RG 13/5.

11. Att. L. Seligsberg to Minnie Sobel, June 30, 1921, HADA, RG 13/5.

12. Morris Rothenberg to Minnie Sobel, September 22, 1921, HADA, RG 13/5.

13. Szold to her sisters, November 5, 1921, CZA, A125/6.

14. Rubinow, parting address, quoted in Shifra Shvarts and Zipora Shehory-Rubin, *Hadassah for the Health of the People: The Health-Education Mission of Hadassah: The American Zionist Women in the Holy Land* (Tel Aviv: Dekel, 2012), 54–55.

15. Yeshayahu Press (1874–1956) was born in Jerusalem, attended the Lämel School, and trained at the Jewish teachers' seminary in Hannover, Germany. He later became principal of the Lämel School and a respected educator. See Mordechai Eliav, *Ha-Yishuv ha-Yehudi be-Eretz Yisra'el bi-re'i ha-mediniyut ha-Germanit* [The Jews of Palestine in German policy] (Tel Aviv: Hakibbutz Hameuchad, 1973).

16. Zipora Shehory-Rubin, "Ha-'kafeteriyah': Mif'al ha-hazanah shel 'Hadassah' be-vatei ha-sefer ha-Ivri'im" [The 'cafeteria': The Hadassah school luncheons program in Eretz Israel], *Cathedra* 92 (1999): 114; Shvarts and Shehory-Rubin, *Hadassah for the Health of the People.*

17. Esther Rubin, *Bouquet of Memories* (Tel Aviv: Steimatzky, 2001).

18. The ESCO Foundation for Palestine was a private family foundation, established by Frank and Ethel Silverman Cohen, for projects in Palestine.

19. Rose Zeitlin, *Henrietta Szold: Record of a Life* (New York: Dial Press, 1952), 68.

20. Szold to her sisters, September 4, 1922, HADA, RG 13 / 26.

21. Zeitlin, *Henrietta Szold*, 64.

22. Szold to her sisters, September 30, 1922, HADA, RG 13 / 26.

23. Szold to her sisters, October 10, 1922, HADA, RG 13 / 26.

24. Szold to her sisters, October 22, 1922, HADA, RG 13 / 26.

25. Szold to her sisters, November 11, 1922, HADA, RG 13 / 26, folder 4.

26. Szold to her sisters, November 27, 1922, December 23, 1922, HADA, RG 13 / 26.

27. Szold to her sisters, November 27, 1922, December 23, 1922, HADA, RG 13 / 26.

28. Szold to her sisters, November 11, 1922, HADA, RG 13 / 26, folder 4.

29. Szold to her sisters, November 11, 1922, HADA, RG 13 / 26, folder 4.

30. A list of Szold's travels, April 23, 1923, AJA, H. H. Szold.

31. Szold to Rose Herzog, October 21, 1932, quoted in Marvin Lowenthal, *Henrietta Szold: Life and Letters* (New York: Viking Press, 1942), 241.

32. Szold Diary, December 19, 1923, AJA, H. Szold Correspondence.

33. Arthur Ruppin, *Memoirs, Diaries, Letters,* ed. Alex Bein, trans. Karen Gershon (New York: Herzl Press, 1972), 213–227; Urofsky, *American Zionism*, 314.

34. Neumann, *In the Arena*, 86.

35. Lipsky's secretary at the ZOA, M. Weisgal, to Zip Szold, chair of the 11th annual Hadassah convention (Washington, DC, July 1–2, 1925), HADA, RG 13 / 26.

36. A list of Szold's travels, November 29, 1925, AJA, H. Szold Correspondence.

37. A list of Szold's travels. Szold arrived in Palestine on March 24, 1926, and departed for the United States on July 15, reaching New York on August 11. AJA, H. Szold Correspondence.

38. Rachel passed away in September 1926.

39. Szold to Mrs. Marx, November 12, 1926, AJA, H. Szold Correspondence.

40. Irma Lindheim was elected president of Hadassah in 1926.

41. Henrietta Szold's will, CZA 125, H. Szold Correspondence.

42. Szold to her sisters, March 8, 1927, HADA, RG 13 / 26, folder 5.

43. Letter from Stanislawow, *Ha'olam*, September 5, 1924; Dan Giladi, *Ha-Yishuv bi-tekufat ha-aliyah ha-revi'it (1924–1929): Behinah kalkalit u-folitit* [Jewish Palestine during the Fourth Aliyah period, 1924–1929: Economic and social aspects] (Tel Aviv: Am Oved, 1973), 201–203; Dan Giladi, "The Economic Crisis during the Fourth Aliya (1926–1927)," in *Zionism: Studies in the History of the Zionist Movement and of the Jewish Community in Palestine,* ed. Daniel Carpi and Gedalia Yogev (Tel Aviv: Tel Aviv University and Massada, 1975), 157–192; Arthur Ruppin, *Three Decades of Palestine: Speeches and Papers on the Upbuilding of the Jewish National Home* (Westport, CT: Greenwood Press, 1975).

44. Nissim Levy, *Perakim be-toldot ha-refu'ah be-Eretz Yisra'el 1799–1948* [The history of medicine in the Holy Land, 1799–1948] (Tel Aviv: Hakibbutz Hameuchad and the Ruth and Bruce Rappaport Faculty of Medicine, 1998), 201–203.

45. Ruppin, *Three Decades of Palestine,* 174.

46. Chaim Weizmann, "Lelo kehal" [The unvarnished truth], *Ha'olam,* June 11, 1926.

47. Weizmann to Neumann, May 23, 1927, quoted in Neumann, *In the Arena,* 90.

48. Amichai Berlad, "Doktor Siegfried Lehmann (1892–1958)—Hogeh hinukhi u-mehanekh yetzirati: Me-hazon le-mif'al hayav bi-Khefar ha-No'ar Ben Shemen (1927–1958)" [Dr. Siegfried Lehmann (1892–1958)—an educational theorist and a creative educator: From a vision to his life's work at the Ben Shemen Youth Village (1927–1958); with English abstract], PhD diss., Hebrew University of Jerusalem, 2013.

49. A list of Szold's travels. Szold's journey took some two months. She left Palestine in March, spent part of April in London, and arrived in New York in May 1927. AJA, H. Szold Correspondence.

50. *Doar Hayom,* July 12, 1927 (two days after the earthquake).

12 IN THE NATIONAL ARENA

1. Marvin Lowenthal, *Henrietta Szold: Life and Letters* (New York: Viking Press, 1942), 59.

2. Szold arrived in New York in May 1927, and the Basel congress took place on August 13 of that same year.

3. Harry Sacher (1881–1971) was a member of the London-based Zionist Political Committee, together with James de Rothschild, Herbert Samuel, Israel Sieff, Herbert Bentwich, Nahum Sokolow, and other Weizmann supporters.

4. Frederick Hermann Kisch (1888–1943) served as an officer in the Royal Engineers in India, holding the rank of lieutenant colonel. His successor at the political department of the Jewish Agency was Dr. Chaim Arlosoroff. See Frederick H. Kisch, *Palestine Diary* (London: Gollancz, 1938).

5. Szold to her sisters, quoted in Lowenthal, *Henrietta Szold,* 221.

6. Isaac Baer Berkson was an American Jewish educator and a student of John Dewey and W. H. Kilpatrick.

7. Harry Sacher, "Zikhronot mi-Yerushalayim" [Memoirs from Jerusalem], in *Sefer ha-Aliyah ha-Shelishit* [The Third Aliyah book], ed. Yehuda Erez (Tel Aviv: Am Oved, 1964), 2:613–616; Lowenthal, *Henrietta Szold,* 221–223. See also Harry Sacher, *Zionist Portraits and Other Essays* (London: Anthony Blond, 1959), which includes a section on Szold.

8. The press conference was held in the offices of Keren Hayesod on June 24, 1928.

9. Rachel Elboim-Dror, *Ha-hinukh ha-Ivri be-Eretz Yisra'el* [Hebrew education in Eretz Israel], vol. 2, *1914–1920* (Jerusalem: Ben Zvi Institute, 1993); Dan Horowitz and Moshe Lissak, *Origins of the Israeli Polity: Palestine under the Mandate* (Chicago: University of Chicago Press, 1978), 120–156.

10. Herbert Charles Onslow Plumer (1857–1932) was a peer and a senior officer in the British Army. See Charles Harington, *Plumer of Messines* (London: John Murray, 2017), 151–169.

11. Szold in Isaac B. Berkson, *Mahleket ha-hinukh shel ha-Hanhalah ha-Tziyonit be-Eretz Yisra'el, sidurah ve-hanhalatah* [The education department of the Palestine Zionist Executive, organization and administration] (Jerusalem, 1929).

12. Berkson, *Mahleket ha-hinukh.*

13. Jonathan D. Sarna, "Two Jewish Lawyers Named Louis," *American Jewish History* 94, nos. 1–2 (2008): 7, 16.

14. Herbert Parzen, "Louis Marshall, the Zionist Organization of America, and the Founding of the Jewish Agency," in *Michael: On the History of the Jews in the Diaspora,* ed. Lloyd Gartner (Tel Aviv: Diaspora Research Institute, 1975), 3:226–253.

15. *Hed ha-hinukh* 13 (15 Iyar 5690 [May 13, 1930]): 245–249.

16. Persitz, in *Hed ha-hinukh* 13 (15 Iyar 5690 [May 13, 1930]): 245–249.

17. H. D. Shahar, in *Hed ha-hinukh* 13 (15 Iyar 5690 [May 13, 1930]): 245–249.

18. A. Globman, in *Davar,* December 19, 1930. Akiva Govrin (Globman) was a member of the executive committee of the Histadrut and, later, a member of Knesset for Mapai, chairman of the Knesset labor committee, and a government minister.

19. Chaim Yassky (1896–1948) was born in Kishinev, Bessarabia (then part of the Russian Empire, today in Moldova), studied medicine in Odessa, and specialized in ophthalmology in Geneva. He immigrated to Palestine in 1919, aboard the SS *Ruslan.*

20. I would like to thank Hadassah Archives director Susan Woodland for these figures.

21. *New York Times,* March 30, 1928, and March 31, 1928.

22. For a firsthand account of the episode by the British officer instructed to remove the screen, see Douglas V. Duff, *Sword for Hire: The Saga of a Modern Free-Companion* (London: John Murray, 1934), 248–254.

23. Zeev Drori, *The Israeli Defense Forces and the Foundation of Israel: Utopia in Uniform* (London: Routledge, 2005).

24. Arthur Ruppin, *Memoirs, Diaries, Letters,* ed. Alex Bein, trans. Karen Gershon (New York: Herzl Press, 1972), 248.

25. Commission on the Palestine Disturbances of August 1929, headed by Sir Walter Shaw (1863–1937), gathered evidence in Palestine from October 24 to December 29, 1929.

26. *Report of the Commission on the Palestine Disturbances of August, 1929, Presented by the Secretary of State for the Colonies to Parliament by Command of His Majesty,* Cmd. 3530 (London: His Majesty's Stationery Office, 1930).

27. Arthur Ruppin, *Pirke hayai* [Chapters of my life] (Tel Aviv: Am Oved, 1968), 3:187.

28. Szold to her sisters, June 12, 1931, quoted in Lowenthal, *Henrietta Szold,* 229.

29. Ruppin, *Memoirs,* 258; Shalom Ratzabi, *Between Zionism and Judaism: The Radical Circle in Brith Shalom, 1925–1933* (Leiden: Brill, 2002); Shalom Ratzabi, "The Political-Cultural Background of Central European Intellectuals in 'Brith Shalom,'" *Journal of Israeli History* 18, no. 1 (1997): 1–27.

30. Ruppin, *Memoirs,* 258.

31. Szold to Rose Herzog (secretary of Hadassah in its early days), October 2, 1931, quoted in Lowenthal, *Henrietta Szold,* 235.

32. Szold to Rose Herzog, October 2, 1931, quoted in Lowenthal, *Henrietta Szold,* 234–235. Gertrude Margaret Bell (1868–1926) worked with Lawrence of Arabia (Thomas Edward Lawrence) during his time as a British military intelligence officer in the Near East. Bell has received greater recognition among scholars today, some of whom have claimed that Lawrence was unjustly given all of the fame and credit that was in fact due to Bell—whose ideas and actions led, inter alia, to the establishment of the Kingdom of Iraq. Szold was an early admirer of Bell and her work.

33. Szold to Rose Herzog, October 2, 1931, quoted in Lowenthal, *Henrietta Szold,* 235.

34. Louis Marshall died on September 11, 1929.

35. Szold to her sisters, June 5, 1931, quoted in Lowenthal, *Henrietta Szold,* 227. See also Zeev Tzahor, "David Ben Gurion's Attitude towards the Diaspora," *Judaism* 32, no. 1 (1983): 9–21.

36. David Ben-Gurion at Mapai central committee meeting, March 23, 1931, Israeli Labor Party Archive, file no. 2-1931-23; Zeev Tzahor, "Yahaso shel Ben-Gurion la-golah ve-la-aliyah" [Ben-Gurion's attitude toward the *gola* (diaspora) and aliyah], in *Kibutz galuyot: Aliyah le-Eretz Yisra'el—Mitos u-metzi'ut* [Ingathering of exiles: Aliyah to the Land of Israel—Myth and

Reality], ed. Dvora Hacohen (Jerusalem: Zalman Shazar Center, 1998), 131–144.

37. Rose Zeitlin, *Henrietta Szold: Record of a Life* (New York: Dial Press, 1952), 84.

38. Szold to her sisters, June 5, 1931, quoted in Lowenthal, *Henrietta Szold*, 225.

39. Szold to her sisters, June 5, 1931, quoted in Lowenthal, *Henrietta Szold*, 226.

40. Szold to her sisters, June 5, 1931, quoted in Lowenthal, *Henrietta Szold*, 225.

41. Szold to her sisters, July 31, 1931, quoted in Lowenthal, *Henrietta Szold*, 232.

42. Szold to Alice Seligsberg, September 10, 1931, quoted in Lowenthal, *Henrietta Szold*, 227–228. See also Moshe Burstein, *Self Government of the Jews in Palestine since 1900* (Tel Aviv: Moshe Burstein, 1934); Szold, 1931, quoted in Zeitlin, *Henrietta Szold*, 89.

43. The expression "Lady Bountiful" denotes a patronizing and self-aggrandizing kind of generosity, based on a wealthy and ostentatiously charitable character in George Farquhar's 1707 play *The Beaux' Stratagem*.

44. Henrietta Szold, "The Future of Women's Work for Palestine." In this report, Szold outlined a program for the institutionalization of social work in Palestine. Quoted in Tammy Razi, *Yaldei ha-hefker: Ha-hazer ha-ahorit shel Tel Aviv ha-mandatorit* [Forsaken children: The backyard of Mandate Tel-Aviv] (Tel Aviv: Am Oved, 2009), 95.

45. Szold to Anna Kaplan, June 7, 1932, quoted in Lowenthal, *Henrietta Szold*, 237.

46. Szold to Alice Seligsberg, September 10, 1931, quoted in Lowenthal, *Henrietta Szold*, 228; Szold to Alice Seligsberg, July 14, 1931, quoted in Lowenthal, *Henrietta Szold*, 231.

47. Szold to Alice Seligsberg, September 10, 1931, quoted in Lowenthal, *Henrietta Szold*, 228.

48. Szold to Alice Seligsberg, July 14, 1931, quoted in Lowenthal, *Henrietta Szold*, 231.

49. Szold to her sisters, September 2, 1932, quoted in Lowenthal, *Henrietta Szold*, 240.

50. Sir Arthur Grenfell Wauchope (1874–1947) was the fourth British high commissioner for Palestine and Transjordan.

51. Gabriel Sheffer, "Sir Arthur Wauchope ve-ha-notablim ha-Aravim ve-ha-Yehudim" [Sir Arthur Wauchope and the Arab and Jewish "Notables"], *Keshet* 51 (1971): 145–160; Gabriel Sheffer, *Moshe Sharet: A Biography of a Political Moderate* (Oxford: Clarendon Press, 1996).

52. Szold to her sisters, June 9–29, 1932, HADA, RG 13 / 26.

53. Szold to her sisters, July 22, 1931, June 9–29, 1932, quoted in Lowenthal, *Henrietta Szold*, 237–238.

54. Szold to Alice Seligsberg, July 14, 1931, quoted in Lowenthal, *Henrietta Szold,*231.

55. Szold to her sisters, July 31, 1931, quoted in Lowenthal, *Henrietta Szold,* 232–233.

56. Szold to her sisters, May 7, 1932, quoted in Lowenthal, *Henrietta Szold,* 235.

13 THE MOTHER OF YOUTH ALIYAH

1. Arthur Ruppin, *Memoirs, Diaries, Letters,* ed. Alex Bein, trans. Karen Gershon (New York: Herzl Press, 1972), 263.

2. Ruppin, *Memoirs,* 263.

3. Victor Klemperer, *I Will Bear Witness: A Diary of the Nazi Years 1931–1941,* trans. Martin Chalmers (New York: Modern Library, 1999), 129.

4. Quoted in Saul Friedländer, *Nazi Germany and the Jews,* vol. 1, *The Years of Persecution 1933–39* (London: Phoenix, 1998), 16.

5. Quoted in Friedländer, *Nazi Germany and the Jews,* vol. 1, *Years of Persecution,* 17.

6. Fritz Albert Lipmann (1899–1986) won the Nobel Prize in 1953. See William P. Jencks and Richard V. Wolfenden, *Fritz Albert Lipmann: A Biographical Memoir* (Washington, DC: National Academy of Sciences, 2006).

7. Friedländer, *Nazi Germany and the Jews,* vol. 1, *Years of Persecution,* 9–14.

8. Ruppin, *Memoirs,* 263; Arthur Ruppin, *Pirke hayai* [Chapters of my life] (Tel Aviv: Am Oved, 1968), 3:219.

9. Monika Richarz, ed., *Jewish Life in Germany: Memoirs from Three Centuries,* trans. Stella P. Rosenfeld and Sidney Rosenfeld (Bloomington: Indiana University Press, 1991), 353.

10. Joseph Walk, "Ha-Hinukh ha-Yehudi be-Germanyah ha-Natzit" [Jewish education in Nazi Germany], in *Toldot ha-Sho'ah: Germanyah* [The history of the Holocaust: Germany], ed. Avraham Margaliot and Yehoyakim Cochavi (Jerusalem: Yad Vashem, 1998), 597–695.

11. Richarz, ed., *Jewish Life in Germany,* 356.

12. Recha Freier, *Let the Children Come: The Early History of Youth Aliyah* (London: Weidenfeld and Nicolson, 1961).

13. Szold to Arthur Biram and Ernst Simon, June 17, 1932, CZA, S 256/2.

14. See Dvora Hacohen, *Yaldei ha-zman: Aliyat ha-no'ar 1933–1948* [Children of the time: Youth Aliyah 1933–1948] (Jerusalem: Yad Vashem, Ben Zvi Institute, and Ben Gurion University, 2011), 17–27.

15. Chaim Arlosoroff to his wife, Sima, May 21, 1933, in *Kitvei Chaim Arlosoroff* [The writings of Chaim Arlosoroff] (Tel Aviv: A. I. Stibel, 1934), 6:262.

16. Szold to her sisters, September 20, 1933, quoted in Marvin Lowenthal, *Henrietta Szold: Life and Letters* (New York: Viking Press, 1942), 250.

17. Szold to her sisters, October 1933, quoted in Lowenthal, *Henrietta Szold,* 256.

18. Szold to her sisters, November 19, 1933, quoted in Lowenthal, *Henrietta Szold,* 256–257.

19. Meeting memorandum, November 27, 1933, Youth Aliyah archives, CZA, 620.20.

20. Szold to her sisters, December 22, 1933, quoted in Lowenthal, *Henrietta Szold,* 258.

21. Szold to her sisters, February 8, 1934, HADA, RG 13/8, H. Szold Correspondence.

22. Moshe Krone, *From Rodges to Yavne* (London: Bahad, 1945).

23. Shlomo Dan, personal interview with the author, August 26, 2009.

24. Interview with Shlomo Dan; report on a gathering of Youth Aliyah graduates [in Hebrew], Hakibbutz Hadati (Religious Kibbutz Movement) Archive, Yavne.

25. Meshulam Windreich, in *Ha-Tzofe,* March 10, 2000.

26. Hacohen, *Yaldei ha-zman,* 140–188.

27. Szold to her sisters, October 19, 1934, quoted in Lowenthal, *Henrietta Szold,* 273.

28. Szold to her sisters, December 28, 1934, quoted in Lowenthal, *Henrietta Szold,* 277.

29. The Nineteenth World Zionist Congress was held in Lucerne from August 20 to September 6, 1935.

30. Ruppin, *Pirke hayai,* 3:219.

31. Ben-Gurion to the Zionist Executive, June 26, 1936, Ben-Gurion Archive. See also Shabtai Teveth, *Ben-Gurion: The Burning Ground* (Boston: Houghton Mifflin, 1987).

32. Chaim Weizmann, Testimony before the Royal Commission on Palestine, in Chaim Weizmann, *The Letters and Papers of Chaim Weizmann,* vol. 2, Series B, *December 1931–April 1952,* ed. Barnet Litvinoff (New Brunswick, NJ: Transaction Books, 1984), 101–106.

33. Szold to Miriam Beyth [in German], October 22, 1943. I am grateful to Miriam Henrietta Beyth, who showed me the letter from Szold.

34. Rahel Yanait Ben-Zvi, *Coming Home,* trans. David Harris and Julian Meltzer (New York: Herzl Press, 1964).

35. Shimon Sachs, *Hamaniyot: Ma'avarim mi-Berlin le-Kiryat Gat* [From Berlin to Kiryat Gat] (Tel Aviv: Papyrus, 1984), 47.

36. Yitzhak Olshan, *Din u-dvarim: Zikhronot* [Memoirs] (Jerusalem: Schocken, 1978), 145.

37. Szold's correspondence with Eddie Cantor, HADA, RG 13/8, H. Szold Correspondence; Children and Youth Aliyah, *Freedom and Work for Jewish Youth—Report for the Third World Youth Aliyah Conference* (London, 1939).

38. *Bene Aliyat ha-noar* [Children of Youth Aliyah] newsletter, Jerusalem, April 8, 1951, 1.

39. Sachs, *Hamaniyot*, 38–39.

40. Dalia Dorner, personal interview with the author, Jerusalem, August 30, 2009.

41. Yehoshua Porath, *The Palestinian Arab National Movement 1929–1939: From Riots to Rebellion* (London: Frank Cass, 1977), 109–161.

42. Szold to her sisters, April 1, 1938, quoted in Lowenthal, *Henrietta Szold*, 329–330.

43. Szold to her sisters, August 27, 1938, quoted in Lowenthal, *Henrietta Szold*, 330–331.

44. Quoted in Yigal Loussin, *Pillar of Fire: The Rebirth of Israel—A Visual History* (Jerusalem: Shikmona and the Israel Broadcasting Authority, 1983), 235.

45. *Palestine Royal Commission Report: Presented by the Secretary of State for the Colonies to Parliament by Command of His Majesty, July 1937,* Cmd. 5479 (London: His Majesty's Stationery Office, 1937).

46. See Itzhak Galnoor, *The Partition of Palestine: Decision Crossroads in the Zionist Movement* (Albany: State University of New York Press, 1995).

47. Henrietta to her sisters, August 27, 1937, quoted in Lowenthal, *Henrietta Szold,* 327–328.

48. Szold to her sisters, October 29, 1937, quoted in Lowenthal, *Henrietta Szold,* 328.

49. Szold to Thomas Seltzer, January 28, 1938, quoted in Lowenthal, *Henrietta Szold,* 328–329.

50. Quoted in Friedländer, *Nazi Germany and the Jews,* vol. 1, *Years of Persecution,* 239.

51. Szold to her sisters, March 18, 1938, quoted in Alexandra Lee Levin, ed., *Henrietta Szold and Youth Aliyah: Family Letters 1934–1944* (New York: Herzl Press, 1986), 29.

52. The British authorities granted "capitalist" certificates, beyond the established quota, to those who possessed a minimum of 1,000 Palestine pounds (equivalent to pounds sterling).

53. Szold to her sisters, May 6, 1938, quoted in Levin, ed., *Family Letters,* 29.

54. Chanoch Reinhold to Szold, November 10, 1935, CZA, S 75/126.

55. Quoted in Friedländer, *Nazi Germany and the Jews,* vol. 1, *Years of Persecution,* 277.

56. See "Kristallnacht," *Holocaust Encyclopedia,* United States Holocaust Memorial Museum, https://encyclopedia.ushmm.org/content/en/article/kristallnacht; Doron Rabinovici, *Eichmann's Jews: The Jewish Administration of Holocaust Vienna, 1938–1945,* trans. Nick Somers (Cambridge: Polity Press, 2011), 81, 164–167.

57. For the period July 1937–March 1938, the British allocated 8,000 immigration certificates, including 900 "capitalist" permits, which previously had been granted beyond the established quota. In the summer of 1938, the British further reduced the number of certificates available for Jewish immigration to Palestine.

58. Greta Kraus, personal interview with the author, Jerusalem, October 14, 2007.

59. Hacohen, *Yaldei ha-zman*, 230–237.

60. Hacohen, *Yaldei ha-zman*, 237–241.

61. *Palestine: Statement of Policy: Presented by the Secretary of State for the Colonies to Parliament by Command of His Majesty, May, 1939,* Cmd. 6019 (London: His Majesty's Stationery Office, 1939).

62. Adele to Thomas Seltzer, undated, quoted in Levin, ed., *Family Letters,* 35.

63. Szold to her sisters, June 14, 1940, quoted in Lowenthal, *Henrietta Szold,* 334–335.

64. Emanuel Neumann, *In the Arena,* 144.

65. Naftali Bezem (1924–2018), personal interview with the author, April 2014.

14 WAR AND CALAMITY

1. John Shuckburgh to Harold Downie, September 16, 1939, PRO CO 733 396/8.

2. Weizmann to Malcolm MacDonald, September 15, 1939, PRO CO 733 396/8.

3. Dvora Hacohen, "British Immigration Policy to Palestine in the 1930s: Implications for Youth Aliyah," *Middle Eastern Studies* 37, no. 4 (October 2001): 206–218.

4. Winston Churchill, Speech to the House of Commons, May 13, 1940, Parliamentary Debates, Commons, vol. 360, cols. 1501–1525, https://api .parliament.uk/historic-hansard/commons/1940/may/13/his-majestys -government-1#S5CV0360P0_19400513_HOC_21.

5. Szold to Bertha Levin, September 28, 1940, in Levin, ed., *Family Letters,* 52.

6. Louis Brandeis died on October 5, 1940.

7. Shimon Sachs, *Hamaniyot: Ma'avarim mi-Berlin le-Kiryat Gat* [From Berlin to Kiryat Gat] (Tel Aviv: Papyrus, 1984), 47.

8. *Me-ha'ir la-kfar: Doh al hevrot no'ar Eretzyisre'eli* [From the city to the country: A report on youth communities in Palestine] (Jerusalem: Jewish Agency and Youth Aliyah, 1947).

9. See Esther Meir-Glitzenstein, "The Baghdad Pogrom and Zionist Policy," in *Al Farhud: The 1941 Pogrom in Iraq,* ed. Shmuel Moreh and Zvi Yehuda (Jerusalem: Magnes Press, 2010), 186–206.

10. Statistical summary, Jewish Agency, Child and Youth Immigration Department, 1951, CZA.

11. Meeting minutes, Jewish Agency executive, May 24, 1942, CZA.

12. Szold to Zvi Cynowitz, May 25, 1942, CZA, S6/3348.

13. The Mossad le-Aliyah Bet was an organization established to facilitate "illegal" Jewish immigration to Palestine.

14. Zipporah Shertok to the Jewish Agency executive, November 19, 1942, CZA, S6/251820.

15. Zipporah Shertok to the Jewish Agency executive, November 19, 1942, CZA, S6/251820.

16. Szold to the Jewish Agency executive, October 6, 1942, CZA, S6/3348.

17. *Ha-Tzofeh, Ha'aretz, Davar,* and other papers, February 19, 1943.

18. Yonah Melaron, *Od tetz'i mi-kan: Yomanah shel na'arah mi-megurashei Transnistria* [You will survive: The diary of a young girl among the Transnistria deportees], trans. Jean Ancel (Jerusalem: Yad Vashem, 1980).

19. Aharon Schechter, personal interview with the author, September 1, 2009.

20. Jean Ancel, *The History of the Holocaust in Romania,* trans. Yaffah Murciano, ed. Leon Volovici (Lincoln: University of Nebraska Press, 2011).

21. Saul Friedländer, *Nazi Germany and the Jews,* vol. 1, *The Years of Persecution 1933–39* (London: Phoenix, 1998), 2.

EPILOGUE: FROM MOUNT SCOPUS TO THE MOUNT OF OLIVES

1. See Norman A. Rose, *Chaim Weizmann: A Biography* (London: Weidenfeld and Nicolson, 1986), 286–293, 384–400.

2. Judah L. Magnes, diary entry for December 27, 1944, Magnes Archive, CAHJP.

3. Judah L. Magnes, diary entry for December 28, 1944, Magnes Archive, CAHJP.

4. Judah L. Magnes, diary entry for February 14, 1945, Magnes Archive, CAHJP; Beyth Family Archive. The dailies *Davar, Ha-Tzofeh,* and *Al ha-Mishmar*; Bracha Habas, "Henrietta Szold einenah" [Henrietta Szold is no more], *Davar,* February 14, 1945.

5. *Ha'aretz, Davar, Ha-Tzofeh,* and others, February 14, 1945.

6. Dvora Hacohen, *Yaldei ha-zman: Aliyat ha-no'ar 1933–1948* [Children of the time: Youth Aliyah 1933–1948] (Jerusalem: Yad Vashem, Ben Zvi Institute, and Ben Gurion University, 2011), 321–322.

7. *New York Times,* February 15, 1945.

8. Tamar de Sola Pool was president of Hadassah during the years 1939–1943.

9. Nancy F. Cott, ed., *No Small Courage: History of Women in the United States* (New York: Oxford University Press, 2000), vii.

10. Alexandra Lee Levin, *Henrietta Szold: Baltimorean* (Baltimore: Jewish Historical Society of Maryland, 1976), 17.

11. Kathryn Cullen-DuPont, *Encyclopedia of Women's History in America* (New York: Facts on File, 2000), 245; Alexandra Lee Levin, ed., *Henrietta Szold and Youth Aliyah: Family Letters 1934–1944* (New York: Herzl Press, 1987).

12. HADA, RG 13 / 1, folder 22.

13. Letter from President Franklin D. Roosevelt, March 2, 1944, HADA, RG 13 / 1, folder 23.

ACKNOWLEDGMENTS

FIRST AND FOREMOST I would like to express my gratitude and appreciation to the late Ruth Bader Ginsburg for her inspiring foreword to this biography of Henrietta Szold. The journey of discovering the life story of Henrietta Szold led me to many places and to a number of special people. Jonathan D. Sarna graciously shared his vast knowledge of the history of American Jewry, where Szold's roots lay, and generously advised, read drafts, and offered corrections where necessary. His comments and insights were invaluable. I would like to thank Jack Wertheimer: my conversations with him shed considerable light on the topics discussed in the book. He also gave me access to the archive of the Jewish Theological Seminary, which is closed to the general public and houses a large number of valuable documents, and I am grateful to him. My thanks to my colleagues and friends who encouraged and helped me along the way, including Motti Golani, Zeev Tzahor, and Avriel Bar-Levav, who kindly read my early drafts, greatly improving the text with their insightful comments. Of course, all mistakes in the book are entirely my own.

I learned a great deal from the copious body of historical research on the Jews of the United States and Mandatory Palestine, and from the newsletters and other publications of the various organizations and institutions in the United States, Palestine, and other countries relevant to Szold's activities. These sources are mentioned throughout the book. I thank the anonymous readers of my manuscript for their helpful comments.

In Baltimore, Henrietta's native city, I was fortunate to meet the granddaughters of Henrietta's sister Bertha Szold Levin, whose children were the Szold family's only descendants. Betsy Levin and Sally Levin came from Washington and toured Baltimore with me, taking me to the streets and houses where the Szold family lived. The family stories they shared with me added a further dimension to Henrietta's rich life and complex personality. I am immensely grateful to them. In Baltimore, I met George Hess, son of one of the city's oldest Jewish families, who kindly took me to the neighborhoods in which members of the Jewish community lived in the past.

I would like to thank the psychiatrist Eliezer Witztum, who helped clarify some of the manifestations of the deep depression that struck Henrietta Szold during the crisis she suffered.

My thanks to my son Aviad Hacohen, who drew my attention to many objects that belonged to Szold and to advertisements of numerous public events in which she took part. My gratitude to my dear cousins Ruth and Robert Oppenheim for their generous hospitality whenever I visited New York. Thanks too to my friends Lisa Clayton Jager, Elliot Jager, and Yohai Goell, who were always willing to lend a hand.

Writing a previously unknown chapter in history is like assembling a giant mosaic from the tiles that are the many and varied documents pertaining to the subject. To do so also requires the skills of a detective. A historian must sometimes face a dearth of documentary sources. In this case, I was surprised to discover thousands of documents well beyond those relating to Henrietta Szold's public activities. Szold wrote countless letters to family and friends, as well as diaries, most of which have never seen the light of day. In these documents I discovered her thoughts and views on many topics, affording further insight into her personality and approach.

During the course of my work I found a wealth of documents scattered in archives on three continents. I spent a great deal of time in these archives, and I am grateful to their directors and staff. At the Hadassah Archive in New York, I was helped by Susan Woodland, the former director of the archive. I thank her for her assistance, dedication, and kindness. During the many weeks I spent at the American Jewish Archives in Cincinnati, I benefited from the help and kindness of Gary P. Zola, executive director of the archive. Thanks to Dana Herman for her advice, and to the former head archivist, Kevin Proffitt. It is thanks to them that I was able to get the best out of my work there. I am grateful to Barbara Selya and to Roger Selya of the University of Cincinnati for their friendship and warm hospitality.

I am grateful to the staff of the Jewish Museum of Maryland and archive in Baltimore, and to the London Metropolitan Archives, the Board of Deputies Archive, and the National Archives in London. I owe a great debt to the staff of the Central Zionist Archives in Jerusalem, to the librarians of the National Library in Jerusalem, and to the staff at other archives at which I worked but which are too numerous to mention here. My thanks to all. My gratitude and appreciation to Shmuel Sermoneta-Gertel for his translation of the manuscript and his meticulous editing.

I am indebted to Kathleen McDermott, executive editor for history at Harvard University Press, for her kindness, support, and dedication throughout the process of publishing the book. I would also like to thank

Kate Brick, senior editor at Harvard University Press, and the publicity staff at Harvard University Press for their hard work and professionalism.

My deepest thanks to Kinneret Misgav, who, with her wisdom, talent, and diligence, helped me find and organize essential material for the book. Working with her made even the most tedious tasks a pleasure. Thank you to the artist-photographer Ariel Hacohen for his help in choosing the images for this book and in improving their resolution.

Last but not least, I would like to thank my family, who listened patiently to the stories and discoveries I made in my research. To my beloved children and grandchildren, who are the joy of my life, I dedicate this book with love.

CREDITS

Page 11
Library of Congress, Prints and Photographs Division, LC-DIG-det-4a10971.

Page 19
Courtesy of the Central Zionist Archive.

Page 22
Courtesy of the National Library of Israel.

Page 40
Library of Congress, Prints and Photographs Division, LC-DIG-ppmsca-10639.

Page 41
Library of Congress, Prints and Photographs Division, LC-DIG-ppmsca-51996.

Page 51
Library of Congress, Prints and Photographs Division, LC-USZ62-50927.

Page 55
Library of Congress, Prints and Photographs Division, LC-USZ62-74997.

Page 76
Courtesy of the Central Zionist Archive.

Page 85
Courtesy of the Library of the Jewish Theological Seminary.

Page 102
Courtesy of the Central Zionist Archive.

Page 119
Courtesy of the National Library of Israel.

Page 120
Courtesy of the National Library of Israel.

Page 121
Courtesy of the National Library of Israel.

Page 150
Courtesy of the Central Zionist Archive.

Page 151
Courtesy of the Central Zionist Archive.

Page 153
Courtesy of the Central Zionist Archive.

Page 155
Library of Congress, Prints and Photographs Division, LC-USZ62-92924.

Page 170
Library of Congress, Prints and Photographs Division, LC-USZ62-93094.

Page 171
Courtesy of the National Library of Israel.

Page 180
Library of Congress, Prints and Photographs Division, LC-M32-13769.

Page 183
Courtesy of the Central Zionist Archive.

Page 192
Courtesy of the Central Zionist Archive.

Page 204
Courtesy of the Central Zionist Archive.

Page 215
Courtesy of Yad Ben Zvi.

Page 222
Library of Congress, Prints and Photographs Division, LC-DIG-matpc-02663.

Page 227
Courtesy of the Central Zionist Archive.

Page 242
Courtesy of the Central Zionist Archive.

Page 245
Library of Congress, Prints and Photographs Division, LC-M33-4123.

Page 246
Library of Congress, Prints and Photographs Division, LC-M33-4110.

Page 251
Courtesy of Yad Ben Zvi.

Page 252
Courtesy of the Central Zionist Archive.

Page 272
Courtesy of the Israel Government Press Office.

Page 274
Courtesy of the Central Zionist Archive.

Page 278
Courtesy of the Beiyth Family.

Page 280
Courtesy of the Central Zionist Archive.

Page 281
Courtesy of the Central Zionist Archive.

Page 289
Courtesy of Yad Ben Zvi.

Page 296
Library of Congress, Prints and Photographs Division, LC-M33-9382.

Page 297
Courtesy of the Israel Government Press Office.

Page 303
Courtesy of the Central Zionist Archive.

Page 309
Courtesy of the Israel Government Press Office.

Page 311
Courtesy of the Israel Government Press Office.

Page 311
Courtesy of the Central Zionist Archive.

Page 312
Courtesy of the Israel Government Press Office.

Page 316
Courtesy of the Central Zionist Archive.

Page 320
Courtesy of the Central Zionist Archive.

Page 321
Courtesy of Yad Ben Zvi.

Page 323
Courtesy of the Central Zionist Archive.

INDEX